Special Forces
in the Desert War
1940-1943

PUBLIC RECORD OFFICE

Public Record Office
Kew
Richmond
Surrey TW9 4DU

© Crown copyright 2001

ISBN 1 903365 29 5

British Library Cataloguing-in-Publication Data
A catalogue record for this book is available from the British Library

Front cover: A Long Range Desert Group patrol resting in the desert,
by Lieutenant Graham, 25 May 1942
Photograph courtesy of the Imperial War Museum, London (E12385)

Printed by St Edmundsbury Press, Bury St Edmunds, Suffolk

Contents

Publisher's Note

This publication reproduces two documents, *The History of the Long Range Desert Group (June 1940 to March 1943)* and *The History of Commandos and Special Service Troops in the Middle East and North Africa (January 1941 to April 1943)*. These histories, written by Brigadier H.W. Wynter for the Historical Section of the War Cabinet, have been preserved in two files, CAB 44/151 and CAB 44/152, which can be consulted at the Public Record Office, Kew.

The original documents included large fold-out maps (some of them in colour), which are here reproduced in reduced form, in black-and-white. Maps that appeared in both documents are here reproduced only once. Similarly, the note about Lieutenant Colonel J.E. Haselden that was printed at the beginning of *The History of the Long Range Desert Group* has been omitted here as it duplicates the note that appears in *The History of Commandos and Special Service Troops*.

Our aim has been to reproduce the wording of the original documents as faithfully as possible. Inconsistencies of spelling (such as 'Bengasi' and 'Bengazi', and 'Haselden' and 'Hasleden') have been retained. However, obvious typing errors have been corrected, and cross-references revised to reflect the pagination of this edition. Footnotes marked * indicate hand-written notes in the original. The Index is a modern addition.

The History of the Long Range Desert Group

June 1940 to March 1943

Brigadier H. W. Wynter, D.S.O.

PREPARED BY THE HISTORICAL SECTION
OF THE WAR CABINET

TO BE KEPT UNDER LOCK AND KEY

Contents

Long Range Desert Group

Introduction.

(March) – is withdrawn to Egypt (April). General Montgomery's letter to Lieut. Colonel Prendergast.

Appendices

1. L.R.D.G. Signals. (Extracts from a report by Lieut. G.B. Heywood, Middlesex Yeomanry, Signal Officer, L.R.D.G.).
2. Extracts from an account of the expedition to Fezzan (December 1940 – February 1941) written by Capt. M.D.D. Crichton-Stuart, Scots Guards, commanding 'G' Patrol.
3. A. List of Officers who served with L.R.D.G. from July 1940 to April 1943.
    B. List of Officers of the Indian Long Range Squadron under Command of L.R.D.G. from October 1942 to April 1943.
4. L.R.D.G. Establishment Authorized on 22nd November 1940. Consisting of H.Q. and Two Squadrons each of Three Fighting Patrols.
5. L.R.D.G. War Establishment February 1942.
6. List of Honours and Awards to N.C.Os and men of the L.R.D.G.

Maps and Sketches[1]

1 *Publisher's Note:* These maps can be seen on pp. 350–51 and 352–53, as they were duplicated in 'The History of Commandos and Special Service Troops'.

Introduction

This narrative describes the formation of the Long Range Desert Group in the summer of 1940, and its various activities in North Africa up to the end of March 1943. The information on which it is based has been taken from the very clear and complete records compiled by Lieut. Colonel R.A. Bagnold, O.B.E., Royal Signals, and Lieut. Colonel G. Prendergast, D.S.O., Royal Tank Regiment, who successively commanded the Group during the period in question. These records are contained in nine volumes, each of two hundred pages or more, and include not only the report on each operation written by the patrol commander who carried it out, but also the orders given for it by the Group or Squadron Commander, relevant instructions by G.H.Q. Middle East and H.Q. Eighth Army, minutes of Command Conferences, establishments and copies of personal letters and G.S. notes bearing on the Group's activities. There are also summaries by the Group Commander of each phase of the operations directly connected with those of the Western Desert Force and Eighth Army, which include also notes on the changes in organization and in type of transport used, on the posting of officers and on other points of importance.

The missions of patrols are described as nearly as possible in chronological order, and where necessary, short summaries of contemporary operations by the main forces of the Allies in North Africa have been inserted. The Patrol Commander's reports and the Commanding Officer's summaries were written in terms of studied moderation, and nowhere is there any sign of overstatement. Nevertheless it is obvious that the standard of training, and the courage, initiative and powers of endurance of all ranks were of the highest order.

There can be little doubt of the value to the Allied Armies in North Africa of the ceaseless activity of patrols of the Long Range Desert Group on the enemy's southern flank, and against his lines of communications; and their skill in desert navigation was more than once exercised in guiding columns of the Eighth Army to their objectives. The help it gave was acknowledged in letters from the Commander-in-Chief, Middle East, the

G.O.C. Eighth Army and from senior general staff officers.

The administrative problems that the Group Commander had to face were very great, for supplies whether from Egypt or from the Sudan, had to be carried some hundreds of miles in transport which was not always adequate for the purpose; and the provision of petrol at forward dumps for the journeys of patrols over distances of 1000 miles or more, required much forethought and very careful organization. Moreover he was often responsible, not only for the movements of his own patrols and those of the Indian Long Range Squadron, which was for sometime under his command, but also for the transport of parties of the Special Air Service, the Inter-Service Liaison Department, the Demolition Squadron and the organization formed to assist the escape of prisoners.

The narrative includes Appendices dealing with the signal problem and with War Establishments, etc.

Map references are to the gridded map of Libya, Cryenaica, Tripolitania and Tunisia, and for convenience the longitude and latitude or the distance and approximate bearing of a locality from some well-known place have at times been added. Accounts of the less successful operations have been cut as short as possible, but it is to be noted that failure was seldom due to errors on the part of patrols. It was much more often the result of bad weather, or of difficulties of ground, familiar though much of it was.

Section I

Origins.

The organization of light motor expeditions capable of covering very great distances, and independent of all supplies including fuel and water, for periods as long as a month, was evolved in Egypt between 1926 and 1932. Its object at the time was to explore the more remote areas of the Libyan Desert of which little was then known. The German explorer Röhlfs penetrated it to the south of Siwa in 1874 but with camels he could not cross the dunes, and was confined to the passages between them. During the last war Light Car Patrols covered much of the eastern part where their tracks are still to be seen. In 1923 Hassanein Bey went to the legendary mountain of Uweinat south of the "Sand Sea". The story of all this is told in "Libyan Sands" by Major R.A. Bagnold, Royal Corps of Signals, who was afterwards the first commander of the L.R.D.G. In 1932, during a journey of 6,000 miles, an expedition led by him made runs of 1,400 miles in fourteen days without refilling or replenishment of any kind. Similar runs were made in 1935 by W.B. Kennedy-Shaw during a 7,000 mile journey, and in 1938 another expedition led by Major Bagnold carried its own supplies for more than a month at a time. During these expeditions much was learnt about the use of mechanical transport in desert conditions. It was discovered that "with light cars and with the technique of channels and ladders[1] for extracting them when stuck, and the adjustment of tyre pressure to suit the consistency of the sand, the dunes could be conquered by motor transport".

Bagnold and his companions, who included Major Prendergast, his successor in command of the L.R.D.G., became experts in navigation and position finding by astronomical observation. They learnt to calculate how

---

1 The "channels" were made of rolled steel troughing used during the last war for roofing. The "ladders" suggested by P.A. Clayton of the Desert Survey, were of rope with bamboo rungs and were lighter and more effective than rolls of wire netting for getting out of sand.

much water and petrol would be necessary for a given distance; the assumption being that the distance must be doubled when estimating requirements for a journey winding through dunes. They learnt the best way to load, the best design for bodies and the necessity for adequate spare parts including spare members of the chassis frames; and they became experts in tracking, and in deducing from tracks the number of vehicles or men who had made them, and how old they were. In many matters they had had valuable help from Dr. Ball and P.A. Clayton of the Desert Survey; the latter afterwards served in the L.R.D.G. It is needless to add that without this experience the work done by the L.R.D.G. in the Libyan Desert, in which not only Bagnold and Prendergast, but also Kennedy-Shaw and Clayton took part, could not have been as successful as it was.

The application to war of this technique for long distance movement across the desert was first suggested in London early in 1939 by Major Bagnold, at the instigation of the Hon. Francis Rodd, who in 1941 succeeded his father as second Lord Rennell of Rodd. The object in view in the event of war with Italy, was the interception of Italian raids across French territory into Northern Nigeria by small and very mobile motor patrols stationed within French territory. The French, however, were induced to increase their garrisons in the intervening desert and the project was dropped.

Outbreak of War 1939.

When war broke out with Germany Major Bagnold who had recently retired from the army returned to it, and was posted to the 7th Armoured Division in Egypt under the command of Major-General P. Hobart. Early in November 1939 a scheme was put up by General Hobart to H.Q. British Troops in Egypt for the formation of a force consisting of small mobile parties whose organization was to be based on the experience gained in the desert during peace time. The suggestion was that such a force could be used for collecting information about the vast interior of Libya, to harass the enemy's communications with the inner oases of Kufra and Uweinat, to survey landing grounds in hostile territory for future use by the R.A.F. in offensive operations, and to keep touch with French outposts on the south-west border of Libya. The scheme however was not adopted then, nor when again put up by General Hobart's successor Major-General O'Moore Creagh, in January 1940, because it was considered that Italy was unlikely to come into the war against us.

Italy declares War June 1940. Long Range Patrol organized.

When Italy declared war on 10 June 1940 Major Bagnold, who was then serving on the staff at G.H.Q., Cairo, put the idea forward once more. General Wavell approved and on 23 June it was decided to organize one

Long Range Patrol Unit, whose operations were to be controlled by the D.D.M.I. The War Office cabled provisional approval on 10 July.

Over and above the obvious necessity that the Long Range Patrol should be capable of traversing great distances and of being away for long periods without having to refill with supplies and petrol, the main requirements were as follows:-

Requirements of Long Range Patrol.

(a) Ability to make the 130 mile crossing of the dune barrier of the Sand Sea.

(b) Sufficient fire power to deal with enemy convoys and their escorts, and with small desert posts.

(c) A reasonable amount of A.A. Defence.

(d) Adequate W/T communications between detachments of the force, and with Cairo at least once a day.

(e) Low inconspicuous vehicles with good camouflage which could be easily concealed from aircraft.

(f) Leaders with experience of the desert country; and navigators trained in dead reckoning by compass and speedometer, and in astronomical position finding.

(g) Steady and self reliant personnel.

It was also decided that the organization must be such as to provide two independent patrols to work the "police trap" method of ambushing convoys on a road, with a third party in identical vehicles to provide immediate reinforcement of men, trucks and technical equipment. Each of these three parties was organized in four troops. The establishment decided on comprised –

HQ., O.C., Adj., Q.M. and intelligence officer.

Two fighting patrols: each including a Major (or Capt.), 1 Subaltern and 23 O.Rs.

'A' Echelon Supply Party of 2 Subalterns, 1 M.O. and 19 O.Rs.

'B' Echelon Supply Party of 1 Subaltern, 4 O.Rs.

The two patrols and 'A' echelon supply party had each ten Lewis guns, four Boys A.T. rifles, one 37 mm Bofors gun (at that time Bren guns were not available in Egypt); and the transport in each case consisted of ten 30-cwt trucks and one 15-cwt pilot car.

Personnel.

It was considered that the best type of men for the purpose would be Australians from Queensland, but General Blamey had instructions from his government that Australian soldiers were not to serve outside Australian formations. The personnel were therefore obtained from the New Zealand Division (including its divisional cavalry regiment and M.G. battalion).

Transport.

Formation of the Unit began on 7 July 1940, but it was found to be impossible to obtain suitable 30-cwt cars of the American type. Finally the unit was allotted the chassis of fourteen 30-cwt lorries and four 15-cwt lorries, all of the Chevrolet pattern, which had recently been brought by the Ordnance Department from the Chevrolet Company at Alexandria; and nineteen Chevrolet trucks which were handed over by the Egyptian Army. These nineteen trucks had suitable bodies, but bodies had to be constructed for the remainder. Special fittings were also necessary for the mounting of Bofors guns, A.T. Rifles and Lewis guns; and brackets for compasses, lockers for tools, spare parts, etc. and racks for carrying two gallon water cans and W.T. sets had to be made. Condensers had to be fitted to the radiators.

By 12 August the thirty three 30-cwt trucks were ready. At about the same time two 6 wheeled-drive Marmon-Harrington lorries were also acquired from an American oil prospecting company, and were used as a 'B' echelon for carrying petrol from the Nile to advanced bases on the east side of the Sand Sea. A trial in Libya between 7 and 19 August proved that the four 15-cwt Chevrolet trucks were too light for the work they had to do, and they were replaced by four Fords fitted out by Thomas Cook & Son which were ready on 2 September.

Navigation and Signals.

Five men with a little knowledge of navigation supplied by the New Zealand Division were trained by Lieut. Kennedy-Shaw. Six wireless operators were supplied by the New Zealand Divisional Cavalry Regiment, and each of the three parties (i.e. the two patrols and 'A' echelon) had a No. 11 wireless set.

Preliminary Reconnaissance.

Little was known about what was going on in inner Libya, but Capt. P.A. Clayton who arrived to join the unit on 16 July had had a long standing acquaintance with useful desert Arabs and at once initiated three schemes for improving our knowledge.

Manoufli, a Shaigi Arab in the employment of the Survey of Egypt, was sent to Uweinat via Wadi Halfa and Shebb with a motor patrol of the Egyptian Frontiers Administration. He was left there with a camel which had been carried in a lorry (the first time this was ever done over a long distance), and was told to find out what he could of the Italian occupation at the western end of the mountain. He was picked up by the patrol on its next trip; and his camel survived a motor-borne journey of 1,000 miles.

The second scheme was to land a former inhabitant of Kufra by air

60 miles from the Oasis, and to pick him up again by car after he had walked into Kufra and out again, bringing with him, it was hoped, some relative who was anxious to get away into Egypt. No one however was found who was willing to do this.

The third scheme carried out by Capt. Clayton himself with five picked New Zealanders and an Ababda Arab, named Abu Fadail, was a reconnaissance of the Jalo-Kufra road with two 15-cwt Chevrolet trucks. Leaving Cairo on 7 August and moving by Mersa Matruh, he reached Siwa on the 8th. He was there reinforced by a section of seven trucks lent him by Colonel Hatton and Major Bather of the Frontier Administration to assist in the carriage of petrol and water, and moved south through the Sand Sea to "Two Hills"* by the route that he had taken on a survey expedition some years before. There the Frontier Administration lorries had to leave him, for as Egypt was not at war with Italy they could not cross the frontier. Clayton then moved W.S.W. as far as the Jalo-Kufra road near which his party lay up to watch for traffic. Unable to move further west owing to the danger of his tracks being observed to the prejudice of future surprise, he sent out a patrol on foot for five miles to find out the width of the traffic lane. It appeared to stretch indefinitely westward, but no tracks fresher than several months old were seen. Later it was discovered that owing to the softness of the marked ground the Italians were using a route considerably further west. The party then returned by Siwa and reached Cairo across country on 19 August. They were congratulated by the C.-in-C. on their success. The reconnaissance had produced valuable geographical information, which included the discovery of a second and formidable "Sand Sea" about 60 miles wide and stretching south-wards, immediately east of the Jalo-Kufra road. It was crossed both on the outward and return journeys.

Before Clayton's reconnaissance a dump of 7,000 gallons of petrol was formed at Siwa by the British Army, and another dump of about 3,500 gallons was formed on the eastern edge of the Sand Sea.

---

* long 25°.20' E – lat 27°.15' N

Section II

Organization and Arms.

On 27 August the unit was inspected by the C.-in-C. and was reported to the War Office as ready to take the field. Its formation, equipment and training had taken only seven weeks from the date of its authorization on 10 July. Moreover preliminary reconnaissances had been made and petrol dumps formed.

Operations by the unit as a whole began in September 1940. The organization which had been slightly modified, was now as follows. It consisted of HQ. and three patrols ('R', 'T', and 'W'). Each patrol had 2 officers and 25 O.Rs, carried in ten 30-cwt Chevrolet trucks, and a light 15-cwt pilot car. All the vehicles were specially fitted and equipped for twenty days and 1,500 miles of self-contained action. The armament of each patrol included one 37 mm Bofors gun, four Boys A.T. Rifles and ten Lewis guns. There was also a supply section consisting of two 3?-ton Marmon-Harrington trucks which was used for forming dumps of petrol and water along the eastern edge of the Sand Sea – Gilf Kebir barrier, a lift of between 350 and 450 miles.

Characteristics of Libyan Desert.

Before dealing in detail with the first operation of the Long Range Patrol it will be convenient to describe the country over which it had to operate. The information is derived from a memorandum written by Major Bagnold at the end of the following month, to which further reference is made later. He points out in the first place that the "desert experience" of British troops in Egypt before the outbreak of war with Italy was confined to the relatively small area within the western frontier and between Mena and Mersa Matruh, in which conditions were vastly different from those of the "Inner Desert" over the Libyan border. It should be remembered too that

18

the British Government had observed all the rules of neutrality, and that the maintaining of agents in Italian territory was not countenanced.

Although many areas exist which can be crossed by motor vehicles at high speed, the main characteristic of the Inner Desert of Libya, which is part of the Sahara, is *Sand* which exists to an extent outside the experience of our Army at that time. There are many great "dune-fields". They can be crossed in certain places by M.T. skilfully piloted, but the vehicles behind must keep closely to the tracks of the pilot vehicle in order to avoid sinking into dry quick-sands. Each vehicle however disturbs the chosen track so much that after twenty or thirty vehicles have passed over it, no more can follow without great loss of speed and consumption of petrol.

Secondly there are many escarpments which often restrict the possible motor routes over them to one pass in every ten or fifteen miles of the escarpment's length. A "pass" often consists of a big sand drift which happens to bridge a vertical cliff and crossing it involves the limitation of numbers for the reasons referred to above. It is therefore almost impossible for a large united force to get through, apart from the delay that must inevitably arise when a great number of vehicles are obliged to traverse any kind of defile in single file.

Finally Major Bagnold points out that the fairly numerous Egyptian oases could not be regarded as a fair sample of the water supplies available further west. In the desert west of Kufra the water in most of the wells is derived from local rainfall. The water seeps in slowly and is not sufficient for the sudden needs of a large number of men.

It was therefore obvious that about thirty vehicles was the greatest number that should normally move together; and the original organization of the force into patrols and later into squadrons, was based on this assumption.

First Operation September 1940.

Orders for the first operation were issued on 4 September 1940. The enemy was thought to be preparing some form of offensive operation from the Inner Desert against Egypt or the Sudan. It was known that he was occupying Jalo and Kufra, that he had W.T. and a few aircraft, and that he was sending patrols to Uweinat. As there was probably a considerable leakage of information from the Egyptian oases and especially from Siwa, great care had to be taken to conceal intentions and movements.

The intention of this operation apart from its training value and the geographical information that would be obtained, was threefold.
(a) To form dumps of petrol, rations and water along the Libyan frontier.

(b) To make long distance reconnaissances N.E., N. and N.W. of Kufra and S.E., S. and S.W. of Kufra.

(c) To raid and destroy any enemy dumps that might exist at Uweinat.

Patrols were to move off on 5 September, 'W' Patrol at 0900 hrs, 'R' at 0930 hrs and 'T' at 1000 hrs.

The O.C. "Marmon" party, i.e. the supply echelon, was to make his own arrangements with Movement Control Abbassia in regard to transport by rail. The C.O., the Adjutant, and Lieut. Kennedy-Shaw accompanied 'W' Patrol. One itinerary (by Siwa) was given to 'T' and 'R' Patrols. Another was followed by 'W' Patrol which moved via Ain Dalla. All three patrols were to concentrate at a final rendezvous east of the Uweinat Mountain so as to carry out a combined reconnaissance of the Uweinat area on 25 September. The return journey was to begin on the 29th.

The report on the operation shows that important information was obtained about the geography of the Sand Sea. 'W' Patrol established that in all probability there was only one practicable east and west route across it south of Siwa. This was a zone about 16 miles wide where the major dune ranges, which are as much as 300 feet high, 16 miles long and entirely impassable, are less densely distributed than elsewhere. Two journeys were made across it from east to west fully loaded, the second in 6? hours running time; and only two trucks got stuck. Further information was gathered about the limits of the previously unknown sand sea discovered by Capt. Clayton during his reconnaissance in August. On 16 September 'W' Patrol visited a small emergency landing ground (No. 4 on the Jalo-Kufra air route) and destroyed a small stock of the enemy's petrol and also the pump and wind indicator. Similar destruction was carried out on landing ground No. 3 further north. Certain well marked tracks were discovered, but there had been no abnormal traffic. Wadi Zighen,* an area of blown sand with a little meagre vegetation and five wells, was also visited. This area is a bottle neck through which all traffic to Kufra from the north must pass in order to get through the Libyan Sand Sea discovered by Clayton. The weather was hotter than anything experienced by members of the patrol who had fifteen years experience of the East, and there were minor cases of heat stroke.

Capture of Italian Lorries.

At landing ground No. 7, some 20 miles S.E. of Wadi Zighen, two lorries were captured belonging to the Trucchi Company, a civilian concern which

---

* 100 miles N.W. of Kufra.

carried Italian military stores. They were carrying two Italians, 2,000 gallons of petrol and a bag of military mail. From this spot; 'W' Patrol drove east to join H.Q. and 'R' Patrol at Wadi El Gubba (or Er Riquba) (about 100 miles) over a hitherto untraversed route.

Owing to the need for saving petrol the two captured lorries were hidden in the hills at a point about 25 miles south of Wadi El Gubba whence they were later recovered; and the eight prisoners were taken to Cairo. From Wadi El Gubba 'W' and 'R' Patrols took different routes. 'W' moved by Jebel Arkenu and Karkur Ibrahim, a valley useful for concealment which runs into the N.W. corner of the Uweinat massif. 'R' Patrol under Lieut. D.G. Steele (New Zealand M.G. Bn.) reconnoitred the line of dunes which runs from a point N.E. of Jebel Biban and thence S.W. between Arkenu and Uweinat towards Bir Sarra. These dunes could only be crossed at one point which, if held, would effectively cut communications between Kufra and Uweinat. 'T' Patrol under Capt. P.A. Clayton left Cairo with 'R' Patrol and both proceeded by an unfrequented route to Siwa. On 10 September the supply dump at Jebel Tibtah was cleared to give the impression that supplies were being withdrawn into Egypt, and on the 11th and 12th new supply dumps were formed, one in the dunes on the route leading to Two Hills, and another at a point in the dunes about 12 miles S.E. of Two Hills. 'T' Patrol separating from 'R' Patrol on 14 September about 40 miles S.S.W. of Big Cairn, moved S.S.W. over a hitherto unreconnoitred route till it reached the Kufra-Uweinat track near Garet Cudi about 120 miles N.W. of Uweinat, where fresh tracks only a few hours old were seen and judged to be those of a single journey from Kufra to Uweinat made by 36 vehicles and *not* a double journey by 18. A landing ground was found but not interfered with as it was desirable not to alarm the Uweinat garrison. The patrol then visited the wells at Bir Bishara and Bir Sarra which were found in their original condition as used by Arabs with no modern improvements. These wells are on the track running S.S.W. from Kufra towards the French frontier.

Contact with French in Chad Territory.

The march was continued in a southwesterly direction, and two cars went as far as Tekro, a French outpost held by native troops who were quite prepared to fight the Italians for whom at first our patrol was mistaken. A note was sent by camel to Lieut. Perron who was in command at Ounianga about 40 miles S.W. of Tekro. The patrol then rejoined H.Q. and 'W' and 'R' Patrols at the prearranged rendezvous near Uweinat arriving at noon on 25 September.

Reconnaissance of Uweinat.

The reconnaissance of the Uweinat area began on 26 September when 'T' Patrol moved south and east of Jebel Kissu to "Peter and Paul" Hills at Long. 25.25 E, Lat. 22.25 N, and 30 miles N.N.E. of Uweinat, where it joined 'W' and 'R' Patrols, who had taken a different route, on the 27th. The day was clear but no aircraft were seen nor did the dust, caused by the patrols, cause any air reconnaissance. The route crossed all possible outlets from Uweinat towards the Sudan and no tracks of enemy patrols were seen. The conclusion was that no Italian ground patrols had been reconnoitring in that direction. On the return journey to Cairo 'R' and 'T' Patrols found a new route to Ain Dalla which was satisfactory and secure from observation, passing west of the Dakhla oasis and thence by Bir Abu Mungar.*

During the expedition only two aircraft were seen and on the first occasion the patrol ('W') was not observed.

The patrols covered 150,000 truck miles without serious mechanical trouble, though one truck turned over on a dune in the sand sea without damage.

Some possible landing grounds were seen and their positions fixed.

'B' Echelon.

During the whole of September 'B' Echelon (Marmon-Harrington trucks), under Lieut. Holliman, was employed in moving supplies of petrol, water and food from Wadi Halfa to the southern end of Gilf Kebir,** where a dump was made for future operations.

---

* About 100 miles N.E. of Uweinat.

** While the patrols were reconnoitring Uweinat a detached party under Lieut. Kennedy Shaw found a new route to Ain Dalla by the east side of the Gilf Kebir, Pottery Hill and Regenfeld.

Section III

Italian Offensive September 1940.

The operations of the Long Range Patrol during September 1940 began just before Marshal Graziani's only offensive operation, that is to say, his advance from the western frontier of Egypt on 13 September, which ended when he dug himself in three days later in the area Sidi Barrani-Maktila, and waited for two months to be attacked. They proved the value of such a force and the impunity with which, if adequately equipped and supplied, it was able to move about the desert. They also revealed defects in organization, and in other respects; and before describing subsequent operations these and other questions will be taken into consideration.

In October responsibility for the Long Range Patrol at G.H.Q. passed from the Intelligence Branch to the D.M.O. (Brig. Whiteley) and the branch dealing with it was known as G (R).

During the September operations it became clear that with the number of men available it was not possible to operate three patrols. The three original patrols ('R', 'T' and 'W') continued to exist and retained their own vehicles and stores, but for operations during the next five months or so they had to be organized as two composite patrols.

Increase in strength of L.R.D.G November 1940.

During Major Bagnold's absence in the desert in September G.H.Q. Middle East asked that the existing unit should be doubled and War Office sanction was given by cable on the 29th of that month. But in view of the experience gained during the first operation it was decided that the increase should not be used to form a second and identical Long Range Patrol, but for the organization of one unit with a centralized Headquarters which was to include a W/T section and a supply section, and two squadrons each consisting of three patrols. The whole unit was to be known as the Long Range Desert Group. Approval in principle of this scheme was cabled from the War Office on 9 November 1940. The next difficulty was to obtain the number of men required (21 officers and 250 O.Rs). Three

serious obstacles had to be overcome. In the first place Major-General
Freyberg, who arrived in Egypt with the remainder of the New Zealand
Division on 10 October 1940, demanded the return of all New Zealand
personnel who formed the great majority of the Long Range Patrol. The
Commander-in-Chief refused to agree, but decided that New Zealanders
must be withdrawn as and when they could be replaced by trained personnel from British and South Rhodesian units; and that this should be treated
as a separate problem from that of expansion. Even so it meant that as men
were withdrawn, the great experience they had gained during more than
200,000 truck miles of desert travel would be thrown away.

New Patrols.

A replacement scheme was approved on 25 October whereby six new
patrols were to be formed, the men for each patrol being drawn from a
specified group of regiments as follows –
    No. 1 Patrol from Footguards.
    No. 2 Patrol from South Rhodesian units.
    No. 3 Patrol from Highland regiments.
    No. 4 Patrol from Yeomanry regiments.
    No. 5 Patrol from Rifle regiments.
    No. 6 Patrol from Home Counties regiments.
The patrols were named accordingly, e.g. No. 4 was "No. 4 (Yeomanry)
Patrol L.R.D.G.". The establishment of each patrol was as follows:-

        Captain (Patrol Leader).....................1
        Subaltern.......................................1
        Sergeant.......................................1 (O.R. included also 3 corporals).
        Bofors gunners..............................2
        Driver mechanics............................1
        Drivers I.C...................................14
        General duty.................................9
        Fitter...1
        First reinforcement (General duty).......4

For reasons which appeared at the time to be avoidable, no action was
taken to put this scheme into effect until after the middle of November.
The second difficulty was the chronic shortage of officers and men in the
Middle East, which made Commanding Officers loth to part with men of
the high standard required for the work they would have to do.

Lastly, the addition of a second squadron necessitated an increase in
transport of 37 Chevrolet trucks which were not available, or even on
order from America. Efforts were made to obtain them from the Egyptian
Army but without success.

Wingate's Plan and Bagnold's modifications of it.

In the middle of October 1940, when the reorganization was beginning, Major (afterwards Major-General) O.C. Wingate arrived in Egypt. He brought with him a scheme, which had some support in England, for the creation of a desert mechanized force of all arms equivalent in strength to a division. In theory the idea was sound enough, but its author had no experience of desert travel in M.T. nor of the consumption of petrol involved. Major Bagnold appreciated the strategical value of the idea; and he submitted a modified scheme which envisaged the gradual evolution of a similar but smaller force of all arms including light tanks, of a strength which was compatible with the limitations imposed on movement and supply by desert conditions.

Italy's declaration of war, and the establishment of a "Vichy French" Government in Algeria and Tunis laid the whole of North Africa open to penetration by the enemy; and a force of the kind that Major Bagnold suggested would probably have had to be based on ports outside the Mediterranean, including those in West Africa. On the other hand, the enemy was obliged by the water problem to scatter his forces along the narrow coastal belt between Jedabia and the Egyptian Frontier. A mobile desert force would therefore constitute a constant threat from the south, while the need for constant reconnaissance would put a severe strain on his Air Force. It would also contribute to co-operation with the Free French in the Chad Territory. Major Bagnold pointed out however that the transport of a force of the kind that he had in mind would require "desert worthy vehicles" of far greater carrying capacity than any then available in Egypt and that its basis should be the 10-ton truck. The scheme was not adopted for many reasons, of which the chief was the provision of men and equipment; but the subsequent operations of the Long Range Desert Group, when it attained its full strength, went a long way towards achieving the strategical objects which its author had in view.

Section IV

Second Operation of Long Range Patrol. October-November 1940.

The second operation carried out by Major Bagnold's command, which was still known as the "Long Range Patrol", took place during the last week of October 1940. Its intentions were –

(a) to harass the enemy by laying mines on parts of the road Uweinat-Kufra-Jedabia,

(b) to gain information about the enemy's air and ground patrol movements between this road and the Egyptian frontier,

(c) to bring in the two Trucchi lorries captured in the September operation,

(d) to capture prisoners.

'T' and 'R' Patrols were employed for the purpose, and supplies were carried from Cairo to Ain Dalla by the 'B' Echelon (Marmon-Harrington trucks). R.A.F. cooperation by No. 216 (Bomber Transport) Squadron was also arranged, with Baharia and other places as advanced bases. 'T' Patrol under Capt. Clayton left Cairo on 23 October, its main objective being the laying of mines round Jalo. It marched by Ain Dalla and thence across the "Sand Sea"; to Big Cairn, where a landing ground was prepared and contact made with the aircraft. From Big Cairn the patrol took a direct course to Jalo, 260 miles to the N.W., thus making a third crossing of the newly found Libyan "Sand Sea" and more useful information was gained as to its limits and the character of its dunes. Passing south and west respectively of Jalo and Aujila, the patrol followed the Aujila-Jedabia road to a point about 72 miles south of the latter place. Here they mined the road (about 30 October) and then turned back towards Aujila in the vicinity of which five more minefields were laid on 1 November, and the fort itself was captured.

Capture of Aujila 1 November 1940.

No resistance was offered, and after the first burst of Bofors and M.G. fire the garrison ran for the adjacent native village. One Libyan prisoner and two heavy M.Gs (Schwaarzloss) were captured. The patrol then returned by Ain Dalla to Cairo making a detour en route in an effort to map the northern boundary of the Libyan Sand Sea. 2140 miles were covered in fifteen days, and of this distance 855 miles were traversed in four days during the operations in and round Aujila. No hostile aircraft were seen.

'K' troop of 'R' Patrol (Lieut. Kennedy-Shaw) left Cairo on 24 October and the remainder of the troop under Capt. D.G. Steele on the 25th. 'K' troop acted as an advanced guard to improve the alignment of the road as far as Ain Dalla.

'R' troop's task was to mine roads in the neighbourhood of Uweinat and to recover the two captured Trucchi lorries. From Ain Dalla the patrol moved on towards Uweinat by Pottery Hill (Abu Ballas) and the east side of the Gilf Kebir plateau, the centre of which is about 115 miles N.E. of Uweinat. From Gilf Kebir 'M' troop (Lieut. Holliman) was detached to recover the Truchi lorries which, as already related, were hidden in September in the hills south of Wadi-El-Gubba. At Uweinat 'K' troop was also detached to make a reconnaissance on foot of the Italian post at Ain Zuwais on the western edge of Uweinat massif. On 31 October H.Q. and the remaining troop ('N'), while selecting places to mine on the dune crossing on the Uweinat-Arkenu road, discovered an Italian dump to the west of Uweinat. They blew up 75 18-k.g. bombs, 640 2-k.g. bombs and 10 forty-four gallon drums of petrol together with detonators and exploders. Later on the same day they destroyed a Savoia-Macchetti S.79 aeroplane standing on the landing ground west of Ain Zuwaia and also 160 forty-four gallon drums of petrol. The patrol (less 'M' troop) then began its return march by the west edge of the Gilf Kebir and while en route were bombed for an hour by three enemy aircraft. There was no casualty and only minor damage to vehicles.

Owing to mechanical breakdowns 'M' troop was unable to get the captured Trucchi lorries further than the Gilf Kebir. 'K' troop, too, had been unable to make its reconnaissance over the top of the mountain at Ain Zuwaia in the time available owing to climbing difficulties, but established the fact that the enemy were still in occupation and using the well, where five lorries were seen.

Apart from the bombing attack made on 1 November on a troop of 'R' Patrol that has been already referred to, only two enemy aircraft were seen by daylight (on 3 and 4 November). During the night of the 5th /6th a few were heard S.E. of Ain Dalla.

R.A.F. Cooperation.

One of our own aircraft, a Vickers-Valentia from No. 216 (Bomber Transport) Squadron R.A.F. cooperated with the patrols from 28 October till 4 November. It was piloted by F/O Farr who had accompanied Major

Bagnold during the September expedition to reconnoitre possible landing grounds. In addition to its crew of six it carried Major E.C. Mitford of the Long Range Patrol and the patrol's Medical Officer with four stretchers and first aid equipment. It was fitted with long range tanks; and fuel had been dumped in advance on the Bawiti landing ground at Baharia, at Big Cairn and at Four Hills (Wadi Sora). After leaving Heliopolis on the 28th the plane operated from one or other of these dumps. It carried 8 days supplies with the usual reserve, but water supply was a difficulty. None had been dumped, and owing to the load already on board it could not be carried in the plane. The passengers were therefore dependent on water provided by the patrols whenever they were in touch. The fuel dumped was only just sufficient for its purpose, and the plane had only one hour's petrol left when it landed at Heliopolis on 4 November. The total distance covered during the operation was about 1.900 miles, the total flying time 24 hrs 40 minutes, and the average speed 78 miles an hour.

W/T Communication.

W/T communication with the R.A.F. station at Ismailia was opened for several periods during each day, and information was successfully passed to G.H.Q. Middle East. Good communication was established with 'R' Patrol, but not with 'T' Patrol which was in touch with the plane only once, and then for a very short time.

Landing grounds were marked out at Big Cairn, Mushroom Rocks and Wadi Sora; and many other suitable places were found.

The visibility of tracks from the air was studied, and the aircraft followed the patrols' tracks over the Sand Sea. These were easy to pick out as the vehicles were following each other in "line ahead", and it was evident that in such cases tracks would always be visible from normal heights. When vehicles are spread out tracks are less likely to be seen, and sudden changes of direction are apt to confuse an aircraft trying to follow them.

The prisoner captured at Aujila gave a certain amount of information. Among other things he said that Marshal Balbo had made a speech to the effect that Italians were not fighting against any Mohammedan troops in Egypt; but the prisoner did not realize that many Indians were of that faith, nor that a Senussi Force was being raised in Egypt. He stated that the garrison of Jalo was only 50 strong and included only two Italians, but that at Giarabub there were about 1,500 men. There were some 2,500 Arab troops in Italian service at Sidi Barrani, and he was of the opinion that they were being pushed on ahead to act as a "shield". He also said that the Italians had spread a rumour that the British killed their prisoners and that the object of our bombing raids was to kill civilians. But the Arabs had ceased to believe the latter accusation as the number of civilians killed had been infinitesimal. The Italians, he said, believed that Siwa was defended so strongly that they could not attack it. As a result of our previous raids vehicles were not allowed to go to Kufra except in convoy and with adequate protection. He also said that the Arabs believed, as we did, that Marshal Balbo's death was not accidental.

Section V

Occupation of Kufra proposed.

In the middle of October 1940, Major Bagnold wrote a memorandum proposing the occupation of Kufra and operations further west in conjunction with the French. It was believed that Toummo (Long. 14°E, Lat. 22°40'N.) which lies near the undemarcated boundary between the Tenere district of French West Africa and the Italian province of Fezzan, about 250 miles N.W. of the centre of the Tibesti massif, was occupied by the Italians. Its possession enabled the enemy to raid Kano either with light mechanized units or by camel; and for a camel raid they could employ the Northern Touareg Tribe who were experts at it and had traditionally raided S.W. from their own territory towards Nigeria.

If Toummo were in Allied hands it would be possible to threaten the important hostile centres at Gatrun, 160 miles to the N.N.E. and Murzouk, 220 miles north. As matters then stood the Free French from Chad could not attack Toummo without passing through the Tenere district which was then in the hands of the Vichy government; but it was thought that the Free French would not object to its occupation by ourselves. Alternatively a small British raiding force might operate from the north of the Tibesti hills based on existing Free French posts, and so avoid contact with the Vichy French. The Free French had a motor machine gun unit but probably no great mobility owing to shortage of petrol; but they were believed to be anxious to consolidate provincial sentiment by attacking the Italians.

Major Bagnold suggested that Anglo French operations, even on a small scale, along the frontier between Tibesti and Toummo concurrently with or immediately after an attack on Kufra, would seriously disconcert the Italians at small cost to ourselves. Little was known in Egypt about the country but it was thought that with the help of the Hon. Francis Rodd in West Africa, and of the French at Fort Lamy (in the Chad territory) enough information would be obtained to enable a decision to be made for or against the proposed action.

Conference at Fort Lamy November 1940.

For political reasons he suggested that representatives from G.H.Q. Middle East should meet Mr. Rodd and the French at Fort Lamy with as little delay as possible. As a result of his suggestion Major Bagnold was sent to Fort Lamy and was there from 8 to 10 November 1940; and in the meanwhile the War Office had proposed to send a mission under Lieut. Colonel Grant to Tibesti to gain adherents there. The objects of Major Bagnold's visit were –

(1) First to find out whether any offensive operations in the area north of the Chad territory were contemplated by Colonel Marchand, who commanded the troops in Chad, General de Gaulle, or Lieut. General Giffard, G.O.C.-in-C., British West Africa; and, if so, what they were.

(2) To find out what was thought of the War Office proposal to send out the mission under Lieut. Colonel Grant.

(3) To discuss with Colonel Marchand a proposal of G.H.Q., M.E. to send two Long Range Patrols to the northern edge of the Tibesti Hills with the object of making raids, in cooperation with French troops, on the Italian posts at Wau-el-Kebir, Gatrun, Murzuk, Tejerri and elsewhere; and, if he agreed, to work out details of the operation.

Lieut. General Giffard sent his G.S.O.2 ("I") Major Burnett, to Fort Lamy to represent his views.

Attitude of Free French.

Colonel Marchand's opinion in which he was supported by his officers, was that the capture of Kufra was of necessity the first major operation to be undertaken; and that the area in which the French could most usefully operate was eastward rather than northward. But he and all his officers warmly welcomed the scheme referred to in sub-para. 3 above for raiding small Italian posts in Fezzen; and Major Bagnold worked out details with him before leaving Fort Lamy. It was proposed that the start from Cairo should be made during the first week of December 1940, and it was expected that the operations would take 36 days from start to finish. The French asked for 12 days notification of the date on which it was to start. Adequate stocks of petrol and rations existed at Zouar in the Tibesti Hills and at Largeau just south of them, details of which were available. The readiness of Colonel Marchand and his officers to fall in with the proposed scheme was due in part to the feeling that it was necessary as soon as possible to justify to their troops and to the native population their recent adhesion to the Free French movement; and that this was best done by military action. They were no less anxious to take an active part as they considered it would have a widespread effect on French subjects in the territory further west which was still controlled by the government at Vichy: and it was hoped that the garrison of Madama, about 120 miles west of the nearest point on the Chad border, might be induced to change sides.

Lieut. Colonel d'Ornano, who was in executive command of the troops, was most anxious to take a personal part in the operation with a picked party of officers and men, both European and native, and would ask permission from General de Larminat. It was not expected that he would raise any objection since General de Gaulle had recently expressed a wish that the troops in Chad should lose no opportunity of taking a part, however small, in the war against the Italians.

Attitude of West African Command.

Major Burnett who, as already stated, was present as the representative of the West African Command, said that General Giffard's attention was at the moment concentrated on defence against possible action by the Vichy French to the north of him, and as his forces were not in contact with the Italians he preferred to leave all action against them to the Free French or to the Middle East Command. Neither he nor Colonel Marchand were in favour of the proposed mission of Lieut. Colonel Grant, for no adherents could be collected, especially by a British Mission, until some solid Anglo-French success such as the capture of Kufra, had been achieved.

Attitude of G.H.Q., M.E.

G.H.Q. Middle East was interested in the capture of Kufra and regarded the Chad province as being a possible base for minor operations against Libya and the Fezzan. The authorities in British West Africa were interested politically because of the possible influence of the Free French in Chad on the Vichy province immediately west of it; and economically because of the trade between Chad and Nigeria. On the military side they were not directly interested from the operational point of view, but were aware that they might be called on to furnish supplies and military stores for operations either by the Free French or the Middle East Command. At this time W/T communication between Egypt, British West Africa and the Chad territory was far from good, and travel even by air was slow.

Section VI

First Operation of L.R.D.G. November and December 1940.

The first operation of the Long Range Desert Group, as it had now become, took place in November 1940.

The intentions in the northern area were –

(a) To examine the sand dune area between Jalo and Jarabub by a traverse from south to north as far as the Jalo-Jarabub road, and in the approximate longitude 23°30'.

(b) To ascertain if the road was used by M.T. and, if so, to lay mines on it.

(c) To retrieve a Ford truck belonging to 'T' Patrol.

(d) To inspect existing dumps; and to form a new petrol dump for M.T. at "Gravel Cairn" in the dunes opposite Mushroom Rock (25°E, 26°30'N.), and one of aviation spirit at the Big Cairn landing ground (25°5'E, 26°58'N).

In the Uweinat area it was intended:-

(1) to reconnoitre the enemy's landing ground S.W. of Ain Dua and if possible damage stores near it,

(2) to take any opportunity of harassing the enemy.

Work in the northern area was to be done by 'R' Patrol under Capt. Steele, in the Uweinat area by 'W' Patrol under Major Mitford. 'B' Echelon (Marmon-Harrington trucks) was to carry M.T. petrol and aviation spirit from Cairo to Ain Dalla dump. The Frontier Administration had given orders that no Egyptian patrol was to visit Uweinat between 26 November and 3 December, and the O.C. 'W' Patrol was instructed, during his return journey, to inform Yusbashi Ayyad Effendi, the Commander of the Egyptian Squadron at Kharga, which provided these patrols, of the situation at Uweinat. Aircraft cooperation was arranged, and detailed instructions given as to intercommunication including ciphers and codes. It appears that Siwa had neither cipher nor code names, and messages to it had to be in clear.

'R' Patrol had some difficulty in its northward traverse owing to the necessity of crossing the sand dunes which run from S.S.E. to N.N.W. The return journey however was made rapidly by running parallel to the dune lines on bearings between 330° and 340°. It was found that north of the sand dunes along the Gardaba track running west from Jarabub there was broken limestone country with good but rough going. South of the dunes the going to Big Cairn was level and very good. Tracks indicated that the road had not been used either by camel or M.T. and no mines were laid.

'W' Patrol left Cairo on 23 November, called at Ain Dalla for water and encamped at the southern end of the Gilf Kebir on the 28th. Owing to the shorter days and some minor breakdowns the rate of travel was less than normal, and the weather was extremely cold from dusk to dawn. It was found that the enemy had bombed the Gilf Kebir dump, but the only damage was the destruction of four tins of water.

On the morning of 29 November the patrol divided into two halves, one under Lieut. Sutherland; the other under Major Mitford which made a wide detour to the east in order to show well marked tracks coming from that direction. Lieut. Sutherland's party was investigated at about 1015 hours by a Ghibli reconnaissance aircraft which sheered off when fired at. The two parties re-united later at Ras-el-Abd on the eastern edge of the Jebel Uweinat, and moved round to the south side of it. They visited Kerkur Murr and noted that there were no recent tacks of hostile vehicles.

Air attack.

At about 1515 hrs when at a point on the open plain about six miles S.W. of Karkur Murr, the patrol was bombed by a S.79 aircraft, and accordingly scattered. Two more aircraft joined in the attack which lasted for 65 minutes. The enemy started at about 1,000 feet, but as a result of fire brought to bear by all the vehicles they rose to 5,000 feet where they were out of range. Over 300 small calibre bombs were dropped but neither men nor vehicles were damaged. The immunity was due to dispersion, and also by vehicles singled out for attack using their speed to move at right angles to the line of flight of the attacking aircraft.

When the last aircraft had flown away the patrol resumed its movement to the west and found an excellent hiding place in some rocks east of Ain Dua. There they spent the night of 29/30th and lay up until 1600 hrs on the 30th when they moved to a camp site on the edge of the gravel plain south and east of Ain Dua. The patrol moved off before sunrise on 1 December and at 0700 hrs arrived with the sun behind it, in the immediate neighbourhood of Ain Dua. One troop was detached to inspect the landing ground which seemed to be empty and the rest of the patrol approached Ain Dua itself.

Attack on Ain Dua 1 December 1940.

There appeared at first to be no sign of life there; but when within about 800 yards the patrol halted, and fired one round from a Bofors gun. This aroused intermittent M.G. and rifle fire from behind walls and rocks.

Major Mitford then attacked. 'D' Troop under Lieut. Sutherland was sent round the enemy's left to make a flank attack on foot, while the rest of the patrol gave covering fire from the front. 'D' Troop's attack was successful and the garrison, believed to consist of about 30 men with 3 M.G.'s, abandoned their strong position and retired up the hill after losing three men, of whom one at least was killed. As a reconnaissance aircraft was expected to make its appearance the action was broken off, and the patrol took cover in the rocks about a mile and a quarter east of Ain Dua. At 1015 hrs two S.79's arrived and at 1045 a Ghibli aircraft. They disappeared in due course, but as it was not certain whether the patrol had been discovered or not, it lay up until 1500 hrs. Major Mitford then decided to make a second attack in spite of the strength of the enemy's position. He hoped to inflict further damage to men and material, and he also wished to show the enemy that one patrol could remain in their immediate vicinity without being spotted by aircraft. This might well create a feeling of uncertainty, and lead them to use up valuable petrol in increased and fruitless patrolling.

The second attack was made from both flanks. 'D' Troop with one Bofors gun attacked the enemy's left over the ground that it knew. Covering fire was given by the H.Q. truck and one Bofors gun. The remainder of the patrol worked round the enemy's right. Orders were issued that the risk of heavy losses must not be taken. 'D' Troop got close enough to inflict further casualties, and silenced two of the three machine guns, but the enemy defended himself stoutly, and the position could not be captured. Lieut. Sutherland and one man got close enough to cause damage with Mills grenades. Trooper Willcox, who was pinned down by M.G. fire, distinguished himself by getting his Lewis gun into a position from which he killed the machine gunner and silenced the gun. The rest of the patrol were unable owing to the difficulties of the ground, to get near enough to engage the enemy. At 1700 hrs when it was beginning to get dark the patrol was withdrawn.

Withdrawal from Ain Dua.

It had had no casualties, but 'D' Troop had killed six of the enemy and wounded another six or possibly more. The patrol assembled in view of Ain Dua and retired due south making very clear tracks. After moving in this direction for a mile or so it turned east and spent the night in the foothills south of the Jebel Uweinat and about 12 miles from Ain Dua. On 2 December the patrol moved east and reached Kharga on the 4th having covered 465 miles in three days over good going suitable for all types of vehicles. No hostile aircraft were seen. The patrol left Kharga at 0830 hrs on 5 December and travelling day and night through the Nile Valley reached Cairo (350 miles) at 0645 hrs on the 6th.

Section VII

Formation of New Patrols and arrival of Reinforcements December 1940 and early 1941.

As related earlier a reorganization and an increase in the strength of the Long Range Desert Group were approved at the end of September 1940; and the scheme envisaged the raising of six entirely new patrols, it being then understood that all the New Zealanders were to be returned to their own division as soon as they could be replaced by trained men. At the beginning of December the group was moved from the Fever Hospital barracks at Abbassia, which were only just large enough for its original strength, to the Citadel at Cairo. The first new contingent arrived on 5 December. It consisted of officers and men from the 3rd Bn. Coldstream Guards and the 2nd Bn. Scots Guards, and was called 'G' Patrol. It was commanded by Capt. M.D.D. Crichton-Stuart, Scots Guards, with Lieut. M.A. Gibbs, Coldstream Guards, as second in command; and took over the vehicles and equipment of 'W' Patrol which ceased to exist. Lieut. J.H. Sutherland of 'W' Patrol went as second in command to 'R' Patrol, and the men were distributed between 'T' and 'R' Patrols. There also joined at the same time a signal officer, 2/Lieut. G.B. Heywood, Middlesex Yeomanry, together with a certain number of Unit and Squadron H.Q. personnel including W/T operators, M.T. personnel, R.A.M.C. orderlies, storemen and R.A.S.C. drivers.

No further reinforcements arrived until 31 January 1941. The Guards Patrol after a short period of training left with 'T' Patrol under Capt. Clayton to carry out the group's fourth operation at Murzuk and in the Fezzan, which started on 27 December 1940 and is dealt with in the next Section.

Heavy lorries.

With a view to the formation of a long range striking force as described in Section III, trials were carried out early in December of various makes of 10-ton lorries. Four types were available, the Foden and the Leyland which were British, and the Mack and the White which were American.

Preliminary trials showed that the two British lorries were not suitable owing to the excessive weight on the front wheels. The two American types were tested during a 300 mile march to Ain Dalla and back between 8 and 15 December, both fully loaded with 10 tons of cased petrol. The test showed that the White lorry was entirely suitable, and Lieut. Colonel Bagnold wrote a memorandum to the General Staff dated the 22nd December 1940, in which he again advocated the establishment of a Desert Striking Force, based either on Wadi Halfa or Kano or on both. As already explained this scheme was not adopted, but the "White" lorries were used as 'B' echelon vehicles in the L.R.D.G.

Second Operation of L.R.D.G. 27 December 1940 to February 1941.

The Long Range Desert Group's next operation began on 27 December 1940 and ended on 9 February 1941. Its "intention" was defined as follows:-

(a) To extend the "nuisance value" of the desert group to areas further west.
(b) To enable the French in Chad territory to cooperate in raids against Libya, and by so doing to influence opinion in the Niger territory which was under the control of the Vichy government.
(c) To spread information of British successes to the natives in Western Libya.
(d) To obtain geographical information for future use.

Sir A. Wavell's attack on Graziani, December 1940.

General Sir A. Wavell's attack on Marshal Graziani began on 9 December 1940 and when the L.R.D.G's operation started he was attacking Bardia which fell on 5 January 1941. The British advance continued without pause throughout January, and Bengazi surrendered on 6 February. There was therefore plenty of good news to spread among the native population.

The operation was to be carried out by 'T' (New Zealand) Patrol and 'G' (Guards) Patrol, under the command of Capt. P.A. Clayton. Ten French officers and other ranks under Lieut. Colonel d'Ornano were to join the force at Kayugi at the north end of the Tibesti "massif", and were to be carried in its trucks for 12 days during the active part of the operation, and dropped at Zouar (south of Tibesti) on the return journey. The French bases at Zouar and Faya were to be used for drawing supplementary rations and petrol.

L.R.D.G. patrols joined by Free French.

'T' and 'G' Patrols left Cairo on 27 December 1940 and marched by Ain Dalla and north of Taizerbo, to point 'A' (Long. 18°E, Lat. 24°22'N), which they reached on 4 January 1941. Capt. Clayton then went to Kayugi and picked up Lieut. Colonel d'Ornano, 2 officers, 2 (French) sergeants and 5 (native) O.R's of the Free French Forces. At the same time 'T' Patrol carried out a reconnaissance of the Italian routes to Kufra through the Jebel Eghei about 120 miles S.E. of Point 'A'. The combined force left Point 'A' on 8 January, moved first N.W. and then turning left-handed about 120 miles away from it, approached Murzuk from approximately N.N.E. They had covered 1,333 miles from Cairo, and during the whole journey through Libya the only human beings seen were three natives leading camels. It was also certain that no sign of the patrols had been seen by the enemy.

Occupation of Murzuk, 11 January 1941.

The patrols entered Murzuk by the main road from Sebha at 1330 hrs on 11 January, and received the Fascist salute from natives who presumably thought they were Italians! The garrison in a fort S.E. of the town, were taken completely by surprise and some of them who were strolling outside it were shot down.

Resistance from the Fort.

Effective resistance however began at once. The fort was engaged by 'G' Patrol, half of 'T' Patrol and the French, with one 37 mm Bofors and two 2" mortars, and with rifle and M.G. fire. The Central Tower was set on fire and burned fiercely for some time. Meanwhile the remainder of 'T' Patrol with its Bofors gun, attacked the aerodrome whose guards surrendered after little opposition. Arms in the hangar were seized, the W/T set was wrecked, and the three aircraft in the hangar were set on fire. Later the roof of the hangar collapsed.

Withdrawal.

When the attack had been in progress for about two hours it became clear that with the force available the fort could not be taken: and the patrols were therefore withdrawn along the Sebha road. The enemy did not pursue, and it was estimated that his losses had been 10 killed and 15 wounded. Two Italians, one of whom was the Murzuk postmaster, were taken prisoner; but the 25 Italians and Libyans who had surrendered on the aerodrome had to be left behind owing to lack of transport.

Death of Lieut. Colonel d'Ornano.

The Allied losses were two killed, one of whom unhappily was the Comte d'Ornano, and three wounded. Lieut. Colonel d'Ornano's death was a grievous loss to the Free French and to ourselves.

Capture of Traghen 12 January.

On 12 January the force surrounded the small town of Traghen, about thirty miles east of Murzuk, and demanded the surrender of the police fort. After a short delay a strange procession left the town headed by the Mudir (headman) and the notables who were followed by some fifty natives carrying banners and beating drums, with two sheepish looking Italian carabinieri bringing up the rear. The Mudir then surrendered the place. The two Italians and all arms from the fort were taken away, and the ammunition was destroyed.

From Traghen the force moved to Um-el-Araneb about 60 miles E.N.E. and thence to Gatrun about 150 miles further south. There were police forts at both these places but their garrisons had by this time been warned by W/T of our movements. Both forts were attacked with Bofors and M.G. fire and casualties may have been caused, but they were too strong to be taken with unarmoured vehicles. An attempt to cooperate with the French "groupe nomade" (Camel Corps) in an attack on Tejerri was unsuccessful as the exact position of the French could not be located. The "groupe's" attack failed because the enemy had been warned by its guides. On 16 January the force left Italian territory by Toummo, and marched to the French post at Zouar en route for Faya which lies S.E. of the Tibesti Hills. Two vehicles were left behind at Zouar owing to mechanical breakdowns after the force had covered a total distance of 1,740 miles.

During the return journey to Cairo another operation was carried out between Faya and Kufra in conjunction with Free French Forces, with the intention of capturing Kufra. 'T' and 'G' Patrols left Zouar on 21 January 1941 carrying a mortar detachment from the French company there, and Capt. Mercer-Nairne,* the British Liaison Officer at Fort Lamy. They followed a route leading S.S.E. from Zouar which skirts the foothills over very bad going, and reached Faya on 24 January. At Faya they took on petrol, rations (on the French scale) and water, left on the 27th and reached Ounianga on the 28th, after being obliged to abandon a Chevrolet truck en route owing to mechanical trouble.

Lieut. Colonel Leclerc's force joins the patrols.

The Free French Force under Colonel Leclerc had left Faya on the 26th, but had experienced delays on their march to Ounianga owing to mechanical defects and lack of experience in this type of transport problem.

'T' Patrol (Capt. Clayton) left Ounianga on 29 January and marching by Tekro, arrived at Sarra on the 30th where it was found that the enemy had blocked the well. They reached Bishara at 1020 hrs on the 31st to find that

---

* Scots Greys.

the well there had also been blocked, and while there they were observed by an enemy aircraft.

Attack by Italians at Jebel Sherif 31 January 1941.

Continuing their march they reached Jebel Sherif some twelve miles further north at 1130 hrs, and took cover among the rocks. At 1340 hrs hostile aircraft reappeared, and at 1400 hrs the patrol was engaged from the south by a ground force of the enemy which included a 20 mm gun. It was probably an "Auto-Saharan" patrol lying up near Jebel Sherif. The enemy's fire with H.E. and machine guns was heavy and accurate. Three of our trucks were destroyed by gun fire, Corporal Beech being killed; and four O.R's were missing, believed killed. Two of the Italian prisoners taken at Murzuk were killed and two others were probably recovered by the enemy. The remainder of the patrol withdrew northwards, and after making a detour were preparing to counter-attack when they were attacked by three aircraft with bombs and M.G. fire. Orders were then given to move to a pre-arranged rendezvous further south. During this retirement Capt. Clayton's car was damaged presumably by air attack and its occupants were taken prisoner. Next day (1 February) the remains of 'T' Patrol moved southwards and met 'G' Patrol, and the two patrols then joined Colonel Leclerc at a rendezvous near Tekro. Colonel Leclerc who was in command of the operation, realized that in view of the altered situation the operation as originally planned could not be carried out. He decided to abandon the idea of an attack on Kufra, and to remain near Sarra for a week or so and carry out harassing patrols. He then intended to concentrate his force at Tekro, and later to occupy Uweinat. He also decided that he could release the British patrols from further service with his force; and expressed his gratitude for their cooperation.

Return journey.

'T' and 'G' Patrols started eastwards on 4 February. They left behind them one truck with a navigator to help the French, and took with them as far as Uweinat two French officers in their own cars, to reconnoitre the enemy's position there. The reconnaissance was made by a small party on the 5th. No enemy were seen, but very recent tracks believed to be those of "Auto-Saharan" vehicles, indicated that the post was still occupied. The patrol reached Cairo by Kharga, on 9 February. Since leaving Cairo on 26 December they had travelled about 4,500 miles. Their losses had been two killed, four missing believed killed and three prisoners. Four cars had been destroyed by the enemy, and two lost owing to mechanical breakdown.

Exploits of 'T' Patrol's navigators.

The navigating truck left with Colonel Leclerc was manned by three men of 'T' Patrol, Lance Corporal F. Kendall, Trooper W. Burnand and Driver Clark, who accompanied the French in their first reconnaissance of Kufra. Lance Corporal Kendall was the navigator, and the three men had volunteered for the duty in response to a call by Captain Ballantyne of 'T' Patrol. They arrived at the French Camp 'S' on 3 February. From noon on 5 February until they reached Gebel-el-Tallab, about 12 miles S.W. of Kufra, they led the French convoy: they also made the first reconnaissance of the ground inside the Kufra "saucer". Later when leading a party of three French trucks to the aerodrome their truck was put out of action by striking a rock. Burnand remained behind to burn it in spite of Italian M.G. fire. Later all three men were thrown out of a 30-cwt Bedford truck which capsized in the dark, and they were also bombed and machine gunned by low flying aircraft. Burnand then distinguished himself by standing on the running board and taking careful aim with a rifle, the only weapon available, with the result that the aircraft sheered off.

The return journey was made by Jebel Sherif which was reached in the afternoon of 9 February. The bodies of Corporal Beech and of the captured Italian postmaster were found by the trucks that had been put out of action on 31 January. Corporal Beech and the prisoner were buried with military honours, the last offices being read by a French priest; and Beech's grave was marked with a cross inscribed with his name and unit. Kendall, Burnand and Clark returned to Fort Lamy with Capt. Mercer-Nairne, and reached Cairo by aeroplane on 27 March.

The adventures of Trooper Moore and others January-February 1941.

It remains to tell the story of four other men who took part in the fight at Jebel Sherif, but were unable to get away when the patrols withdrew. Their names were Trooper R.J. Moore, Trooper Easton, Fitter A. Tighe, R.A.O.C. and Guardsman A. Winchester. Details of what occurred are taken from notes made in conversation with them by Capt. Mercer-Nairne.

About 1600 hrs on 31 January these four men and one of the Italian prisoners took refuge in the rocks above the spot at which Corporal Beech's and Trooper Moore's trucks had been destroyed. Enemy aircraft were about during daylight and after dark all five men started to walk in the direction of Bishara. At one time they saw lights which they thought might be those of 'T' Patrol, but it is more likely that they belonged to Italian vehicles. They slept in the open desert. Next day, 1 February, they returned to Jebel Sherif to look for food and water. They found a one-gallon tin of water in the wreck of Corporal Beech's lorry, but no food, so they again started south without the prisoner. On 3 February they found a 2-lb pot of jam and some lentils but the latter were rotten and made

Winchester ill. They continued their journey on 4 February, but on the 5th Tighe was so tired that he had to be left behind. He was given his share of water – there was no food – but did not discover till later that it was in a bottle that had contained some salty substance and was undrinkable. On 6 February the other three arrived early at Sarra in a sandstorm, after walking 125 miles from Jebel Sherif. There was no food but they found some motor oil with which they bathed their feet. They spent the day in a hut and were able to make a fire at night. On the 7th Tighe, who had walked all the previous day, rejoined them but was unable to go further. The remainder continued their southward journey towards Tekro, and found great difficulty in keeping to the trail owing to the effects of the sandstorm. At dusk on the 9th a French patrol found Tighe at Sarra, and he was able to explain to them that he had three companions. Lieut. Dubat, who was in command, at once organized a search in the dark, but without success. On the same day two French aircraft flew over Moore and Winchester and dropped food and a bottle of lemonade. Unfortunately they were unable to find the food and the cork came out of the lemonade bottle. Easton had already had to drop out owing to exhaustion. On 10 February a French plane again came over and a second French search party found Easton about 56 miles south of Sarra, Winchester about 12 miles further on, and finally Moore who was still walking on when the trucks overtook him. At about 1930 hrs that evening Easton died and was buried near Sarra well two days later. A French chaplain read the committal prayers and a cross was erected over his grave with his name and unit stamped in metal on it.

Capt. Mercer-Nairne's report emphasizes the fact that Moore was unquestionably the leader of the party, and was game enough to be so in spite of a wounded foot with a splinter still in the flesh. Easton had a bullet wound in the throat and had suffered terribly from it. Before he died his body was so withered up that the Doctor who did all he could with the means available, could hardly extract a drop of blood from his body. Winchester had become almost insane. Tighe though he had been alone and without water for nearly four days and was a nervous wreck, at once thought of his three companions when he was found by the French patrol. Moore was back in Cairo on 27 March, but Tighe and Winchester had to remain in hospital at Khartoum.*

'R' and 'T' Patrols at Jarabub January-March 1941.

Soon after the departure of 'T' and 'G' Patrols to carry out the Murzuk operation the successes of the Western Desert Force had the effect of cutting off the Italian garrison in the Jarabub oasis, to which the garrisons of other posts along the frontier had retired. In order to help in containing

---

* Further reference to this expedition is made in App.2.

them 'R' Patrol (Capt. Steele) was put under command of the G.O.C. British Troops in Egypt, and was given orders to patrol the western approaches to the oasis. It left Cairo on 1 January 1941, marched by Ain Dalla and Big Cairn, and reached the Jarabub-Jalo track by a route through the northern area of the Sand Sea that had been reconnoitred in November 1940. The Jarabub garrison however were rationed by air and did not surrender as soon as was expected. 'R' Patrol was relieved by 'T' Patrol on 2 March and returned to Cairo on the 26th by which time the oasis had been taken by an Australian force sent from the north. The Kufra Oasis was captured by the French under Colonel Leclerc on 1 March.

Section VIII

Reorganization continues.

While the operationsdescribed in the last Section were in progress the reorganization of the Group went on. The second of the new patrols, known as 'S' (South Rhodesian) Patrol, came into being on 31 January 1941. In addition to men from Southern Rhodesia, it included drafts from the Northumberland Fusiliers and the Argyll & Sutherland Highlanders. Its formation was delayed by the fact that at the beginning of January the battalions concerned were engaged in the battle of Sidi Barrani, and their commanders were naturally reluctant to part with any men. At the end of January General Freyberg, G.O.C. New Zealand Division, agreed that the two New Zealand patrols ('T' and 'R') should remain with the Group, and be kept up to strength by the New Zealand Expeditionary Force.

On 25 February the Yeomanry Patrol arrived under the command of Capt. P.J.D. McCraith, Notts Yeomanry (Sherwood Rangers). It was drawn from units of the 1st Cavalry Division in Palestine. Many of the men proved to be unsuitable and some were ex-cavalry reservists of bad character. They had to be replaced, and the formation of the patrol was consequently delayed until 9 March.

An artillery section formed March 1941.

The Murzuk operation, described in Section VII, had shewn that stone forts might have to be captured, and that this could not be done without a much heavier weapon than the 37 mm. Bofors gun. It was therefore decided to form a small artillery section in place of one of the patrols that had been authorized. The men for this section arrived on 21 March and the Group was complete by the 31st, except that "B" Squadron had no commander, and was also short of a Squadron Sergt. Major and two N.C.Os.

Group H.Q.

Major Bagnold, who had been promoted Lieut.Colonel, remained in command with Major G.L. Prendergast, R.T.R., as second-in-command.

Group Headquarters included also one officer as Adjutant and Quarter Master, an Intelligence Officer (Lieut. W.B. Kennedy-Shaw), an Administrative Officer for Group H.Q., a Signal Officer and a Medical Officer. It had 47 O.Rs in all, some of whom (Wireless Operators and Medical Orderlies) were detached to squadrons and patrols.

'A' Squadron under Major E.C. Mitford included 'G' (Guards) Patrol, 'S' (South Rhodesian) Patrol, and 'Y' Yeomanry Patrol.

'B' Squadron whose headquarters was as yet incomplete, included the original New Zealand Patrols 'T' and 'R'.

The R.A. section which was armed with a 4.5 howitzer and a light tank was known as 'H' Section. The intention was that the light tank should act as an armoured O.P. besides using its own weapons when necessary.

Signals.

Signal arrangements had been very much improved as the result of experience, and the original operators were replaced by men lent by the Royal Corps of Signals including a Signal Officer (2/Lieut. G.B. Heywood, Middlesex Yeomanry), a Signal Sergeant and an instrument mechanic.

Transport Changes.

By the end of January 1941 it had become clear that the 30-cwt Chevrolets would not last much longer, owing to the exceptionally heavy work they had done. No more were available in the Middle East, and as the War Office policy was to abolish all 30-cwt trucks it was unlikely that any more would be sent out there. There was however a consignment of Ford 30-cwt four wheeled-drive trucks which had been originally built for the Canadian Army. They had been in Egypt for some time but orders had been received that they were not to be used even for trials, until a defect common to all of them had been remedied by replacement of the defective parts. As there was no alternative the Group was obliged at the end of February to accept 70 of these vehicles without trial, and the necessary modifications and fittings were completed by 20 March. It was realized that they would not be as suitable as the Chevrolet owing to their greater weight and to the complications introduced by the front wheel drive. In the meanwhile use was made of twelve Italian trucks captured from the "Auto Saharan" units. It was soon found, however, that they were not reliable enough, though excellent when in running order. The two six-wheeled Marmon-Harrington lorries of 'B' echelon were replaced by four 10-ton White lorries, two of which were fitted to carry a 4.5 howitzer and a light tank for "H Section".

L.R.D.G. Base moves to Kufra, April 1941.

After the Italians had been finally driven out of Cyrenaica as a result of the battle of Solluk (5 to 7 February) and the surrender of Bengazi on 6 February 1941, it became clear that the Long Range Desert Group could no longer operate from Cairo but must have a base further west. The neighbourhood of El Agheila on the Gulf of Sirte was at first considered, but the arrival of German forces at Tripoli, and their subsequent active patrolling in the Agheila area made this impossible. Though Kufra itself was occupied by the French it was shortly to be handed over to the Cyrenaica Command. The outlying oases were open to occupation by the enemy at any time; and it was therefore obvious that Kufra was a suitable place for the L.R.D.G.

Reconnaisance of Kufra March 1941.

The Group's next operation which began on 9 March was therefore a reconnaissance of the area carried out by Lieut.Colonel Bagnold, accompanied by the new 'S' (South Rhodesian) Patrol. Its objects were as follows:-
(a) To make contact with the French.
(b) To enable the political and medical officers who were to take over the district to get a knowledge of the oases.
(c) To establish a W/T ground station at Kufra for direct communication with Cairo and Cyrenaica.
(d) To reconnoitre the country to the west of Taiserbo and Ribiana and between Taiserbo and Cyrenaica.

Besides its operational objects, the expedition was also intended to provide training and experience for newly joined men, and existing dumps were to be inspected.

Before the end of March the Italians were again in occupation of Marada and El Agheila with German aircraft cooperating. The Germans were believed to be using ground patrols in eight-wheeled trucks carrying light guns; and the enemy's attitude was aggressive. The situation at Kufra and in the neighbouring oases at that time was as follows. The fort of El-Taj at Kufra itself was held by a Free French garrison of some 250 native troops without A.A. weapons or any form of mobile defence. The outlying oases, Taiserbo, Zighen, Ribiana, etc. were unoccupied. With the exception of Zighen they were inhabited by natives who, though peaceable, could not be trusted to refrain from giving the enemy information. Our intention was to occupy and hold all the oases of the Kufra group as soon as possible.

'R' Patrol occupies Taiserbo Landing Ground 9 April 1941.

The first task was the occupation of the landing ground at Taiserbo to deny it to hostile aircraft, to prevent its occupation by the enemy and to give warning of any preparations for an attack in Kufra. 'R' Patrol of the L.R.D.G. therefore left Cairo on 1 April, and moving by the Sand Sea and

Zighen reached Taiserbo on the 9th. Its arrival had been observed by an Italian who was picked up by a plane on the edge of the oasis on the same day.

German counter-offensive April 1941.

In the meanwhile the Germans had taken the offensive in the north, and by 7 April the whole of Cyrenaica except Tobruk, was in their hands. Orders were then given for the remainder of the L.R.D.G. less 'A' Squadron ('G' and 'Y' Patrols), to proceed to Kufra as soon as possible, and Lieut.Colonel Bagnold was made Commander of the mixed British and French garrison. A "directive" sent to Lieut.Colonel Bagnold by the General Staff at Cairo gave him the following instructions :-

(a) He would be Military Commander of all troops in the Kufra-Taiserbo group of Oases.

(b) He would be under command of the C.-in-C. Middle East from whom he would receive all orders as to Military Policy.

(c) He would exercise operational command of the French at Kufra through the local French Commander. For matters of internal Military Administration French troops would be under the Administrative Branch of the French Command in Chad territory.

(d) In political matters he was to act in accordance with the instructions given him by the Chief Political Officer of Occupied Territories: and would be assisted by a British Political Officer and the local French Commander.

(e) The Kufra garrison was to deny the oases to the enemy. If evacuation of the oases appeared necessary Colonel Bagnold was empowered to carry it out on his own responsibility. No air or ground assistance could be expected.

The L.R.D.G. was accompanied by two Political Officers, (Major Barnes and 2/Lieut. Herman) and 30 Libyan police, and moved in four columns (A, B, C and D), the first of which left Cairo on 9 April. Lieut.Colonel Bagnold accompanied 'B' column and arrived at Kufra on the 19th. The first column to leave ('A') moved by a separate route (Kharga-Gilf Kebir). It included the Heavy Section (B echelon) of four 10-ton White lorries, and the Political Officers and police were also with it. Owing to being too heavily loaded the lorries gave much trouble in traversing some hundreds of miles of blown sand and they did not arrive at Kufra until 25 April, a week later than was intended.

For purposes of reconnaissance and defence the available troops were distributed as follows:- 'R' Patrol at Taiserbo, 200 miles N.W. of Kufra, and 'S' Patrol at the uninhabited oasis of Zighen 120 miles to the north, formed the outer defences. The inner defences were manned by the French infantry garrison of the El-Taj fort, a platoon in Bedford trucks for local mobile defence; and there were two Lysander aircraft. 'T' patrol was in reserve.

Administration at Kufra.

The native population of the area numbered 5,900. Of these 800 lived at Taiserbo, 400 at Rebiana, 80 at Bzema and the remainder in the "home oases" within 10 miles of El-Taj fort. They were of diverse origin, and there was a trading element of Arabs: for though it produced nothing exportable Kufra had been an entrepôt where merchandise from Cyrenaica and Egypt was exchanged for hides, ostrich feathers and live stock from Chad. Since the beginning of 1941 however there had been no civil administration, trade was at a standstill and the gardens were mainly untended. The French had not instituted any form of administration though they had requisitioned food, materials and labour.

The new administration was faced with three main problems which were vigorously tackled by the Political Officer, Major Barnes. Effective control had to be instituted in order to prevent the leakage of information. Trade had to be started again, and the inhabitants induced to work once more in their gardens so that the troops might be supplied with vegetables and fresh meat. Lastly Libyan prisoners of war whom the French had allowed to live at large in the oases, had to be rounded up and removed. Fifteen of them were recruited to augment the local police. The Political Officer's efforts had the result of stopping the requisitioning of food and other goods soon after the L.R.D.G. arrived, and goods which the traders had buried began to appear in the market; currency in francs was sent by air from Equatoria; sheep began to arrive from Tibesti and trade between Chad and Wadi Halfa was reopened. R.E. and supply services had at first to be carried on by Officers of the L.R.D.G. and the political staff; but early in May a R.E. Officer (Capt. Buchanan) arrived from Wadi Halfa, and at the beginning of June a Supply Officer was posted. On 24 May Major R.N. Harding-Newman, R.T.R. arrived to take up the appointment of G.S.O.2 to the Garrison Commander.

Supplies from the Sudan.

Supplies for the Kufra garrison became the responsibility of the Sudan Command, which had lorries set free during the later stages of the campaign in Abyssinia. The magnitude of this problem had not been fully appreciated either at Cairo or Khartoum. The journey from the base at Wadi Halfa to Kufra was 700 miles mainly over blown sand, the monthly "lift" was very great and petrol consumption high. The lorries at first used, 3-tonners and 30-cwt., were part-worn and had unsuitable tyres, the route was unknown, maps were inadequate and the native drivers had no experience of the desert. The first convoy, about a hundred vehicles, set out from

Wadi Halfa on 28 April under Capt. Lonsdale. He had with him Corporal Brown who had been sent by the L.R.D.G. to act as navigator and to give advice in desert technique. The 3-ton lorries caused much trouble during the first half of the journey, and 20 of them broke down owing to lack of spare parts which were unobtainable. Capt. Lonsdale unloaded them near Jebel Kamil, and for the last 300 miles the supplies were carried in the 30-cwt lorries which made two trips. The first instalment arrived on 7 May and the second which brought the total to 70 tons, on the 13th.

When the difficulties which had to be faced are taken into consideration the arrival of even part of the convoy was a remarkable feat.

The deficiencies at Kufra, both of rations and petrol, had become very serious for the L.R.D.G. had brought only enough rations to last until 23 April; and had only the petrol that remained after its 700 mile journey from Cairo. 'B' echelon which had left Cairo on 9 April, carrying a month's supplies, did not arrive until the 25th, and then with supplies for two weeks only. The remainder had had to be dropped half way through the journey in order to lighten the loads. The total amount of petrol available after the arrival of 'B' echelon would, it was calculated, last till 1 May; and the risk of not having enough petrol even to begin an evacuation had to be accepted. Capt. Lonsdale's convoy brought 40 tons only, though the Group had been promised 60 tons as a month's reserve by 1 May. Owing to patrolling, and to unavoidable journeys to Taiserbo and Zighen the daily consumption of petrol was high, and the fighting reserves carried by patrols were only enough for 300 miles. Apart from these reserves there was no petrol left, nor was there any aviation spirit to refill R.A.F. aircraft which might be sent to assist the garrison in the event of attack. By the middle of May, however, G.H.Q. Cairo had realized the position, a supply column of twenty 10-ton lorries was hurried to Wadi Halfa, and additional lorries were provided from Khartoum. The situation improved, and by the end of June the Kufra convoy was in working order.

Air cooperation at Kufra.

Air cooperation with such a force as the L.R.D.G. was clearly necessary. Apart from its value for reconnaissaince, it would enable the C.O. to visit outlying detachments and supervise their work; the evacuation of sick and wounded would be facilitated; and urgent information could be quickly exchanged between Cairo and patrols in the field. While the unit was operating from Cairo aircraft were borrowed from time to time, but as the theatre of operations moved westwards it became more and more obvious that the unit must have aircraft of its own. The R.A.F. however found themselves unable to supply any, and after some delay sanction was given for the purchase in March of two privately owned "Waco" Aeroplanes which were for sale in Cairo. They were flown by Major Prendergast who had fifteen years experience, and Trooper Barker of the New Zealand Army; and two navigators were trained. Owing to the risk of breakdowns it was preferable to fly the two aircraft together, and the fact that one was much slower and had a shorter range than the other was a handicap. Moreover both were unarmed, and owing to the amount of work that had to be done on them (by Misr Airways, the R.A.F. would not undertake it) they were not ready for use until May.

Later the R.A.F. agreed verbally to undertake the maintenance of the two "private" machines and to regard them as a "special section". All spare parts however had to be obtained from the U.S.A., and sanction to order them had to be asked for from London.

In accordance with an agreement made in March 1941 a R.A.F. flight of six aircraft was to be sent to Kufra as soon as the cessation of the Abyssinian Campaign made them available: but the campaign dragged on, and during April, May, and June the only aircraft at Kufra were the two Wacos and one French Lysander. On 1 May it was agreed that the eventual R.A.F. flight was to consist of three Lysanders and three Gladiators. In order to get them to Kufra intermediate landing grounds had to be prepared and stocked with petrol. The L.R.D.G. undertook to do this and two landing grounds were prepared by 2/Lieut. Croucher and Lance Corporal Kendall, one at "Eight Bells" east of the southern end of the Gilf Kebir, and the other at Bir Terfawi about 200 miles further east.

Arrival at Kufra of 237 Sqn. R.A.F. May 1941.

At the end of May the 237th (South Rhodesian) Squadron arrived in Wadi Halfa from Eritrea. The ground party left for Kufra in ten 3-ton lorries on 20 June; the composite flight itself, escorted by F/O. Farr in a Bombay, flew to Kufra on the 30th. Both types of aircraft in the flight were far from suitable owing to their limited range, and to the inability of their pilots to find their way without navigators. The Lysanders without extra tanks could not do the journey to Taiserbo and back, 400 miles, without refilling, and the Gladiators being single seaters could not carry a navigator.

During the period April to July enemy activity was very slight. For a short time Italian planes paid daily visits to Taiserbo, but these ceased when the French Lysander was seen on the landing ground there. On the other hand the L.R.D.G. could do but little reconnaissance owing to the acute shortage of petrol. Of four reconnaissances only one made by Lieut. Ellingham and five trucks of 'T' Patrol at the end of June and beginning of July was opposed. They were attacked from the air while on a track marked by petrol drums and known to the Italians as the "Fustificata Leo" which lies between Taiserbo and Haruj some 250 miles to the north west. As the party had orders not to show themselves and there were signs of enemy activity on the ground, the reconnaissance was curtailed.

S.D.F. to garrison Kufra.

G.H.Q. Cairo had for some time past intended to relieve the L.R.D.G. and the French garrison of Kufra by troops from the Sudan Defence Force, but like the arrival of the R.A.F. flight the relief was delayed by the long drawn out operations at the end of the Abyssinian Campaign. When the new garrison arrived the French troops were to return to Tekro, and the L.R.D.G. was to resume its duties of long range reconnaissance under the direct orders of G.H.Q., Cairo.

Section IX

Operations of 'A' Squadron in Cyrenaica, April-July, 1941.

It will be remembered that when the L.R.D.G. was sent to occupy Kufra, 'A' Squadron under Major Mitford, which consisted of the Guards and Yeomanry Patrols, was detached from the unit and remained at Cairo. From April to July 1941 it operated in Cyrenaica, first under the command of the G.O.C. Cyrenaica (Lieut. General Neame, V.C.) and later under his successor, the G.O.C. Western Desert Force. By the middle of March it became clear that the enemy, now under German Command and reinforced by German troops and aircraft, intended to attack Cyrenaica. A small German force had occupied Marada about 80 miles south of El Agheila, and it became necessary to watch for any movement eastward towards Jalo and Jarabub. 'A' Squadron was put under General Neame's command for this purpose. 'G' Patrol left Cairo on 24 March followed by the rest of the Squadron on the 25th, and they marched to Barce, about 70 miles N.E. of Bengazi.

Lieut. General Neame's instructions to 'A' Squadron.

On arrival on 30 March the squadron received an Operation Instruction from Cyrenaica Command, the contents of which may be summarized as follows:-

1. Squadron H.Q. to be based on Jalo, and, if possible, to be always established near a suitable landing ground, which was to be marked; and its position was to be signalled to H.Q. Cyrenaica Command.

2. The squadron was to operate in the area between Long. 17°E and 21°30E and Lat. 29°50N and 28°30N.

3. Its tasks were:-

   (a) To give warning of any movement by the enemy eastward from Marada.

   (b) To obtain information of any movement into Marada from the west and N.W.

   (c) To collect information about hostile activity, the state of tracks and

52

nature of the going, and the tactical features in the area Marada, Zella,[1] Tagrifet;[1] and as far north of the track Marada-Tagrifet as patrols could penetrate without risk of capture.

'G' Patrol reconnoitres Marada April 1941.

In accordance with these instructions Major Mitford sent half 'G' Patrol under Capt. M.D.D. Crichton-Stuart (Scots Guards) to make a complete circuit of the Marada Oasis, to look for signs of hostile activity on the ground and in the air, and to report on the going.

The party left Barce on 31 March, three days after our army had begun its retirement from the El Acheila area. In this connection it is interesting to note a remark made by Capt. Stuart in an outline of the actions of 'G' Patrol between 25 March and 25 August 1941, to the effect that the "Information" paragraph in the orders given him for the Marada patrol contained the statement, "Enemy will not be ready to move for a month".

The party carried petrol for 600 miles, and food and water for 7 days. It encircled Marada from the north and by the west and then turning eastwards arrived at Aujila, the prearranged rendezvous with the rest of the squadron on 6 April without having seen any signs of hostile activity either on the ground or in the air. The rest of 'A' Squadron however had not arrived at the rendezvous, and attempts to get in touch with it by W/T were unsuccessful.

British retreat from El Agheila area April 1941.

By this time of course the British forces were in full retreat and near the coast road the enemy were already east of Bengazi. The party encamped during the night 6/7 April in the S.W. corner of the Aujila oasis. The fort was empty, and the inhabitants were friendly. On 7 April a W/T message was received from Squadron HQ to say that they were surrounded by the enemy. Capt. Crichton-Stuart therefore decided to make for Jarabub, which was more than 200 miles to the east. By this time however petrol supplies had been reduced to 54 gallons which he considered was enough to enable one truck to reach Jarabub.

'G' Patrol has to abandon trucks and retire on Jarabub.

All rations, petrol and water were therefore loaded on the W/T truck together with navigation kit, fitters' tools and accessories, machine guns, rifles with the necessary ammunition, blankets and medical kit. The breech of the Bofors gun was removed, and it was left behind with the remaining trucks, only three of which were completely serviceable. The march started

1 Tagrifet is about 120m. west of Marada (long. 17°20'E. lat. 29°15'N).
Zella is about 120 miles S.W. of Marada (long. 17°30'E. lat. 28°30'N).

at 0930 hrs on 9 April with the 15 men of the party and their Commander sitting on the top of the lorry; and as Capt. Crichton-Stuart remarked, "the springs appeared to feel the strain". There was a following "Khamseen" and the water in the radiator boiled fourteen times before sunset. G.H.Q. Cairo were informed by W/T of the party's position and the march was continued by moonlight until 0100 hrs on the 10th when there was a halt until daybreak. The journey was continued along the Gardaba track until the petrol was exhausted at a point about 15 miles from Jarabub fort. With two volunteers Capt. Crichton-Stuart walked to the fort, "somewhat deterred by cannon-fire, machine gun fire and a rifle shot". He found however that the garrison commander was expecting him and he returned with the petrol necessary to bring the party in. The rest of 'A' Squadron arrived at Jarabub in the same afternoon.

Capt. Crichton-Stuart's report on this expedition gave valuable information as to signs of enemy ground activity which were few, the geography, and the performance of his lorries.

'A' Squadron's retirement from Barce to Jarabub April 1941 and operations en route.

Major Mitford with the remainder of 'A' Squadron, namely Squadron H.Q., 'Y' Patrol and half 'G' Patrol, left Barce for Aujila on 1 April, the day after Capt. Crichton-Stuart started for the Marada reconnaissance. The intended route was by Tecnis-Msus-Saunnu and Gasr-el-Sahabi. This route is parallel to and about 60 miles inland from the east coast of the Gulf of Sirte, and Gasr-el-Sahabi is about 100 miles east of El Agheila. Going was rough which made progress slow, and at 1700 hrs the Squadron was no further than Bir-el-Malez, ten miles east of Msus. At this point a party of six trucks with four or five men in each, was sighted through the mirage. They were approaching in line, but when the Squadron turned to meet them they went about at great speed and scattered in an easterly direction. Capt. McGraith was wounded in the arm by the explosion of a "thermos" bomb under his truck, but the vehicle remained serviceable. The Squadron halted for the night 25 miles east of Msus, but too late to get into W/T communication with Cairo.

On 2 April the Squadron moved west into Msus where they found a French Motor Company with an English liaison officer, Capt. Hore-Ruthven. Major Mitford warned them of the party he had seen the night before, and also informed the Cyrenaica Command, who appeared to think that the trucks in question were our own which was unlikely. Orders had been given by Cyrenaica Command that the Squadron was to communicate with them every half hour on 2 April and no movement on that day was possible. On 3 April Lieut. M.A. Gibbs, Coldstream Guards, with half 'G' Patrol reconnoitred east and N.E. of Msus in case the hostile trucks seen the day before should interfere with convoys coming to Msus. At midday information was received from the R.A.F. that a hostile column was advancing north from Antelat which lies about 35 miles S.S.W. of Msus, and a R.A.F. ground party retired through that place. Capt. Hore-Ruthven therefore decided to destroy the dump and withdraw the French troops, who were clear by 1600 hrs. Five enemy armoured cars then appeared from the south and 'A' Squadron withdrew to the east. On its way it picked up Lieut. Gibbs's party and the night 3/4 April was spent 14 miles east of Msus.

On 4 April the Squadron moved S.E. to Trigh-el-Abd, a likely line of advance for the enemy but saw nothing; and a halt for the night was made at Bir Ben Gania about 80 miles E.S.E. of Msus. There the Squadron was observed by a German aircraft. On 5 April it moved north and N.E. towards Mekili. No ground troops were seen but two squadrons of German dive-bombers flew over and engaged a target to the north. The going was very bad and a halt was made for the night 5/6 April 20 miles S.W. of Mekili. On 6 April the Squadron marched to Mekili and arrived just west of it when an Italian column was attacking from the south. Major Mitford reported his arrival to the Commander of an Indian Motorized Brigade, and explained that though theoretically under the direct orders of the Cyrenaica Command, he had been out of touch with them for three days. The brigadier asked him to operate on the enemy's western flank. Major Mitford divided his force into two parties, one under his own command, the other under Lieut. Gibbs. With his own party he stalked a gun position, made the gun limber up and later captured an Italian officer; Lieut. Gibbs fired on an enemy H.Q. Both parties were then chased away by A.F.Vs and halted in a dust storm four miles S.W. of Mekili. On 7 April our troops were still holding Mekili; and the Squadron went there to draw supplies, and to get the radiator of a Ford P.U. mended by the I.A.O.C. Its driver, Trooper Cave, remained with the vehicle. Major Mitford reported to Brigade H.Q. and was told to continue operating on the enemy's western flank. After filling up with petrol and water the Squadron again moved west leaving Trooper Cave and his vehicle with the I.A.O.C. They sighted a small party of hostile vehicles and captured one of them which had got stuck, and a German prisoner. Another column of some 40 vehicles was fired on, dispersed and driven off to the west. An A.A. gun and two more lorries were destroyed, and four more German prisoners were captured and sent to Mekili. It appeared that the whole of this column was German. The Squadron then lay up for the night in the escarpment six miles west of Mekili. On 8 April the enemy again attacked Mekili at 0600 hrs, and British transport could be seen escaping to the west and being bombed. A truck of the 3rd Regiment R.H.A. was picked up carrying an officer who had become separated from his regiment, and said that Mekili had fallen as the result of an attack from the south, east and north. Major Mitford decided to get away to the east by the north of Mekili and then to go S.E. His movement was concealed by a dust storm, and though a German patrol was seen he was able to lie up for the night three miles north of Gadd-el-Ahmar which lies forty miles or so E.S.E. of Mekili. A hostile column had been sighted on the track to Gadd-el-Ahmar.

On 9 April Major Mitford moved S.E. to investigate the hostile column seen overnight, and found that it consisted of 40 or 50 vehicles and had halted. The Squadron lay up in a depression, and tried to get in touch with some part of our forces by W/T. They were seen by a hostile aircraft which attacked them hitting the radiator of a truck and wounding one man; and they were attacked on one flank by the enemy's trucks. These were engaged and casualties were inflicted. The Squadron then retired S.E. over country devoid of any cover and on the way had to abandon the truck that had been hit. Eventually it reached a point (long. 23°40'E. lat. 30°30'N.) where there was sufficient cover from the air to lie up and carry out very necessary maintenance. That evening the Squadron received instructions to go to Jarabub, and it also heard from Capt. Crichton-Stuart's detachment of 'G' Patrol that it was on its way to the same place, and had had to abandon all but one truck. On 10 April the whole Squadron was concentrated at Jarabub. W/T communication with Cyrenaica Command had been effected every day from the time it left Barce on 1 April until the 9th, the day before its arrival at Jarabub.

Escape of Trooper Cave April 1941.

It will be remembered that on 7 April Trooper Cave of the Yeomanry was left with his truck in the I.A.O.C. depot at Mekili in order that repairs to it might be carried out. Mekili was taken by the enemy on the following day, and Trooper Cave, with some 1,500 others, British, Australian and Indian, became a prisoner of war. Six days later they were transferred to a Prisoner of War Camp at Derna. They were short of food, the Italian barracks in which they were quartered were insanitary, and there were cases of dysentery and typhoid. The German soldiers were civil enough but the Italians were not. Cave and one of the Australians decided to try and escape after darkness fell, and they accumulated food and water. At about 1900 hrs on 21 April the Australian told Cave that the guards who patrolled outside the barracks were nowhere to be seen. There were however machine guns at intervals of 50 yards all round which had to be avoided. Luckily it was a moonless night, and aided by the cover given by large boulders they crawled out between the M.G. posts and after going some 400 yards found themselves in a disused quarry. Avoiding the road they scaled the Derna Escarpment which took over four hours to negotiate, and after half an hour's walk found a cave in which they sheltered until daylight on the

22nd, and this enabled them to get their bearings. They found themselves due west of Derna and had to make a detour inland to avoid the airport at the top of the Derna pass, of whose position they had previous knowledge. They declined an invitation from some Arabs to "dine and sleep", but were told by them of a track that led to a friendly Bedouin encampment. On the advice of two other Arabs, who gave them a welcome cup of tea, they left the track and crossed the Wadi-Derna only to find themselves on the edge of the airport, and they watched it being bombed by our own aircraft. After walking 5 or 6 miles inland they made their way back to the main road and thence to the coast. It was too cold to sleep at night and next day they walked in sight of the sea and got a few hours sleep in a wadi. They started again before dawn on the 24th and after a few miles Cave's "chaplis" gave out. He had however been prepared for this and had picked up an old pair of boots; and though they were too small managed to walk in them after cutting off the toecaps and heels. About midday they met an Arab boy with three horses who lent them each a mount, and they arrived soon afterwards at an Arab encampment near Ras-el-Tin, which is on the coast and 30 miles E.S.E. of Derna. There they found three British soldiers and a Canadian, and were treated with the greatest hospitality by the Arabs. They heard too that in a neighbouring cave were an officer and three other men, one wounded, who had hired an Arab guide to take one or two of them through the enemy's lines into Tobruk, about 80 miles further east along the coast road. They hoped that a boat might then be sent to bring away the rest of the escaped prisoners. The attempt was made by the officer and one man, but the Arab guide returned to say that they had been captured at Gazala. Meanwhile two more officers arrived who had escaped from Derna, and an Arab trader who had come from Tobruk by Acroma and said that he had met hostile patrols. The Arab trader agreed to take the two officers with him on his return journey provided they wore Arab dress and paid him £30 each. If they got to Tobruk they would try to obtain a pinnace, but said that if this failed to arrive the remaining escaped prisoners were to do as they thought best. After a wait of 14 days there was no sign of a boat; food was very scarce, and as the wounded man had recovered sufficiently to walk the eight remaining men decided to divide into small parties and try to walk to Tobruk. Cave, the Australian who escaped with him from Derna, and two others started on 22 May. By midday they had covered some 15 miles and had reached the escarpment at Bomba. The road below on which there was constant traffic, had to be crossed. The road seemed clear but just as they were about to cross it, they heard the sound of an approaching lorry. Being unable to move either way without being seen they had to stay where they were, lying flat on the ground. But the lorry passed without any one of its occupants even turning his head. Late in the evening they sighted the "White house" at Tmimi seven or eight miles further on, which was familiar to them. They intended to spend the night near it but as it was too light to move they had a bathe in the sea! They then tried to reach the house along the shore, but were held up by a succession of creeks running half a mile or more inland and had to spend a cold night in the open. Next morning (23 May) they found they were within 200 yards of the White house. As there seemed to be no one about they made a dash for it and reached cover about a mile and half further on. They again made for the coast and walked along it without interference until when on the coast road about 20 miles from Tmimi, they came in sight of Gazala Point. They also saw, but were not seen by, a party of Italians pumping water with a small engine about fifty yards from the shore. At about 1900 hrs the Italian party left with the exception of two who appeared to live in a tent near at hand. An hour later they crept up to the well to fill their own water bottles. To do so Cave had to go down the water pipe into the well and the bottles were lowered to him. The water stank and later they were to regret having drunk it. Three hours afterwards they found themselves near a large car park; and the bad water had begun to make them feel ill. Nevertheless they climbed the escarpment which took them four hours during the night; and when they reached the top just before dawn they were too exhausted to go further. When daylight came they could see the car park below them and Gazala airfield covered with aircraft and men. They continued their journey that day and on 25 May, with frequent halts to take cover from observation by the enemy who had several camps along the route they took. On 26 May at midday they reached yet another camp and Cave and his Australian companion shared their last drop of water. They made up their minds to try and get water from the camp and after lots had been drawn it fell to Cave to do the work. Unfortunately he was seen, and though he contrived to get away along the coast he lost touch with his companions. Late in the day he found an Arab camp where he was given food and water. He had had nothing to eat for 48 hours, his feet were badly cut, and he was feeling ill from drinking too much water at a time. On the 27th he was too ill to move more than a mile. On the 28th he continued his journey with bare feet over rocky ground, and by midday had made only four or five miles. Then he saw a machine gun post which was in fact the German front line. He lay up in a small cave and with difficulty prevented himself drinking his last drop of water. His mind wandered and at one time he was on the point of surrendering. After dark he again moved on, crawling across wadis on his hands and knees. He regained the coast and found himself in front of barbed wire on the sand. Instinctively he dropped, and for a time failed to realize that the wire protected a British position. He crawled through it and found Indian troops whose conversation, which he had overheard, had alarmed him not a little. Next day his three companions turned up, and having passed the same

Arab encampment they knew that Cave was ahead of them. Three days later Cave arrived at Alexandria, and five days after that rejoined 'Y' Patrol at Siwa.

'A' Squadron operates from Siwa. Rommel's advance continues April-June 1941.

During the period 11 April to 9 June 1941 'A' Squadron operated from Siwa under the orders of H.Q. Western Desert Force. Rommel's advance continued; Sollum was lost on 28 April, and the enemy reached the frontier of Egypt. Sollum was retaken on 15 May, but the enemy retained the Halfaya Pass and Fort Capuzzo. Minor but valuable offensive operations by our forces in the middle of June forced Rommel to disclose his strength; but we continued otherwise to remain on the defensive until November when our forces, which had been under the command of General Auchinleck since 1 July, were sufficiently strong to attack once more.

When 'A' Squadron concentrated at Jarabub on 10 April it was short of trucks – six out of eleven had been lost by 'G' Patrol alone. 'Y' Patrol had no officers as Capt. McCraith had been wounded near Mekili at the beginning of the month, and it was therefore employed on garrison duty.

The Squadron left Jarabub on 12 April and arrived at Siwa on the following day. Major Prendergast (second in command) arrived by air on the same day, and what remained of the Squadron was reorganized into two small patrols, one commanded by Capt. Crichton-Stuart and the other by Lieut. Gibbs, and a reserve to garrison Siwa. This arrangement lasted rather more than a month.

On 15 April Capt. Crichton-Stuart's patrol left Siwa for Aujila in order if possible to recover the trucks abandoned during the retirement to Jarabub earlier in the month. Marching by Jarabub and the Gardaba track on the north edge of the Sand Sea, the patrol encamped for the night 16/17 April at a point 45 miles east of El Gueaed and about 100 miles short of Aujila. It arrived at the Aujila depression from the east at 1430 hrs on the 17th. Capt. Crichton-Stuart states that it was the clearest day he had ever known in the desert, and he saw a large convoy of trucks round the Aujila fort five miles away; fresh tracks had been seen not long before on the Aujila-Jedabia track. Keeping under the cover of trees and scrub he approached the spot in the S.E. corner of the depression where he had left the trucks. Through his glasses he could see a Ford 15-cwt truck which he knew had a broken rear spring and was more or less immovable, but no sign of the other trucks. At this moment an enemy truck appeared from the direction of the fort, stopped about 400 yards away and then hurried back. Capt. Crichton-Stuart therefore withdrew northward without loss of time and camped for the night 18 miles east of El Gueaed.

The watch on the Gardaba track.

From 18 to 24 April 'G' Patrol kept watch on the Gardaba track from a point about 55 miles west of Jarabub, in order to give warning of any enemy movement from Aujila, or Jalo which they had also occupied; but no movement was seen. On the 20th the patrol was immobilized by a very bad sandstorm. On 25 April it was withdrawn and reached Siwa "about teatime". From 28 April to 11 May the watch on the Gardaba track was kept by Lieut. Gibbs's patrol. 'G' Patrol guarded the immediate approaches to Jarabub whose inhabitants had been evacuated; and it was told to be prepared for attack by airborne troops. The weather during this fortnight was very hot and water was limited as the Jarabub wells had been destroyed or polluted. On 9 May an Australian demolition party completed the destruction of the wells, and also destroyed many tons of Italian Breda ammunition which could have been salvaged. Capt. Crichton-Stuart persuaded them not to destroy the mosque! No signs of the enemy were seen and the men suffered from heat, flies, mosquitoes and inaction. On 11 May Lieut. Gibbs returned from the Gardaba patrol, with many men who were suffering from heat exhaustion and had to be sent back to Siwa. A day or two later Major Mitford arrived. He gave information of the limited offensive that was to begin on the 14th in the Sollum area, and resulted in the recapture of that place.

Our attack on Sollum May 1941.

The 11th Hussars has been ordered to watch the enemy's southern flank. To do so they were going to patrol to the west from Bir Sheferzen which lies on the wire entanglement marking the Italian frontier, about 110 miles north of Jarabub and 20 miles S.W. of Sollum. 'G' Patrol (Capt. Crichton-Stuart) was ordered to join the 11th Hussars at Bir Sheferzen, and to patrol as arranged with them, and beyond their western limit.

The patrol with six trucks marched about midday on 13 May, moved along the wire and bivouacked five miles north of the ruins of Fort Maddalena, having covered a distance of about 85 miles. On the 14th they reached a point on the wire immediately opposite Sheferzen (their rendezvous with the 11th Hussars) at about 0800 hrs. There they saw in the distance a number of armoured cars and at least two tanks. The latter looked like British "cruiser" tanks but being covered and camouflaged could not be identified through glasses. Capt. Crichton-Stuart approached well ahead of the other trucks and Guardsman Fraser gave the recognised signal, a steel helmet held aloft on a rifle.

'G' Patrol in action at Sheferzen 14 May 1941.

They were at once fired on by a number of machine guns both heavy and light, and there were a few shots from a tank gun. Luckily the shooting was poor and only Capt. Crichton-Stuart's truck was hit, but Fraser received two bullets through the arm. The truck was reversed and moved back about half a mile to a covered position, in order that Fraser's arm might be bandaged and a bullet-riddled tyre might be removed. Keeping one of the trucks with him Capt. Crichton-Stuart ordered the remaining four to go five miles to the south and await events. There was, however, no time to change the tyre as the enemy were approaching and the truck had to be abandoned. The patrol Commander and his men got away in the other truck when the enemy with three armoured cars were within 300 yards of them. For a time the enemy kept up at 45 miles an hour, and even gained a little, firing as they went. However, in Capt. Crichton-Stuart's words, "it was found that a really frightened truck could get up to 50 miles an hour", and very gradually they drew ahead. They were chased for thirty miles losing another truck owing to a bullet having hit the tyre, but eventually were able to halt five miles south of Fort Maddalena. A W/T message was sent to Siwa and the patrol received orders to go to the Egyptian frontier post at Shegga which is close to Fort Maddalena, and to await an ambulance and further orders. There they encamped, still not entirely sure whether they had been fired at by the enemy or by the 11th Hussars! On the morning of 15 May an ambulance came for Guardsman Fraser; and about midday Lieut. Easonsmith arrived with certain spare parts, and took back to Siwa a full account of what had happened. A reconnaissance was made northwards to within five miles of Bir Sheferzen but no trace was seen of the two abandoned trucks. On 19 May the patrol was ordered back from Shegga to Siwa and in the words of the diary "arrived lunchtime". On 21 May Capt. Crichton-Stuart learned that he had in fact been fired at by the enemy and that their armoured cars had stopped at Fort Maddalena until late in the afternoon on the 14th.

"The operation at Sheferzen was a failure because unarmoured vehicles cannot be expected to operate against tanks and armoured cars. It was a misuse of the L.R.D.G."

'G' Patrol had now only three of its original trucks left. Lieut. Gibbs had been evacuated on account of illness, and there was an epidemic of malaria. The patrol therefore remained at Siwa, and was used for drawing supplies from Mersa Matruh and taking them forward to Jarabub, where the defensive patrolling was done by 'Y' Patrol under Lieut. Easonsmith.

Reorganization of 'A' Squadron June 1941.

On 6 June Capt. McCraith who had recovered from his wound returned with new trucks from Cairo. On the following day 'Y' Patrol came in from Jarabub and the Squadron was reorganized. Three patrols were formed, 'G', 'Y' and 'H', each of six trucks, 'H' Patrol drawing its men from the other two patrols. For the next month patrolling was done by 'Y' and 'H' Patrols, and 'G' Patrol remained at Siwa. Equipment was deteriorating owing to lack of supervision and the O.C. L.R.D.G. immobilised at Kufra, short of staff, and lacking supplies was powerless to help.

Representations as to the misuse of the L.R.D.G. Patrols had been made to G.H.Q.; and coincided with new requirements by the Intelligence Branches both at G.H.Q. Cairo and at H.Q. Western Desert Force, which led to the employment of the patrols in more suitable tasks. They were now charged with the conveyance of agents to the interior of Cyrenaica, and the collection of their reports, and with gathering geographical information about the country south of the Jebel-el-Akhdar.[1]

'H' Patrol to Gambut June 1941.

On 10 June 'H' Patrol consisting of 9 guardsmen and 9 yeoman, under Lieut. R. Easonsmith, left Siwa in three trucks to drop two Arab agents as near as possible to Gambut, an aerodrome about 35 miles W.N.W. of Bardia; and to report on the state of the main tracks. The first night was spent at Weshka, about 100 miles north of Siwa. On 11 June the going was in places bad and deep dust made it difficult to judge whether there had been traffic recently or not. At 1400 hrs (G.M.T.) the Arabs were dropped about five miles S.W. of Gambut. Lieut. Easonsmith then moved north up to a point whence the Bardia-Tobruk road was visible (448401 on sheet Tobruk 1:500,000). Traffic was visible about 2? miles away. There were 16 heavy lorries widely dispersed in the valley and the patrol Commander decided to attack them as the light was failing that evening. There was little resistance and the attack was successful; three lorries were partially demolished with grenades and a considerable amount of .455 Tommy-gun ammunition was fired into the engines of six more. Two prisoners were taken and the remainder of the enemy fled. Later in the evening Lieut. Easonsmith went down again into the valley on foot, and finding the enemy had not returned he set fire to three more trucks making a total of twelve put out of action. On the way back the steering arm of one truck broke; it had to be towed nearly 250 miles and the patrol did not get back to Siwa until 1500 hrs on 13 June.

---

1   The line of hills running parallel to the coast of Cyrenaica between Bomba and Barce.

Rescue of Pilot Officer Pompey by 'H' Patrol June 1941.

At 1230 hrs (G.M.T.) on 14 June 'H' Patrol went out again with orders to find an Air Force pilot who, it was believed, was being sheltered by Bedouins at Bir Bidihi, a well about two miles south of the Trig-el-Abd track, and about 20 miles W.N.W. of Sheferzen. The well was reached on the 15th but there was no sign of life. A reconnaissance of the area was made and about five miles W.N.W. Lieut. Easonsmith found a dry well shaft. A Bedouin climbed out of it and confirmed that the patrol was at the spot it had intended to reach; but he denied all knowledge of a lost pilot. Luckily the conversation was heard by a French Hurricane pilot, P.O. Pompey, who also emerged from the well. It then transpired that the Bedouin, Muhammed Tayib of Jedabia, who was also "wanted" by the enemy, had made up his mind that Lieut. Easonsmith and his men were Germans because they were wearing beards! Both men were taken back to Siwa, which the patrol reached on the 16th. Pompey's earlier adventures while escaping received considerable publicity in the newspapers and on the wireless.

Reconnaissance at Mekili by 'H' Patrol, June 1941.

On the 19th 'H' Patrol left Siwa to carry a British Intelligence Officer and two Senussi Officers to a point in Jebel el Akhdar, and while the latter carried out their mission, to find out whether there was any main convoy route west to east through Mekili. On 21 June they encamped five miles south of Gerdes-el-Gerrari in the foothills of Jebel-el-Akhdar about 50 miles east of Barce. The Intelligence party was dropped on the 22nd, and the patrol then reconnoitred the Mekili area and had covered the N.W. sector by nightfall. On the 23rd broken country and wadis enabled them to reach a concealed position three miles to the north of Mekili fort, and then to go on foot. They were unable however to go forward more than a mile as the garrison was at work on the defences. Two planes were seen on the aerodrome and there was a little traffic on the Derna road. That night the patrol lay up in the Baltet-er-Ramla, a mudpan about 8 miles south of Mekili, and narrowly escaped detection by an Italian Patrol. On the 24th the circuit of Mekili was completed and it was established that there was no main convoy route from west to east. The only regular traffic was on the Derna and El Adem tracks further north. While they were examining an abandoned Bedford truck which, as its badge showed, had belonged to the 2nd Armoured Division, Guardsman Hopton was killed, and Trooper Wise wounded by the explosion of a booby trap. The truck caught fire and after burying Hopton, the patrol moved away as quickly as possible. Later in the day the Intelligence party duly arrived at the rendezvous with two men of the Northumberland Fusiliers who had escaped and had been sheltered by Arabs. The patrol then returned to Siwa and arrived there on 26 June.

'H' Patrol to Mersa Lukk July 1941.

'H' Patrol's last expedition in this series began on 2 July. It had orders to take two Arab agents to Mersa Lukk on the coast about 50 miles east of Tobruk, and then to examine the state of the Trigh-el-Abd track. Lieut. Easonsmith visited Bir Bidihi en route and was told by a young shepherd that a R.A.F. pilot who was escaping had passed through the day before with two Senussi. There were also fresh tracks of 30 vehicles running past the Bir, but no information about them could be obtained. The Trigh-el-Abd itself was being very little used. On the way north the patrol passed near a camp which, it was afterwards learned, was occupied by 50 tanks and 150 other vehicles, and dropped the agents at Bir Micail about 25 miles south of Mersa Lukk. During the return journey to Siwa which was reached on 4 July two armoured cars were seen "on a most unpleasantly flat" stretch but the patrol was not interfered with. It may be added that the patrol was warmly congratulated by H.Q. Western Desert Force on the success of its expeditions to Gambut and Mekili in a telegram dated 26 June 1941.

'G' Patrol July-August 1941

'G' Patrol resumed its active work early in July. From the 15th to the 22nd it made a reconnaissance of the Jebel-el-Akhdar. As Capt. Crichton-Stuart was taken ill with malaria on the 14th the patrol was commanded by Lieut. A.M. Hay, Coldstream Guards, who had arrived a few days before and Lieut. Easonsmith went with him as "instructor".

On 26 July Capt. Crichton-Stuart took out the full patrol of six trucks having with him Major David Lair of the U.S. Army, and camped that night 35 miles N.W. of Siwa. Next day he reconnoitred Jarabub aerodrome to find an aeroplane that had been reported by a R.A.F. tactical reconnaissance, but found nothing and encamped 70 miles further north. On the 29th he arrived from the west on the landing ground at Bir-el-Gseir, which is about 100 miles N.N.W. of Jarabub and about 60 miles south by east of Tobruk.

Destruction of the enemy's petrol at Bir-el-Gseir.

The landing ground was empty, but there were fresh tracks of vehicles from the north and N.E., and two dumps of petrol and oil. The drums were broken open with picks and it was estimated that the enemy lost rather more than 2,000 gallons of petrol and 500 gallons of oil. The patrol encamped that night at Garn-ul-Grein, about 80 miles S.S.E. and returned to Siwa next day.

On 30 July 'G' Patrol went out again in a bad "Khamseen" with orders to sweep up both sides of the frontier wire to a point 10 miles south of Fort Maddalena, in search of a party of the enemy reported to be in that neighbourhood. The Khamseen continued, but by midday the distance had been covered and there was no sign of the enemy within half a mile of the wire on either side. The patrol then returned to Siwa.

Capt. Crichton-Stuart evacuated with malaria.

Capt. Crichton-Stuart had again been attacked by malaria, and having a temperature of 106° was evacuated to Cairo. He and Lieut. Gibbs, who had gone down with malaria about two months earlier, were then recalled to their regiments.

'G' Patrol's casualties December 1940-July 1941.

From its formation on 6 December 1940 to the time when Capt. Crichton-Stuart left the casualties in the Guards patrol had been: one Guardsman killed, one died of wounds, and three wounded or injured. Only one Guardsman had applied to return to his unit.

'Y' Patrol July-August 1941.

On 25 July 'Y' Patrol under Capt. P.J. McCraith left Siwa at 1520 hrs to convey an officer and a party detailed by G.H.Q. to the area of Bir Raggia, and to bring them back. Bir Raggia is a well in the foothills of the Jebel-el-Akhdar (approximately at long. 21°45'E, lat. 32°15'N). The route taken was that used by Lieut. Hay's patrol in mid-July by Garn-ul-Grein and Bir Tengeder.

The patrol arrived at Bir Raggia at 1600 hrs on 27 August. No enemy movement was seen on the outward journey, but M.T. were heard to the south of Bir-en-Nisi on the night 29/30 July. Some fresh tracks of tyred vehicles were seen during the return journey overlying those made by the patrol a few days before. No aircraft were seen. The wreck of a Wellington bomber which had been hit by A.A. fire zwas found on a mud flat, and an unnamed well with good water was located about a mile and a half east of Bir-en-Nisi (about 7 miles S.E. of Bir Raggia). The patrol returned to Siwa at 1930 hrs on 2 August.

Reconnaissance for landing grounds.

On 7 August 'Y' Patrol under Lieut. Easonsmith went on a reconnaissance with two tasks. The first was to find and plot the positions of three potential landing grounds in an area bounded on the east by long. 23°40' and on the west by long. 22°40'; and within 30 miles of lat. 31°. The second was to find three more landing grounds in the same latitude, but somewhat further west. The centre of the first named area is near the track leading

S.S.W. from Bir Hakim to Jalo, and about 45 miles from Bir Hakim. F/O Holland, R.A.F., accompanied the patrol. Three landing grounds were found in the first named area, but only one with a somewhat rough surface in the other. Their locations were as follows:-

No. 1 at long. 23°35'E. lat. 31°N.
No. 2 at long. 23°25'E. lat. 31°5'N.
No. 3 at long. 23°3'E. lat. 31°5'N.
No. 4 at long. 21°35'E. lat. 30°56'N.

No sign of the enemy was seen either on the ground or in the air.

Section X

H.Q. L.R.D.G. moves to Kufra April 1941.

As described in Section VIII the Long Range Desert Group less 'A' Squadron moved to the Kufra Oasis in the middle of April, and was still there at the beginning of July 1941. During this period there was very little activity either on the enemy's part, or by patrols of the L.R.D.G. In accordance with instructions given him at Cairo in April, Lieut.Colonel Bagnold drew up a defence scheme for the Kufra Oasis area, including an appreciation of the possibilities of attack along the few available routes across the western part of the Libyan Desert. Ground attacks on Kufra might come from Marada by Taiserbo and Zighen; from Marada or Jalo direct to Zighen; or from the Fezzan by Wau-el-Kebir (long.16°40'E. lat. 25°20'N.), S.E. through Tekro (long. 21°10'E. lat. 23°30'N.), and thence N.E. to Rebiana, a long and difficult route but possible for a raiding party.

Proposals for increased raiding forces.

Early in 1941 the desirability of increasing our striking power on the desert was again considered.[1] The German lines of communication from Tripoli to Sollum were by that time 900 miles long, and frequent raids against them from Kufra would certainly tie up a large number of the enemy's troops for their defence, and so weaken his effort along the coast. At that time too there was still the possibility of a German attack through Turkey or Syria on Basra. Hence it might pay to create several small raiding forces similar to the L.R.D.G., for use both in the African and Syrian Deserts. At a G.H.Q. conference held at Cairo, but in the absence of the B.G.S. (Brigadier Whiteley) in the U.S.A., and of Lieut.Colonel Bagnold at Kufra, a decision in principle was arrived at which contemplated the formation of five such units.

---

1 Originally suggested by Major Wingate and with modifications, supported by Lieut.Colonel Bagnold (See Section III).

Lieut.Colonel Bagnold goes to General Staff at Cairo and Major Prendergast succeeds to command of L.R.D.G. August 1941.

It was also decided to bring Lieut.Colonel Bagnold back from Kufra to undertake the raising and training of the new units; though it seemed that the conference had no clear idea of how the necessary troops and equipment were to be found. There was however another factor which led to this latter decision. While the L.R.D.G. was operating from Cairo it was possible for Lieut.Colonel Bagnold, Capt. Clayton and Lieut. Kennedy-Shaw who alone were qualified to advise on matters connected with the interior of the Libyan Desert, to combine advisory work at G.H.Q. with active control of the patrols in the field. When the headquarters of the L.R.D.G. moved to Kufra this was no longer the case. Moreover Major Prendergast who was an experienced pilot had arrived as second-in-command; and his ability to fly enabled him to use the newly acquired aircraft to visit distant patrols in a way which Lieut.Colonel Bagnold could not emulate. Lieut.Colonel Bagnold therefore went to the special section of the Operations Staff at Cairo with the rank of Colonel, to reorganize the raising of the new units and to control all independent desert operations; and Major Prendergast, who was promoted Lieut.Colonel on 1 August 1941, took over command of the L.R.D.G. with Major E.C. Wilson, V.C. (East Surrey Regiment) as second-in-command.

Eighth Army formed September 1941.

On 24 September 1941 the Eighth Army was formed under Lieut.General Sir Alan Cunningham, to take the offensive in the Western Desert, and the L.R.D.G. was put under his command. At the same time the decision to form other similar units was abandoned partly owing to difficulty of finding men and equipment, and partly because of the prevalent feeling that the Germans would shortly be driven out of Africa altogether. All that materialized was one "Indian Long Range Squadron" which was formed during the winter of 1941/1942; so in that respect there was little for Colonel Bagnold to do.

Sudan Defence Force takes over defence of Kufra.

On 10 July 1941 G.H.Q. Middle East issued instructions for the relief of the L.R.D.G. from garrison duty at Kufra by troops of the Sudan Defence Force, and as described in Section VIII, the new garrison arrived on 18 July. The group remained at Kufra but resumed its original duty of long range reconnaissance.

Duties of L.R.D.G.

Its commander was told that except when he had orders from G.H.Q. for a specific operation, he was to use his own initiative in supplying intelligence under the four headings described below in order of priority; and in so doing was to conceal as far as possible the presence or movements of his patrols, and the scope of his activities.

Reconnaissance Areas.

The information required was as follows :-

(a) Of the enemy's movements in the neighbourhood of Zella (long. 17°35'E. lat. 28°33'N.), Marada, and Jalo, and to the south of these Oases.

(b) Of the best routes into, and the possibilities of movement by M.T. over the Sirte Desert, from the coast of the Gulf southwards to Jebel-es-Soda which is west of Zella; and as to the geography of that area.

(c) Of the routes between the plain of Kufra and the Fezzan which might be useful later for offensive operations.

(d) Of the nature of the Haruj as an obstacle to military movement; and of its inhabitants, if any, and their normal routes and water holes. The Haruj is a range of hills running from S.E. at long. 18°E. to N.W. at long. 17°30', between latitudes 27°30'N. and 28°N.

Survey work.

In order that full advantage should be taken of the opportunity of improving existing maps a Survey Officer and a topographical draughtsman were sent to Kufra, and another Survey Officer came from Khartoum. The L.R.D.G. had already done a good deal of topographical work. When it first began to operate in the autumn of 1940 the country south of latitude 29°N. and west of the Egyptian frontier on the 25th meridian east of Greenwich, was entirely unknown and unmapped; though of the area further west there were Italian maps which were "somewhat sketchy and imaginative", especially in regard to scale and sheet lines. The improved maps available at the end of October 1941 were to a great extent due to the efforts of the two Survey Officers, Lieuts. Lazarus (L.R.D.G) and Wright (S.D.F).

The Commander L.R.D.G. was given permission to ask the R.A.F. Commander at Kufra for air cooperation: but as the latter's primary task was the Air Defence of Kufra it was left to him to decide whether aircraft for reconnaissance could be spared. The two Army Aircraft (Wacos) being unarmed were to be used for communication purposes only.

Northern Boundary for L.R.D.G. Operations.

The operational boundary between the L.R.D.G. patrols and those of the Western Desert Force was to be a straight line from El Agheila to Jikerra (both places inclusive to L.R.D.G.) and thence along the north edge of the

Sand Sea to the Egyptian frontier. Jikerra (long. 21°40'E. lat. 29°15'N) is 25 miles E.N.E. of Aujila. Lastly the O.C. L.R.D.G. was made responsible, by means of personal visits by air, for keeping H.Q. Western Desert Force and its patrols informed of the general scope and results of his activities; and he was authorized to make periodical visits to G.H.Q. when in his opinion it was necessary to do so. The G.H.Q. Instruction was amplified by Colonel Bagnold in a letter addressed to the O.C. L.R.D.G. from Cairo and dated 16 July 1941.

After the group had been relieved of its garrison duties at Kufra leave was granted to parties of 20 or 30 men. 'G' and 'Y' Patrols which with H.Q. 'A' Squadron had been at Siwa since April, had suffered considerably from malaria, and their equipment was badly in need of overhaul. It was therefore decided to relieve them and also to form the two New Zealand Patrols 'T' and 'R' into a New Zealand Squadron under Capt. Steele who had hitherto commanded 'R' Patrol. The relief began on 6 August and was completed on the 25th when 'A' Squadron arrived with 'G' and 'Y' Patrols at Cairo. 'S' Patrol remained at Kufra.

Reconnaissance by 'T' Patrol July-August 1941.

The first reconnaissance to obtain the information asked for by G.H.Q. was carried out during the last week of July and the first week of August 1941 by 'T' Patrol. It was to cover the Sirte Desert between the coast and Jebel-es-Soda within the following boundaries:-

North: The coastal belt between El Agheila and Buerat-el-Hsun (about 50 miles west of the port of Sirte).

East: The line Ain Sidi Mohammed (long. 20°10'E. lat. 29°5'N. and about half way between Aujila and Marada) – El Agheila.

South: The line Ain Sidi Mohammed-Marada-Zella-Hon (in long. 20°10'E. lat. 29°5'N. and about 140 miles W.N.W. of Zella).

West: The line Hon-Bou Njem (long. 15°35'E. lat. 30°37'N. and about 110 miles N.N.W. of Hon) – Bouerat-el-Hsun.

Emphasis was laid in Lieut.Colonel Prendergast's instructions to the patrol, on the importance of concealing movement from the enemy. No aggressive action was to be taken beyond the capture of prisoners for interrogation, if this could be done without the fact being revealed to the enemy. It was believed that there were Italian detachments of varying strength at Jalo, Marada, Tagrifet (50 miles north of Zella), Zella, Hon and Bou Njem. The patrol was ordered to march as a whole to the Bir Zelten area. Bir Zelten is a well in long. 19°75'E. lat. 28°28' and is 60 miles S.E. of Marada. On arrival in this area it was to divide into three parties, 'A' party of 15 men and 4 vehicles, commanded by Captain Ballantyne who had with him Captain Wilson, V.C., as Italian interpreter; 'B' party of 12 men and 4 vehicles under Lieut. Ellingham with Capt. W. Kennedy-Shaw as

70

navigator and interpreter; and a rear party under a N.C.O., of 18 men (including Capt. F.B. Edmundson, M.O.) and 7 vehicles. 'A' and 'B' parties were to carry out the reconnaissances and the rear party was to remain at Bir Zelten and act as a rallying point in case of need. The vehicles included three 15-cwt Fords, the remainder being 30-cwt C.A.S. type Fords. Each party had a No. 11 W/T set.

The patrol left Taiserbo at midday (G.M.T.) on 30 July and moving N.N.W. reached a suitably concealed harbour for the rear party about 60 miles E.S.E. of Bir Zelten, on the same day. On 31 July, 1 August and 2 August 'A' and 'B' parties marched together, and on the 1st had to make a considerable detour eastwards to avoid an area of dune filled depressions stretching some 60 miles eastwards from the vicinity of Marada to Ain Sidi Mohammed. From the latter place they moved on a bearing of 285° which brought them to the Marada-El Agheila road at a point about 40 miles south of El Agheila. At midday on 2 August the two parties parted company when about 50 miles west of the road, at long. 18°25'E. lat. 29°30'N. 'A' party moved due west for the remainder of the day, and on 3 August turned S.E. at a point approximately at long 16°25'E. lat. 29°50'N., in the high ground about 100 miles south of the town of Sirte and 60 miles N.N.E. of Hon. Its movement for the next six days was generally south east and it reached Taiserbo on the 9th. The route followed was parallel to and about 40 miles N.E. of Jebel Haruj. Capt. Ballantyne intended to pass between Tagrifet and Zella but bad going prevented it. Taiserbo was approached from the west along the "Fustificata Leo", the track marked by the Italians with petrol drums, which had been reconnoitred in June by a troop of 'T' Patrol.

After leaving 'A' party, 'B' party moved on bearings that varied from 290° to 300° till on 3 August it reached its most westerly point at long. 16°20'E. lat. 30°40'N, 40 miles S.W. of the town of Sirte. The going was generally good. Five miles east of this spot the party found what seemed to have been a German training camp. There were no signs of recent use, but the camp appeared to have been hurriedly evacuated as a certain amount of serviceable material (camp beds, chairs, clothing and camouflage netting) had been left behind. There was also the wreck of a German single engined plane. The party then turned E.N.E. towards the coastal plain and on 4 August encamped about 20 miles from the coast and 80 miles S.E. by east of Sirte. It continued its return journey parallel to the coast, and on 5 August about long. 19°20' was within 10 miles of the sea near El Agheila. Owing to the presence of natives it was decided in order to get nearer to the coast to turn back; and at long. 18°35' the whole party came within 8 miles of the sea, one lorry going down a wadi to within a mile of the coast road. The going here was practicable for 30-cwt lorries and a complete patrol could have got to the road unobserved. The party then returned to the rear party's rendezvous by a route slightly to the north of, and better than that followed on the outward journey; and reached it on 8 August. On the 9th acting on W/T orders from Capt. Ballantyne, 'B' party and the rear party moved to Zighen. 'A' party joined them on the 10th and the patrol arrived at Kufra on the 11th.

Three lorries and a car were seen by 'B' party on the coastal road, but no M.T. were seen inland. One Italian aircraft flew over and apparently disregarded 'B' party on 4 August but no others appeared. 'B' party passed a few camel herdsmen south of Sirte, but no Europeans or natives were seen by 'A' party.

The topographical information collected was reported in detail and covered the coastal zone extending 10 to 15 miles inland, a central zone extending 20 miles further south, and a southern zone extending southwards from the central zone to the Haruj and Jebel-es-Soda.

Shortly after its return from the Sirte Desert reconnaissance 'T' Patrol returned to Cairo to rest and refit, arriving there on 25 August, and as already related 'A' Squadron arrived there from Siwa on the same day. This left only two patrols in the field; 'R' under Capt. Easonsmith, which had gone from Kufra to Siwa on 6 August, and 'S' under Capt. Holliman which remained at Kufra.

'S' Patrol 2–9 September 1941. Reconnaissances to Jalo-Jedabia road.

Between the 2 and 9 September 1941 'S' Patrol carried out from Kufra, a reconnaissance to obtain accurate information on the possibilities of an advance along the Jalo-Jedabia line. Reports were asked for on the best routes for movement by A.F.Vs and columns of 3-ton lorries; on sites for landing grounds; and on the water supplies in an area which extends for some 55 miles to the east of Jalo-Jedabia road and about 45 miles along it, and is bounded on the north by the Wadi el Faregh which crosses the road about 35 miles S.E. of Jedabia. A reconnaissance was also to be made for possible routes on both sides of the road, of the bad country between Maaten-es-Shegeig to the east of the road and Gasr-el-Sahabi which lies on it, about 60 miles S.E. of Jedabia. The patrol was divided into two parties, 'A' under Capt. Holliman and 'B' under 2/Lieut. Olivey. Each party consisted of 15 of all ranks travelling in one 15-cwt Ford lorry, and three 30-cwt C.A.S. type Fords. Capt. C.D. Buchanan, R.E., was with 'A' party and Capt. Kennedy-Shaw with 'B' party. No troops of the enemy were seen, but single aircraft were observed on the 6, 7, and 10 September. Recent tracks of M.T. were found which indicated varying degrees of movement north and east from Jalo, N.W. of Aujila and near El Gueaed. Information was given by natives that short range patrols were often made from Jalo, particularly to the east, but otherwise there was no movement off established routes. Convoys from the north went to Jalo about once a month. All native seen were friendly and it was thought they were unlikely to report the presence of British patrols, unless they lived near enough to the enemy to run the risk of punishment if they failed to do so. All complained of the lack of food, sugar, cloth, etc., and many asked how far along the coast the British had advanced.

The movement of the patrols was on two parallel routes, the more westerly on a bearing of 340° from Zighen, the other along which 'B' party returned home, on the same bearing from a point about 45 miles further east. Aujila and Jalo were "by-passed" to the east, and the most northerly point reached was about 45 miles east of Jedabia (near Saunnu).

'R' Patrol to Jebel-el-Akhdar August 1941.

As described earlier, 'R' Patrol relieved 'A' Squadron at Siwa during the first week of August 1941. On the 13th the patrol, under 2/Lieut. C.H.B. Croucher started for Jebel-el-Akhdar with four objects in view:

(a) To take two Arab agents to Jebel-el-Akhdar, and if they returned within a maximum of four days to bring them back.
(b) To collect a note at the well at Bir Raggia.
(c) To repair and bring back a car left by a previous patrol.
(d) To reconnoitre Medwar Hassan, a dune area with a Wadi running east to west through it, which is about 110 miles N.W. of Jarabub at long. 23°E, lat. 30°54'N.

The Arab agents were left six miles north of the Bir Raggia well at 0900 hrs on 15 August. A rendezvous with them at the well itself was arranged for at 1700 hrs on the 18th. The car was repaired, but again had to be abandoned on the way home owing to a broken radiator. The patrol waited till the agents were twelve hours overdue and started home without them, but with two other natives who had useful knowledge of the country and of the enemy's positions. Medwar Hassan was reconnoitred en route and a report on it written. No enemy on the ground nor aircraft with the exception of one monoplane were seen; though there was considerable air activity at night in the Bir Raggia area.

Reconnaissance of Landing Grounds by 'R' Patrol August–September 1941.

A second reconnaissance for possible landing grounds was made by 'R' Patrol under Lance Corporal Hamilton at the end of August. The area investigated was west of Jarabub as far as long. 22°, and south of the Jarabub-Jalo road. Six possible sites were found.

No enemy were seen on the ground, but a Ghibli aircraft fired two bursts of M.G. fire at the patrol and then flew away. As no theodolite was available during this reconnaissance the exact positions of the possible landing grounds were not exactly fixed. This was done by 'R' Patrol under 2/Lieut. D.I. Ross during the second week of September. The exact location of Medwar Hassan was also determined, and a truck abandoned in an earlier reconnaissance was repaired and brought in. Aircraft and fresh tracks were seen but no enemy M.T.

Section XI

Further reorganization September 1941.

When 'A' Squadron ('G' and 'Y' Patrols) returned to Cairo towards the end of August in order to rest and refit, a second squadron HQ under Major Steele was formed at Siwa; and 'R' Patrol was also quartered there. In order to suit the requirements of H.Q. Western Desert which commanded the L.R.D.G. detachment at Siwa, the new squadron was called 'A' Squadron. The former 'A' Squadron then at Cairo was renamed 'B'. 'T' Patrol which had also gone to Cairo to refit was part of Major Steele's 'A' Squadron, but did not return to Siwa until the middle of October. Group H.Q. remained at Kufra with H.Q. Signals (less a detachment at Siwa), 'S' Patrol, and the Heavy Section which was commanded by Lieut. Morris of the New Zealand Army. This still had four 10-ton White lorries, but their reliability was becoming doubtful.

Deterioration of vehicles.

It had become increasingly apparent that the vehicles, and in particular those detached at Siwa, were not getting adequate maintenance. This was due not only to the fact that there was no officer fully qualified to take charge of repair, but also to a dearth of fitters and a lack of spare parts.

Repair Section.

When he went to G.H.Q., Colonel Bagnold took the matter up and during the autumn of 1941 a separate light repair section R.A.O.C. with its own war establishment was formed and attached to the L.R.D.G. under the command of Capt. Ashdown, R.A.O.C., an electro-mechanical engineer.

Signal Section.

The L.R.D.G. Signals were also reorganized at this time. As in the case of the light repair organization, a separate signal section came into being. This enabled the Signal Officer, Capt. Heywood, to cope more successfully with the problems of long range intercommunication.

Waco Aircraft and Air Routes.

The two "Waco" aircraft, piloted by Lieut.Colonel Prendergast and Sergeant Barker and navigated by Lance Corporal Arnold, did much flying; and enabled the C.O. to visit his detachments and to attend conferences at Cairo and at H.Q. Western Desert Force at Bagush. They were however not really reliable, for their engines were old and had not been improved by sand and great heat. They had therefore to be used together in case either of them was forced to land. In order further to safeguard the occupants the same route to Cairo, by the Gilf Kebir plateau about 180 miles S.E. of Kufra, was always followed if possible; and along it dumps of food and water were made at intervals of fifteen miles. There was also an emergency landing ground known as Jebel Ailam between Gilf Kebir and the Kharga oasis, which was the next aerodrome. This route had been reconnoitred by Capt. Kennedy-Shaw while navigating a leave party to Cairo. Another air route to Siwa was made later by Jebel Thalma, which was similarly stocked with food and water, and also with petrol. Navigation in the air over desert country is always difficult owing to the risk of sand storms at certain times of the year, and of the absence of landmarks. It was carried out in the normal manner by time and drift, but it was at times necessary to land on the nearest stretch of firm looking sand, and fix the position from the sun with a sextant. Food, water and spare parts were invariably carried. Track following was impracticable owing to glare, bumps and overheating. Later, when the flying routes had been surveyed by an expert and the crews had had experience of them, navigation became easier.

Operations of L.R.D.G. August to November 1941.

The operations carried out from August to November 1941 were of two kinds:-
(a) Those organized by L.R.D.G. H.Q. under orders from G.H.Q. Middle East and
     undertaken from Kufra.
(b) Those organized by the O.C. 'A' Squadron at Kufra under orders from H.Q. Western Desert Force (later the Eighth Army).

'S' Patrol reconnoitres coast road in Tripoli September 1941.

In September an important operation by 'S' Patrol (2/Lieut. J. Olivey) in the former of these categories took place. Its object was in general to reconnoitre the coast road west of El Agheila; and, in particular, to obtain accurate information in regard to traffic as follows:-

(1) The number and types of A.F.Vs, guns and lorries using the road.
(2) Whether the vehicles were those of fighting units or merely supply convoys.
(3) The time and date on which movement by M.T. was seen and its direction.
(4) The type of escort vehicles accompanying supply convoys and where they were placed in the columns.

The enemy was known to have garrisons at El Agheila, Nofilia, Sirte and Bouerat-el-Hsun on the coast. At Jalo there were believed to be 150 Italian troops mostly artillery, with about 40 vehicles and two Ghibli aircraft. Marada was said to be unoccupied.

The patrol consisted of 2/Lieut. Olivey, with 2/Lieut. L.H. Brown, D.C.M., as navigator and intelligence officer, and 16 O.Rs. For transport they had one 15-cwt lorry and four of 30-cwt.

Owing to the necessity for concealing movement aggressive action was forbidden. If the patrol was attacked the O.C. was to decide whether to continue the reconnaissance or return with any information he had obtained. The patrol was not strong enough to fight for information, and half the required information brought back was better than none at all. The party was to lie up near the coast road in the neighbourhood of Ras Umm el Garanig (some 50 miles west of El Agheila); the road was to be kept under observation night and day, and a record was to be kept of every vehicle seen.

The patrol left Zighen on 15 September and moved east of Ain Sidi Mohammed (half way between Aujila and Marada) to Alem-el-Mgaad 32 miles north of Marada on the road to El Agheila, thus avoiding the danger areas round Jalo and Marada. Watch on the coast road was maintained day and night from a hill at long. 18°39'53"E, lat. 30°21'10"N for 168 hours (18-25 September). The hill is about 160 feet high and 2? miles from the road, near the spot later known as "Marble Arch" (x) A5492 near Ras Lanuf. The party was seen by some natives with camels on the 17th, near Ain Sidi Mohammed. For the night watch the observers at first moved on foot down to the road, but there was so little traffic during darkness that to record it by sound and lights from the hill was considered enough. On 21 September a German aircraft circled round the "harbour" area, but as there was plenty of warning and everyone was under cover it was concluded that the party had not been observed. On the 24th 2/Lieut. Olivey went down to within 200 yards of the road during daylight in order to make a close examination of traffic. On the 25th when 2/Lieut. Browne was within 300 yards of it two men got out of a car and started to shoot hares! The party moved off that evening and went back 10 miles, having left nothing but tracks to show that they had been there. On the 26th they reached the neighbourhood of Ain Sidi Mohammed and signalled to Kufra information as to the amount of traffic seen. They then hurried on in case their message had been intercepted at Jalo, and after a certain amount of delay owing to breakdowns, reached Zighen at sunset on the 27th and moved on to Kufra next day. During this 168 hours watch the following vehicles had been seen:-

Lorries varying from 3 to 10 tons	– eastbound	1218
	– westbound	764
Military and civilian cars	– eastbound	131
	– westbound	59
Motor cycles, D.R.	– eastbound	111
	– westbound	13
Motor cycles (solo and combination) of German fighting troops		
	– eastbound	556
	– none passed towards the west.	

Thirty 4-wheeled armoured cars were seen and also twenty seven tanks (1 heavy, 1 medium and 25 light) all going east.

Forty four guns were seen, also going east.

Lieut.Colonel Prendergast's report on the expedition to the coast includes general remarks on the report made by the Officer in command of the party. He points out that the observers were not trained to recognise enemy equipment; so that the details given of tanks, etc., could not be regarded as reliable, but it could be taken that, in the case of M.T., the sizes and the numbers were accurate. Traffic by night was very slight; the majority of it passed between dawn and 1030 hrs, and between 1600 hrs and dusk. Some lorries carrying circular fuel containers were seen. The majority of the traffic seen moved in convoy, and seemed to be supply columns and not fighting units. A good many guns however were seen, and two German motor cycle units. An interesting point was that heavy and medium lorries going west (and presumably empty) had another lorry of the same size in tow. Judging by the method of attachment it appeared that towing was not caused by breakdowns, and the inference was that fuel was short. Tanks and guns were carried on trailers. On two occasions convoys encamped for the night near the observers; and all traffic was checked in by two police posts within sight. Enemy aircraft were seen on eleven occasions mostly going westwards.

'R' Patrol to Mekili September 1941.

At about the same time Capt. J.R. Easonsmith with a party of 'R' Patrol carried out an expedition from Siwa under the orders of H.Q. Western Desert Force. Its object was to drop two agents west of Mekili and to bring them back; to bring back two other agents from the same area; and to retrieve a Ford light van abandoned during a previous expedition.

The party with three trucks, left Siwa at midday on the 15th, and returned in the evening of the 19th. The route crossed the wire at Weshka and passing through Bab-es-Serir, crossed the Trigh el Abd twenty miles S.W. of Bir Tengeder (S) UO630; thence to Wadi Tamanlu nineteen miles due west of Mekili. The two agents who went with the party duly returned after an absence of one and a half days. The other two had started back with camels on their own initiative and arrived at Jarabub a week or two later. The route followed on the return journey lay somewhat more to the south west, and came into Weshka from Hatiet Etla about 55 miles due west. Some useful topographical information was reported. Nothing of the enemy was seen on the ground, except the tracks of a few light vehicles, and few aircraft appeared.

Tripoli Road Watch by 'S' Patrol October 1941.

At the beginning of October a further reconnaissance of the coast road west of Agheila was ordered by G.H.Q. Middle East. It was carried out by Capt. C.A. Holliman with a party of 'S' Patrol. He had with him 2/Lieut. Browne, D.C.M., as navigator and Intelligence Officer, and 16 O.Rs. There were five 30-cwt lorries, one carrying W/T.

The information about traffic required by G.H.Q. was given at some length in the form of a "questionnaire". In particular it asked for details about the construction and armament of tanks, and armoured cars; and also about guns and trailers. It also asked for an opinion as to the nature of any columns seen, and what sort of head dress the men wore; whether, for instance, they wore German or Italian helmets, berets, feathered hats, etc.

The watch on the road was carried out between 9 and 16 October from the point chosen by 2/Lieut. Olivey three weeks earlier. Information had been received that G.H.Q. expected important traffic to pass from 8 October onwards, and the O.C. L.R.D.G. gave orders that observers were if possible to be placed so as to enable them to note details of the traffic as well as numbers.

Traffic Census.

The report made by Capt. Holliman went into very great detail. The catalogue of guns, tanks, lorries, motor-cycles, etc., had nineteen headings; and a list was added with a description of every group of vehicles or single vehicle, and giving its direction, the date and time at which it was seen, and whether troops or loads were being carried or not. In the general remarks made when he forwarded the report Lieut.Colonel Prendergast notes –

(a) That the majority of vehicles appeared to be new.

(b) That there was little traffic at night, and most of it staff cars (mainly late model Fiats) which appeared to be unarmed.

(c) That 70% of the traffic was eastbound.

(d) That as before, lorries proceeding westwards frequently had another lorry in tow.

He stated also that on 11 October three convoys of 28, 29, and 12 heavy vehicles respectively were seen going east all carrying European troops. The remaining troop movement was irregular and in small parties.

No opinion could be given as to the nationality of the men seen, nor was there any uniformity of dress except that the majority were wearing a type of forage cap. The only formed body of troops consisted of motor cyclists, a column of whom were going east on 15 October.

During daylight observation was carried out from a shallow sand pit about 500 yards south of the road. In addition, a continuous watch was kept for 168 hours, from a hill 100 feet high and 2? miles from the road. No traffic passed unrecorded; and it may be added that throughout the period of observation only six aircraft were seen. It is very remarkable that on two occasions our men should have been able to bring their vehicles so close to the enemy's principal line of communications and to stay there for seven days without revealing their presence. It is no less strange that the enemy had not discovered any trace of 2/Lieut. Olivey's expedition to observe traffic a few weeks previously, for its tracks could not have been obliterated.

'S' Patrol to Jalo October 1941.

The next reconnaissance from Kufra was made by a party of 'S' Patrol under 2/Lieut. Olivey with 2/Lieut. B. Herman as interpreter, and 15 O.Rs, carried in one 15-cwt lorry and four 30-cwt lorries. It had two tasks:-

(a) To ascertain by the capture of an Italian prisoner the strength and composition of the garrison at Jalo.
(b) To obtain topographical information of the country in the vicinity of the Jalo oasis.

The garrison of Jalo was believed to consist of about 150 Italian troops mostly artillery, with about 40 vehicles and two Ghibli aircraft. Officers were said to live in the office of the District Administration (Zona) and the troops and vehicles were in the palm groves. The Airforce personnel occupied the school. One of the aircraft went daily to Jedabia, the other carried out local reconnaissances. Patrols of 11 vehicles reconnoitred at frequent intervals round the oasis. The aircraft were parked on the landing ground south of the main village. The W/T station was in the barrack building of the "Zona". The landing ground was not wired. In the fort, which was wired, there were said to be 50 men with two 75 mm guns in emplacements. There were no troops or police in Jikerra or Aujila.

The party left Kufra on 9 October, and moved by Zighen to a point in the sand dunes east of Jalo. On the 12th it proceeded westwards between

Jikerra and Jalo, to the western outskirts of the hamlet of Es Scerruf, about 5 miles north of Jalo. During the night 12/13 October two officers and two O.Rs entered Jalo on foot from the north, and saw some 8 vehicles with a sentry among palms on the northern edge of the oasis. Recent tracks showed that the Jikerra-Jalo and Aujila-Jalo tracks were much used. It is probable that the arrival of the patrol was given away by natives of Es Scerruf, for on the morning of the 13th an aircraft searched for the party and eventually located it west of Jikerra. The plane went back to Jalo and the L.R.D.G. party moved off to the west. They were then discovered by another machine which attacked them with bombs and M.G. fire for half an hour, but without causing casualties. A second entry into Jalo was made from the direction of Bir Bettafal, about 18 miles to the S.W., on the night of 15/16 October.

No prisoners were taken but natives said that the water in Jalo was undrinkable, and that supplies were therefore brought from Es Scerruf on alternate days. Food in Jalo was short, tea and sugar being almost unobtainable.

A certain amount of topographical information was also obtained and forwarded to G.H.Q.

The party returned to Kufra on 17 October.

'R' Patrol to Gulf of Bomba October 1941.

An operation which began on 30 September was carried out from Siwa by a detachment of 'R' Patrol under Capt. Easonsmith with two trucks. Two Arab agents were taken into the area bounded on the west by Sidi Tmimi (on the Gulf of Bomba) and on the east by Ain-el-Gazala, which is near the coast road and about 40 miles west of Tobruk. The agents duly returned after an absence of four days and the detachment reached Siwa on 9 October. On the return journey an abandoned Wellington bomber was found about 20 miles S.E. of Bir Hakim. It appeared to have landed without injury to the crew, and had been most effectively wrecked by them. Five men had walked off on an approximate bearing of 260°, but the tracks were "stale". From discarded equipment it appeared that the names of four of the men were Sergeants Dodd, McCormick, Leach and Collier.

No M.T. or troops were seen and there were no fresh tracks east of meridian 23°E. There was a good deal of patrol activity mainly by Ghibli aircraft near the coast. Capt. Easonsmith also reported a certain amount of topographical information.

'B' Squadron at Kufra 20 October 1941.

'B' Squadron ('G' and 'Y' Patrols) arrived at Kufra from Cairo on 20 October. It was now commanded by Major E.C.T. Wilson, V.C., East Surrey Regiment, as Major Mitford, its former commander, had left. There were no more operations from Kufra, for before the end of October it had been decided to concentrate the whole group at Siwa in readiness for the projected offensive which started in the following month.

More reconnaissances from Siwa were carried out by 'R' and 'T' Patrols of 'A' Squadron, before the group concentrated there, the last of which terminated on 1 November. Like others before them they were to some extent of a routine nature, and as several British and Arab agents were conveyed to and brought back from the Jebel-el-Akhdar, 'A' Squadron acquired the name of "Libyan Taxis Ltd.".

'R' Patrol to Mekili Area October 1941.

The first expedition was a reconnaissance by a detachment of 'R' Patrol under Capt. Easonsmith with the following objects:-
(a) To map the eastern end of the Wadi Mra near Medwar Hassan.
(b) To meet a British Officer (Capt. Hasleden) either at Abd-el-Krim or at the landing ground N.W. of Ain-bu-Sfia, and to send him back as soon as possible to Siwa.
(c) To obtain all possible information about Mekili.
(d) To traverse the area south of Mekili known as Dahar-el-Hallab, which was an obstacle to troop movement from N.E. to S.W., and to find out whether the Wadi-es-Shiaaba, 40 miles S.W. of Bir Hakim, was an obstacle to A.F.Vs or M.T.

The detachment consisting of 15 of all ranks with two Arabs, and divided into two parties, 'A' and 'B', left Siwa in five trucks on 14 October. They crossed the wire at Weshka and moving by the Wadi Mra, arrived on the 16th at the first rendezvous at Abd-el-Krim (S)O.1602, where they were due to pick up Capt. Hasleden. Three British O.Rs, who had escaped from Bengazi a week before, were found hiding in the ruins at Garet Tecasis, 12 miles south of Abd-el-Krim, and picked up early on 17 October. Having waited the appointed time and searched the area, the party, on 19 October, went on to Ain-bu-Sfia, (S)O.7806, the second rendezvous. Two trucks were left at Garet Tecasis, which could take Capt. Hasleden back to Siwa if he arrived later; and the two Arabs were sent on to look for him at Marsua about 20 miles to the north. The second rendezvous which is about 25 miles east by north of Abd-el-Krim, and is marked on the Cyrenaica map as Abiar-bu-Sfeia,[1] was reached at midday; and a short reconnaissance on foot revealed the presence of four enemy trucks and two light tanks close at hand.

Capt. Easonsmith made a further reconnaissance and discovered a camp at the place he believed to be Ain-bu-Sfia. He went back and having hid his

1 Abiar, plural of Bir, means "wells" or "cisterns" – Ain means "spring" and the places are probably identical.

truck, sent out the two Arabs to search the locality for Capt. Hasleden. He then went out on foot with three days supplies to search on his own account for Capt. Hasleden, and to locate a landing ground marked on the 1:500,000 map dated 7 February 1941. At 0700 hrs on the 20th he reached a flat area large enough for an emergency landing ground, whose position agreed with the map, and he stayed there two days and nights. This search proved to be waste of effort as the Arabs whom he had sent to look for him elsewhere, found Capt. Hasleden on the 19th and brought him in to the rendezvous on the 22nd. He went straight back to Siwa with 'B' party and arrived there on 24 October.

'A' party left its "harbour" at 0400 hrs on 22 October and by 0700 hrs had reached a point on an escarpment N.E. and in view of the enemy's camp at Ain-bu-Sfia. There were about 30 to 40 vehicles and four light tanks, parked round the base of a small circular hill with the ruins of a fort on the top which was being used as a look-out post; and on another rise there appeared to be low bivouac tents which perhaps contained stores. There was a constant stream of traffic passing through the camp in the direction of Mekili, and Capt. Easonsmith decided to make a small "Cutting out" expedition.

Attack on Italian Convoy.

On 23 October, before the enemy's traffic had begun to move, he took his three trucks to some dead ground close to the track. After a short reconnaissance on foot he sent two trucks to some rising ground commanding the track, and about three to four miles from the camp, and took the third truck to another point on the track about two miles away. His intention was to attract the enemy's notice by simulating a breakdown, and he therefore turned back along the track dropping some "specially doctored" boxes of Italian machine gun ammunition as he went. Unluckily he had not noticed that there was dead ground in the direction from which enemy's vehicles were coming, and near the spot chosen for the "breakdown". They were not seen until they were about 200 yards away and the "breakdown" had to be "staged" rather hurriedly. Of the crew of four, two bent over the engine, the machine gunner hid under a tarpaulin and Capt. Easonsmith held up his hand. The leading lorry stopped and Capt. Easonsmith walked up to it and opened the door of the cab. The Italians were suspicious but apparently not convinced that Easonsmith was not one of themselves. He relates that he produced his tommy gun rather clumsily, and that as he was standing too close to the driver the latter fell out on to him and got hold of the tommy gun. There was a hand to hand tussle, and the driver got away and ran off with the tommy gun, but did not use it. Easonsmith then had a shot at him with a hand grenade which he described as "fairly lucky". An Italian officer who was a passenger, had "in the meantime used up all his revolver ammunition and run". He was killed or wounded. In Easonsmith's words "things became quite fast and furious. Fortunately none of the leading Italian trucks had a machine gun but quite a supply (sic) of men with rifles was appearing by now." As the sound of firing could be heard in the camp there was no time to lose. Two Italians were pulled out from under trucks, and the leading Italian truck was put out of action with a grenade. The other two trucks of the party "were doing good work with a Lewis gun and a rifle", though their Vickers gun had jammed. Capt. Easonsmith decided that it was "time to clear off " and did so. He had had no casualties, and the only damage was from a revolver bullet which had hit the radiator of his truck. The impression gained was that five or six Italians were killed and about a dozen wounded. One of the two prisoners was wounded and died about two hours later. The party got away without interference, and by nightfall had covered about 140 miles. Owing to the extra men that were being carried and the damaged radiator, water was getting low, and the programme had to be curtailed. They returned by Wadi es Sciaaba, 32 miles S.W. of Bir Hakim, and satisfied themselves that it was not an obstacle to M.T.; and they reached Siwa at 0900 hrs on the 25th. Few hostile aircraft were seen, but in the Wadi-es-Sciaaba an abandoned S.M. 82 aircraft was found which appeared to be capable of repair, and a number of papers were removed from it.

As usual a good deal of useful topographical information was obtained, although owing to the lack of water it had not been possible to visit Mekili or reconnoitre the Dahar-el-Hallab.

'T' Patrol to Jedabia area October 1941.

On 16 October Capt. Ballantyne left Siwa with a detachment of 'T' Patrol for the Jedabia area. His tasks were:-
(1) To drop two Senussi officers at Bir et Tomba, about 17 miles S.W. of Jedabia; and while waiting for their return,
(2) To survey the country round Jedabia and as far south as (excl) Wadi-el-Fareg.[1]
(3) To survey the escarpment between Benina and Antelat which lies to the east of the line Bengasi-Soluk.
The escarpment is about 30 miles inland from the east coast of the Gulf of Sirte.

Six trucks were used and the detachment operated in two parties, one of which (the "Southern party") was commanded by 2/Lieut. Ross who had

---

1   30 to 40 miles S.E. and south of Jedabia.
    References are to Cyrenaica 1:500,000 sheets 13 and 15.
    "   "   " Libya 1:500,000 sheet 2.

with him 2/Lieut. Costello, was to carry out tasks (1) and (2). This party also had orders to drop German and Italian belt boxes at places on the main roads so as to give the impression that they had fallen off a truck. The detachment marched by Garn-ul-Grein and Hatiet-el-Etla (where there was a supply dump) and split into two parties just south of Garet-el-Esc (XC 9595). They were to rendezvous at the same place on 24 October, or not later than the morning of the 25th. The northern party, under Capt. Ballantyne, then moved north and struck the escarpment at (S)S.4205 near Abiar el Cremeisa. They found that the escarpment as far north as Es-Sheledeima ((S)S.4115) about 20 miles S.E. of Soluk, could be crossed easily from east to west or vice versa. It appeared too that the enemy sent salvage parties from time to time to collect spare parts from abandoned vehicles, and one of these parties was captured in the area west of Msus. The local natives who were numerous, appeared to be friendly, and gave information about the enemy's dispositions.

The Southern party did not arrive at the rendezvous and on 27 October had still not returned to Siwa; but it came in later.

Capt. Hunter's reconnaissance south of Tobruk November 1941.

'A' Squadron's last independent operation from Siwa was carried out between 1 and 4 November 1941. Its object was a reconnaissance of the area south of Bir Hakim (45 miles S.W. of Tobruk) and Bir-el-Gubi (38 miles south of Tobruk) to ascertain –

(a) The nature of enemy activity.
(b) The number and type of vehicles.
(c) The type of armament.

Capt. A.D.N. Hunter was in command and he had with him 2/Lieut. Croucher with 13 O.Rs of 'R' and 'T' Patrols. There were four trucks. It was originally intended to divide the detachment into two parties, one going to Bir Hakim, the other to El Gubi. Soon after leaving Jarabub however one truck damaged a spring and had to be sent home; so the three remaining trucks operated together. They moved by Jarabub, Saniet ed Deffa (25 miles N.W.) and Hatiet-el-Etla to a point within 15 miles of Bir Hakim (Reference 356360 on map Cyrenaica 1:500,000 sheets 14 and 15). Here six aeroplanes passed over them going S.E. They lay up till the evening by which time the weather was so hazy that neither the well nor the village of Bir Hakim could be seen. They moved N.E. to a landing ground just north of it, and thence S.E. for about 5 miles.

Capture of an enemy patrol.

Here they captured a motor cycle patrol of five men with their machines and a W/T set. The W/T set was brought back but the M.Cs had to be broken up and left. The prisoners were unprepared for action and seemed glad to be captured. It was then decided to take them to Siwa, and not to go on to Bir-el-Gubi.

Results.

The reconnaissances from Kufra and Siwa were generally speaking very successful, and provided G.H.Q. Middle East and H.Q. Western Desert Force, which at the end of September 1941 became the Eighth Army, with a great deal of valuable information both tactical and topographical. The expeditions to report on traffic along the coast road west of El Agheila made on two occasions by detachments operating from Kufra were very daring and of the greatest importance. Capt. Easonsmith's exploits in ambushing an Italian convoy, and Capt. Hunter's capture of prisoners near Bir Hakim on his first patrol, showed a very high degree of skill and courage, and their moral effect on the enemy must have been considerable. It has to be remembered too that although the Siwa Oasis is quite a pleasant place to live in, it lies below sea level and is not only enervating but also highly malarial. The going in its immediate vicinity was extremely bad, and the vehicles were not in good mechanical condition; steering gear, for instance, often broke down. Any reconnaissance from Siwa, though it might be devoid of "incidents", involved a journey of several hundred miles behind the enemy's lines with the ever present danger of being spotted from the air.

All these factors conduced to very great strain both mental and physical, on all who took part in the very frequent operations that had to be undertaken.

Section XII

L.R.D.G comes under Eighth Army October 1941.

On 1 October 1941 the whole of the L.R.D.G. including the squadron at Kufra, came under the G.O.C. Western Army whose headquarters were established in the desert at Maaten Bagush on 24 September. Shortly afterwards the "Western Army" became the "Eighth Army", under Lieut. General Sir Alan Cunningham. The O.C. L.R.D.G. attended several conferences at Army H.Q. to discuss the Group's role in the forthcoming offensive in Cyrenaica, which eventually started on 18 November.

Conference at Army H.Q.

In the minutes of a Conference held at H.Q. Eighth Army on 29 September the role of the L.R.D.G. before and during future operations was defined as follows:-

(a) To obtain information of enemy movement on certain tracks and in certain areas; and to watch his reactions to any offensive by us.

(b) To provide further information as to the going.

(c) To try at all times to harass the enemy as far as possible, and as the Group Commander thought fit; provided the patrols did not get too deeply involved in fighting.

(d) To send in tactical information as early as possible: and when doing so just before or during an operation, to take the risk of W/T messages being picked up by the enemy which would not be justified in other circumstances.

Group concentrated at Siwa November 1941.

For the time being H.Q. L.R.D.G. remained at Kufra, but Lieut.Colonel Prendergast himself went to Siwa so as to be in closer touch with Army H.Q. It became clear however that the whole group would be better placed at Siwa and it was concentrated there early in November. At Siwa they were reconnoitred by enemy aircraft every day, and occasionally bombed:

but no serious harm was done, and the two "Waco" aircraft which occupied the small and exposed "Town landing ground" were not harmed.

Patrols are reorganized October-November 1941.

Towards the end of October the patrols were reorganized. It had become increasingly clear that a patrol consisting of one 15-cwt lorry and ten 30-cwt lorries was too large to be used in one body, particularly on account of the difficulty of concealing it from the air; and it had become the habit to divide a patrol into two parties, each under an officer, and acting independently. A new W.E. was, therefore, devised which gave the L.R.D.G. ten "half patrols", each of six 30-cwt lorries. The 15-cwt lorries were unsuitable for carrying a load and often broke down; and they were therefore dropped. Thus in effect the L.R.D.G. doubled the number of its patrols; 'G' Patrol split into 'G' 1 and 'G' 2, 'S' into 'S' 1 and 'S' 2, and so on. The number of operators and the amount of signal equipment had of course to be increased. At the end of September Colonel Bagnold informed Lieut.Colonel Prendergast that a mobile medical unit for the L.R.D.G. had been authorised, but it had not yet come into existence.

Relations with Higher Formations. Provision of supplies.

As far as General Staff questions were concerned the relations between the L.R.D.G. and H.Q. Eighth Army were simple enough; but the Group was still administered by G.H.Q. Middle East. Colonel Bagnold, in a letter dated 24 September 1941, expressed the opinion that when the theatre of operations was further to the west, all supplies necessary would have to be drawn from the Q.M.G's branch of the Eighth Army. Eighth Army agreed on 29 September that L.R.D.G. should indent on them for all equipment other than navigational stores which were to be obtained from Cairo; and that all stores would be consigned to Siwa. As far as 'A' matters were concerned, it was likely that the Group would continue to deal direct with Cairo; in any case 'A' questions were not numerous. Maintenance of the "Waco" aircraft was still a difficulty, for the R.A.F. naturally regarded them as relatively of little importance. Lieut.Colonel Prendergast suggested the provision of a two-engine aircraft such as the "Anson", to be maintained by the R.A.F. and flown by himself, and Eighth Army promised to make enquiries.

On 21 October Lieut.Colonel Prendergast wrote a personal letter to Major R. Harding-Newman, who had been G.S.O.2 to Colonel Bagnold when the latter was in command of the Kufra Garrison, but was then at H.Q. Eighth Army. In it Lieut.Colonel Prendergast asked for information as to what was expected of the L.R.D.G. both before and during the coming offensive. He also emphasized that patrols would have to be withdrawn to refit and refuel about fourteen days before 'D' day; and made certain suggestions as to the tactical role of the L.R.D.G. which expressed his own opinions, and those of Capt. Kennedy-Shaw. Major Harding-Newman's reply is dated 25 October. He said that instructions had been written by the General Staff but they were not at the moment prepared to issue them; and his personal opinion was that 'D' day would not be for three weeks or more. He described however what he thought the General Staff's wishes were for the time being. No attacks on aerodromes were to be carried out, though if an opportunity of destroying aircraft arose in the course of other operations, there would naturally be no harm in taking advantage of it. He added that he had some suggestions which he could make personally as to explosives which could be carried as a matter of routine.

The ambushing of convoys should begin as soon as possible.

Major Harding-Newman went on to say that he had not had any direct instructions on the subject, but he had no doubt that "Traffic census" operations could be undertaken; and he knew that the Intelligence Branch would like a continuous watch on the roads in question. He also sent a list of the points on which information was required, topographical or otherwise.

Dispositions at end of October 1941.

At the end of October 1941, the L.R.D.G., now reorganized in "half patrols" as described previously, was stationed at Siwa and Kufra. H.Q. 'A' Squadron with R.1., R.2., T.1., and T.2 (half) patrols was at Siwa; H.Q. 'B' Squadron with G.1., G.2., S.1., S.2., Y.1., and Y.2. patrols was at Kufra. Group H.Q. was also at Kufra, though the Group Commander was usually at Siwa.

Concentration at Siwa 9 November 1941

By 9 November the whole Group was concentrated at Siwa, with the exception of S.1., which had left Kufra on a prolonged operation on 30 October and had not returned on 24 November, and S.2., which left Kufra on 6 November to carry out another task, and arrived at Siwa on 11 November.

'S'1. Patrol to Hon-Misurata road October-November 1941.

S.1. Patrol's primary object was to raid enemy transport on the road from Hon (or Hun) to Misurata. The latter place is in Tripolitania at the N.W. corner of the Gulf of Sirte; Hon (long. 16°E. lat. 29°5'N.) is also in Tripolitania and is about 230 miles S.S.E. of Misurata. If this operation was successful and if the patrol was not too greatly encumbered by prisoners, it was to make a second raid on transport on the coastal road between Sirte and Buerat el Hsun.[1]

The patrol's tasks in particular, and in order of priority were:-

(a) To ambush and destroy a convoy between Bu Njem and Gheddshia which are respectively 130 and 80 miles south of Misurata.

(b) To ambush and destroy an enemy convoy on the coast road between Sirte and Buerat-el-Hsun.

(c) To reconnoitre the approaches to the coast road between Sirte and Buerat-el-Hsun.

All available information as to the location of the enemy's garrisons and aircraft in eastern and southern Tripolitania was given in 'B' Squadron's operation instruction. Capt. C.H. Holliman commanded the detachment, and had with him Lieut. P. Arnold as Intelligence Officer and interpreter; and there were 16 O.Rs. One 8-cwt lorry and five 30-cwt trucks were taken, one of the latter carrying a W/T set and another a Bofors gun.

The outward journey was to be made by Taiserbo-Bir Zelten-Abu Naim (about 30 miles S.W. of Marada) - Jebel-bu-Hosa;[2] and thence on a direct course to the Hon-Misurata road between Bu Njem and Gheddshia.

The patrol commander was to select a suitable spot for the ambush and if successful, or if no enemy convoy from Misurata appeared within three days, he was to carry out a similar ambush on the coast road. But the decision as to the second task was left to him. The reconnaissance ordered as the third task was to be contingent on the success of the raids. Prisoners were to be brought back, and lorries searched for documents. If mines were laid their positions were to be recorded, as they are double edged weapons.

The party left Kufra on 30 October, and after travelling on a general bearing of 310° for three days, reached a point about 45 miles S.W. of Marada. The auxiliary gear box of the W/T lorry had begun to heat up badly, so the W/T apparatus was removed, and the car was hidden and abandoned. The party then took a more northerly course, leaving Tagrifet 30 miles to the south, and at 1600 hrs on 6 November it arrived on the Hon-Misurata road at a point about 18 miles north of Bu Njem. There they found a small camp and a gang of native workmen, who had to be collected and kept in camp while the patrol took up a well covered position west of the road. After dusk they moved forward to within fifty yards of the road and put a barricade across it.

1 Marked on the French sheet "Tunisie" 1:2,000,000, "Bouerat-el-Soun".
2 Long. 18°3'E. lat. 28°50'N. 80 miles N.W. of Abu Naim, and where 'A' party of 'S' Patrol had encamped on 16 October.

Capture of a lorry and prisoners.

At 0500 hrs on the 7th, a heavy Diesel lorry (Lancia), containing five Italians and seven natives, was captured. The natives were put for the time being into the workmen's camp. Rain came on, and as the evidence available indicated that the road was but little used, it was decided to go on to the coastal road. Five mines were laid and the party then went N.E. towards Tmed Hassan which is on the coast road some 40 miles west of Sirte. After going 18 miles they blew up the captured lorry and released the natives, and reached the vicinity of Tmed Hassan at 1750 hrs. A reconnaissance towards the coast road was made in the 8-cwt lorry, and the remaining trucks "harboured" about 2? miles south of it. The reconnaissance located a "roadhouse" at which traffic was seen to draw up.

Attack on "roadhouse" at Tmed Hassan 8 November 1941.

It was then decided to capture the roadhouse, to lay mines on the road, and to hold up and destroy any passing traffic. Parties were detailed for the various tasks, and at 2015 hrs (local time) the 8-cwt lorry and the Bofors truck went down towards the roadhouse which was locked up. Capt. Holliman then sent for the mine laying party and ordered them to reconnoitre the roadhouse, while he examined a heavy truck with a trailer some 50 yards away. On his return the mine layers showed him armed men in the courtyard of the roadhouse. Meanwhile, unknown to Capt. Holliman, the second half of his party had found an entrance behind the house, and it was they who had been pointed out to him. He shouted to them in English to stop, but they were too intent on their hunt for Italians to pay attention. As they continued to move about the men with Capt. Holliman opened fire, with the result that one of his own men was hit in the shoulder. Two Italians were taken prisoners, but one broke away and was severely wounded, and the other was later released. Capt. Holliman then decided to return with his other prisoners to Siwa, and the journey home was made without incident.

When the patrol arrived at Siwa on 24 November the prisoners were interrogated by Major Wilson. His methods are described as varying "from the threats of a Free French prison camp to an overdose of gin", and they elicited some useful information. One of them, an airman, said that the carefully controlled "jinking" employed by our cars during an air attack, made accurate bombing most difficult.

'S' Patrol to Jalo 6 November.

The last operation from Kufra was a special mission in the Jalo area undertaken by a detachment of 'S' Patrol under 2/Lieut. L.H. Browne, D.C.M., and began on 6 November. In the instructions given him he was informed that the enemy were holding Jalo, and were probably patrolling actively both on the ground and in the air; and that a half patrol of L.R.D.G. under Capt. Shaw had left Siwa on 2 November to reconnoitre the same area. On completion of his missions 2/Lieut. Browne was to bring his party into Siwa.

"Planting" a faked map.

The object of the expedition was to "plant" near Jalo a faked map prepared at H.Q. Eighth Army,[1] which was intended to give the enemy the impression that a large British force was about to move on Jalo from the east. It was marked with notes about the going and calculations of distances on the margin.

The patrol which included 10 O.Rs and was carried in three 30-cwt Fords, moved by Zighen, and on 9 November arrived at a point within sight of the northern edge of Jikerra oasis, 20 miles E.N.E. of Jalo. Here a native was seen riding a camel towards the waterhole of El Aseila, about 15 miles east of Jikerra. The patrol then went towards El Aseila, overtook the native, and "planted" the map at the water hole. After lighting a fire and having a meal which was watched by the native, they moved off, leaving evidence which included a map board, scale and protractor to indicate that they had departed in a hurry. They travelled N.N.E. and at 1045 hrs an unidentified aircraft "banked" overhead, and then made off towards Jalo. Half an hour later an aircraft was seen about 5 miles behind apparently following the tracks. At 1145 hrs they sighted two natives and a camel, and drove across to speak to them. At first the natives levelled their rifles, but being apparently satisfied that the patrol was British they laid down their arms. They said that they were "military" and had the ranks of Lieut. and 2/Lieut.; and that they were waiting to be picked up and taken to Jarabub or Siwa. They were therefore taken on by the patrol, which arrived at Siwa without further incident on 11 November, having covered 797 miles.

When Jalo was captured by Brig. Reid's force a fortnight later the details on the faked map were found to have been copied on to a large map in the Italian Commander's office. The "plant" had been successful.

Shaw's reconnaissance towards Jalo 3-11 November 1941.

Capt. Shaw's reconnaissance referred to above took place between 3 and 11 November. Three 'T' patrol trucks were used, and Lieut.Colonel J.S. Jenkins, commanding a Punjab battalion then at Jarabub, and a R.A.F. officer accompanied the party. The intention was to reconnoitre a line of advance to Jalo with a view to an attack in that area.

---

1 By Captain Kennedy Shaw.

Section XIII

L.R.D.G.'s role in Eighth Army offensive 18 November 1941.

The part that the L.R.D.G. was to play in the Eighth Army's offensive which opened on 18 November was defined in Eighth Army Operation Instruction No. 18, dated 11 November 1941.

The Group's primary role from D-1 day until it was modified by further instructions, was the observation and reporting of enemy movement:-

(a) along tracks in the area Bir Hakim–El Adem–Mekili–Bir Tengeder (S)U.0530;

(b) along the Trigh el Abd from the track junction at (S)U.5965 – Bir Tengeder – Giof el Etel (SX.8525);

(c) the approaches to Jalo from the north.

Force 'E'.

The Group Commander was informed that a mixed force of all arms, including armoured cars, to be called Force 'E', and commanded by Brig. D.W. Reid, D.S.O., M.C. (Indian Army) would be operating from Jarabub towards Jalo. The Group would remain under command of the Eighth Army, but was to report to H.Q. Force 'E' any information that directly affected them; and without prejudice to its primary role the Group was to give Brig. Reid all possible assistance.

Another strong force of armoured cars would be operating at the same time from landing ground 125 (E5884) at long. 22°53'E. and lat. 30°23'N. The Group was to endeavour to maintain communication with this force, whose role could be more clearly defined when the best targets became evident.

S.A.S. party to be collected.

The Group was also ordered to detail a patrol of suitable size ('R' 1 was chosen) to collect a party of 55 men under Capt. D. Stirling of the Special Air Service Battalion (S.A.S.) from a certain rendezvous. The S.A.S. men

93

were then to be taken back to a second rendezvous, the position of which like that of the first was to be arranged with Capt. Stirling by Capt. Easonsmith, the Patrol Commander. If they did not appear at the first rendezvous between 0600 hrs and 0700 hrs, G.M.T on D3, the patrol would have no further responsibility for transporting them, but were to leave 12 gallons of water and two 4-gallon tins of dates at the rendezvous. This operation was the first in which the L.R.D.G. cooperated with the S.A.S.

Capt. Hunter with T.2 patrol in addition to other duties, which are referred to later, had the task of dropping Capt. Hasleden and a small party in the Mekili area and bringing them back to Siwa at the end of November.

Owing to unforeseen developments of the fighting, these orders were drastically altered by the Eighth Army in an instruction which reached the L.R.D.G. on 24 November, and is dealt with later.

Group Instructions.

In accordance with Eighth Army's orders, Lieut.Colonel Prendergast issued a verbal instruction for the action of his patrols as shown below:-

Patrol.	Date of start.	O.C.	Area of operations.
T.2	7 November	Capt. A.D. Hunter	Mekili (S)U.0486
Y.1	15 "	Capt. F. Simms	Garet Meriem (S)U.5860
Y.2	15 "	Capt. D. Lloyd Owen	Bir Tengeder (S)U.2334.
T.1	15 "	Major L.B. Ballantyne	South of Bir Hakim 365382[1]
G.1	15 November	Capt. A. Hay	Bir Ben Gania (S)Y6586
G.2	15 "	Lieut. J. Timpson	Maaten el Grara (S)X8525
R.2	16 "	2/Lieut L.H. Brown D.C.M.	Medwar Hassan (S)Z.8042
R.1	17 "	Capt. J. Easonsmith	Garet el Asida (S)U.3525

S.1 Patrol (Capt. C.A. Holliman) and S.2 Patrol (2/Lieut. J.R. Olivey) remained in reserve at Siwa. Special instructions to which reference has already been made were issued to Capt. Hunter (T.2) and Capt Easonsmith (R.1). All patrols were ordered to report any movement of the enemy seen on the tracks in their respective areas. In addition to giving the time, place and direction of movement they were to state whether convoys or individual vehicles were concerned, and their nationality, whether troops or supplies were being carried, and (including A.F.Vs and guns) what the type of vehicle was. All patrols but T.2 and R.1 were to be in position by the evening of 17 November.

An interesting point was an order that Arab headdress was not to be worn, and that clothing should be as much like that worn by the enemy as possible.

1 Reference to Egyptian "purple grid".

Twenty one days supplies of food and water were to be taken and each 30-cwt lorry was to carry 30 cases of petrol. Signal procedure was as usual given in detail in a separate instruction. On this occasion the call signs were in French. No messages were to be sent in clear and in English, except in the greatest emergency.

Information about the enemy was given by Capt. Kennedy-Shaw as Intelligence Officer. Colonel Prendergast's instruction gave the information about our own troops which was included in the Eighth Army Instruction already referred to. Except in the case of R.1 the action of each patrol will be described successively in the order given above, which corresponds more or less with the order of leaving Siwa.

Instructions to T.2.

The special instructions given to Capt. Hunter of T.2 Patrol were as follows: He was to take with him Capt. Hasleden, three other offices and two Arabs and to drop them at (S)O.5514 by 10 November, or as soon after as possible. He was then to remain in hiding until the evening of 17 November, when he was to begin observation of the road from Mekili to Bengasi. At about that time a code word would be sent him indicating that he was to start reporting his observations. The road was to be kept under observation until 29 November, on which date the patrol was to return to the point where Capt. Hasleden and those with him had been dropped, and they were then to be brought back to Siwa. If they were not at the rendezvous by 0600 hrs (G.M.T.) on 1 December the patrol was to return without them.

Capt. Hunter's Patrol started from Siwa at 1400 hrs on 7 November and included 2/Lieut. P.R. Freyberg and 17 O.Rs, besides the passengers. On the 9th it encamped 35 miles S.E. of Bir Tengeder. Next day the going at first was bad; and the Trigh-el-Abd which was crossed about 15 miles from the start, showed signs of fairly recent use. Air activity mostly by German machines flying from east to west, was considerable; but there was no sign that the patrol had been noticed, though some of the aircraft passed directly overhead at 3,000 feet. Owing to the difficulty of the country movement on a bearing was not possible but with the help of the local knowledge of Capt. Hasleden and an Arab, the patrol reached the Wadi el Heleighima which crosses the road to Bengazi about 25 miles west of Mekili, and found good cover a mile from the road. Capt. Hasleden and one Arab left that night; the remainder of his party stayed with the patrol which remained in hiding. On 13 November an Arab arrived with a note from Capt. Hasleden saying that the Trieste Division had left Slonta (about 50 miles E.N.E. of Barce, on the road from Bengazi to Derna) three weeks before, going east. As this was not known to the Eighth Army a week earlier and was of great importance, it was decided to break the wireless silence and send the information. The remainder of Hasleden's party left that night. Next day (14 November) the patrol left the Wadi and moved N.E. over rough and hilly country. About three hours after starting, they crossed the Mekili-Slonta road about 20 miles N.W. of Mekili. There were no signs of the enemy, though Arabs said that the road had recently been much used. They then lay up in a Wadi about 5 miles west of the road, and remained there during the 15th. Capt. Hunter reconnoitred on foot and found anti-tank mines piled along the road from Mekili to Chaulan (about 15 miles further north). They moved a little further east on the 16th, and on the 17th split up into three parties which went to positions of observation, all about 20 miles from Mekili. Capt. Hunter with headquarters and two trucks were two miles west of the Chaulan road; Corporal Porter with two trucks watched the road from Mekili to Giovanni Berta (about 45 miles north) from a point 8 miles east of the headquarters position; 2/Lieut. Freyberg with one truck watched the Mekili-Slonta tracks from a point 5 miles west of headquarters. Heavy rain fell all through the day and continued during part of the night of the 17/18, with the result that the roads were not under continuous observation till the 18th. On that day an old camp was located and some letters were picked up, the latest postmark (from N.E. Italy) being dated the middle of October. There was no movement by the enemy on the 18th, 19th or 20th though there was considerable air activity. Late on the 21st a 10-ton truck and four motor cyclists were seen to encamp near the road to Giovanni Berta; and moved on next morning.

Capt Hunter captured 22 November.

In the evening of 22 November the party on the Giovanni Berta road reported that Corporal Porter had not returned from observation duty, and on the 23rd Capt. Hunter who went on foot to look for him, with Corporal Kendall and Trooper McIver, was attacked by 20 Italians in two trucks, with a Breda gun. Capt. Hunter shouted to his Bofors truck to go back and give warning; and he and his two men were last seen firing at the enemy. The Bofors truck got away to the position occupied by 2/Lieut. Freyberg on the Slonta road, having collected the other H.Q. truck which had been with Capt. Hunter's party, on the way. 2/Lieut. Freyberg then decided that it would be better to leave the area, as the positions the patrol had occupied were linked by tracks and there was risk of being betrayed by natives; so on the night 23/24 November he moved into more open country, crossed the Mekili-Bengazi road east of Wadi-el-Heleighima, and camped 10 miles south of it. The patrol continued its southward move on the 24th and lay up near a salt-marsh. 2/Lieut. Freyberg then got in touch by W/T with Group H.Q. at Siwa. On hearing his report Group H.Q. ordered him to return to Siwa immediately; and at the same time arranged for 2/Lieut. Croucher to take three H.Q. trucks to the Mekili area and pick up Capt. Hasleden's party.

T.2 returns to Siwa.

T.2 patrol had not, of course, been informed of the change in the Eighth Army's plans which was made known on 24 November, as it had orders to wait for the return of Capt. Hasleden and his party on the 29th. At 1530 hrs on the 26th 2/Lieut. Freyberg arrived at Jarabub with T.2. patrol, and there met 2/Lieut. Croucher who had left Siwa that morning. Trooper White of T.2 was transferred to the outgoing party in order to guide it to the rendezvous with Capt. Hasleden: and T.2 patrol went on to Siwa, arriving there on 27 November.

Escape of Capt. Hunter 1 December 1941.

2/Lieut. Croucher's journey to the north was successful and without incident; but it was slow owing to bad going and mechanical trouble, and he did not arrive at the rendezvous near the Mekili-Bengasi road till 1 December. There, however, he found not only Capt. Hasleden and the whole of his party, but also Capt. Hunter of T.2 who had evaded capture. The return journey was more rapid, and the party reached Siwa early in the morning of 4 December, having done a good deal of night marching.

R.1's mission in co-operation with S.A.S.

As related earlier, R.1 patrol under Capt. Easonsmith was ordered to carry out a special mission connected with an operation by 55 Officers and O.Rs of 'L' detachment of the 1st S.A.S. Bde under Capt. D. Stirling, Scots Guards.

Orders to S.A.S.

Capt. Stirling had orders to raid both the aerodromes at Tmimi, and also those known as Gazela No. 1 and Gazela No. 2. The raid was to take place during the night D-1/D, at an hour decided by himself, with due regard to the fact that all the aerodromes named were to be bombed by the R.A.F. during the whole of the night D-2/D-1, at dusk on D-1, and after moonrise on the night D-1/D. He and his party were to be dropped by parachute in the Bir Temrad area (20 miles W.S.W. of Gazala) between 2030 hrs and 2130 hrs on D-2.

After completing its task his party was to go to a rendezvous selected in consultation with Capt. Easonsmith, commanding R.1 patrol of the L.R.D.G., where it would be picked up by lorries of the L.R.D.G. The party was to reach the rendezvous between 0600 hrs and 0700 hrs (G.M.T.) on D3; and it was added that for reasons of security the L.R.D.G. lorries would not wait after 0700 hrs on that day. There was to be a second rendezvous (also arranged between Capt. Stirling and Capt. Easonsmith) at the northern end of the Wadi-el-Mra, about (S)U.3418, and within walking distance of the first, at which two S.A.S. lorries would be left by the L.R.D.G. on their way north from Siwa. After picking up the S.A.S. party at the first rendezvous R.1 patrol's lorries would take it to the second; and from this point Capt. Stirling and his men were to go in their own transport to Jarabub, and report their arrival there to Battle H.Q. Eighth Army.

Instructions to R.1.

Instructions to the same effect were given to Capt. Easonsmith in which the first rendezvous is described as being at Garet Meriem (S)U.6148, a low hill at the point where the Trigh Capuzzo crosses the 23rd meridian E. After disposing of any parachutists he had collected he was to inform Group H.Q. by W/T and await instructions at the second rendezvous.

Capt. Easonsmith left Siwa on 17 November at 0530 hrs (G.M.T.) i.e. 0730 hrs Egyptian standard time, with six 30-cwt trucks of R.1 patrol. He took with him also two 15-cwt Bedfords left by the S.A.S. and a 3-ton Bedford truck belonging to the L.R.D.G., in case, as was more than likely, the S.A.S. transport was insufficient. This truck unfortunately blew a gasket during the first day's march and had to be left behind. They reached rendezvous No. 2 in the Wadi-el-Mra at 0800 hrs on 19 November, left the two S.A.S. trucks and pushed on N.N.E. to rendezvous No. 1. On their way they met Y.2 patrol who were operating in the Bir Tengeder area. In the evening they reached rendezvous No. 1 which was reported as being three miles S.E. of the Gadd-el-Ahmar cross roads on the Trigh-Capuzzo. The first party of the S.A.S. (Lieut. Lewis, Welsh Guards, and 9 O.Rs) came in soon after. At 0100 hrs on the 20th they were followed by Capt. Stirling and a sergeant. At dawn the patrol moved to cover leaving a smoking fire on a hill on which two hurricane lamps had been hung during darkness. This brought in Lieut. Mayne and 8 men. No other S.A.S. men appeared, nor had any been seen by Y.2 patrol which was again met; and in the late afternoon after waiting at rendezvous No. 1 eight hours longer than had been intended, Capt. Easonsmith withdrew to rendezvous No. 2 in the Wadi-el-Mra. During 21 November no more men came in though trucks were spread over an 8 mile front to look for them. At midday on the 22nd, a W/T signal was received with orders for Capt. Stirling's men to be handed over at Bir Tengeder to R.2 patrol which would take them to Siwa. On the way R.1 patrol was machine gunned by a Savoia 70 aircraft. No casualties were caused but apparently the Savoia went off for help as a Heinkel III appeared about 40 minutes later; but it failed to locate the patrol and bombed what were probably derelict trucks about three miles away. The patrol camped about three miles from Bir Tengeder on the 22nd but failed to get in touch with R.2; and movement on the 23rd was restricted owing to the presence of hostile aircraft. On 24 November orders were received to bring the S.A.S. party in. The return journey was made through rendezvous No. 2, were Lieut. Fraser was still encamped, but no more men of the S.A.S. had come in. Capt. Stirling's party was dropped at Jarabub at 1230 hrs on the 25th, and the patrol reached Siwa at 0700 hrs on the 26th.

The intended raids on the aerodromes were not carried out for the parachutists were dropped over a very wide area, and never got together. This was also no doubt the reason why only 21 of the 55 men who were to take part were picked up.

Course of the Eighth Army's offensive 18-24 November 1941.

Before relating the action of the other patrols it will be best to describe briefly the course of the battle in the coastal belt up to 24 November; and the circumstances which caused the tasks originally allotted by H.Q. Eighth Army to the L.R.D.G. to be drastically altered.

General Auchinleck's attack began on 18 November on a sixty-five mile front from Sollum to Jarabub. For the first two days all went well. Our armoured troops had reached the escarpment of Sidi Rezegh (32 miles S.E. of Tobruk) and captured the aerodrome there on the 19th. An armoured brigade had severely handled the Italian Ariete Division near Bir el Gubi, and the 29th Indian Inf. Bde. with South African troops, was pushing forward from Jarabub. But on 20 November the enemy struck back and recaptured Sidi Rezegh. After a series of long and confused tank actions without decisive result, the crisis of the battle was reached on the 24th. By this time the Tobruk garrison was forcing its way out, the New Zealand Division had turned the fortified line and wheeled to the north to take Gambut, the 4th Indian Division had captured some of the enemy's positions at Sidi Omar 20 miles S.W. of Sollum, and the 29th Indian Inf. Bde. had taken Jalo and Aujila. Rommel, however, then delivered an unexpected blow by sending a column of tanks and motorized infantry across the Egyptian frontier in the neighbourhood of Sidi Omar, which turned north and attacked our communications. They did a good deal of damage and then moved westwards again by Halfaya to join the remainder of the enemy's armoured forces east of Sidi Rezegh.

L.R.D.G.'s instructions changed 24 November 1941; and disposition of patrols.

The Eighth Army's instruction which changed the role of the L.R.D.G. was received at Siwa on 24 November and ordered the Group "to act with the utmost vigour offensively against any enemy targets or communications within reach"; adding that the most effective areas were Mekili,

Gadd-el-Ahmar[1] to El Adam, and the coastal road in the neighbourhood of Jedabia. When this order was received the patrols were disposed as follows:-[2]

T.2 north of Mekili, having lost its commander (Capt. Hunter) the day before.

Y.1 on its way north from Siwa with a new W/T truck.

Y.2 at Gadd el Ahmar.

T.1 returning to Siwa.

G.1 at Bir Ben Gania.

G.2, half en route to Maaten el Grara, the other half en route to Jalo with an urgent message from the R.A.F. to Brig. Reid.

R.2 at Bir Tengeder.

S.2 at Medwar Hassan.

R.1 returning to Jarabub with Capt. Stirling.

In his instruction No. 22 sent by W/T and dated 24 November, Lieut.Colonel Prendergast informed his patrols that their object was now to attack transport and any other target within reach. He allotted areas with the object if possible of bringing "half patrols" together, as shown below:-

Y.1 and Y.2 – (S)U.6065 – Gazala-Derna-Mekili.

G.1 and G.2 – Road Bengasi-Jedabia.

S.2 and R.2 – Road Marsus-Barce-Bengasi.

As already stated, T.2 and R.1 were otherwise engaged. S.1 was still in reserve at Siwa, and T.1 returned there on the day that the new orders were issued.

Y.1 to Garet Meriem.

Y.1 patrol (Capt. F.C. Simms) which was to be responsible for observing the Garet Meriem area (some 35 miles S.W. of Gazala, and 60 to 70 miles west by south from Tobruk) made an unfortunate start. At about 1100 hrs on the 17th, when they were near the "Segnali" cross roads at (S)U.6253 on the Trigh-el-Abd, they were machine gunned by three R.A.F. aircraft who took no notice of the T panel put out to indicate their nationality; and the wireless truck was burnt out. Luckily the patrol got in contact later in the day with Y.2 patrol, who took over its duties on the 19th and enabled it to return to Siwa for another W/T truck. On 23 November it left Siwa for the second time and reached Bir Habesh 25 miles south of Garet Meriem, at 1800 hrs on the 24th. There the patrol remained till the following day in order to get into wireless touch with Group Headquarters.

---

1   30 miles W.S.W. of Gazala on Sheet Bengasi-Aujila 1:1,000,000, but not shown on gridded map.

2   The action of several of these patrols previous to 24 November has yet to be described.

Y.1 and Y.2 join 26 November.

On the 25th they were told of the change of plan and moved off at 0630 hrs on the 26th. They joined Y.2 that day in a reconnaissance for suitable sites for an ambush along 25 miles of the Trigh Enver Bey (otherwise known as Trigh Capuzzo) and two were selected. At 0600 hrs on the 27th the whole of Y Patrol left for one of these sites but found no traffic. On the 28th Y.2 went to reconnoitre roads in the Gadd-el-Ahmar – Tmimi – Gazala area but got stuck in the mud S.W. of Tmimi and returned next day. In the afternoon of the 28th Y.1 went towards Afrag at (S)U.5393 on the road from Gazala to Mekili and 30 miles east of the latter place, with the intention of attacking convoys between Mekili and Derna, but without result. Independent patrolling carried out on 29 and 30 November and on 1 December, led to the discovery by Y.1 of a large camp at a road junction on the Derna-Mekili road about 20 miles S.W. of Derne.

Y.1's attack on M.T. park.

At about 1900 hrs on 2 December, when in the neighbourhood of Abier-el-Aleima (about 10 miles east of Afrag along the road to Gazela) the patrol found itself in the middle of a M.T. park of about 30 vehicles. They were able to damage fifteen of them before withdrawing; but it was found that the navigator, Lance Corporal Carr, was missing and though the patrol waited at the first rendezvous he did not appear. He eventually escaped however, as will be described later.

The patrol returned to Siwa by Gadd el Ahmar (Segnali cross roads) and arrived there on 6 December, less two trucks which had gone to Hatiet el Etla to help R. Patrol, and reached Siwa on the 7th.

Y.2 patrol under Capt. D. Lloyd-Owen left Siwa at 0810 hrs on 15 November. On their way to Bir Tengeder on the 17th they met Y.1 patrol which, as already described, had lost its W/T truck. On the 18th Y.2 patrol watched the Trigh el Abd and, late on the same day, received orders to take over Y.1's duties about Gadd el Ahmar. The patrol reached this area at 1030 hrs on 19 November and remained there for five days without seeing any movement except by hostile aircraft which were mostly German. On 26 November Y.1 patrol joined them, bringing the revised orders for attacking convoys; the reconnaissance was continued and some stores in a small Italian bivouac were destroyed. The night 28/29 was spent with Y.1 patrol at Afrag. On the 29th both patrols moved at 0700 hrs towards Grara es Saadi, about 28 miles to the N.W. and on the road from Mekili to Derna.

Y.2 patrol captures prisoners.

About 0715 hrs Y.2 patrol operating independently captured a Ford lorry with three Italians and two Libyans. One prisoner stated that he was on his way to Derna to collect rations for men in a fort whose position he indicated, and was afterwards found to be in long. 22°40'E. lat. 32°16'30"N. about seven miles east of the Shrine of El Ezzeiat. Capt. Lloyd-Owen decided to investigate, and took his lorries to within 600 yards of the fort. He then deployed, and again advanced. When the trucks were about 200 yards from the fort the enemy opened fire with M.G's and rifles. Capt. Lloyd-Owen then gave orders for an attack on foot, leaving his machine gunners in the trucks to give covering fire. The attacking party moved forward into the cover afforded by the outer defences which were not manned, and sent a prisoner to offer terms to the garrison which were refused.

Y.2 captures fort near El Ezzeiat.

After a short discussion it was decided to continue the attack. "This was too much for the enemy who then surrendered at 0830 hrs." Ten Italians and two Libyans were captured, and two of the enemy were killed. The wireless section in the fort and three M.G's, together with ammunition and stores were destroyed, and documents were collected. The patrol left the fort at 0915 hrs and lay up for the day, as it had been discovered that before surrendering the Italians had communicated by W/T with Mekili. From the prisoners it was learnt that there were two Italian Divisions in Derna and three or four hundred men at Mekili. They also knew that we had recently dropped parachutists. They complained of the want of warm clothing and said that their food was not good. At nightfall, having disposed of its prisoners, the patrol received fresh orders, and moved to a position eight miles south of Tmimi aerodrome in order to attack convoys on the Tobruk-Derna road.

The patrol moved off at 0615 hrs on 30 November and at sunrise they found themselves nearer the aerodrome than they had intended to be. There was much activity, and there were many aircraft on the ground. It was decided to move N.W. to the Wadi Maalegh (S)P.7616, near Bomba, where the trucks were concealed, and a reconnaissance was then made on foot. There was a great deal of air activity from Tmimi and Martuba, but little movement on the roads. At 2000 hrs Capt. Lloyd-Owen took the trucks towards the Derna-Tobruk road, and left them about three miles away from it. He and his party then walked to the road and arrived there at about 2100 hrs.

Attack on traffic near Wadi Maalegh.

At midnight, after watching the passage of a little traffic both eastward and westward, the patrol fired at a large petrol tanker at about 5 yards range, but although undoubtedly hit it went on. Three quarters of an hour later a 10-ton lorry was fired at and its tyres and petrol tank were punctured. It stopped and two hand grenades were thrown into the back. Two officers jumped out from the front and were shot, as was a man who got out behind. The truck was damaged by more grenades and nine of the enemy were left dead. The telephone wires along the road were cut and the party then returned to the trucks. During the withdrawal the trucks were pursued by the enemy and one which had trouble had to be abandoned. The patrol lay up during 1 December, moved at night to Hatiet el Etla and returned to Siwa on 3 December.

Escape of Lance Corporal Carr 3 December 1941.

Lance Corporal S.M. Carr who was left behind by Y.1 patrol on 2 December decided to make for the coast road near Grar el Ambar, a nullah about six miles N.W. of Gazala, which was the proposed scene of the next raid. At dawn on 3 December he found a Senussi camp where he was sheltered and fed for a fortnight, while the battle went on all round him. By 17 December our troops were advancing and he and a wounded R.A.F. officer to whom the Senussi had also given shelter, were picked up by the 31st Field Regiment R.A. and taken to H.Q. 4th Indian Division near Derna. They were then sent back by road and air to Mersa Matruh, and Lance Corporal Carr reached Siwa on 23 December.

G.1 to Bir-ben-Gania 15 November 1941.

G.1 patrol under Capt. A.M. Hay left Siwa at 0700 hrs on 15 November with orders to patrol the area about Bir-ben-Gania (SY.6586) on the Trigh el Abd, and some 240 miles W.N.W. of Siwa. It lay up in that neighbourhood, without seeing any transport until the 24th, when it received orders to join G.2 patrol at (S)X8525 (Maaten el Grara, 45 miles east of Jedabia), and carry out an attack on the Bengasi-Jedabia road. It left Bir-ben-Gania at 1500 hrs on the 24th, but the patrol commander read the map reference wrong and headed for Beda Fomm (approximately (S)X2585). On the 25th the patrol found itself obstructed by the mud pan known as Balat Abd el Hafid, and had to go nearly as far north as Msus to get round it. The area was boggy, and progress was slow and made slower by air attack, though there were no casualties. The patrol eventually reached Beda Fomm at nightfall. Capt. Hay then communicated with Group H.Q. and the patrol lay up in a Wadi at (S)X5183 about 20 miles east of Beda Fomm, until 28 November when they were ordered to attack the road without waiting for G.2 patrol which, owing to breakdowns, was in fact immobilized near Jalo.

G.1 patrol then moved to a small hill overlooking the road at Point (S)X0591 about 60 miles north of Jedabia, and saw a convoy of tankers going south with intervals of as much as two or three miles between vehicles, and occasional trucks going north. The patrol commander having reconnoitred to find a better target, located a M.T. park of 30 vehicles off the road about 4 miles to the south, and near a rectangular white building at which motor vehicles stopped for a short time as they passed.

Attacks on enemy M.T.

After sunset the patrol moved off with its vehicles in single file towards the white house and passed 8 Italian vehicles, one of which carried a 20 mm A.A. gun manned by Germans. On reaching the building the patrol turned off the road. The patrol commander's truck was leading, and 12 grenades were thrown from it at the vehicles in the M.T. park. The other trucks of the patrol then drove past and the machine gunners fired 300 rounds. Owing to the light it was impossible to assess the damage, but the enemy did not return the fire.

The patrol then returned to the Wadi and received orders to carry out another raid next day. On the 29th it left the Wadi at 1530 hrs, as there had been a good deal of air reconnaissance earlier in the day. Owing to the failure of the tyres the patrol commander's 8-cwt truck had to be left behind. The road was approached at Point (S)X0877 a few miles further south, and as on the previous day the flat country made concealment difficult; but a small hill was found about 200 yards from the road, and the Lewis guns were taken off the trucks and put on it. A large tanker which was one of a convoy again going south, was fired at and left the road. The crew of two men who jumped out were both killed, and 250 rounds were fired into the vehicle. The remaining lorries on the road reversed and went in the opposite direction.

Orders were received that night to go to Bir Maaten el Grara, and on 1 December the patrol was ordered back to Siwa where it arrived at midday on the 3rd.

G.2 to Maaten el Grara 15 November 1941.

G.2 patrol under Lieut. J.A.L. Timpson left Siwa on 15 November. It consisted of 1 officer and 13 O.Rs with four 30-cwt trucks, and its orders were to patrol the area about Maaten el Grara, (S)X8525, 45 miles east of Jedabia. Nothing of importance was seen until 22 November when at 1420 hrs (local time) an Italian aircraft (Fiat B.R.20) landed near the well at El Grara with engine trouble.

Attack on Italian plane.

It was attacked, the pilot officer and pilot sergeant were killed and the remainder of the crew, three in number, were made prisoners. All papers were removed and the plane was set on fire. Soon afterwards another aircraft appeared and circled the burning Fiat for ten minutes, but the patrol was not observed and moved off to landing ground 125 (long. 22°53'E. lat. 30°23'N.) where they arrived next day and disposed of their prisoners.

104

Message to 'E' Force near Jalo.

Late that afternoon the Wing Commander asked Lieut. Timpson to take an important message to the Commander of 'E' Force (Brig. Reid) who was presumed to be somewhere just north of Jalo. Lieut. Timpson was unable to get through by W/T to Siwa, and eventually decided at about 0800 hrs on 24 November to send two of his trucks back to Maaten el Grara, and to take the other two to Jalo with the message. As one of these, however, would not start he went off in the other, and camped that night at Jikherra, 20 miles north of Jalo. His remaining truck also broke down next morning (25th), and he had to deliver the message on foot. The remainder of his patrol reached Maaten el Grara on the same day. He himself spent 26 November trying to repair his truck, but as it again broke down, he was forced to go back to Jalo on the 27th, and send a message to Siwa to say that he was immobilised. This message did not reach Group H.Q. till 1 December.

On 28 November the rest of the patrol at El Grara were ordered to search for their commander, and reached Jalo on 1 December. On 2 December Lieut.Colonel Prendergast arrived by air with the necessary spare parts, but repairs were not finished until the next day. The patrol started on its return journey on the 4th and arrived at Siwa on the 6th.

R.2 patrol to Bir Tengeder 16 November 1941.

R.2 patrol commanded by 2/Lieut. L.H. Browne, D.C.M., left Siwa on 16 November, its strength being 1 officer and 10 O.Rs, with four 30-cwt lorries. The patrol moved north, and at 0800 hrs on 19 November arrived at the Wadi Mra in the vicinity of Medwar Hassan. There they received a message ordering them to relieve Y.1 patrol whose W/T truck, as already related, had been destroyed by the R.A.F. They failed to find Y.1 on the 19th at the rendezvous they had been given, but on the 20th got a message from Group H.Q. stating that Y.1 had been relieved by another patrol, and ordering them to observe movement on the Trigh el Abd in the neighbourhood of Bir Tengeder. At midday on the 20th they took up a position about two miles east of that place. R.1 patrol passed them on the 22nd without making contact, but they saw no other movement on the ground during the 20th, 21st, 22nd, 23rd and 24th. There were however many hostile aircraft, some of which were flying low and obviously looking for our vehicles. At 1000 hrs on the 24th R.1 patrol arrived carrying Capt. Stirling and his parachutists and a message from Siwa ordered R.1 to return there and R.2 to remain in the Bir Tengeder area.

Joint reconnaissance with S.2 to Mekili-Bengasi road 26 November.

At 0900 hrs on 25 November S.2 patrol arrived from Siwa under 2/Lieut.

Olivey with 11 O.Rs and three 30-cwt trucks. He carried verbal orders from the Group Commander for a joint reconnaissance by S.2 and R.2, of movement on the Mekili-Bengasi road, 2/Lieut. Olivey being in command.

The combined patrol moved off at 0700 hrs on 26 November leaving S.2's W/T truck behind. They marched N.N.W. and arrived on the Mekili-Bengasi road at 1600 hrs, averaging only four miles an hour for three hours across the "Stone belt" on the plateau known as Dahar el Hallab. They encamped just south of the road and about four miles east of the Wadi el Helegheima.

The change of orders for L.R.D.G. 27 November.

It was not until 27 November at 0900 hrs that they heard from Group H.Q. that the role of the L.R.D.G. had been changed, and that their orders were to take aggressive action on the road and railway between Barce and Bengasi. On the night of 28/29th the two patrols encamped in a deep gully in the foothills of the Jebel el Akhdar, about 8 miles S.W. of Maraua, where much interest was taken in them by the local shepherds.

Attack on enemy M.T.

On 29 November they moved eastwards along the road removing lengths of overhead wire; and at about 2000 hrs the moon being nearly full, they took up a position near a cutting at Kilometre post 44, the trucks being halted 30 yards apart with their bonnets away from the road. Here they engaged a west bound lorry carrying troops. After about a minute's heavy firing several of the enemy were killed or wounded, and the remainder scattered. Shortly afterwards another lorry coming from the west was engaged and put out of action. Both patrols then moved west along the road and accounted for four more lorries; but a motor cyclist who was among them escaped towards Maraua. They then took up another position near Kilometre post 35, the trucks being formed up 50 yards apart and south of the road. There they destroyed two heavy lorries with trailers and an oil tanker; and all the occupants but one who was wounded, were killed.

At 2145 hrs the patrols left the road, moved S.S.W. and at 0300 hrs on 30 November lay up in a Wadi about 30 miles east of El Abiar (SS.4484), on the road from Barce to Bengasi. The tracks leading into the Wadi and the vehicles themselves were carefully camouflaged, and the patrol rested during daylight on the 30th. Plans were made for a night attack on traffic on the road between Barce and El Abiar, and for derailing a train seven miles north of Sidi Mahius (S)S5892. At 1200 hrs on 1 December, however, orders came from Group H.Q. ordering S.2 to Jalo, and R.2 to Hatiet el Etla. The patrols moved together at 1300 hrs on 1 December and arrived at Bir Tengeder at 1300 hrs on the 2nd. S.2 picked up the W/T truck left there on 26 November and moved on towards Jalo. R.2 set course S.E. and arrived at Hatiet el Etla (long. 23°47'E. lat. 30°40'N.) where a supply dump had been formed, at 1330 hrs on 3 December. Here they found Y.2 patrol and the Heavy Section ('B' Echelon) under Lieut. Arnold. They were given orders to remain at El Etla until the arrival of R.1 patrol about 6 December, and to send any casualties to Siwa in the Heavy Section. The only casualty was the W/T operator who had fever. On 7 December they were given orders to return to Siwa and arrived there on the 8th.

Section XIV

Second Phase of Eighth Army offensive 9 December 1941.

The operations described in the last section brought to an end the first phase of the L.R.D.G's operations in cooperation with the Eighth Army. The second phase began on 9 December 1941, and on that date the patrols were distributed as follows:-

Distribution of Patrols.

H.Q. 'A' Squadron (Major Steele) was at Jalo with S.1 (Capt. Holliman), S.2 (2/Lieut. Olivey, T.2 (2/Lieut. C. Morris) and the R.A. Section now armed with a 25 pr., under 2/Lieut. P. Eitzen. They had left Siwa on 1 and 2 December and were under the orders of Brig. Reid, commanding 'E' Force, with which they remained until 22 December.

The following patrols were at Siwa: G.1 (Capt. Hay), G.2 (Lieut. Timpson), R.1 (Capt. Easonsmith), R.2 (2/Lieut. Croucher), Y.1 (Capt. Simms) and Y.2. (Capt. Lloyd-Owen). T.1 under Major Ballantyne had left Siwa on 2 December and was at Point 425361 (ref: "Egyptian purple grid" 1:500,000) with "Marriott Force", a detachment under the command of Brig. Marriott (22nd Guards Brigade). This patrol's task was to guide "Marriott Force" to the Bengasi-Jedabia road. The force did not move westwards until 20 December and by that time had been joined by R.1 and R.2 patrols.

Role of L.R.D.G. Patrol areas.

Apart from special tasks the role assigned to the L.R.D.G. by H.Q. Eighth Army was to harass the enemy's transport, and the remaining four patrols (G.1, G.2, Y.1 and Y.2) were sent out to do so.

Lieut.Colonel Prendergast's Operation Instruction No. 23 given verbally on 9 December 1941, ordered the patrols that were still under his command to move as soon as possible to the areas in which they were to attack enemy traffic. These were allotted as follows:-

108

G.1 patrol   Bengasi-Jedabia road
G.2 patrol   Barce-Bengasi road
Y.1 patrol   Bengasi area.
Y.2 patrol   Tobruk-Derna road
R.1 patrol   Mekili area.

R.2 patrol which was eventually to join "Marriott Force", was ordered to Hatiet el Etla there to await further instructions. R.1 patrol which was also to join "Marriott Force" would receive orders to do so later.

G.1 and Y.2.

G.1 patrol under Capt. Hay left Siwa in accordance with the orders described above, and in the morning of 14 December met Y.2 patrol near Abiar el Charaz (SX4980) (6 miles north of Antelat and 30 miles N.E. of Jedabia). Plans were made for co-ordinated attacks at different points in the evening of the 15th. The patrol after again meeting Y.2 at Cardasi el Oti about 20 miles north of Antelat, marched some 25 miles north west to a point on the Jedabia-Bengasi road five miles south of Magrun (S)S.0202. After waiting an hour they destroyed a staff car and a lorry that was towing it. The patrol then left the road moved about 75 miles S.E. travelling all night.

Capt. Hay captured.

At sunrise next morning it ran into the enemy; and Capt. Hay was captured. Only two trucks under Sergeant Roebuck got away, and reached Siwa on 18 December.

G.2 to Barce-Bengasi road 11 December 1941.

G.2 patrol under Lieut. Timpson, consisting of 1 officer and 16 O.Rs in five 30-cwt trucks, left Siwa at 0800 hrs on 11 December for the Barce-Bengasi road. On the 14th they reached cultivated land with many inhabitants about four miles south of Gerdes el Abid (SS.8298), a village 16 miles south of Barce and about 11 miles east of the Barce-Bengasi road and railway. The natives were very friendly and told the patrol that there was an Italian post at Gerdes el Abid, and also at El Abiar 20 miles to the south west. On the 15th the road was observed from a point about a mile and a half S.E. of Sidi Mahius (15 miles N.E. of El Abiar) which the natives had said was not occupied by troops. It had rained during the night and the cultivated country confined the patrol to tracks. There was no traffic either on the road, or the railway, which appeared to be almost unused.

On the 16th one of the men, Guardsman Wann, developed appendicitis and the patrol commander's intention was to leave him behind with one truck and go on to the road from Bengasi to Tocra, a place on the coast about 20 miles west of Barce. Group H.Q. however refused to allow the patrol to be divided, and on the 17th Wann was in such great pain that the patrol commander decided that he must be evacuated. On the 19th the patrol lay up for the day near Msus in the hope of being able to raid the aerodromes there during darkness, but the enemy's vehicles were too numerous, and the patrol had to extinguish its lights while passing through them. The sick guardsman was taken to Siwa from Landing Ground 125 by air, and the patrol arrived there on 21 December.

Y.1 to Bengasi 13 December 1941.

Y.1 patrol left Siwa on 13 December for the Bengasi area, picked up Capt. Hunter at Jarabub, and at 0700 hrs on the 17th reached the escarpment east of Soluk which is 35 miles S.S.E. of Bengasi, and is the terminus of the railway from Barce. After watching the road for some hours and seeing very little traffic, the patrol drove into Soluk and opened fire on some soldiers in the village street and in a camp near by. Fire was returned, and the patrol withdrew N.E. across country for about 16 miles and halted for the night. Further operations had to be abandoned, as in the evening of the 18th orders were received to return to Siwa. On the way home the patrol was fired at by British A.F.Vs but without damage; and it reached Siwa on 23 December having been forced to abandon one vehicle.

Y.2 to Antelat area.

Y.2 patrol which had orders to attack the enemy's transport on the road from Derna to Tobruk and on desert tracks east of the line Derna-Mekili, left Siwa on 11 December. It consisted of one officer (Capt. Lloyd-Owen) with 13 O.Rs and four 30-cwt trucks. By this time however the Eighth Army had reached a line west of Gazala, which is some 40 miles west of Tobruk along the road to Derna; and on 13 December when the patrol was at a point near Medwar Hassan its orders were cancelled, and it was told to go at once to the Bengasi-Jedabia road.

Joins G.1.

On 14 December it met G.1 patrol near Abiar el Charaz (6 miles north of Antelet) and, as already related, plans were made for attacks on different points of the road that night or the next. At 1700 hrs that afternoon Y.2 patrol arrived within half a mile of the road, after passing several Bedouin camps whose occupants professed their hatred of the Italians. There was a considerable amount of widely dispersed traffic, mostly moving south. Many vehicles were "packed with troops", and guarded by A.F.Vs. At 1900 hrs the patrol could see firing to the south which was presumed to be due to the action of G.1 patrol. The enemy traffic halted, and lights were extinguished before moving on.

Attacks on M.T.

At 1920 hrs the patrol fired on a 10-ton lorry moving southward and towing a large tanker, set both vehicles on fire and shot the occupants. The patrol then drove along the convoy and attacked other vehicles whose occupants had taken to their heels. There were two more 10-ton lorries each towing two large tankers, and all four vehicles were set on fire. The patrol then cut the telegraph wires and cables and withdrew about 40 miles E.S.E. Fires and explosions could still be seen two hours after leaving the scene of the attack. The patrol lay up during the morning of 15 December, and at 1530 hrs moved towards the point on the road selected for the next attack. At Cardasi-el-Oti they again met G.1 patrol. As already related Capt. Hay said there had been patrol activity in front of his position; and vehicles visible to both patrol commanders were moving about between them and the road. Capt. Lloyd-Owen decided to move at dusk (1700 hrs). He took his trucks towards the road, and when about a mile from it came across a burnt out petrol dump which was thought to be on the landing ground at long. 20°10'E. lat. 31°30'N. Firing was again seen to the south and the enemy's traffic on the road halted. Capt. Lloyd-Owen decided that it was better not to attack, and marched all night to the neighbourhood of Balat Abd-el-Hafid, a swamp lying to the south of Msus. The patrol remained here during the 16th and 17th, and on the 18th received orders to return to Siwa. They arrived there on the 21st having destroyed a Caproni aircraft that had been shot down near the Trigh-el-Abd.

T.1 with "Marriott Force" December 1941.

T.1 patrol under Major Ballantyne left Siwa to join Brig. Marriott's Force on 2 December. It reached the rendezvous area (Pt. 465335 Egyptian "purple grid" 1:250,000)[1] on 4 December but there were no signs of the 22nd Guards Bde which formed the principal part of the Force.

It was in fact involved in the fighting at Tobruk, and did not arrive until a fortnight later. Major Ballantyne was informed however by a signal unit that Headquarters "Marriott Force" was at 431338,[2] about 60 miles W.N.W. of Fort Maddalena.

Advanced H.Q. was found to be on the point of moving to Bir el Gubi, some 25 miles N.N.W., but the patrol remained at rear H.Q. and except for occasional attacks from the air, nothing important occurred. Rear H.Q. went slowly forward navigated by the patrol. On 8 December it reached Pt. 425361;[3] and on the 11th it moved 35 miles to the N.W. and leaguered at Bir Lefa on the Trigh Capuzzo, about 8 miles west of El Adem.

1   Reference to Sheet Salum-Tobruk 1:250,000 G.S.G.S. No. 4386 1943.
2   See Note 1 above.
3   See Note 1 above.

Relief of Tobruk 8 December and retirement of Rommel.

During the ten days that followed T.1 patrol's departure from Siwa on 2 December, the Eighth Army had gradually advanced. Tobruk was relieved on 8 December, and Rommel fell back on to the line Bir Hakim–Gazala which he held for three days. He then retired again, and by 13 December had collected his remaining tanks and German lorry borne infantry about 30 miles further west, in the area Gadd el Ahmar at the west end of the Trigh Capuzzo.

On 12 and 13 December the patrol was bombed and 2/Lieut. Freyberg was wounded in the back. On the 13th acting on a message from H.Q., L.R.D.G. Major Ballantyne asked Brig. Marriott to be allowed to with-draw his patrol until "Marriott Force" was concentrated. The Brig. agreed but said that it would be necessary to ask H.Q. Eighth Army for permission, and H.Q. L.R.D.G. were informed of this.

On 14 December "Marriott Force" was ordered to concentrate further to the east in the area of Square 3739[1] just north of Bir Hakin, and Force H.Q. moved back accordingly.

Major Ballantyne was called to Eighth Army H.Q. and remained there during the 15th. On the 16th he returned to the assembly area and found that Capt. Easonsmith and 2/Lieut. Croucher had arrived with R.1 and R.2 patrols. On the 18th the advance westward was discussed with Brig. Marriott, and it was decided to go south until clear of the rough country round the Wadi el Mra, and thence direct to Antelat. On the 19th the Brig., Major Ballantyne and Capt. Easonsmith met the G.O.C., Eighth Army (Lieut.General Ritchie) at El Adem. Marriott Force was ordered to move direct on Antelat. The axis of advance was to be as follows:-

Axis of Advance "Marriott Force" 20 December 1941.

From the assembly area on a bearing of 255° to a point south of Hallebet-el-Ezba [(S) U.1519], thence 270° to south of Roubet-el-Ageremia [(S) T.6014]. At this point a column was to be detached to go by Msus to Esh-Sheledeima 28 miles further west on the road to Soluk. The main body was to continue its march on a bearing of 250° to Antelet. This route was clear of any obstacle except the Wadi El-Mra which would have to be crossed.

R.1 and R.2 as flank guard.

The 11th Hussars were to go ahead and cover the advance; and R.1 and R.2 patrols acting as a flank guard, were to move parallel to the column and some 50 miles to the north, through the areas Abiar Omeil [(S) G.2254] –

---

1 Reference to Sheet Salum-Tobruk 1:250,000 G.S.G.S. No. 4386 1943.

Bir El Gerrari [(S) T.5142] – Wadi El-Gabr [(S) G.8353]; and to report any movement by W/T to Major Ballantyne. The 11th Hussars moved at dawn on 20 December; R.1 and R.2 patrols at 0730 hrs; the advance guard (Scots Guards and some artillery) at 0800 hrs, and the main body at 1100 hrs. The navigation party provided by T.1 patrol was divided into two parties; one of two trucks under Corporal Tinker with the advance guard, the other with Force H.Q. at the head of the main body. There was no difficulty in crossing the Wadi el Mra, and no interference by the enemy throughout the march during which the force maintained an average pace of ten miles an hour. The Scots Guards column which had acted as advance guard, moved away towards Msus on 21 December; and a battalion of the Cold-stream Guards took its place. The main body of the force halted for the night 21/22 December about 16 miles short of Antelat. Early on the 22nd the 11th Hussars came in contact with the enemy west of Antelat, and later in the morning they took Saunna 15 miles S.E. of it. R.1 and R.2 patrols on the right flank reported no sign of the enemy but that they were in contact with British troops; and Major Ballantyne visited H.Q. Support Group, 7th Armoured Division at (S)X.6395. On the same day the patrols received orders to return to Siwa and left at 1130 hrs on the 23rd. T.1 patrol arrived at Siwa on Christmas Day, R.1 on 26 December and R.2 on the 24th.

R.1's operations before joining "Marriott Force".

R.1 patrol had left Siwa on 10 December, and before joining "Marriott Force" had operated for about four days west of Gadd-el-Ahmar. On arrival in that area on the 12th they realized that fighting was in progress not far away, and their commander (Capt. Easonsmith) considered, to use his own words, that "the area was too populated with soldiers to be ideal for convoy attacks". He therefore moved further west, but before doing so decided to have a "hit and run" attack on the troops closest to him. Just before dark he managed to get within 300 yards of the enemy who apparently mistook the patrol for some of their own troops. Each truck fired from 50 and 100 rounds before the enemy took any action, and two small explosions were observed. By this time the light had failed and they made off to the south without any casualties.

On the 14th and 15th they reconnoitred N.W. and north in heavy rain and bad going, and on 16 December reached their rendezvous with Marriott Force. In the evening of 20 December R.1 and R.2 reached the eastern end of the area along which they were to patrol so as to cover the right flank of the march of "Marriott Force" and got in contact with the 12th Lancers "without damage to either party"!

On the 21st they moved west with R.2 patrol to an agreed point at Gur-el-Agaba, about 25 miles north of Msus, from which R.1 was to operate forward to the west, and R.2 back towards the east. Except for meeting units of the Eighth Army and "arranging not be shot", R.1's flank guard operations were without incident. They reached Garat el Bezem (ref. Bengazi 1:500,000 (S/S2849)) about 35 miles S.E. of Bengazi, on 22 December, and there received the order to return to Siwa.

R.2 patrol, now commanded by 2/Lieut. C.H. Croucher, left Siwa on 13 December with orders to report to "Marriott Force". After separating from R.1 at Gur el Agaba, it patrolled the area eastwards to Bir el Gerrari. The only troops met were our own, and on 22 December the patrol was ordered back to Siwa.

Rommel retires to Jedabia 16 December.

Rommel, who had counter-attacked the 4th Indian Division from 13 to 15 December without success, was finally forced to retire, leaving much material behind him. On the 18th our troops entered Derna, and on the 19th patrols entered Apollonia and Cyrene. El Abiar was taken on Christmas Eve, Bengazi was occupied next day and Rommel retired to Jedabia, where for a time he held his ground.

'A' Squadron's operations first three weeks of December 1941.

As stated earlier 'A' Squadron H.Q. with S.1 and S.2 and T.2 patrols and the R.A. section had left Siwa on 1–2 December to join Brig. Reid, commanding 'E' Force, and when L.R.D.G. Operation Instruction No. 23 was issued on 9 December[1] they were under that officer's command at Jalo. Their activities during the first three weeks of December have now to be described.

S.1 and S.A.S. to Sirte 8 December 1941.

On 8 December S.1 patrol, under Capt. Holliman, left Jalo with a party of the 1st S.A.S. (parachute) Brigade to carry out a raid on the landing grounds at Sirte, and at the mouth of the Wadi Tamet, about 28 miles further west. They had also the subsidiary tasks of mining the road west of Sirte, and attacking traffic on the road. The party consisted of Capt. Holliman and nineteen O.Rs of S.1 patrol, with Capt. D. Stirling, Lieut. R.B. Mayne and eleven O.Rs of the 1st S.A.S. Bde.

Passing between Marada and El Agheila they reached a point about 40 miles south of Sirte on the morning of the 10th. Owing perhaps to the interception of a W/T message, the patrol was discovered on the morning of the 11th by a Ghibli aircraft near the Zella-Sirte road. The aircraft attacked but was driven off without loss. The party had to take cover, but two Ghibli planes which arrived later failed to discover it, though they bombed and machine gunned ground not far away. As time had been lost it

1. See p. 108 above.

was decided to drop the S.A.S. men three miles from Sirte aerodrome the same night; but a detour made on information given by a friendly Bedouin, in order to avoid a small Italian post, and difficulty in crossing unexpected sand dunes caused so much delay that the raid had to be postponed. Capt. Stirling and Sergeant Brough were dropped to do a reconnaissance on foot, and the remainder of the party lay up in the Wadi Tamet a few miles further west. It was arranged that Capt. Stirling was to be picked up 5 miles from Sirte in the evening of the 14th, when the raid would be carried out. On the 13th the trucks moved north down the Wadi to a point about 15 miles from the coast and again lay up. During the 14th a reconnaissance was made further down the Wadi in an 8-cwt Ford to within four miles of the coast road. From this point several aircraft were seen on the ground at the north end of the Wadi. The party was then split up. Two trucks under Lieut. Mayne went to attack the landing ground at the end of the Wadi. The remainder were to go to the coast road and drive down it to the point where Capt. Stirling should be waiting. All went well. Capt. Stirling was picked up about 4½ miles from Sirte having discovered that there were no aircraft on the landing ground. The main road was mined, and an ammunition truck was seen to blow up on it a few minutes later. Twenty four aircraft, a petrol dump and a bomb were destroyed by Lieut. Mayne's party on the Tamet landing ground, and a house containing about 40 of the enemy was "soundly shot up". The two parties got away separately, and met 80 miles south of Sirte at 0700 hrs on the 15th. One 30-cwt lorry whose steering gear had broken, had to be destroyed near the coast road. The return journey to Jalo, reached on the 16th, was uneventful. This was a highly successful operation.

T.2 and S.A.S. to Tripoli coast 10 December 1941.

On 10 December T.2 patrol under 2/Lieut. C.S. Morris left Siwa on a similar mission with 13 of his own men and 12 of the 1st S.A.S. Brigade. Five patrol trucks and one Lancia which carried the S.A.S. men were used. The patrol was given the following tasks:-

(a) To take the S.A.S. men to El Agheila where they were to raid the landing ground.

(b) To attack Mersa Brega which lies on the coast 25 miles N.E. of El Agheila.

(c) To attack traffic on the coastal road as far west as (exclusive) Nofilia (100 miles N.W. of El Agheila).

(d) To capture a prisoner in the area described.

The patrol crossed the Marada-El Agheila road on the 11th, and went on to the neighbourhood of the Salt marsh S.W. of El Agheila known as Sebka Kebrit. The going was bad and one track was mined. The original plan was that the raiders were to be dropped about 11 miles S.W. of El Agheila; but owing to the difficulty of circumventing the marsh 2/Lieut. Morris decided on the 12th to go back, and take them to a point at the same distance from the village but to the south east of it. On the night of the 12/13th the party encamped about 4 miles west of the Marada-El Agheila road. Next morning the trucks were hidden a mile from the road and 2/Lieut. Morris went forward to examine it, as much traffic had been heard going south during the night. Fresh tracks were found including those of five tanks. Rain began to fall, and taking advantage of the weather the patrol crossed the road, moved 8 miles east and then headed north. Several aircraft were seen but the trucks were not detected. The S.A.S. were duly left with their Lancia truck and two L.R.D.G. lorries fully manned, 12 miles S.E. of El Agheila; and arrangements were made to pick them up again after the raid. The rest of the patrol then went N.E. towards Mersa Brega through undulating scrubby country.

On 14 December the trucks were left about 12 miles S.W. of Mersa Brega and 2/Lieut. Morris continued the journey on foot with three other ranks carrying explosives. Unfortunately they missed the way, and being unable to cross a marsh returned to their trucks arriving about 0145 hrs on the 15th. Meanwhile the S.A.S. men had returned having discovered that the El Agheila landing ground was empty; but they had blown up a large truck full of ammunition and wrecked the telephone communications. Natives stated that the enemy's aircraft had been moved to Jedabia; and it was also discovered that about 300 Germans and some aircraft had gone to Marada. A great deal of traffic was seen on the road between Mersa Brega and El Agheila.

On the 16th another effort was made to get to Mersa Brega; this time along the road from Marada owing to the roughness of the open country. During the evening of 16/17 December the patrol moved north and arrived near the coast road at 2000 hrs.

Attack on enemy's M.T. 17 December 1941.

For more than an hour 2/Lieut. Morris watched the convoys moving S.W. along the road, i.e. toward El Agheila, in groups of twelve. He then took his own trucks on to the road, having removed the dimmers on the lamps. The lamps were then turned full on every ten seconds, so as to give the impression to traffic going the opposite way that the trucks were coming over a slight rise a few hundred yards away. The Lancia which had no lights led, followed by 2/Lieut Morris's truck whose lights were the most dazzling. In this way the patrol covered the remaining nine miles to Mersa Brega, passing nearly 50 of the enemy's vehicles on the way! The road was good, but so narrow that there was seldom more than a yard between passing vehicles. It was noticed that many of the enemy's vehicles were Fords and Chevrolets. At midnight they reached buildings previously seen through glasses, and drew up at the nearest of them, alongside 22 enemy vehicles carrying German and Italian troops. In his report 2/Liuet Morris says "Unfortunately we were unable to commence proceedings at once as two of my trucks had not arrived, and we waited another five minutes. Almost immediately after their arrival a shot was fired at us so we commenced. Most of the firing between the enemy and ourselves was carried out at an average of from 25 to 30 paces. We suffered no casualties although the enemy tried unsuccessfully to encircle us. After careful enquiries made by me later, it appears that we must have killed about fifteen besides wounding several. I myself actually saw four destroyed. ... Reinforcements seemed to be arriving so we moved out, my truck now leading with headlights full on, followed by the Lancia". A mildly worded account of a remarkable feat! The S.A.S. men in the Lancia threw four time bombs into the enemy's trucks during the fight, and during the withdrawal mines were dropped on the road by the last truck "and" to quote the report, "judging by reports heard did a good job of work ... I estimate from explosions easily heard, that 7 trucks were blown up". The patrol moved 10 miles north along the road to Jedabia, and then took to the open country to the east. At the point where they left the road four telegraph posts were blown up. Turning south the patrol drove through the night over rough country mostly in second gear, and camped at 0630 hrs on the 17th. They reached Jalo at 1000 hrs on 19 December. Two prisoners were captured, a Libyan corporal by the S.A.S. men at the El Agheila aerodrome, and an Italian driver at Mersa Brega.

S.2 and R.A. Section to El Gtafia 13 December 1941.

Between 13 and 23 December an operation from Jalo was carried out by S.2 under 2/Lieut. Olivey and the R.A. Section under 2/Lieut H.P. Eitzen. This was the first operation in which the R.A. Section took part. It was originally armed with a 4.5 howitzer carried in a 10-ton lorry, and had also a light tank to be used as an armoured O.P. The 4.5 howitzer however was handed over to Colonel Leclerc of the French Army when the defence of Kufra became the L.R.D.G.'s responsibility in April 1941, (see Section VIII), and some time afterwards the R.A. Section was re-armed with a 25 pr. also "porté".

The tasks allotted to the patrol and the R.A. Section were as follows:-
(a) To reconnoitre the area Maaten Bettafal (X)B.6350, (in the Wadi el Faregh 40 miles E.S.E. of El Agheila) – Haseiat, 30 miles S.E. of Jedabia – Bir Bu Gedaria (X)B.8581. This area is roughly due east of El Agheila at an average distance of sixty miles, and some forty miles south of Jedabia.
(b) To attack the fort of El Gtafia, at the track junction 25 miles S.S.W. of Jedabia.

(c) To attack traffic on the Jedabia-El Agheila road.

(d) To reconnoitre the country south and west of Jedabia.

Leaving Jalo on 13 December the R.A. Section went N.W. while 2/Lieut Olivey with two trucks moved somewhat further north by Bir Gwetin (75 miles N.W. of Jalo), and rejoined the section later in the day. On the 14th the detachment encamped in the hills north of Bettafal, and reconnoitred the landing ground at Bir Bilal (X)B.8580, 25 miles to the N.E., finding it in good condition but unused. On the 15th further reconnaissance took place of the Wadi el Faregh, and also of the fort at Gtafia, which was sited in a hollow and was in bad repair. The attack on the fort was made next day. The R.A. Section with the W/T truck approached it from the S.W.; two trucks (S.5 and S.10) took up a position S.E. of it; and 2/Lieut. Olivey with the two remaining tucks moved round the west side to positions north and N.E. The artillery opened at 1630 hrs and fired 14 rounds, with the result that four soldiers left the fort and went along a Wadi to the N.W. where they were captured, and the rest of the garrison having fled, the fort was entered and searched. No wireless or telephone was found; but two Fiat guns were taken, and the ammunition was put into the well. Papers were removed and everything of value broken up. The party then camped 10 miles S.E. of the fort, lay up during the 17th and signalled results to Group H.Q. Next day (18 December) the patrol was ordered to leave its R.A. detachment in the Wadi el Faregh, and reconnoitre the country north of Qasr el Sahabi which lies some 40 miles further east. An A.F.V. and some lorries carrying troops were seen, but as they were thought to be British, fire was not opened, nor was any contact made with them. On the 19th the patrol moved on again, and on the 20th camped in the Wadi el Faregh at Ain Naga about 40 miles south of Jedabia. Here by previous arrangement they met a party of S.A.S. troops who had been given the task of raiding the landing ground at Jedabia.

S.A.S. raid on Jedabia landing ground 21 December.

The S.A.S. men were taken to a point about 5 miles from Jedabia on the road from El Haseiat, where they were given their position and the bearing to the landing ground; and a rendezvous for the return journey was fixed. The raid was highly successful, 37 aircraft being destroyed and an ammunition dump blown up. The raiders were duly collected on the 22nd, and the party returned to the Wadi el Faregh where they found Brig. Reid's force.

While signalling to Group H.Q. on the same day, the patrol was attacked by two Blenheim aircraft bearing British markings and flying very low, with the result that two men, Corporal Ashby and Private Riggs, were killed.

On 23 December the patrol returned to Jalo.

Section XV

Instructions from Eighth Army 21 December 1941.

On 21 December 1941 the O.C. L.R.D.G. visited H.Q. Eighth Army at Tmimi Derna and received fresh instructions. The patrols under the command of Brig. Reid ('E' Force) and Brig. Marriott reverted to the command of H.Q. L.R.D.G.: and the L.R.D.G.'s role was defined in Eighth Army Instruction No. 32, dated 22 December 1941, which included the points enumerated below.

(a) To carry out offensive patrols as far behind the enemy's lines as possible, and act aggressively against his L. of C. in areas where such action was unlikely to be expected.

(b) To note details of the topography of Tripolitania which might be of value in the future.

(c) To watch the enemy's movements, and in particular to report as soon as possible whether a position was being prepared in the neighbourhood of Buerat-el-Hsun.

(d) To supply information as to the "going" along the "coastal strip" north of the line Marada-Zella-Hon, of the garrisons in those places and of water to be found there. In particular the Army wished to know which garrisons were German.

The L.R.D.G. was also told that it might at times have to transport Intelligence personnel, and start them on their tasks.

When carrying out offensive action major opposition was to be avoided. If Jedabia were taken the L.R.D.G. would be based on it.

These instructions opened the third phase of the Group's action in cooperation with the Eighth Army.

Effect on enemy of L.R.D.G. raids.

Information obtained from captured German documents showed that the reports made by victims of the L.R.D.G.s exploits during the second phase had given the enemy an exaggerated notion of the strength of its patrols; and had caused them great anxiety about the safety of their L.of C. As a result aircraft, men and vehicles had been directed from the main front to protective duties. The enemy had also formed the entirely erroneous opinion that there was close and constant cooperation between the L.R.D.G and the R.A.F. This was far from being the case as no such arrangement existed, and the patrols had on more than one occasion been shot at by our own aircraft!

W/T set sent to French December 1941-January 1942.

Before dealing in detail with the action of the L.R.D.G. patrols during the third phase, it should be recorded that on 29 December the L.R.D.G. was ordered to take a wireless set and 20 anti-tank weapons to Zouar in the Tibesti district of the Chad territory, the H.Q. of General Leclerc, who was preparing to advance into the Fezzan. The wireless set was to be used as a link between the Free French H.Q. and H.Q. Eighth Army.

General Leclerc's force was small. It consisted of two mobile infantry companies, a "groupe" of artillery consisting of two 75 mm guns and one 4.5" howitzer carried in trucks, and two "groupes Nomades", one of lorried infantry and the other of "Méharistes" who rode camels. He also had the support of six somewhat antiquated aircraft. General Ritchie's instructions, dated 26 December 1941, to the French who were shortly to come under his command are of interest, apart from their importance to the L.R.D.G., as they given an idea of the intentions of the G.O.C. Eighth Army at that time.

General Ritchie's Instructions to French 26 December 1941.

He stated that his object was to cut off what was left of the enemy in Cyrenaica; and that it was not clear whether they intended to make a stand in Tripolitania, or if so where. He went on to say that little was known of the enemy's strength in ground troops or aircraft, though the Germans had lost heavily and the Italians were completely disorganised. Nor could he estimate the possibilities or extent of reinforcement, but information would be given as soon as it was available.

General Ritchie's intention was to operate against the enemy in Tripolitania as soon as the supply situation made it possible. He recognised that General Leclerc's force was not strong enough to attack strongly held posts. The French were therefore to operate in the area bounded on the north by latitude 28°N, on the east by latitude 18°E and on the west by the line Tummo-Ubari[1] and thence due north, which corresponds approximately with the 13th meridian east. On no account were the Vichy territories of Tunisia and Southern Algeria to be entered. Operations were to

---

1   Tummo long. 14°5'E. lat. 22°40'N.
    Ubari long. 12°50'E. lat 26°35'N.

begin on 9 January 1942, or as soon after as possible. At a later date to be communicated in due course, and dependent on the general situation, General Leclerc was to operate against the enemy's L. of C. between Hon and Misurata; and to prevent him from interfering with the L. of C. of the British forces based on Cyrenaica. The L.R.D.G. would be operating north of latitude 28° and would keep General Leclerc informed of the activities of its patrols.

Situation on Main Front.

The general situation during the first month of the third phase of the L.R.D.G's operations on the left of the Eighth Army was as follows:-

On 21 and 22 December, Rommel had received strong tank reinforcements by sea, and had concentrated his strength in the Jedabia-El Agheila area. Bengazi was still held by the enemy but was abandoned by him on 24 December. On Christmas Day our advanced troops were at Bengazi, Saunnu, Antelat and Soluk, with Brig. Reid's 'E' Force further to the south. They were lacking in infantry, and the supply problem made it difficult to increase the strength by bringing troops up from further east. Bardia, Sollum and Halfaya were also still in the enemy's hands, but Bardia was taken on 2 January 1942, and Halfaya and Sollum on the 12th.

Rommel's counter stroke 21 January 1942.

On 6 January Rommel withdrew from Jedabia, and by the 14th was fighting a rearguard action behind minefields on the line Marada-El Agheila. Further reinforcements had however reached him during the first week of January 1942, and he was preparing to counter attack. He began to do so on 21 January, and by the 22nd had retaken Jedabia, Antelat and Saunnu. On the 25th we were forced to evacuate Bengazi.

The area for which the L.R.D.G. was to be responsible was bounded on the north by the sea, on the east by the line Marada-El Agheila, on the south by latitude 28°N. and on the west by the eastern frontier of Tunisia.

L.R.D.G. Patrol areas.

This area was subdivided by Colonel Prendergast into five smaller ones bounded by meridians of longitude and parallels of latitude as shown below:-

Area.	Boundaries.			
No.	North.	East.	South.	West.
1.	32°N.	12°E.	30°N.	10°E.
2.	32°N.	14°E.	Nil.	12°E.
3.	Sea.	16°E.	29°30'N.	14°E.
4.	Sea.	18°E.	29°30'N.	16°E.
5.	29°30'N.	18°E.	Nil.	16°E.

S.1 and S.A.S. to Sirte 24 December 1941.

The first patrol to go out during this period was S.1 under Capt. Holliman which left Jalo on 24 December carrying a party of S.A.S. troops to make another attack on the landing grounds at Sirte and Wadi Tamet. On arrival in the area the party divided into two sections. One went to the Wadi Tamet where it destroyed 27 aircraft. The other reached the coast road at a point 11 miles west of Sirte, and then drove along till it was 4 miles from the town. Here the trucks were parked between two camps of the enemy's M.T., and the party set off on foot towards Sirte. Unfortunately a sentry saw them and gave the alarm, so that the raid on the landing ground had to be abandoned. The party regained their trucks and drove along the road shooting at the vehicles parked alongside it with small arms and a Bofors gun, and they also put thermite bombs in two large lorries. The two parties reunited south of the coast having driven 70 miles in the dark, and evaded two fighter aircraft which were obviously searching for them.

T.2 and S.A.S. to Marble Arch 25 December 1941.

On Christmas Day T.2 under 2/Lieut Morris, M.C., left Jalo with two S.A.S. parties to raid the landing ground near the "Arco dei Fileni" better known as the "Marble Arch" at (S)V.5492 about 40 miles west of El Agheila; and at Nofilia, some 60 miles further along the coast to the west. He took with him 15 men of the L.R.D.G. and 10 of the S.A.S. On the 27th he dropped Lieut. Fraser and 4 other S.A.S. men about 6 miles from the Marble Arch aerodrome. Troops and lorries were visible just south of it. At about 1500 hrs on 28 December the remaining S.A.S. men under Lieut. J. Lewis were dropped close to Nofilia. The trucks then lay up about ten miles to the south, and remained there throughout the 29th.

Lieut. Lewis killed.

At about 1800 hrs on the 30th, Lieut. Lewis and his party were picked up at the place where they had been dropped, and on the morning of the 31st the trucks were taken on to the Marble Arch. At about 1000 hrs they were attacked by a Messerschmidt aircraft from a height of about 60 feet. The trucks were scattered and the aircraft went back to the landing ground which was close at hand. A second low level attack was then made with bombs, "cannon" and machine guns using incendiary bullets, by two Stukas and a reconnaissance plane. In spite of concealed positions and camouflage their fire was effective; two trucks were destroyed and Lieut. Lewis was killed. During the course of the morning there were further attacks and all the trucks but one were destroyed, though no more casualties occurred.

Escape of Corporal Garvin and others.

2/Lieut Morris got away with the remaining truck and some of his patrol, and reached Jalo on 1 January; but 9 men of the L.R.D.G. and one of the S.A.S. were left behind. All however reached Augila (close to Jalo) except the S.A.S. man who, as his feet were almost raw, had been obliged to fall out near the Marada-El Agheila road. They had then walked more than 200 miles in eight days. Their total resources were three gallons of water, one packet of biscuits, one emergency rations, a compass and a map of the eastern part of the area; and for one night they were sheltered and fed by Arabs. They suffered much from the cold, which forced them to march at night, and from their footwear falling to pieces on the rough going. One of them, Corporal Garvin arrived at Augila with a piece cut from a greatcoat on one foot, and part of the canvas cover of a Lewis gun on the other.

The stories told by the survivors of the march, of whom Corporal Garvin was the leader, show how much the human frame can endure; but also that travelling in M.T. is not the best of training for a long walk. Eight of the party were New Zealanders, the other two were English. The principal trouble seems to have been with feet. Of the crew of T.9 truck, two men were wearing boots, one sand shoes and one "chaplis". Corporal White who was wearing sand shoes, was the S.A.S. man who failed to reach Augila. But every form of footwear seems eventually to have given out, and one of the party Trooper Martin, was of the opinion that the slipper worn by natives is the most suitable type, and better than "chaplis", at any rate as made in Egypt. Some of the men were lucky in getting water one day from the tank of an abandoned armoured car. They had passed this car on their outward journey, and when they found it, realized that they were on the way to Jalo and not far from it.

L.R.D.G. Instructions for raiding 23 December 1941.

In an Instruction dated 23 December 1941, Lieut.Colonel Prendergast allotted the areas he had defined to other patrols as follows:- No. 1 to T.1, No. 2 to Y.2, No. 3 to G.2, No. 5 to R.1, and he gave a list of possible targets in each area. All the patrols in question were based on Siwa, and were ordered to leave for their respective areas as soon as possible, moving by Jalo. R.2 patrol was ordered to Zouar where it was to come under the orders of General Leclerc. Y.1 patrol was to go to Jalo where it would be in reserve.

Kufra ceases to be the base 30 December 1941.

On 30 December 1941, Kufra though still garrisoned by the Sudan Defence Force ceased to be a base for any part of the L.R.D.G.; except that a W/T set was left there to form a link between R.2 at Zouar and Group

H.Q., which moved to Jalo during the first ten days of January 1942, as Siwa was considered to be too far back. The Heavy Section under Lieut. Arnold with the Survey Officer (Lieut. Lazarus) reached Jalo on 6 January and left on the 23rd for Matruh and Tobruk, reinforced by five Lancia lorries which had been salvaged at Jalo. In the middle of January S.1, S.2 and T.2 left Jalo for Cairo to refit and obtain new vehicles, and were still there at the beginning of February. It was apparent from the experience of all the patrols at this time that the C.A.S. Fords were reaching the limit of their service.

Y.2 to Central Tripolitania, 24 December 1941.

Of the patrols based in Siwa the first to operate was Y.2. It left Siwa on 24 December 1941 and in addition to 13 O.Rs the patrol commander, Capt. Lloyd-Owen, had with him Capt. S.V. McCoy (2nd Lancers I.A.) and one Indian O.R. from the Indian Desert Squadron, which had been formed in Cairo but was then in Syria.

The patrol's area of operations, No. 2, was in Central Tripolitania, south of the Djebel Nefusa (or Neoussa), a range of hills which runs from east to west about 80 miles south of Tripoli and then north to the Gulf of Gabes. Moving by Jalo, they crossed the road from Hon to Sirte on 31 December at a point about 50 miles south of the latter place. The road was well made with an artificial surface, but showed no signs of use. On 1 January 1942 they crossed the Wadi Tamet, and camped about 20 miles west of it and 70 miles from the coast. On 2 January they crossed the road from Bou Njem (long. 15°25'E. lat. 30°33'N) to Misurata, also well made and much used. It had now rained for three days, the going was difficult and there had been mechanical trouble. On 5 January the patrol reached the neighbourhood of the fort at Chemech (R)R.1700, about 100 miles S.S.E. of Tripoli. An attack was planned but the fort was found to be empty, though the natives (who were told that the patrol was German) said that a German patrol had been there that morning. The fort was wired and there was a landing ground alongside it.

The return journey was uneventful, except that one truck broke its main drive and had to be abandoned. Useful information had been obtained about an area which the L.R.D.G. had not previously visited; and the patrol commander paid a well deserved tribute to the skill of his navigator Lance Corporal Denniff, who during a journey of 1,500 miles had guided the patrol successfully through many rainy days and nights when the sun and stars were invisible.

G.2 to Hon-Misurata road, 26 December 1941.

G.2 under Lieut. Timpson left Siwa on 26 December 1941 with the Hon-Misurata road as his principal objective. He destroyed a Diesel lorry near

Bou Njem and captured the driver, but bad going and mechanical trouble made it necessary to return home and the patrol reached Siwa on 15 January 1942.

R.1 to Zella-Hon road, 7 January 1942.

On 7 January Capt. Easonsmith left with R.1 patrol for Area 5, intending to raid traffic on the road from Zella to Hon which was reached on 10 January. In the country that had just been crossed, known as Es Sodaia, the going is powdery limestone ("fesh-fesh") and so soft that tracks are very noticeable. As a result the patrol was located by aircraft and attacked next day. As the going was too soft for "zig zagging" the men had to dismount and scatter. There were no casualties but three tyres were hit. The aircraft eventually moved off, but the dust was then seen of vehicles approaching from Zella. The patrol, however, shook off its pursuers, probably an Italian "Auto Saharan Company", and got back to Jalo on 14 January. On 20 January the patrol with H.Q. 'A' Squadron left for Cairo to refit, and they were followed shortly afterwards by T.1 (Major Ballantyne) which had started for Area 1 on the 8th, but owing to constant mechanical breakdowns and lack of petrol, failed to reach its objective.

Y.1 with XIII Corps, January 1942.

On 3 January 1942 H.Q. Eighth Army sent Lieut.Colonel Hasledon with a letter to the O.C. L.R.D.G. ordering the attachment of a patrol to the XIII Corps, a matter which had already been the subject of correspondence.

The XIII Corps which was in the Antelat area was to carry out an operation towards the "Marble Arch", moving by the Wadi el Faregh. As it was to assist in navigating the force, it was desirable that the patrol selected should have a knowledge of the area.

The order also emphasized the importance of obtaining information of M.T. and supplies going forward to the enemy at Ras el Ali (on the coast 25 miles W.N.W of El Agheila) and of delaying or stopping them.

Y.1 patrol (Capt. Simms) was detailed for this duty and on arrival at Corps H.Q. was sent to obtain information about the garrison at Marada. While trying to do so, Capt. Simms and another man were taken prisoner. Capt. Lloyd-Owen (Y.2) who had just returned from Chemech, took his place, and with the whole of Y Patrol was sent by XIII Corps on a reconnaissance N.W. of Marada.

Rommel advances to Msus.

On 21 January while Y Patrol was engaged on this duty, Rommel's counter offensive began and it was recalled to Jalo. By 24 January 1942 the enemy had reached Msus and were still progressing eastwards.

H.Q., L.R.D.G. leaves Jalo.

On the advice of H.Q. Eighth Army, H.Q. L.R.D.G. which had recently joined 'A' Squadron at Jalo left there on 26 January, taking 'A' Squadron with it. In the hope that the situation might improve only a short withdrawal was made, and H.Q. was reopened at Maaten Ghetmir, 20 miles N.E. of Jalo where cover and water were good, and there was a strong defensive position. The enemy however continued to make progress and on 1 February H.Q. reopened at Siwa. Most of the stores accumulated at Jalo were moved to a dump on the western edge of the Sand Sea, east of Ghetmir. Those that could not be moved owing to lack of transport, together with any vehicles that the enemy might be able to repair, and a quantity of ammunition left by the Italians at Jalo were destroyed. These demolitions were carried out by Lieut. Timpson whose patrol remained at Jalo to await the return of G.1 patrol which had started on an expedition to Buerat-el-Heun on 17 January.

Capture of Capt. Carr 26 January 1942.

An unfortunate result of the German counter offensive was the capture of Capt. R.P. Carr, Adjutant of the L.R.D.G., with 14 men and 7 vehicles. He had left Jalo on 24 January to bring a load of petrol from Msus. As he had no W/T, it was impossible to warn him of the enemy's rapid advance, and when he arrived at Msus on 26 January he found that it was in the enemy's hands and the whole party was taken prisoner. Later in the day, while they were being removed, the convoy was attacked by two of our armoured cars and seven men contrived to escape, but Capt. Carr and the other seven remained in the enemy's hands.

G.1 patrol and S.A.S. to Bouerat 17 January 1942.

As stated above G.1 patrol, under Capt. A.D.N. Hunter, left Jalo to attack Bouerat el Hsun on 17 January. It consisted of 1 officer and 13 O.Rs of the L.R.D.G., 1 officer (Capt. D. Stirling) and 12 O.Rs of the S.A.S., 1 officer and 1 O.R. of the "Folbot" (folding boat) company and 1 officer and 1 O.R. of the R.A.F.

They crossed the Kufra-Marada road at Bir Zelten (60 miles south of Marada) and then struck N.W. through Abu Naim (X)F.7523, and El Hofra (X)F.0546 (S.W. and west of Marada respectively), to the Wadi Tamet which runs down to the coast about 30 miles east of Bouerat el Hsun. Progress was slow owing to breakdowns and difficult country, and while crossing the Wadi the patrol was attacked from the air and the vehicles dispersed. When the party was about to move on again it was found that the W/T operator and three L.R.D.G. men were missing and they had to be left behind as there was no time to make a long search for them. On the evening of the 23rd the patrol reached the sand dunes just east of the Hon-Misurats road near El Gheddahia,* and the S.A.S. and "Folbot" party went on to carry out their attack. They returned at 0800 hrs on the 24th having completed their task and destroyed several vehicles, but without the Folbot officer and one man. They however were picked up in the evening of the 25th by Capt. Hunter and Capt. Stirling, who with 9 O.Rs went north to attack the coastal road. There was little traffic, but one tanker with a trailer was destroyed, and telephone poles were mined.

During the return journey the party was ambushed, but had no casualties, though it was fairly certain that some were inflicted on the enemy.

The party started for Jalo on the night 26/27 January and arrived there without incident on the 31st.

* (R) X.3794

Section XVI

Dispositions of patrols 1 February 1942.

At the beginning of the fourth phase of the L.R.D.G.'s operations about 1 February 1942 the patrols were disposed as follows:-

G.1 which had reached Jalo from Bouerat el Hsun on 31 January, en route to Siwa.

G.2 en route from Jalo to Siwa.

R.1 at Cairo.

R.2 at Zouar with the Free French Forces.

S.1 and S.2 at Cairo.

Y.1 and Y.2 at Siwa.

T.1 and T.2 at Cairo.

The patrols at Siwa were under the immediate command of Major E.R.C. Wilson, V.C., commanding 'B' Squadron. The patrols at Cairo were refitting, and during the next six weeks the remaining patrols also went there from Siwa for the same purpose; but at no time during this period were there less than two patrols in the field.

30-cwt Chevrolets replace Fords.

At Cairo the 30-cwt C.A.S. Fords were handed in, and replaced by 30-cwt Chevrolets which consumed less petrol. Certain changes in armament were also made, and each patrol received in due course two .5 Vickers guns, three .303 Vickers "K" guns, one .303 Vickers gun, five Lewis guns, and one 22mm Breda dual purpose gun.

10 Macks replace White lorries.

In the Heavy Section the "White" lorries were replaced by four 10-ton "Macks", and the two "Waco" aircraft were sent in for overhaul.

Reorganization and changes among officers.

There were also changes in establishment. The Group was now to consist of Headquarters, one H.Q. Squadron of six patrols, and one "Detachable Squadron" of four patrols. A Light Repair Section, R.A.O.C. and a Signal Troop were attached to Group H.Q. It was also proposed to form a "Sabotage platoon".

Capt. L. Cranfield (R.A.C.) became adjutant in place of Capt. R.P. Carr who was taken prisoner at Msus. Lieut. Hon. R. Gurdon, Coldstream Guards succeeded Capt. Hay in command of G.1, and Capt. Morris, M.C., (N.Z.E.F.) succeeded Major Ballantyne in command of T.1. Before going to Cairo G.2 and Y.2 patrols under Lieut. Timpson and Capt. Lloyd-Own respectively, made one more expedition each from Siwa.

By this time the enemy had re-occupied Cyrenaica as far east as the line Bir Hakim-Gazala. The Army Commander's intention was to use the L.R.D.G. to obtain immediate information as follows:-

(a) As to what extent the enemy was using the roads Cyrene-Barce-Bengazi, and El Faidia[1]-Maraua-Barce-Bengazi.

(b) Whether fuel or other dumps were being made in the area east and north east of Jedabia (which might indicate an intention to advance on Tobruk).

Eighth Army's position 6 February 1942.

In his Operation Instruction No. 25, dated 6 February, for the action of G.2 and Y.2 patrols (issued to Major Wilson, V.C., commanding 'B' Squadron), Lieut. Colonel Prendergast gave information of the position of our own troops as follows: "Eighth Army is holding the line Gazala-Bir Hakim with strong patrols consisting of armoured cars, guns and lorry borne infantry, patrolling westward as far as Charruba".[2] G.2 patrol was ordered to observe and make a census of traffic continuously for four days and four nights on the two roads in question. The patrol's route to the area was to pass west of Charruba; it was to avoid all contact with troops; and no arrangement was to be made for recognition signals except from ground to air. Wireless silence was to be maintained unless the number of A.F.V's, guns, etc., observed made it clear that an immediate attack on our main position was impending. Such information was to be signalled immediately.

The patrol commander was however to let H.Q. Eighth Army know when he left Siwa, and to give the probable dates between which the census would be carried out.

Y.2 was to find out if dumps were being formed at the following places which were given in order of probability:- Msus, Antelat, Soluk, Jedabia, Maaten-el-Grara (S)X.8324, Saunnu, Esh-Sheledeima (S)S.4116. As these

1 El Faidia is 8 miles due south of Cyrene.
2 Charruba or El Kharruba 52 miles due east of Bengazi.

places were likely to be protected, the patrol was to watch the tracks lead-ing to them from the coastal road. Wireless silence was not to be observed, and both positive and negative information was to be signalled.

Both patrols were warned that the success of their operation was on no account to be jeopardized by aggressive action.

G.2 Traffic Census 9 February 1942.

G.2 patrol left Siwa to take the traffic census at 1500 hrs on 9 February 1942, and Capt. J.E. Hasleden, M.C., of the General Staff went with them. In his report the latter says that in view of the unsettled state of Cyrenaica he thought it advisable to take with him Hussein Eff Taha, the ex-Mudir of Slonta (at (S)O.4833 on the southern road from Derna to Barce), to advise on the reliability of Arabs in the area; and an Arab guide, Tayeb el Barani, a native of Slonta, who had been a refugee in Egypt for some years. On arrival at Baltat-ez-Zelagh, 30 miles south of Mekili, information was received from an Arab that there was no enemy movement in the area, and that Gerdes-el-Gerrari, about six miles S.E. of Slonta, was unoccupied. At midday on 12 February the trucks were hidden in a wadi near Bir Embescer, some six miles south of Slonta. At 1500 hrs on the 13th Lieut. Timpson went, with one party, to observe the southern road to Barce near El Cueifat, 5 miles S.W. of Slonta; and Capt. Hasleden took four other men to a point about 20 miles W.S.W. of Cyrene to observe the northern road. No traffic on the northern road was seen until the early morning of the 15th. A detailed list of traffic on both roads was made; and Capt. Hasleden noted in it that about one vehicle in five was British, and that captured British vehicles were in very much better condition than the enemy's vehi-cles. A good many guns, tanks and A.F.V's were seen among the east bound traffic. Local Arabs gave a good deal of information about the movements of the enemy's troops; and Capt. Hasleden was also informed by a man of the Barassa tribe, whom he met at Bir Embescer, that several British officers and men had been seen on the previous day (11 February) going east. Some of them were located; and Major J.T. Gibson and Capt. Hammond of the Welch Regiment, Capt. Dodds, R.A., with 2 O.Rs of the Welch Regiment, 11 O.Rs of the 3rd Bn. Libyan Arab Force, and a drum-mer boy of the Royal Sussex Regiment were rescued and taken back to Siwa. Capt. Hasleden recorded that on the whole the Arabs were loyal, particularly those of the Barassa and Obeidat tribes, and had helped many British stragglers. He also said that there had so far been no reprisals against Arabs, though as they themselves admitted, they had done a good deal of looting from Italian Colonists! Major Gibson wrote a report which gave information about the enemy, and confirmed the poor condition of German vehicles. He believed that about 200 British officers and men were attempting to make their way back, and mentioned as among them,

Lieut.Colonel R. Peake of the Royal Dragoons, who in fact did eventually escape. All were being aided and fed by the Senussi. During the return journey to Siwa G.2 patrol carried 47 passengers, who included besides the rescued officers and men, two wives and one child of the Mudir of Slonta, not to mention some chickens and a goat!

Y.2's reconnaissance to Jedabia 11 February 1942.

Y.2's reconnaissance for dumps east and N.E. of Jedabia was a difficult task for the country is very open. The patrol left Siwa on 11 February 1942, and at Weschet el Heira where it camped that night, the latest information from H.Q. Eighth Army was dropped from a Lysander aircraft. Observation began on 14 February about 18 miles E.S.E. of Jedabia on the track leading to Maaten el Grara. 100 stationary vehicles in a camp were seen through a telescope, but owing to the nature of the country it was not possible to get within five miles of them. Next day the patrol moved northwards towards Antelat, passing many derelict British tanks and M.T. vehicles which were being salvaged by Italians; and small convoys were seen between Antelat, Jedabia and Saunnu. Early in the afternoon the patrol was chased by two lorries, but after 20 miles they were left behind, and the patrol having turned west towards Cardasi el Oti encamped about 13 miles S.E. of Esh Sheledeima, which is on the road from Msus to Soluk. More traffic of all kinds and salvage parties were seen on the 16th. Again the country was so open that it was difficult to remain long in one place, and the patrol was often visible to the enemy. The homeward journey began on 17 February and the patrol arrived at Siwa on the 19th with useful information.

Tripoli road watch. 25 February to 29 April 1942.

The census on traffic on the Bengasi-Tripoli road was resumed on 25 February by S.2 (2/Lieut. Olivey) which had returned from Cairo. S.2's watch began on 2 March, and from then onward until 28 April the coast road was under almost continuous observation by S.2, T.1, R.1, T.2, G.2, T.1 patrols in succession. Every patrol observed from the same place; which had first been used during a similar operation in July 1941. It is some 35 miles west of El Agheila and five miles east of the "Marble Arch" (near Ras Lanuf). There is high ground south of the road from which a wadi leads down towards the coast. In the wadi there is good cover, and trucks could be effectively camouflaged. At its N.E. end the wadi leads to a flat plain, which the road crosses about 2? miles from the mouth of the wadi. There is a certain amount of small scrub on the plain which enabled a man to conceal himself; but once in position he had to remain in his place throughout the hours of daylight. The usual procedure was as follows: the trucks were hidden in the wadi, and at about 3.30 a.m. daily two men went down and took cover within 300 yards or so of the road and remained there until nightfall, lying at full length. At night observers could approach to within 30 or 40 yards of the road. The risk of being seen was considerable. Arabs with camels and goats occasionally came down the wadi. On several occasions convoys pulled off the road for a meal, or to encamp for the night; and on another occasion a party of school children got out of a bus, and started a game of rounders within a short distance! The reports sent in classified M.T. vehicles according to tonnage; and tanks, guns, etc. were identified as accurately as possible. During the period referred to 260 tanks were recorded. Divisional signs and unit numbers were also noted as far as possible.

As had been noticed in July 1941, west bound traffic was arranged so as to economise petrol. Capt. Easonsmith's report states that a common arrangement was for a 10-tonner with an empty trailer loaded on it, to tow a second trailer with a truck in it. A quotation from the same report gives an idea of the difficulties that had to be faced. "Reports on the day (21 March) are accurate up till 12.30 hrs. From then onwards until darkness the road pickets were unable to look up or move … as a convoy pulled in behind them with the nearest vehicle at 150 yards. The approximation for the remainder of the day is based on the reports of camp picquets, and on the average traffic in the afternoons".

S.1 Traffic Census. 25 February 1942.

S.1 patrol (Capt. Holliman) after its return from Cairo was sent out to take a similar census of traffic on the northern and southern roads which run eastwards from Barce and re-unite at Lamluda about 25 miles west of Derna. The patrol was accompanied by Capt. R. Melot (a Belgian business man then on the General Staff and afterwards in the S.A.S.) who acted as Intelligence Officer, and it left Siwa on 25 February. Owing to the enemy's increased activity on and between the two roads the trucks could not be taken far forward. Transport was to be provided by Arab agents, but it failed to materialise. The reconnaissance of the northern road had therefore to be abandoned, but a census was taken on the 2nd, 3rd and 4 March from a point on the southern road. When the observing party returned to the wadi where they had left the trucks, they found that a cloud burst on the Jebel-el-Akhdar had caused a flood which had smashed one truck against a rock and temporarily submerged two others. The clutches of the two latter burnt out after 14 miles had been covered on the return journey, and they had to be abandoned. The party, nineteen in all, returned to Siwa in the two remaining vehicles.

Return of R.2 from Chad Territory 1 March 1942.

On 1 March 2/Lieut. Croucher returned from Zouar with R.2 patrol, as our loss of Jedabia had made it necessary to postpone the action of the Free

French against the Fezzan. They had been there for seven weeks (9 January to 17 February 1942).

Eighth Army Instruction 9 March 1942.

On 9 March 1942 H.Q. Eighth Army sent an instruction (No. HQ/8A/91/39/G(O)) to XIII and XXX Corps, L.R.D.G. 'C' Squadron Middle East Commando and Capt. D. Stirling, S.A.S. Bde, on the subject of operations behind the enemy's lines, which may be summarized as follows:-

(1) During the interim period before major offensive operations were resumed every effort was to be made to weaken the enemy's main forces, to cause him to disperse his effort and, in particular, to lower his morale.

(2) Intensive "sabotage" was to be directed at the enemy's aerodromes, L. of C. and bases, the objects being:-
   (a) To make the enemy realize that his L. of C. were far from secure.
   (b) To make him disperse his available resources to guard his L. of C., aerodromes and bases.
   (c) To destroy M.T. and A.F.Vs in transit.
   (d) To damage supply dumps particularly P.O.L.
   (e) To damage repair facilities.

(3) Information was required which would facilitate the attainment of the objects enumerated above.

(4) The responsibility for sabotage would be divided as below:
   (a) Within the enemy's forward area, by forward troops under arrangements made by XIII Corps.
   (b) Further west, between (excl) the line Martuba-Mekili and (excl) Bengazi, by Commandos acting under orders of H.Q. Eighth Army.
   (c)South and west of Bengazi, by S.A.S. detachments under orders of H.Q. Eighth Army.

(5) The L.R.D.G. was to be employed primarily on reconnaissance, and when necessary for guiding or collecting sabotage parties, with whose operations the activities of the L.R.D.G. must be closely coordinated.

(6) Certain minor operations might be undertaken by personnel of the General Staff (R).

It will be seen that the L.R.D.G. took a prominent part in the operations of the Commandos and the lately formed S.A.S. detachments, and of the latter in particular. These detachments known at first as the Special Air Service Brigade, had been formed chiefly through the efforts of Capt. (later Lieut.Colonel) D. Stirling, Scots Guards, after the disbandment of the three British Commandos (Nos. 7, 8 and 11) which had come to Egypt in March 1941. The Middle East Commando referred to in the Eighth Army's letter was a "reincarnation" of three others which had been formed in

Egypt and took part in the Abyssinian and Madagascar campaigns. It was originally intended that the S.A.S. detachments should be trained as parachutists and be taken by air to the scene of their activities. One operation of this character was tried and has been referred to in Section XIII above. It was not a success and S.A.S. detachments were for some time to come navigated by the L.R.D.G., and to a great extent carried in its transport.

S.1 and S.A.S. to Barce 16 March 1942.

On 16 March Capt. Holliman went out with S.1 to take Lieut. Fraser and six men of the S.A.S. to raid a landing ground near Barce. On his return journey he was to go to Cheda bu Maun and await the arrival of S.2 patrol (2/Lieut. Olivey) which, as related below, had gone out at the same time on a similar mission in the Berca-Bengasi area. He also intended to salvage two vehicles abandoned near Mekili during his last mission.

Operations with S.A.S. March 1942.

As a result of these orders three expeditions to be carried out in conjunction with parties of the 1st S.A.S. Brigade, left Siwa in the middle of March 1942.

(a) S.2 (2/Lieut. Olivey) was to take a S.A.S. party under Capt. Stirling to raid the aerodromes at Barce and Benina, and to attack shipping in Bengazi harbour. On the way home S.2 was to meet S.1 at a pre-arranged rendezvous, and then pick up a S.A.S. party under 2/Lieut. Dodds (see (b) and (c) below).

(b) T.1 (Capt. Morris) was to take a similar raiding party under 2/Lieut. Dodds to the area S.E. of Slonta, and to bring back a Commando party under Capt. Chapman, that had been operating in the same area, leaving Dodds's party to be brought back by S.2.

(c) S.1 (Capt. Holliman) was to carry a party of S.A.S. men under Lieut. Fraser to the area south of Barce, and bring them back to Siwa. On his return journey he was to wait for S.2 patrol who should also be on their way home in the area (S)S.9468 – (S)T.0575 (between Charruba and Cheda bu Maun).

The arrangement was somewhat complicated and, as will be seen later, did not work well.

T.1 to Slonta 16 May 1942.

T.1 patrol left Siwa on 16 March. With the aid of local Arabs they found the Commando party at 2300 hrs near Sidi Musa (S)0.5705, and at 0100 hrs on the 20th the S.A.S. party left to carry out their task in the Slonta area. An hour later the patrol started for home, and reached Siwa on the 23rd. On the way they were chased for a few miles by a heavy armoured car and a staff car, which were escorting a north-bound convoy along the Trigh el Abd, but were able to shake them off.

S.1 to Barce 16 May 1942.

S.1 patrol also left on 16 March, and on the 18th, when about 25 miles S.W. of Bir el Garrari, at (S)T.5642, they received a W/T message from Group H.Q. stating that the enemy's patrols were active between Bir el Garrari and Msus, 40 miles to the S.W., and their tracks were in fact noticeable. On the 19th Capt. Holliman left three trucks under Corporal Eastwood at Sidi Zamut (S)S.8475, which is about 55 miles due east of Bengazi, and went on to a point (S)N.8110, in the hills about 8 miles S.E. of Barce and dropped the S.A.S. party there on the 20th. Owing to the difficulty of the going the average speed during the latter part of the journey had been only one mile an hour.

Meanwhile Corporal Eastwood had noticed ground and air activity on the enemy's part near Sidi Zamut, and accordingly moved his three trucks to a pre-arranged rendezvous at Cheda bu Maun, five miles to the S.E. He was joined there by Capt. Holliman on the 21st, and during the next few days the two trucks that had been submerged in a flood a fortnight earlier were brought in and repaired. On the 27th a truck was sent to Sidi Zamut to bring back Lieut. Fraser's party, who joined the patrol at Bir el Amia (S)Y.6181 on the 30th. Their raid had been successful and they had destroyed one aeroplane and four workshop lorries. S.2 patrol with Major Stirling's party, joined S.1 on 28 March and reported their arrival by W/T to Group H.Q. On the 29th they received orders to bring back Major Stirling at once, which made it impossible for them to pick up 2/Lieut. Dodds's party as originally arranged. Capt. Holliman therefore sent three of his trucks to the camp of a local Arab agent, Hamed bu Serawaliya, who undertook to guide them to Sidi Musa, which was the rendezvous for Dodds's party. When however the trucks arrived at Hagfet Gelgaf, about 10 miles south of it, news came that Sidi Musa was occupied by Germans. Arabs were therefore sent forward on foot to find the S.A.S. men, bring them back to Hagfet Gelgaf and tell them that another patrol would come out to pick them up about 8 April. S.1 then returned to Siwa and arrived there on 31 March.

S.2's mission 15 March 1942 with S.A.S.

The main object of 2/Lieut. Olivey's mission with S.2 patrol which left Siwa on 15 March has already been stated.

The S.A.S. and Folbot party consisted of Major Stirling and Capt. R. Mayne, with six O.Rs of the S.A.S., and three officers with three O.Rs of the Folbot section. The patrol carried also an Arabic speaking officer of the General Staff (Capt. Melot), two O.Rs of the Senussi Regiment, and fifteen

O.Rs of the L.R.D.G. The S.A.S. and Folbot parties were to raid the aerodromes at Benina and Berca, and to damage or destroy shipping in the harbour at Bengasi. Included in the transport was a captured German staff car which was to be used to facilitate entry into Bengasi.

On 17 March the German car struck a "thermos" bomb and had to be abandoned. Lieut. D. Sutherland and Sergeant Moss of the Folbot party were wounded and had to be sent back in a truck to Siwa.

On 18 March the patrol reached Gasr-el-Gehese at (S)S.2161 and 16 miles S.E. of Bengasi. The two Senussi were then sent forward on foot to reconnoitre the aerodrome at Benina, and the main and satellite aerodromes at Berca which are on the S.E. outskirts of Bengasi, while Major Stirling, Capt. Melot and 2/Lieut. Olivey reconnoitred the escarpment in a 15-cwt lorry. On the 19th a party went forward on foot for further reconnaissance of Bengasi.

S.A.S. raid on Berca 20/21 March 1942.

On the 20th the two Senussi returned with information; and Lance Naik Ahmed Din of the 4th/16th Punjab Regiment who had been in hiding with Arabs for two months, also arrived at the patrol's position. That night, guided by Corporal Merrick, the L.R.D.G. navigator, Capt. Mayne with 2 officers and 16 O.Rs, went to the two Berca aerodromes. Major Stirling and 2 O.Rs travelled in a 15-cwt lorry – which had to be "helped" down the escarpment – to Benina, 10 miles east of Bengazi and on the railway and inland road to Barce. At midnight 20/21 March the R.A.F. made a covering attack on Bengasi. At 0510 hrs Major Stirling and his men returned, having been unable to find any aircraft at Benina. The party then returned to Gasr-el-Gehese where it encamped. On the 22nd the two Senussi who had again gone out, were expected to reappear but did not. The patrol then went to Chedu by Maun, where part of S.1 was found but not its commander. On the 23rd a search was made for T.1 in the neighbourbood of Sidi Musa, but as already related, T.1 had left that area three days before, and by the 23rd had arrived at Siwa. Capt. Mayne's party and Corporal Merrick returned safely at 0900 hrs next day (24th) having destroyed fifteen aircraft. Major Stirling again left in his own 15-cwt lorry for Bengasi, and encamped for the night 24/25 at Siret-Aslia (S)S.2481, about 13 miles further north. He took the "Folbot" party with him, and on the following night drove into Bengasi.

S.A.S. raid on Bengasi and Benina 25/26 March 1942.

In the meanwhile 2/Lieut. Olivey with the remainder of the party went to a point on the El Abiar-Bengasi road, 6 miles east of the edge of the escarpment at Regima. The Folbot party returned from Bengasi at 0400 hrs on the 26th, having reached the quayside but failed to damage any shipping.

At 0900 hrs on the 27th Major Stirling also returned. During his return journey from Bengasi he had destroyed five aircraft in their hangars on the Benina aerodrome, and a good many telegraph poles.

On 28 March the patrol and its passengers arrived at Cheda bu Maun where they found S.1, and on the 29th received instructions from Group H.Q. to return. On 31 March Major Stirling with three O.Rs left them near Hatiet er Retem (long. 23°15'E. lat. 30°52'N) and went north to El Adem. The remainder of the party arrived at Siwa at 1600 hrs on 1 April.

Y.2 to Slonta 31 March 1942.

On 31 March Y.2 (Capt. Hunter) took a Commando detachment of 16 men to the neighbourhood of Slonta, and while waiting to bring them back, did a certain amount of mapping in the Wadi Mra area. The Commando men did not achieve much, and the patrol returned to Siwa on 13 April.

R.2 to Hagfet Gelgaf 5 April 1942.

2/Lieut. Croucher, commanding R.2 patrol was given the task of bringing back 2/Lieut. Dodds and his S.A.S. men who, as already related, should have been picked up by S.2 a fortnight earlier. They were still at Hagfet Gelgaf (S)T.5386 to which place they had been directed in the message sent them by Capt. Holliman of S.1 patrol.

R.2 were also to take a commando party of 3 officers and 12 O.Rs under Major Glennie to the neighbourhood of Ghedir Bu Ascher (S)T.4060, six miles north of Baltet ez Zelagh; and carried as well an Arab speaking officer of the General Staff, and two O.Rs of the Libyan Arab Force.

The patrol left Siwa on 5 April and arrived at Baltet-ez-Zelagh on the 7th. There they met the Arab agent Hamed bu Serawaliya who informed them that 2/Lieut. Dodds and his party would be at Hagfet Gelgaf, 20 miles to the north, in the evening of 8 April. As this place was nearer Major Glennie's objective than Ghedir bu Ascher it was decided to drop his party there. Hagfet Gelgaf was reached after dusk on 8 April; and there, in addition to 2/Lieut. Dodds and his 6 S.A.S. men, the patrol found Capt. Chapman of the General Staff, an officer of the Libyan Arab Force, a corporal of the Royal Signals, attached to the General Staff, and six men of the R.A.F. who had been brought in by Arabs. As these additions to the party greatly increased his load, 2/Lieut. Croucher decided to return to Siwa at once, and come back again for Major Glennie and his commando detachment. The patrol reached Siwa on 10 April and left again on the 11th. On the 13th they picked up the Commando party and also 3 O.Rs of the Libyan Arab Force, and arrived at Siwa on the evening of the 15th. A good many hostile aircraft were seen or heard during the journey; and Arabs gave the information of a German patrol which had been seen in the

Wadi bu Ascher area, and was looking for British patrols. Two other patrol operations were carried out during April. G.1 took two Arab agents to the neighbourhood of Jalo, and picked them up four days later after they had obtained much useful information about the garrison there. Y.1 was away from the 10th to 18 April and took four officers of the XXX Corps to reconnoitre the country south and south-east of Bir Tengeder. The Survey Section under Lieut. Lazarus did survey work south east and south of Marada.

In a telegram dated 28 March 1942 the Army Commander congratulated all ranks of the L.R.D.G. on the success of their recent operations.

Section XVII

Fifth Phase April-May 1942.

The fifth of the phases into which its Commander has divided his record of the L.R.D.G. began on 19 April 1942, and ended just before Rommel once more attacked on 27 May. The 19 April is an arbitrary date, and as far as the L.R.D.G. was concerned the period was one of routine activity. They continued the traffic census on the coast road, now known as the "Tripoli Road Watch"; they dropped Intelligence agents; and they transported parties of Commando and S.A.S. troops.

Eighth Army Instructions 23 April 1942.

A second road watch, on the track from Mekili to Msus, was ordered in Eighth Army Operation Instruction No. 60 dated 23 April 1942. The instruction states that it was estimated that more than half the enemy's maintenance tonnage for Cyrenaica was coming by road from Tripoli to Bengazi. Information about his road movements not only from Tripolitania to Cyrenaica but also between Eastern and Western Cyrenaica, was therefore of great importance. In order that activities behind the enemy's lines both in Tripolitania and Cyrenaica might be closely coordinated, the Commander L.R.D.G. was given control of all such operations in the two territories; and in order to increase his strength 'A' and 'C' Squadrons of the Middle East Commando were put under his orders. Personnel of G(R) and agents employed on special missions to collect information would report to the Commander L.R.D.G., who would be responsible for their operations from the time at which they reported until they returned. Any other parties detailed for operations behind the enemy's lines in the two areas would also be placed under his command; and he was to be responsible for approving their plans and coordinating their activities.

It was also emphasized that the obtaining of information had "absolute priority", and that the interruption of the enemy's supplies was on no account to be allowed to interfere with it. Subject to any recommendations the Commander L.R.D.G. might make, offensive action was to be confined to two areas as follows:-

Area of L.R.D.G. operations

(a) The area west of meridian 20°30'E and north of latitude 30°30'N.

(b) The area west of long. 17°E.

The first named area which is in Cyrenaica includes the coastal belt along the eastern shore of the Gulf of Sirte only; approximately from El Abiar 30 miles east of Bengazi on the north, to an east and west line through Mersa Brega on the south. The second area, in Tripolitania and the Fezzan, lies roughly west of a north and south line through Sirte, and includes Hon and Wau el Kebir (long. 16°40'E. lat.25°20'N.).

The main objectives were to be petrol, motor transport and tanks. Besides being limited to certain areas, "offensive action" was further restricted by the priority given to road watching; for an attack on enemy traffic in a "road watching area" might cause an intensive search to be made by the enemy, and lead to the discovery of road watchers. An effort was made to vary the type of attack by placing time bombs in enemy vehicles unobserved by their crews. This however proved to be impracticable, and patrols had to revert to the tried and simpler method of "shooting up".

Towards the end of the period the demands on the L.R.D.G. became more and more numerous and exacting. In Colonel Prendergast's words, "An increasing stream of Commandos (European and Arab), 'L' detachment (S.A.S.), I.S.L.D., G(R), bogus Germans, lost travellers, escape scheme promoters, stranded aviators, etc. continued to arrive at Siwa, needing petrol, rations, maintenance, information, training and accommodation". These demands were usually met, but not without putting a strain on the unit's resources and personnel.

M.E. Commando.

'A' Squadron of the Middle East Commando, when it came under the command of the L.R.D.G., was at Jarabub, and was organized into three patrols, each of which had five new 15-cwt Chevrolet trucks. This organization resembled that of the L.R.D.G., but the circuit of action of the Commando patrols was only 250 miles. Three "sabotage sections" were also formed to work on foot or transported by M.T. It was originally intended that the road watching duty in the Mekili-Msus area should be performed by men of the Middle East Commando; but for reasons which are dealt with later this plan had to be abandoned.

On 11 May two patrols of the Long Range Indian Squadron[*] under Capt. Rand and Lieut. Nangle arrived from Syria. Each did a short trip from Siwa to the Trigh el Abd to get accustomed to the local conditions.

[*] I.L.R.S.

Survey.

The Survey Section under Lieut. Lazarus completed during April and May a "car and compass" survey of some 25,000 square miles of country in the area Bir Zelten-Taiserbo-Bir Maaruf (long. 18°40'E. lat. 25°2'N), which was well behind the enemy's lines.

Escape Dumps.

The Heavy Section under Lieut. Arnold in addition to bringing supplies from Mersa Matruh, laid a line of "escape route dumps" of food, water, shoes, etc. westward from Jarabub to Bir Etla (45 miles north of Jalo), a distance of some 200 miles. They were intended for the use of men of the L.R.D.G. who, as happened in one case to T.2 patrol, had to abandon their vehicles and walk home.

Waco aircraft.

The L.R.D.G. "airforce" did not operate during this period. The two "Wacos" had been sent in to Heliopolis to be fitted with new engines, which had to be ordered from America and did not materialize. Another type of engine was tried, which was not powerful enough for the larger of the two planes, but was eventually fitted to the smaller one and worked satisfactorily.

There were at this time a great many cases of burst tyres mainly of the same type, and one mission had to be abandoned in consequence.

Officers.

There were several changes among the senior officers. Major Wilson was posted home, and Capt. Easonsmith took his place as second in command. Major Steele (Commander 'A' Squadron) returned to the N.Z.E.F. and Capt. Morris succeeded him. Lieuts. Wilder and Guild took over command of 'T' and 'R' Patrols respectively.

Tripoli Road Watch, April-May 1942.

The watch on the coast road near the Marble Arch went on without interruption. T.1 did this work from 16 to 28 April, S.1 from 29 April to 22 May and R.2 from 13 May to 26 May. The reports as before covered many pages of foolscap.

The enemy took to laying mines on old L.R.D.G. tracks near Marada and one of S.1's trucks was wrecked, but there were no casualties. The road observers were on two or three occasions seen by Arabs; and in one case an Arab tried to extract money, presumably as blackmail. Though he did not get it, there were no untoward results; but for two days the observers were posted further from the road.

Road Watch Mekili-Msus.

A watch on the Mekili-Msus track was also maintained during the period 28 April to 29 May, from a point a few miles east of Bir el Gerrari, by Y.2, R.1 and T.1 in succession. No traffic was seen, and the only incident worthy of record was the rescue by T.1 (Lieut. Crisp) on 28 May of six men of the crew of a Wellington Bomber which had made a forced landing east of Msus.

On 24 April S.2 patrol which was carrying two Arab agents was shelled from an enemy post at El Haseiat in the Wadi el Faregh about 26 miles S.E. of Jedabia. There were no casualties but the agents appeared to have been much shaken and after an absence of five days produced no information of any value.

G.2 to Bengasi area 2 May 1942.

On 2 May G.2 patrol (Lieut. Hon. R. Gurdon) was ordered to take Capt. Melot, G.(R) and Lieut. Segal, both Intelligence officers, and two Arabs, to Wadi el Gattara, and after dropping them to return to Siwa. This Wadi which is near Sidi Mohammed el Emeilet, (S)S4539, about 37 miles S.E. of Bengasi, was found to be too far south for Capt. Melot's purpose, and he was dropped in the Wadi Ftilia (S)S3555, 15 miles to the N.W. Arrangements were made for him to be picked up again in the same neighbourhood on 4 or 5 June. On the return journey a good many Senussi were seen which was regarded as unfortunate, but there was no incident.

G.1 and T.2 experiment with bombs. 14/15 May 1942.

G.1 patrol (Capt. Timpson) left Siwa on 8 May to try and destroy vehicles on the coastal road between the Marble Arch and Sirte, by placing time bombs in them. If this was not feasible, they were to destroy vehicles in M.T. parks or attack traffic at night near Sirte. T.2 was to be operating with similar orders between Bengasi and Jedabia, and it was desirable that both patrols should begin operations on the night 14/15 May. In his report Capt. Timpson pointed out that in order to place bombs in moving vehicles it was necessary to force them to slow down, and thus give the attacker time to jump out from a covered position at the side of the road, and run up to the rear of the lorry in order to "lob" the bomb in. It had been found at practice that to throw a bomb from some distance at a fast moving vehicle was not only inaccurate, but liable to arouse men in the rear of the vehicle. The patrol carried 45 gallow drums for blocking the road; and in the hope of creating the impression of a stretch of road under repair two long poles were to be put across the drums, and two red lamps were hung on them with the notice "Achtung! Strassenbau".

G.1

The stretch of the road selected was near the Wadi Cahela which runs into the sea about 20 miles N.W. of Ras Lanuf ("Marble Arch"). After a certain amount of reconnaissance, a spot in the road was found where there was a large heap of road metal – a suitable excuse for the road block; and Capt. Timpson went there in a truck with six O.Rs carrying 25 bombs after dark on 14 May. The truck was left 150 yards from the road with the driver and two machine-gunners. Two other ranks armed with a Tommy gun, a rifle and some hand grenades were in position 50 yards from the road. These two parties were to give covering fire. Five drums were placed round the heap of road metal which was shovelled further into the road. The first trucks to pass however did not slow up, and the barrels and stones had to be put further and further into the road; but no one succeeded in getting a bomb into a truck. Attempts were made by a man squatting behind a barrel, but when two or more vehicles passed together he was liable to be shown up by the lights of the second vehicle, and the idea was abandoned. The only alternative position was behind a bank on the side of the road; but in this case the bomb thrower had to go over the bank, jump the ditch and then catch the vehicle up. A third difficulty was the height of the trucks. This entailed throwing the bomb, a rather clumsy missile, whereas it had been intended to drop it.

As no success was achieved by 0200 hrs on the 15th Capt. Timpson decided to try chasing a vehicle in his truck without lights; and Sergeant Fraser sat on the bonnet with a bomb, in readiness to throw it. The first vehicle they followed was found halted in front of the road block, and it was explained by two gesticulating Italians that it had been in tow and that the tow rope had broken. The lights of an approaching vehicle however appeared in the distance so the party was forced to go on to the west; and in spite of a puncture they managed to rejoin the rest of the patrol after daybreak on the 15th.

G.1 attacked 15 May 1942.

It seems that the patrol's presence had by this time become known to the enemy, for at about 1300 hrs on the 15th the sentry saw a lorry come over the ridge about 200 yards away, and gave warning of the approach of hostile troops. The enemy, about 24 in number, had apparently seen the wireless aerial which was raised for the midday call, and got quickly into action with L.M.G. and rifle fire. The patrol's trucks were so well camouflaged with nets and tarpaulins that two minutes elapsed before they opened fire. The enemy, who were Italians, had exposed themselves, and as the patrol's available weapons included two Vickers .303 and three Vickers "K" machine guns, one Browning and one Lewis gun, their enthusiasm and fire soon slackened. With some difficulty the trucks were got out of the Wadi, and by the time the last left it, half an hour after the "incident" started, fire had ceased except for an occasional rifle shot. As the leading truck emerged from the Wadi, about 20 Italians were seen walking slowly away and were fired on at 200 yards range. They fell down flat and made no attempt to return the fire. If the enemy had been more resolute, or had kept up their fire and waited for reinforcements, the patrol might well have been destroyed, for the road was only three miles away and the trucks were in full view as they left the Wadi. Guardsman Matthews, who had been the first to man his weapon, was killed, and was the only casualty.

Attack on road near Sirte 22 May 1942.

On the 16th the Patrol Commander was given permission to attack the road, but it was to be done west of longitude 17°E, that is to say about 100 miles along the road towards Sirte. Information was also given of the location of a petrol dump that had been formed by Capt. Lloyd-Owen. This was searched for on the 17th, but was apparently not found either then or later. By the 19th the patrol had reached a "harbour" from which on 21 May Capt. Timpson proposed to make his raid on traffic near a road-house at longitude 16°57'E; and it was hoped later to find and capture the occupants of a German Staff car west of Buerat el Hsun. One truck, whose brakes were not working, and two men were left behind. About three hours after the start, however, the steering gear of another truck broke down and the raid had to be put off till 22 May. The patrol started once more at 2200 hrs., and on reaching the road cut the telegraph wires. On arriving at the roadhouse they opened fire with everything they had on six large supply trucks parked on both sides of the road. They then went on for half a mile and cut more wires. By this time one truck had gone astray and though it turned up at 0630 hrs next morning time was lost in looking for it. When they approached their original harbour the two men left there with the truck that had damaged brakes, mistook them for the enemy. They took to their heels and two days elapsed before they were found. Eventually the patrol started for home on the 25th with only 32 gallons of water left, and arrived at Siwa on 28 May.

On 8 May Y.1 (Capt. Lloyd-Owen) left Siwa with 3 men of the I.S.L.D. one of whom an alleged Italian "anti-fascist" called Ottavio Martinez, a civilian prisoner of war, had been released for special work. By the time the patrol had reached the neighbourhood of El Hagfet about 20 miles north of Marada so many tyres had burst that it was ordered home. On the way back the Italian escaped and was only recaptured with difficulty. He made the excuse that he was disappointed with the failure of the expedition and wanted to continue the journey on foot. This explanation, however, was not accepted and he was re-interned in Palestine.

S.2 to Jebel el Akhdar 9 May 1942.

On 9 May S.2 (2/Lieut. Olivey) was sent to the area north of Hagfet Gelgaf (S)T.5290, in the foothills of the Jebel-el-Akhdar, to drop a party drawn from a Middle East Commando and the Libyan Arab Force, and also 3 officers of G(R); and to bring back a similar party taken there in April by Y.2 patrol when on its way to watch the Mekili-Msus track. The intention was that the Commando party should carry out the road watch. On 14 May the Commando party previously dropped by Y.2 came in, and reported that the enemy were searching the area. Group H.Q. therefore gave orders that both Commando parties were to return, and they were brought back to Siwa. Experience showed that for lack of knowledge of field craft, and for other reasons the Commando men were not capable of doing the work of road watching. It was therefore decided that the watching of the roads in the Jebel-el-Akhdar area should in future be done by Major Peniakoff of the Libyan Arab Force, helped by officers and W.T. operators of G(R).

G.2 and S.A.S. to Bengasi 15 May 1942.

In the middle of May Major Stirling with three officers[1] and four O.Rs of the S.A.S. Bde, now known as 'L' Detachment S.A.S., made another raid on Bengasi; and were taken there by G.2 patrol under Lieut. the Hon. R. Gurdon. The patrol had the additional task of mining the Barce-Bengasi railway. They left Siwa on 15 May with five 30-cwt trucks of the L.R.D.G. and a Ford utility staff car belonging to the S.A.S. detachment. At 0945 hrs on the 17th while on the march, they met Lieut. Wilder with T.2 patrol, and were told by him that the enemy had been "planting" hostile Arabs in the Jebel-el-Akhdar locality. The route was therefore altered, and the patrol encamped that night in the Wadi-el-Mra. On 19 May, while moving to the west they found and reported a collection of deserted vehicles, including seven carriers, in excellent condition. On the 21st the patrol lay up all day near Haua (S)S.7575, about 45 miles east of Bengasi. At 1730 hrs Major Stirling moved off in the staff car, taking with him two L.R.D.G. trucks with Corporal Wilson and other Guardsmen of G.2 patrol. When he had reached the road from El-Abiar to Bengasi, Major Stirling went on with his S.A.S. party in the staff car to Regima on the escarpment east of Bengasi.

Railway mined near El Abiar 22 May 1942.

Corporal Wilson waited until the moon set at 0100 hrs on the 22nd and then went down on foot to the railway between the stations of Bu Mariam

---

1 Capts. F. Maclean, Alston and R. Churchill.

and Gabr el Gira, seven and ten miles S.W. of El Abiar respectively, taking with him Corporal Bennett, Grenadier Guards and Guardsman Knight. A 40lb. charge of dynamite was put under the rails to be exploded by means of a pressure cap. They waited for Major Stirling until 0345 hrs but he did not return, and they rejoined the rest of the patrol at 0515 hrs. Major Stirling and his party reappeared at 0600 hrs on 23 May. They had spent two nights in Bengasi, and in spite of some encounters with Italians which Colonel Prendergast describes as "Gilbertian", their identity was almost certainly undetected. But for various reasons their intention, which was to sink ships in the harbour and damage the H.Q. of the German Transport Control Staff, could not be carried out. On their way back however they blew up some machinery on the Benina aerodrome. One train passed along the railway but no explosion took place. It was believed that the mine had been detected, as it was unlikely that the cap would fail to work.

The party began its return journey at 1430 hrs on 23 May and drove all the following night. It reached Siwa at 0745 hrs on the 26th.

T.2 to Jedabia-Bengasi road 10 May 1942.

On 10 May T.2 patrol, now under Lieut. N.P. Wilder, left Siwa to make another attack on traffic along the coast road between Jedabia and Bengasi. If possible the attack was to take place on the night 14/15 May and to synchronize with a similar attack by G.1 in the neighbourhood of Sirte which had already been described; and here too the method of using time bombs was to be tried. If this proved impracticable traffic, whether parked or on the move, was to be attacked in the usual way.

By nightfall on 13 May the patrol reached the escarpment 20 miles east of the coast road between Antelat and Esh-Sheledeima. On the 14th they were seen near Bir Belhasen (S)X.5187, 12 miles north of Antelat, by an Arab who acted suspiciously, and possibly by the occupants of a staff car; and therefore moved about ten miles further north to Got Bu Hamida and lay up. Again they came in sight of Arabs who were later seen talking to the occupants of another staff car, and it appeared that their presence had been given away. They therefore moved west across the plain, and struck the Jedabia-Bengasi road about 12 miles S.W. of Soluk. There were few vehicles about, and when drums were placed on the road they went all the faster, but one vehicle moving south was stopped by fire and blown up with bombs. Subsequently a search was made for vehicle parks and for traffic on the road from Msus to Antelat, but without success; and the party then returned to Siwa arriving there on 18 May.

Section XVIII

Rommel resumes offensive 26/27 May 1942.

The sixth phase of the L.R.D.G.'s operations synchronizes with Rommel's resumption of the offensive. After 15 May the enemy grew more active, and air reconnaissances showed that he was preparing the attack which began during the night of 26/27 May. On 26 May Main H.Q. Eighth Army, in a personal letter numbered M8A/18/G(P), sent Lieut.Colonel Prendergast instructions for the future action of the L.R.D.G. which are summarized below.

Eighth Army Instructions 26 May 1942.

1. The "Jebel road watch" (Mekili-Msus) was to continue.
2. Suitable targets for sabotage were to be selected in the Lamluda-El Ghagab area.[1] The time at which they were to be attacked would be fixed by Army H.Q. and then signalled to the Jebel road watch, through G.(R) with a copy to H.Q. L.R.D.G.
3. One L.R.D.G. patrol was to be provided to take a "Buck" party[2] party and Free French paratroops to attack Martuba landing ground (16 miles S.E. of Derna). The patrol was to be ready to leave Siwa on or after 2 June.
4(a). Two Middle East Commando patrols were to "prepare forthwith to proceed to the Maraua area". Their task was to "beat up both roads as energetically as possible and for as long as possible". (The roads in question are the two which run parallel through the Jebel el Akhdar, and are referred to in the note to sub-para 2 above). The Commando patrols were to be guided by a L.R.D.G. patrol into and out of the Jebel el Akhdar; but the latter was not to take part in any offensive

1 Lamluda (S)O.8956 is 28 miles west of Derna and 5 miles west of Giovanni Berta near the junction of the northern and southern roads which run through the Jebel el Akhdar from Berta to Barce. El Ghagab (or Acquaviva) (S)O.7746, is 10 miles W.S.W. of Lamluda on the southern road.
2 Irregulars under Capt. Buck.

action. The Commander, L.R.D.G. was to warn Eighth Army H.Q. at least 48 hours in advance of the "earliest time that the Commandos would be ready to proceed".

4(b). Two further patrols were to be prepared to take Major Stirling's S.A.S. detachment to destroy aircraft on the landing grounds at Berca, Benina and Barce. They would not be required until 2 June, and G.H.Q. had yet to decide whether the S.A.S. operation was to take place or not. If not, the two patrols would be at the disposal of the Commander L.R.D.G.

5. The Tripoli road watch was to be maintained.

6. If the "beat up" referred to in para 3(b) above was successful the Commando patrols were to be prepared to repeat it at short notice.

7. The Commander L.R.D.G. was to "endeavour to maintain during June one patrol always in reserve, ready to obtain specific information in the desert of Cyrenaica".

In accordance with those instructions the Tripoli road watch was maintained by Y.2 from 27 May to 9 June, by S.2 from 10 June to 23 June and by Y.1 from 24 June to 4 July.

In the first of these periods there was no incident, but the report notes that even among eastbound traffic motor vehicles were seen towing other motor vehicles. It was the practice to have lookout men sitting on the loads, but machine guns were not seen except on troop carriers and A.F.Vs. Of trucks going east half were driven by Italians. Traffic almost ceased at night, and vehicles normally moved at distances of half a mile to a mile, except in the case of a complete unit, or of a number of armoured cars.

During S.2's watch 137 tanks mostly Italian, were seen going eastwards. In his report Lieut. Olivey remarks that the "escape dumps" which had been established by the Heavy Section were hard to find, because the panorama sketches of them had been made looking towards the west instead of from the west, which would be the usual point of view of anyone trying to escape to the east!

A great many prisoners of war were seen especially during the early part of the period, and 500 horses were counted going east with native troops.

Y.1 patrol's watch from 26 June to 4 July was uneventful. It was given the further task of attacking traffic on the coast road west of the sixteenth meridian east, but this part of the programme could not be carried out.

Course of Main Battle, May-June 1942.

The course of the main battle up to the middle of June was as follows:-

On the night of 26/27 May, in order to carry out the first two stages of Rommel's plan which were the capture of Bir Hakim and the envelopment of our left flank, the Afrika Corps (15th and 21st Armoured Divisions) passed south of Bir Hakim, and then moved rapidly north towards

Acroma, El Duda and Sidi Rezegh. They were followed by the 90th German Division and the Italian 20th Mobile Corps. The attack on Bir Hakim by the Italian Mobile Corps was beaten off by French troops, and this delayed the enemy's advance which was also engaged successfully by British Armoured Divisions and Heavy Tank Brigades.

On the 27th, our main positions south of Gazala were attacked with little, if any success. Heavy and confused fighting continued for several days; but until 3 June the situation appeared to be in our favour, and although Rommel had forced a gap in our minefields he was having great difficulties with his supplies.

On 3 June however the 150th Brigade of the 50th Division was heavily attacked and overrun, and a counter attack failed with considerable losses. Bir Hakim was then attacked again, and was defended with great tenacity by its French garrison; but on 10 June the garrison was withdrawn. With the forces thus released, the enemy pressed his attack further north in the "Knightsbridge"-El Adem area, and the 1st South African and 50th Divisions had to fall back from their positions south of Gazala, under cover of our armoured divisions. The enemy continued his attack near El Adem on 13 June, and on the 17th General Ritchie decided to withdraw to the El Adem-El Duda area; and to concentrate his main forces towards the Egyptian frontier, leaving what was considered to be an adequate garrison in Tobruk.

Jebel road watch Y.1, 30 May 1942.

The road watch in the Mekili-Msus route was continued until 15 June. From 30 May to 9 June it was undertaken by Y.1. On its way out the patrol carried a party of the Libyan Arab Force under Major Peniakoff, which consisted of three officers and fourteen O.Rs, and dropped them at the road watch position 10 miles south of Baltet ez Zelagh. No traffic was seen.

G.1 9 June 1942.

Y.1 was relieved by G.1 on 9 June. The instructions given to G.1 included information that 'A' Squadron M.E. Commando with 18 vehicles were operating in the road watch area. The patrol was not to initiate any offensive action, but if called upon for assistance by the Commando Squadron it was to do its best to help. No traffic was seen during the period of the watch. On 13 June Group H.Q. sent Capt. Timpson information and orders to the following effect:-

Eighth Army had ordered that two patrols were to go immediately to attack traffic and harass the enemy's L. of C., west of the line (all inclusive) Tmimi-Afrag-Asida. The last named place is at (S)U.3525 in the northern end of the Wadi Mra and about 20 miles east of Bir Tengeder.

The task was to be carried out by G.1 reinforced by R.2 patrol, whose Commander Lieut. Croucher would bring all available information about the enemy. There were no British or Allied troops in the area. It was left to Capt. Timpson to decide whether to use the patrols together or separately, and a cipher was sent for use by both patrols in case the latter course were adopted.

Before dealing with the combined action of G.1 and R.2, it is necessary to go back to the end of May and describe operations carried out earlier by various detachments in the order in which they occurred.

Indian (I) to Bengasi area 30 May 1942.

On 29 May the Commander L.R.D.G. issued orders to the Commander of No. 1 Patrol of the Indian Long Range Squadron (known as Indian I. Patrol) as follows:-

(1) The patrol was to leave Siwa on 30 May 1942 to drop Lieut. Losco and two O.Rs of the I.S.L.D. at Zaueiat Umm-es-Schechaneb ((S)S.5355) about 27 miles S.E. of Bengasi. It was to pick up and if necessary bring back to Siwa Capt. Melot of G(R) who would be either at Umm-es-Schechaneb, or at Sidi Mohammed el Emeilet ((S)S.4539) 13 miles further to the south east, throughout 4 and 5 June.

(2) If Capt. Melot approved, a mine was to be laid on the Barce-Bengasi railway 8 or 9 miles S.W. of El Abiar.

The patrol reached the rendezvous at 0200 hrs (G.M.T.) on 4 June. Capt. Melot was not there but his position – two and a half miles to the north – was reported by two of his Arabs later in the morning. The patrol started for the railway at sunset on the 6th and reached it at Point (S)S.3279 between 8 and 9 miles S.W. of El Abiar, at 0200 hrs (G.M.T.) on the 7th. 10lbs of gelignite were placed under the rails. On the way home they were chased and fired at by five vehicles, but shook off their pursuers and arrived at Siwa on 9 June, bringing Capt. Melot with them.

'A' Squadron M.E. Commando 3 June 1942.

'A' Squadron Middle East Commando organized as H.Q. and two patrols, left Siwa on 3 June to attack transport in the neighbourhood of Barce. The patrols operating separately were successively attacked from the air and lost nearly all their vehicles without achieving any results.

T.1 and T.2 to Jedabia-Bengasi area 4 June 1942.

On 4 June T.1 and T.2 patrols left Siwa together under the command of Capt. Wilder to make attacks on the road and in the area between Jedabia and Bengasi. The party included 2 officers and 30 O.Rs, with ten 30-cwt trucks and two W/T sets. On 7 June Capt. Wilder decided to separate the two patrols. T.1 was to ambush the coast road south of Sidi Ad-el-Magrun

(50 miles north of Jedabia) and T.2 to do likewise between El Magrun and Bengasi, after repairing a truck which had been damaged in a minefield. On the night of 7/8 June T.1 ambushed the enemy four miles south of the landing ground at El-Magrun. One patrol truck and one troop carrying vehicle with 25 to 30 men were destroyed and the enemy had a good many casualties. A few minutes later three ten-ton trucks and a trailer parked by the roadside were also destroyed. Their drivers having heard the firing had abandoned them. T.2 did not operate that night owing to the damaged truck, and no traffic was seen during the night 8/9th.

On 9 June the two patrols encamped about five miles south of Msus; and it was decided that both patrols should attack the blockhouse on the main road near Abd el Aati, (S)X.0982, 36 miles north of Jedabia. Under orders from Group H.Q. this attack was postponed to the night of the 10/11th. On reaching the escarpment some miles east of the road, the patrols ran into a hostile patrol in a 3-ton truck. After a short fight one officer and five men were taken prisoner, and two of the enemy were killed. T.2 was then sent back to Siwa with the prisoners, and T.1 returned two days later after laying mines on the road south of Saunnu, and reached Siwa 2030 hrs on 14 June.

G.2 and S.A.S. to Benina 8 June 1942.

On 8 June G.2 patrol (Lieut. Hon. R. Gurdon) left Siwa to convey parties of 'L' detachment S.A.S. commanded by Major Stirling, to the Benina-Berca area and to bring them back on completion of their tasks. The information given in the group instruction shows that no less than eight detachments of the L.R.D.G., or under its command, were operating in much the same area; and Lieut. Gurdon was told that if he required assistance urgently G.1 patrol which was near Bir Belamed (S)T.5735, could be asked to give it. The party consisted of 33 of all ranks of whom 3 officers and 10 other ranks belonged to 'L' detachment S.A.S.; and there were seven 30-cwt Chevrolet trucks, and Major Stirling's Ford utility car. The S.A.S. detachment worked in three parties, one of which was French and commanded by 2/Lieut. Zirneld. On 9 June the patrol met Indian (I) Patrol bringing back Capt. Melot. G.2's experiences on 10 and 11 June exemplify the dangers of minefields in the now much frequented tracks, and the mechanical difficulties that had to be faced. On the 10th Major Stirling's car hit a "thermos bomb" and was put out of action and "G.11" truck split a brake drum. It was therefore decided to send some of the party back to Siwa with G.11 and another 30-cwt truck. On the 11th another truck (G.7) hit a thermos bomb, and had for the time being to be abandoned. Nevertheless at 1930 hrs that evening the party reached Gasr-el-Gehesh ((S)S.2361) on the escarpment near Regima, and the S.A.S. parties were dropped there. The patrol then moved back to harbour in a wadi 4 miles

N.W. of Zauiet-umm-esh-Shechaneb ((S)S.3255) at which place the S.A.S. parties were to rendezvous on their return.

On 13 June Major Stirling and his party returned safely at 1100 hrs, and on the 14th Capt. Mayne brought in the rest of the S.A.S. detachment, except Corporal Warburton who was missing. At 1700 hrs on the 15th the patrol again moved, and reached Haua-ben-Chesciar ((S)S.7474) at 0800 hrs on the 16th. At 1745 hrs on the same day two trucks were taken to the El Abiar-Bengasi road. One carried Major Stirling and the men of 'L' detachment S.A.S., the other Lieut. Gurdon and 7 O.Rs of the L.R.D.G. At Regima Major Stirling dropped his French party which was to raid one of the Berca aerodromes, and he himself went on to raid Bengasi. Lieut. Gurdon and his party mined the railway about Point (S)S.3279 with 50lbs of ammonal; and then made contact with the French. The two parties waited for Major Stirling until 0330 hrs on the 17th, 15 minutes later than the agreed time. As he did not appear, they returned to Haua, and lay up until the late afternoon. At 1700 hrs the patrol moved off for Zauiet-Umm-es-Shechaneb which had been agreed on as a secondary rendezvous, and slept in the open on the way. Early next morning "a hostile aircraft, possibly a M.E.110, nearly surprised the patrol at breakfast, and systematically quartered the surrounding country". Local Senussi reported an Italian post in the neighbourhood, and as this was confirmed by Group H.Q., the patrol harboured in the Wadi Ptilia just east of Umm-es-Shechaneb. Lieut. Gurdon and two O.Rs went on to the rendezvous where they found Major Stirling and his party in a cave. At 1700 hrs they moved S.E. to Bir el Gueisa, (S)S.5941, for the night. At midday 19 June they met Major Eason-smith, the Group's second in command, at a prearranged rendezvous, and with G.7 truck which had struck a mine on the outward journey in tow, they continued their homeward march. They arrived at Siwa two days later.

The results of the expedition were by no means inconsiderable though the raid on one of the Berca landing grounds on the night of 12/13 June was seriously hampered by an ill-timed attack made on it at 2315 hrs on the 12th by the R.A.F. At Benina Major Stirling's party set three hangars on fire and destroyed a number of aircraft and 2/Lieut. Zirneld's party destroyed eleven aircraft and killed fifteen men on the other aerodrome at Berca. The charge of ammonal placed on the railway was seen to explode some hours later. During his raid on Bengazi itself on the night of the 16/17th, Major Stirling and his party destroyed a number of petrol dumps, and other stores.

S.1 to Barce 8 June 1942.

A similar operation at the same time was carried out by S.1 patrol (Capt. Holliman) with 14 O.Rs of the L.R.D.G., and a Free French party of five of all ranks of 'L' detachment S.A.S., commanded by Lieut. Jacquier.

Leaving Siwa on 8 June they reached Cheda-bu-Maun ((S)S.8571) in the evening of the 10th. Two trucks went forward on the 11th taking the 'L' detachment party to (S)N.8405, a point about 11 miles S.E. of Barce; and thence the S.A.S. men and three O.Rs of the L.R.D.G. went on foot to the escarpment overlooking Barce. There they captured a Libyan soldier and sent him back to the trucks. The aircraft on Barce landing ground were so well guarded that it was impossible to do any damage to them, but a bomb dump was destroyed. The two trucks then returned to Cheda-bu-Maun and a plan was made for an attack on the railway north of El Abiar. Two trucks and six men of the L.R.D.G. accordingly set out and on the way met some Senussi who told them of an Italian camp at Ain Gebara ((S)S.5878). This place is on the road to El Abiar, and the going off the road was so bad that the trucks could not avoid it by moving across country. It was therefore decided to enter the camp and do as much damage as possible with the few bombs available. Here again, however, the vigilance of the sentries defeated the raiders who were compelled to abandon their project. The patrol then returned to Siwa arriving on 17 June.

R.1 and S.A.S. to Martuba and Derna.

The third mission in cooperation with 'L' Detachment S.A.S. was undertaken by R.1 patrol under Capt. A.I. Guild. The patrol consisting of 1 officer and 12 O.Rs of the L.R.D.G. left Siwa on 8 June and carried with them Lieut. Jordan and 14 (French) O.Rs of 'L' detachment S.A.S. and Capt. Buck with 14 "bogus Germans". The latter were Palestinian Jews of German origin who wore German uniforms, used German vehicles and were employed on special missions. Capt. Buck was to be in command not only of his own men but also of the S.A.S. detachment; and was to be conducted by the patrol as far as Hagfet Gelgaf (S/T.5290), whence his party would operate independently. The patrol was then to move south, lie up and await their return. Capt. Buck's objectives were the landing grounds at Martuba and Derna. His party was actually dropped 10 miles north of Baltet-ez-Zelagh (S)T.6555, on 11 June and it was arranged that the patrol would await their return until the evening of the 18th. On 14 June, under instructions from Group H.Q. the patrol picked up four men of the R.A.F. and two Libyans, at a rendezvous given them by G.1 patrol which was road watching in the neighbourhood.

The attack on the aerodromes was only partially successful for it was betrayed by one of the Palestinians. The whole of the French party was captured, but not until they had destroyed about 20 planes; and later Lieut. Jordan who spoke German perfectly contrived to bluff the sentries in charge of him and escaped. The remainder of Capt. Buck's party were duly picked up on 15 June and brought back to Siwa. It is interesting to read in

Capt. Guild's report, that on 14 June his party saw the destruction by aircraft about five miles away, of the lorries of 'A' Squadron M.E. Commando which as described earlier were operating in the same area. They themselves were well concealed and therefore not detected.

These attacks on the enemy's landing grounds, like others made at various times, were not haphazard operations. They were in this case part of an extensive plan to assist the arrival of a convoy at Malta by reducing the scale of the enemy's air attacks; and similar attacks were made elsewhere at the same time.

Indian (2) to Jalo-Jedabia road, 11 June 1942.

"Indian (2) Patrol" under Lieut. A. Nangle watched the road from Jalo to Jedabia during the period 11 to 18 June in the hope of ambushing a convoy and capturing prisoners, but no traffic was seen.

As already related (on pages 149–50) Capt. Timpson while carrying out a road watch with G.1 patrol along the Mekili-El Gerrari-Msus track, received an instruction from Group H.Q. for a new task to be carried out in cooperation with R.2 patrol under Lieut. Croucher, which joined him on 14 June. The substance of this instruction has also been given.

G.1 and R.2 to Derna area, 14 June 1942.

The first objective of the two patrols was the track running N.N.W. from Afrag ((S)U.6995) to El Carmusa ((S)U.2835), the latter place being some 20 miles S.W. of Derna. This track was reported to be used as a main supply route but was found to have no tracks fresher than a week old. Capt. Timpson then decided to attack the coast road. Natives reported a camp of the enemy in the Wadi el Maalegh south and S.W. of the Martuba landing grounds, and another near the coast road north of Tmimi. The spot finally chosen for the attack was near Sidi Scisher Ruhai. This point, S(O)9338, is about three miles south of the coast road at Giovanni Berta. It is on a track which after running westward for several miles from El Carmusa, turns north to Giovanni Berta, and was said to be used intermittently during day-time. The date chosen for the raid was the night of 18/19 June. The two patrols reached the main road at 2000 hrs and formed up on the south side of it, R.2 on the eastern flank and G.1 on the western. The plan was that after the first vehicles to arrive had been destroyed R.2 should move east and G.1 west and attack traffic as it came along. No traffic appeared until about 2100 hrs when two Italian lorries arrived with trailers carrying M.13 tanks. Both lorries were stopped and prisoners were taken. Capt. Timpson inspected the vehicles and having done so found that he had lost touch with R.2 patrol, and in his own words, "At about 9.45 p.m. a civil war developed, G.1 and R.2 shooting each other up, without casualties, but spoiling the party!" He also states in his report that, as he heard later, Major Peniakoff and a party of the L.A.F. had raided a petrol dump on the previous night, which might account for the scarcity of enemy vehicles. If this was so, it is at least a proof that patrol operations behind the enemy's front were upsetting transport arrangement on his lines of communication.

On the 19th the patrol received orders to return to Siwa and arrived there on 22 June.

T.2 to Jebel el Akhdar 19 June 1942.

The last patrol operation in this phase took place between 19 and 25 June and was carried out by T.2 patrol under Lieut. J.E. Crisp. His orders were:
(a) To pick up at Bir Hanascia ((S)T.7298), a wounded airman who had "baled out" after a raid on Bengasi and after being looked after by local Arabs, had found his way to Major Peniakoff's party.
(b) To take up to the Jebel el Akhdar 12 men of the Libyan Arab Force under Capt. Grandguillot, who was to set up an organization for helping British airmen, prisoners of war and others to return to our lines.

This operation was successfully accomplished without incident, and the patrol returned to Siwa on 25 June.

The enemy crosses the Egyptian Frontier, 23 June 1942.

The fall of Tobruk on 21 June 1942 was followed by a further German advance, and by 30 June the Eighth Army stood on a line extending southwards from the coast at El Alamein to the Qattara Depression, which effectively covered its left flank.

L.R.D.G. withdrawn from Siwa 23-29 June 1942.

The Germans had crossed the Egyptian frontier on 23 June and their advance made Siwa no longer tenable as the H.Q. of the L.R.D.G. It was therefore decided that 'A' Squadron L.R.D.G. should be sent to Kufra, and that the remainder of the Group should go to the Eighth Army area, that is to say the Nile Valley. The movements of the patrols to their new destinations were somewhat complicated and took a considerable time; but there is no necessity to deal with them in detail.

The evacuation of Siwa had many disadvantages. Although an unhealthy place, it was an excellent base for patrol operations in Libya, and after it had been evacuated the only westward route open to patrols was through the El Alamein lines, or across the very bad going in the Qattara Depression. It must be remembered too that the Tripoli road watch was still being maintained, from a point nearly 800 miles "as the crow flies" from Cairo, and 600 miles from Kufra; and it was not until 21 July that it was finally cancelled by G.H.Q. Middle East. At about this time 'A' and 'C'

Squadrons of the Middle East Commando which had been under command of the H.Q. L.R.D.G. since April, were withdrawn and took no further part in L.R.D.G. operations.

Section XIX

Seventh Phase July-September 1942.

The Seventh Phase began with the withdrawal of the L.R.D.G. from Siwa during the last week of June 1942, and ended on 30 September, when the L.R.D.G. ceased to be under the Eighth Army and reverted to the direct command of G.H.Q. Middle East.

On 29 June the group was disposed as follows:-

Group H.Q. near Alexandria.

'A' Squadron H.Q. at Cairo.

G.1 and G.2 Patrols near Alexandria.

R.1 Patrol en route to Tripoli road watch.

R.2 Patrol en route from Siwa to Kufra.

S.1 Patrol en route from Siwa to Eighth Army area.[1]

S.2 Patrol en route from Tripoli road watch.

T.1 in Cairo.

T.2 en route from Siwa to Kufra.

Y.1 at Tripoli road watch.[2]

Y.2 near Alexandria.

Group H.Q. had left Siwa on 23 June and later camped at Kom Aushin in the Fayoum district south of Cairo. H.Q. 'A' Squadron moved to Kufra by Cairo and the Kharga oasis, and was eventually joined there by R.1, R.2, S.2 and T.2 patrols.

S.A.S. activities.

The chief events of the period were a series of operations in conjunction with Major Stirling's 'L' detachment of S.A.S. behind the enemy's position. At the end of June Major Stirling was preparing a force from 'L' detachment to operate west of the El Alamein position. He was now acquiring transport of his own, but his men were not yet fully proficient in naviga-

---

1 See page 155.
2 See page 148.

tion and the use of W/T, and the L.R.D.G. patrols in addition to taking part in the raids, provided navigators and signallers.

As already stated the Tripoli road watch at the "Marble Arch" was continued until 21 July and will be dealt with first.

R.1 on Tripoli road watch 4 July 1942.

R.1 patrol (Capt. Guild) left Siwa in the afternoon of the 26th and relieved Y.1 patrol on the coastal road on 4 July. Capt. Guild's report noted that the traffic was mostly Italian and well camouflaged; for instance, canvas covers were left loose and allowed to flap, which destroyed the outline of the load and made observation difficult; and the windows of buses were painted so that their occupants could not be seen. The report included useful sketches of new types of vehicles armoured and otherwise, and covered 25 pages.

Throughout the period great difficulty was experienced in communicating with Group H.Q., and with H.Q. 'A' Squadron at Kufra; and batteries had to be charged for as much as five hours a day to obtain enough power to get through. Tyres again gave trouble; and the men suffered a good deal from desert sores and, towards the end of the period, from "desert weariness", or "cafard" as the French call it.

R.1 was relieved by T.2 in the evening of 19 July, and arrived at Kufra without incident on the 23rd.

T.2.

T.2 left Kufra on 12 July and after watching the road for one day received orders on the 21st to the effect that the road watch was cancelled, and that the patrol was to attack traffic west of longitude 18°15'E, which cuts the coastal road 20 miles N.W. of the "Marble Arch".

On the night of 22 July the patrol lay up near Point (X)A.6580. They stopped a motor cyclist and a 10-ton Alfa-Romeo truck with a trailer, with the result that the enemy lost three men killed or mortally wounded, and two wounded. One of the latter was a civilian, the other, an Italian, was taken prisoner. The truck and trailer, and the motor cycle were destroyed. Owing to lack of petrol the patrol was unable to make a second attack and had to return to Kufra.

The Tripoli road had been under continuous observation at the same place since 2 March except for one or two breaks of a few hours. The information obtained enabled the Intelligence branch at G.H.Q. to form an idea of the extent of the enemy's activities, and was of considerable value. When the enemy began to use the harbour at Tobruk, as well as Bengasi, the importance of the road watch in Tripoli diminished, but the General Staff hoped to start a similar watch on the road east of Tobruk, which will be referred to later.

G.2 and Y.2 operate behind the enemy's lines, 1 July 1942.

On 1 July 1942 G.1 and Y.2 patrols left Dekheila Camp, near Alexandria, with orders to attack enemy M.T. convoys, particularly lorries carrying water and petrol. The boundaries given to them were as follows:-

(a) G.1 patrol.   West-long. 27°30'E.
                   East-El Alamein line.
(b) Y.2 patrol.   West-unlimited.
                   East-long. 27°30'E.

Long. 27°30'E is about 80 miles west of the El Alamein position which is approximately parallel to the meridian. On completion of the task the patrols were to return to Cairo by the Qattara Depression, unless otherwise ordered.

Y.2.

Y.2 moved westward through the British position on the El Alamein line by a route that was slightly north of the Qattara Depression, and passed through the battle area without incident. On 3 July the patrol's original orders were cancelled and it was ordered to go to Qaret Tartura and await the arrival of G.1 patrol and a party of 'L' detachment S.A.S. Qaret Tartura (long. 27°E. lat. 30°15'N.) is on the north western edge of the Qattara Depression, and about 80 miles south of Mersa Matruh on the road from that place to Siwa. It is somewhat west of long. 27°30'E which was originally to be the operational boundary between the two patrols.

G.1.

G.1 started by the same route as Y.2, but when trying to pass through the British line came under artillery and other fire from our own troops and had to go back. It then moved along the northern edge of the Qattara Depression, but owing to the difficulty of the ground had to go as far south as Qara (long. 26°30'E. lat. 29°35'N.), 60 miles N.E. of Siwa on the Mersa Matruh-Siwa road, in order to reach Qaret Tartura to which it also had been directed. The two patrols and the S.A.S. detachment and also G.2 patrol concentrated at Qaret Tartura on 6 July.

G.1, Y.2 and S.A.S. to coast road 6 July 1942.

The whole force then came under Major Stirling's orders, and less G.2 patrol which is dealt with later, set off to attack the coast road between Galal[1] and Fuka, which are 50 and 57 miles west of El Alamein respectively.

---

1   At 810316. Sheet El Daba 1:250,000. G.S.G.S. No. 4386.

After a march of more than 60 miles through the enemy's "back areas" the force reached a point just south of the railway which was chosen as a rallying point, and then split up.

Y.2.

Y.2 was located west of Galal, but saw no traffic. It then returned to the rendezvous with 'L' detachment who had joined it during the return journey. Next morning a force of tanks which they could not identify passed them within a mile. During the night of 9/10 July a hostile plane spotted their position and a move was made to Bir el Quseir (841281) about 25 miles S.E. of Galal.

On 11 July Y.2 patrol left Bir el Quseir with a party of 'L' detachment S.A.S. to attack landing grounds and the road in the neighbourhood of Fuka. Three aircraft were destroyed during the night on landing ground 68, but one truck which fell into a hole in the dark had to be abandoned. On the 13th July Y.2 patrol received orders to return to its base escorting three 3-ton trucks and a staff car belonging to 'L' detachment. On the way they were attacked from the air, and the staff car and one S.A.S. truck were destroyed, but the remainder of the journey was accomplished without incident.

G.1.

On the first night of the operations G.1 was ordered to take two S.A.S. parties under Major Schott and Capt. Warr to attack the landing grounds 121 and 05, which lie just south of the coast road and a few miles east of Sidi Barrani. It appears that Major Stirling was under the impression that the enemy were about to retire, as he gave orders that the landing grounds were not to be attacked unless they had a considerable number of aircraft on them; his assumption being that they might fill up later as the enemy retired.

The patrol marched to a Wadi in the escarpment east of Sofafi (569333) about 30 miles S.S.W. of Sidi Barrani, and on the way found a dump of about 3,000 gallons of petrol which they appropriated. Next evening the two S.A.S. parties were dropped within four miles of their respective objectives, and Capt. Timpson left two of his men to observe the water-point at Km post 101 (on the main road in square 5937), formerly used by the British forces, with a view to raiding it later. Capt. Schott returned the following evening having found that landing ground 121 was unused. Capt. Warr did not reappear till three nights later. Landing ground 05 was used in daytime only by a ferry service of Ju 52's and was closely guarded.

Meanwhile Capt. Timpson had received orders to raid the road. An attempt to reach the area of Buq Buq had to be given up owing to bad going, and another point was selected; but no sign of the enemy was seen.

The water-pipe lines which were working at full pressure were blown up and the patrol then returned by Qara to its base in the Fayoum. The Sheikh of Qara told Capt. Timpson that the enemy were not in Siwa.

G.2 and S.A.S. 3 July 1942.

G.2 patrol (Lieut. Hon. R. Gurdon) which had also been given orders to work under Major Stirling, was to operate against the enemy's L. of C. and landing grounds west of the El Alamein line; and it left camp near Alexandria on 3 July. Major Stirling and his party went with the patrol. They met G.1 and Y.2 patrols at Qaret Tartura on 6 July, having been to H.Q. Eighth Army on the way. On 7 July they moved to the Fuka area, Major Stirling being still with them. The plan was that while the S.A.S. party raided the El Daba landing grounds, G.2 patrol was to attack the road at 0130 hrs on the 8th. Owing to mechanical trouble three lorries had to return to the rendezvous at Qaret Hireimis (731269) about 50 miles south of Mersa Matruh; but Lieut. Gurdon with the remainder piloted the S.A.S. party to the starting point for their attack on the landing grounds which was fairly successful.

After dropping the S.A.S. party Lieut. Gurdon, with a party carried in two trucks, reconnoitred the roads in the immediate vicinity of Fuka station, and at 0130 on 8 July he began his attack. A vehicle park was first dealt with and there was no opposition. The party then fired at a large tanker and at a number of tents and huts. Again there was no opposition; and the party rejoined its remaining vehicles at the rendezvous at 1030 hrs. The other parties returned later including Y.2 patrol, and lay up in the hills. Unfortunately Y.2 had been seen from the air and the force had to move next morning. A harbour was selected near the western face of the escarpment about point 700275. The vehicles were dispersed there, and the crews rested throughout 10 July.

Lieut. Gurdon killed 12 July 1942.

In the evening of 11 July G.2 patrol started with a French party of the S.A.S. under Lieut. Martin to raid a landing ground near the coast at Fuka. Next day, while on the way to Minqar Sida (787627) the patrol was attacked by three Macchi aircraft. Lieut. Gurdon was mortally wounded and died next day: and Guardsman Murray was badly hit. One truck was destroyed, and the raid had to be abandoned.

T.1 to Qara-Mersa Matruh road 7 July 1942.

The fourth patrol to take part in operations under Major Stirling's orders at the beginning of July 1942 was T.1 (Capt. Wilder). Its original orders were to attack traffic on the coast road between the Egyptian frontier and Tobruk, and it left the Fayoum on 7 July. On the 9th however these orders were cancelled, and it was told to report to Major Stirling at Bir el Quseir (689283). Finding it impossible to pass through the El Alamein lines the patrol marched through the Qattara Depression, and reached the rendezvous on 12 July. Major Stirling had to go to Cairo that night, and while awaiting his return a road watch was organized on the "barrel route" between Fuka and Sidi Haneish (757328), about 18 miles along the coast road to the W.N.W. The watch was maintained from 14 to 19 July, but there was practically no traffic on the road. The enemy's aircraft however were very active. Major Stirling returned on 23 July. On 26 July T.1 patrol with a detachment of S.A.S. troops attacked landing grounds 12 and 13 in the neighbourhood of the Mersa Matruh-Qara road, and lost a truck in a minefield. The attack on the landing grounds was very successful, and 36 planes (all German) were destroyed before the patrol withdrew. Next morning at 0800 hrs about long. 27°15'E. lat 30°30'N, near Qaret Hiremas, part of the patrol was attacked by aircraft one of which was shot down, and also by six trucks, four of which were carrying infantry. The patrol had previously split up, and the only three trucks available to fight gradually withdrew and shook the enemy off. The march continued throughout the night of 27/28 July and the patrol reached its base on the early morning of the 29th.

Between 11 and 20 July S.2 and R.2 patrols were employed in transporting officers and O.Rs of G(R), of the I.S.L.D. (Interservice Liaison Department) and of what was known as the "Popski" party[1] to and from the Bengazi area. These missions were successfully accomplished, but once more many burst tyres were reported during the journey of 1,450 miles.

On 12 July in response to an urgent request from Major Stirling, Lieut. Lazarus and Lieut. Arnold, with four 3-tonners of the Heavy Section took petrol, food and ammunition from Cairo (Mena) to Qaret Tartura (7136, 2294). They reached this place on the 15th and returned to Mena without incident. The journey was made across the Qattara Depression.

While Major Stirling was at Cairo he received an Instruction from H.Q. Eighth Army (No. 99, dated 16 July), a copy of which was sent to the Commander L.R.D.G. He was ordered to discuss with Colonel Prendergast the formations of a base at Qara on the N.W. edge of the Qattara Depression; and was given the order of priority of objectives for raiding as tank workshops, tanks, aircraft, water, petrol. He was further told to prepare for future operations as follows:-

(a) The formation of a traffic block at Sollum on the coastal road. This block was to be held until a party of Royal Marines had been landed to exploit the situation and maintain the block for 48 hours.

---

1 A band of Arab irregulars under Major Peniakoff, a Polish Officer whose "cover name" was "Popski"; also known as "P.P.A." or "Popski's private Army".

(b) A second detachment was to block Halfaya, and keep the road closed for 48 hours. The action of this detachment was to be coordinated with that of the detachment which made the block at Sollum.

(c) He was also to be prepared to "initiate traffic blocks on the coast road at Garawla and Bagush", which are respectively 12 and 30 miles S.E. of Mersa Matruh.

A copy of this Instruction was also sent to G.H.Q. Middle East. On 17 July D.D.M.I., G.H.Q. sent his remarks on the Instruction to H.Q. Eighth Army, and a copy of them to the L.R.D.G. He considered that a base at Qara would be insecure, and said that arrangements were being worked out by the R.A.F. for dropping or landing supplies required by Major Stirling. He did not think the proposed joint action with the Royal Marines (as suggested in sub-para (a) above) was feasible. Synchronization would be difficult and "handing over" virtually impossible. He recommended that the block should be formed by Major Stirling, and that when he was clear of the area the R.A.F. should "do the rest".

Y.1 to Gambut area, 20 July 1942.

On 20 July Y.1 patrol (Capt. Lloyd-Owen) was given orders to watch the coast road between 450 and 490 Eastings, which is a stretch of some 25 miles midway between Bardia and Tobruk, and just north of Gambut (462412). The patrol was to be relieved after 10 days. It was found however that a watch on this part of the road was impossible owing to the open nature of the country; and after picking up an Indian soldier of the 3/2nd Punjab Regiment and making an unsuccessful search for the crew of a Blenheim that had been lost near Tobruk, the patrol returned home.

Y.2 and G.2 to Qara and Umm-es-Schechaneb.

On 4 August Capt. W.B. Kennedy-Shaw, M.B.E., Intelligence Officer of the L.R.D.G. left the Fayoum with Y.2 patrol (Capt. Hunter) and G.2 patrol under Lieut. K. Sweeting, Coldstream Guards, who had succeeded to the command after the death of the Hon. R. Gurdon. Capt. Shaw's task was to get in touch with the Sheikh of Qara, to get from him all possible information of the enemy's movements, and to arrange that he should give us warning if the enemy occupied Qara.

The patrols were:-

(a) To drop four men of the I.S.L.D. with a W/T set and 750 pounds of gear, in the Regima area about (S)S.2270, and arrange to pick them up again at a later date.

(b) To go on to Point T.8989 in the Wadi Belater about 15 miles west of Mekili, and deliver two million lire to Major Peniakoff; and to bring back Capt. Chapman and such other members of the party as Major Peniakoff might wish to send, up to a total of thirty.

The party crossed the Qattara Depression and reached Qara on 6 August. Capt. Shaw remained there for the rest of the day, and then returned home.

Y.2 and G.2 continued in company till the morning of 7 August when they parted at the top of the Naqb el Ahmar (643143). Marching by Hatiet el Etla (395276), where G.2 remained until Y.2's return, and the Wadi Mra, Y.2 patrol dropped the I.S.L.D. party at Umm es Schechaneb on 11 August. Major Peniakoff's party were duly found and twenty of them were taken on board for the return journey on 13 August. On the march back a petrol and ammunition dump was found and destroyed in square (S)U.64, near Garet Meriem on the Trigh Capuzzo, sometimes known as "Trigh Enver Bey". Y.2 rejoined G.2 on 16 August at Hatiet el Etla where orders were received for both patrols to go to Kufra, and they arrived there on 20 August. Some useful information was obtained as to the enemy's posts, and it was established that Mekili was not occupied by the enemy.

On 24 August G.2 received orders to return to the Fayoum and arrived there on the 29th.

T.2 to Bir Gahau July 1942.

At the end of July T.2 patrol now commanded by Lieut. J.R. Talbot took Capt. Grandguillot and three O.Rs of the L.A.F. to Bir Gahau ((S)S6647). The journey both ways was uneventful, but in his report Lieut. Talbot writes that on 2 August a fog from daybreak to 0800 hrs reduced visibility to 300 yards. He reported also a high percentage of burst tyres.

R.1 to Tarhuna 29 August 1942.

On 29 August R.1 (Capt. Guild) left Kufra with Lieut. Losco and three O.Rs of the I.S.L.D. for Tarhuna (R)L8917, or as near to it as possible. This place lies some 40 miles in a direct line S.E. of Tripoli, and the journey was therefore a very long one. There was but little reliable information about the country west of the Hon-Misurata road, and the patrol commander was told to bring back a "going" map, of this area in particular. He was also warned that Tarhuna was a large place and that there would probably be defences in the neighbourhood. In his report on the operation Capt. Guild describes his destination as Giafara, probably El Giaafra, which lies some 25 miles S.W. of Tarhuna.

On 24 August the patrol camped five miles east of the Hon-Misurata road, and the road was crossed next morning. The going on the west of the road was so bad and the tyre position so serious that Capt. Guild after discussing the question with Lieut. Losco, decided to leave two of his four trucks in the Wadi el Chobir, (W)C.09, about 30 miles west of Bu Njem on the Hon-Misurata road, and to drop the I.S.L.D. party at Bir Talah (long. 14°27'E. lat. 31°37'N.) which is about 75 miles S.E. of Tarhuna and about the same distance E.S.E. of El Giaafra. Having done so, and arranged a rendezvous, he returned with his two trucks to the Wadi el Chebir where the other two had been left.

On his way back to Kufra Capt. Guild had to send a message asking for fresh tyres, and did not reach the base until 31 August. He produced a detailed report on the "going", which was better on the more easterly route by which he made his return journey.

D.M.O's Conference 23 August 1942.

On 23 August the D.M.O. (Brig. G.M.O. Davy) held a conference at G.H.Q. which was attended by Lieut.Colonel Prendergast, and by Major Freeland representing 'L' detachment S.A.S.

The object of the conference was to decide on the best system of coordinating the enterprises of the various organizations, which included not only the L.R.D.G. and S.A.S., but also the I.S.L.D., the L.A.F., the surviving Commando detachments and the "military portion of G(R)".

The D.M.O. said that there were two alternatives –

(1) to have a Staff Officer at G.H.Q. (D.M.O's Branch) whose duty would be to coordinate the various operations,

(2) for all raiding forces to be under a single Controller at G.H.Q., who would control all raiding operations, and advise on the composition of the forces employed. This scheme would necessitate a special signals organization.

Lieut.Colonel Prendergast preferred that things should be left as they were, though he agreed that there should be a Staff Officer at G.H.Q. responsible for planning and coordination. Control was particularly necessary in the case of operations by the L.R.D.G. and 'L' detachment S.A.S.

The D.M.O. then proposed –

(a) That the L.R.D.G. should be primarily responsible for carrying personnel of the various organizations, and for long distance reconnaissance. The destruction of long range targets would be a subsidiary role.

(b) That 'L' detachment should be used for the destruction and sabotage of close range targets; by stealth if possible, but by force if necessary. Reconnaissance was not their duty.

(c) The military portion of G(R) should not undertake reconnaissance as such, for this was the work of the I.S.L.D. Nevertheless, they could gather much useful information incidentally, and should of course report it.

Colonel Prendergast agreed, as also did Major Freeland, who however pointed out that until 'L' detachment had its own signals it would have to rely on the L.R.D.G. for intercommunication.

It was also agreed that "Folbot" (folding boat) parties should be under the command of 'L' detachment S.A.S. Colonel Prendergast then recommended that Headquarters L.R.D.G. should be at Kufra, and the D.M.O. replied that this point, and the question of the L.R.D.G. coming under direct control of G.H.Q., were under consideration.

Posting of Officers August 1942.

During August 1942 there were further changes among the officers. Capt. Holliman returned to the R.T.R. and Lieut. Lazarus took over S.1. Lieut. H.K. Sweeting as already stated took over G.2 after Lieut. Gurdon was killed. Lieut. Crisp returned to the N.Z.E.F., and Lieuts. Talbot and Cramond joined. Capt. Cranfield was succeeded as adjutant by Capt. Poole. Lieut. Croucher took over the L.R.D.G. office at Cairo.

The smaller of the two "Waco" aircraft was returned to service after extensive repairs; and the unit acquired a number of "jeeps" then in the experimental stage, and some 80-gallon petrol carrying trailers.

Section XX

By the middle of August 1942 the fronts of both armies had stabilized on the El Alamein position and the general situation was as follows:-

General Situation.

Shortly after the Prime Minister's visit to the Eighth Army in the first week of August, General the Hon. H. Alexander succeeded General Auchinlech as G.O.C.-in-C., Middle East, and General Montgomery became G.O.C. Eighth Army. The Army was reinforced by the 44th and 51st Divisions from England, and two new Armoured Divisions, the 8th and 10th, also became available. Rommel too had received reinforcements of German infantry and artillery, but owing the attacks by the Royal Navy and the R.A.F. he was in difficulties with his supplies. Nevertheless he was determined to take the offensive once more, and did so on the night of 31 August/1 September 1942. By the morning of 3 September it was clear that his attack had failed, and he began a withdrawal to the line Deir el Angar – Deir el Munasib – Himeimat. Except for small and successful operations by the Queen's Royal Regiment at Deir el Munasib on 3 September, by the Royal Sussex Regiment on 5 October, and by the Greek Brigade on 6 October, the situation on the main front remained unchanged until the Eighth Army attack from the El Alamein position on 23 October.

Operations "Bigamy", "Agreement", "Nicety", September 1942.

In August Rommel was receiving the bulk of his supplies through Bengazi and Tobruk; and G.H.Q. Middle East therefore planned simultaneous operations against the enemy's L. of C. at those two places and also at Barce; and a third operation was to be an attack a few days later on Jalo.

"Bigamy".

The attack on Bengazi known as "Operation Bigamy" was to be carried out by 'X' Force under Lieut.Colonel D. Stirling, which included detachments of the Royal Navy and S.A.S., a folding boat detachment of the

167

"Special Boat Section"[1] and S.1 and S.2 patrols of the L.R.D.G.

Its object was to block the harbour, sink shipping and destroy oil storage facilities and pumping plant. An attack on Benina landing ground was to be made at the same time.

The attack on Barce was to be made by G.1 and T.1.

"Agreement".

The attack on Tobruk which had similar objects, included naval cooperation from the sea and an attack from the landward side was to be made by 'B' Force[*] which included Y.1 patrol. The code name of this operation was "Agreement".

"Nicety".

The attack on Jalo, known as "Operation Nicety" was to be made by a detachment of the Sudan Defence Force from the garrison at Kufra, and Y.2 patrol was to take part in it. The object of the capture of Jalo was to use it as a base for subsequent operations by Lieut.Colonel Stirling's 'X' Force against the enemy's L. of C., and it was to be held for three weeks, unless attacked by very superior forces.

In all these operations the patrols were responsible for navigating the forces to which they were attached, but they also took a share in the fighting.

Operations "Bigamy" and "Agreement" were to take place on the night of D.1/D.2. Giolo was to be attacked on D.4, or at least by the morning of D.5.

S.1 and S.2 with 'X' Force September 1942.

The attack on Bengazi by 'X' Force including S.1 and S.2 patrols commanded by Capt. Olivey, M.C., which was known as "Bigamy" took place on the night of 13/14 September and was unsuccessful. The failure was thought to be due to lack of security measures during preparation, and also to the fact that some of the S.A.S. troops employed had not been sufficiently trained for desert work. The two patrols were withdrawn on 15 and 16 September, marched by landing ground 125 (X)E.6884, and reached Kufra about five days later.

Y.1 with 'B' Force September 1942.

The attack on Tobruk from land and sea on the same night in which Y.1 patrol (Capt. Lloyd-Owen) took part, also failed. The patrols guided 'B'

---

1 The special boat sections were formed from personnel of the disbanded British Commandos (7, 8 and 11) for combined operations.

* Under Lieut.Col. J. Haselden, who was killed on 14 September.

Force to the neighbourhood of El Duda and 'B' Force then went on to Tobruk, leaving the patrol to carry out its tasks, one of which was to hold the perimeter on the east side of Tobruk throughout D.2 day (14 September), a formidable problem for 20 men. On its way there Y.1 destroyed one of the enemy's lorries and killed 8 men; and on arrival on the perimeter destroyed a German Staff car that was trying to get out, with all its occupants. By 0630 hrs on the 14th no news had come from 'B' Force, and it was impossible to get into W/T communication with H.Q. L.R.D.G. in order to find out what was going on. It was also obvious that the attack from the sea had failed, and Capt. Lloyd-Owen therefore decided to withdraw to Sidi Rezegh, 12 miles to the S.E. The withdrawal was carried out with difficulty owing to minefields and numerous hostile posts, and the patrol had to go 20 miles beyond Sidi Rezegh before it was possible to communicate with Group H.Q. Headquarters told them of the failure of the attack from the sea, and that there was no news of 'B' Force. After further efforts to get into contact with 'B' Force by R/T, the patrol withdrew and marching by landing ground 125 arrived at Kufra on 25 September.

The subsidiary operation "Caravan" at Barce 13/14 September 1942.

The attack on Barce aerodrome which was made by 'B' Squadron L.R.D.G. with T.1 and G.1 patrols was part of "Operation Bigamy", and the detailed orders for it were given by Lieut.Colonel Stirling. Its code name was "Caravan". The two patrols were under the command of Major J.R. Easonsmith, M.C., who was second in command of the L.R.D.G. and also in command of 'B' Squadron. Major Peniakoff and two O.Rs of the Libyan Arab Force were attached during the period of the operation.

Both patrols were in the Fayoum, as also was S.2, which accompanied them during the first ten days of the outward march, and then left to join S.1 near Bengazi for the operation known as "Bigamy".

'X' Force and S.1 patrol were to march on 1 September from Kufra to Bengazi. 'B' Force and Y.1 patrol also at Kufra, were at the same time to go to Tobruk for the operation known as "Agreement". It was therefore necessary in order to avoid congestion, that Major Easonsmith's party should go by an independent route.

There were two alternatives, the first across the Qattara Depression, the second by a southerly loop which would necessitate a double crossing of the Sand Sea; east to west from the Farafra Oasis to Big Cairn (long. 25°E. lat. 26°58'N.) and south to north for about 70 miles to Garet Khod (long. 22°25'E. lat. 29°43'N.), between Jarabub and Jalo. It was reported that the enemy were occupying, or at any rate watching the western edge of the Depression; and as surprise was of great importance the second alternative was chosen, though it entailed an outward journey of 1,150 miles. The vehicles used were five "jeeps" and twelve 30-cwt Chevrolets. The "jeeps" were self supporting for 900 miles and the Chevrolets for about 1500. To cover the additional mileage, two 10-ton "Macks" accompanied the column for the first 200 miles, and supplied all petrol for that part of the journey. A second refill was obtained after the seventh day's march at Howard's Cairn on the western edge of the Sand Sea, from lorries of the Heavy Section which had been sent up from Kufra, 170 miles to the south. On the third day Capt. Timpson's vehicle capsized; he and Guardsman Wann were badly injured, and with one other man had to be sent home by air. As the men now available were hardly enough for the number of vehicles, one 30-cwt lorry ("G.5") containing enough petrol to get it to Kufra and also hard rations and water, was hidden at (S)T.6641, about five miles east of Bir el Gerrari. Its position being known to all ranks it was available for stragglers on the return journey and called "rendezvous G.5".

On 13 September the party reached Benia ((S)S.7298) about 15 miles south of Barce; and as they had seen only one aircraft, it was thought they had not been observed. Major Peniakoff and his two Senussi soldiers then went forward to collect information from their friends. At dusk the party moved forward to the track from Benia to Gerdes el Abid, five miles to the east, cutting the telephone wires in case anyone should have seen them; and then northwards for seven miles to Sidi bu Raui, where a police post was found, and the party was challenged by a Tripolitanian soldier. The lights were switched on to dazzle him, and he was seized, disarmed and put in a truck; and later proved to be quite a good guide! The party "shouted for help on their captive's behalf", and this produced an Italian officer from the post, about 200 yards off the road, who was shot. Some men also came out, but could not be seen in the dark and gave no trouble. Unfortunately two trucks collided, one being T.1's Breda gun truck, and they had to be stripped of gear and abandoned. At Sidi Selim about 7 miles further north, Major Peniakoff was waiting, but without his two Senussis; and here the telephone wires were again cut. A wireless truck was left at Sidi Selim so that touch could be kept with Colonel Stirling, the M.O. (Capt. Lawson) remained with it, and the place was made a rallying point.

At 2300 hrs they reached the road running eastward from Barce to Maraua "in good order". They then turned westward along the road with lights on, and at the top of the escarpment some five miles east of Barce two light tanks were seen, one on each side of the road. Not knowing whether the patrols' vehicles belonged to friend or foe the tanks were unable to open fire. The patrol fired first, and the whole party got through unscathed.

The two patrols entered Barce at midnight, and then separated; T.1 to deal with the aerodrome and its buildings, G.1 to cut the telephone wires to Bengazi and Tobruk, then to go down to the barracks two miles east of the town, do all the damage they could there and finally attack the railway station. They were given two hours for their tasks.

Driving round the airfield in single file, T.1 patrol burnt 24 aeroplanes and damaged 12 others. They also destroyed a considerable quantity of petrol in 44-gallon drums, and a petrol tanker and trailer; and they damaged several M.T. vehicles. There is little doubt too that they inflicted casualties, but they could not be counted. On their way back through the town they found the road blocked by four light tanks, two opposite the railway station and two a little further on, which were firing up and down the street. Capt. Wilder, the patrol commander, drove his 30-cwt truck at full speed into the nearest tank to try and push it out of the way, and in doing so cannoned off it into the second tank. "This", in his own words, "had the desired effect of clearing a way through for the remainder of the patrol".

As they were out of ammunition Capt. Wilder and one of his men put hand grenades under the tracks of the tanks in the hope of immobilizing them; and they were then picked up by one of the jeeps and went on. The jeep was overturned at a roundabout, and in Capt. Wilder's words "The crew were thrown out, but I was pinned underneath and became unconscious through breathing petrol fumes ... The crew righted the jeep and put me into a 30-cwt ... I very soon came to".

No casualties had occurred on the landing ground, but during the retirement through the town, one jeep with six men became separated and was not seen again, and two 30-cwt trucks were lost, one of which was Capt. Wilder's.

G.1 patrol, which since Capt. Timpson's accident had been commanded by Sergeant Dennis, had a more difficult target to locate. When they reached the barracks after cutting telephone wires along the road, there were men on the roof and there was no surprise. A grenade throwing party went in, covered by fire from the rest of the patrol; but it was impossible to say what damage was done, and their activities were cut short by the arrival of two light tanks. The latter followed them during their withdrawal, and they had to leave the town without attacking the railway station. In his report Sergeant Dennis states that while they were cutting the telephone wires, there was a group of Italian soldiers about 75 yards away who took no notice of them, and that while approaching the barracks he passed two pairs of sentries but disposed of them by dropping a 4-second grenade between the men of each pair.

The occupants of the two jeeps of Squadron H.Q. too had not been idle. One party threw grenades among some occupied buildings to the east of the town, the other, after failing to gain an entrance into what was believed to be the officers' mess, threw grenades on the roof of the building. They also opened fire on two light tanks, but had trouble with their machine guns; fortunately the tanks did not pursue. Further damage was done to eleven vehicles in a M.T. Park, and a small party of Italians were taken by surprise and bombed by the driver of a jeep, while the gunner was trying to rectify the mechanism of his machine gun.

Squadron H.Q. and the two patrols reassembled at Sidi Selim at 0400 hrs on 14 September, with three jeeps and seven 30-cwt trucks still serviceable; and Major Easonsmith decided to go south and pick up the two 30-cwt trucks left during the outward journey at Sid bu Raui. The road ran through a valley, and when about a mile and a half short of Sidi bu Raui the column was fired on by a party which, as was found later, consisted of 3 Italian officers and 150 Tripolitanian soldiers. Their marksmanship was poor, and though they hit one truck it was taken in tow, as also were the two 30-cwt lorries that had been left on the outward journey. Fire had to be kept up until this done; and the party then resumed its journey with six sound 30-cwts and three in tow. The enemy's fire then increased and three men were wounded, but no more vehicles were damaged. Some five miles further on the party pulled off the road, but had to go another five miles before cover was found, and the fitters were able to get to work on the damaged vehicles.

Before much repair work could be done however a party of mounted Tripolitanians came up, and though they turned tail when they sighted the trucks, it was obvious that a move was necessary. Petrol and other things were removed from the damaged trucks, but while this was being done some fifty or sixty Tripolitanian foot soldiers opened fire with rifles. A jeep was sent out, and by using folds in the ground, and appearing in unexpected places it was able to disconcert the enemy, who fell back about two miles. The march was continued without further interference, time bombs having been placed in the trucks which had to be abandoned. After about 7 miles of bad going had been traversed, G.1 patrol's W/T truck stripped a rear axle pinion on the top of a very bare hill, and at the same time a reconnaissance plane came over and stayed in the neighbourhood for three quarters of an hour. All the other trucks were under cover at the bottom of the hill, and the damaged W/T truck was pushed down a deep Wadi, but six fighters arrived a little later and machine-gunned various patches of cover. No reply was made by the patrol in the hope that the position might not be given away. Fighters in varying numbers remained in the neighbourhood from 1030 hrs till dusk, but the only casualties were Capt. Wilder and one guardsman of G.1 patrol who were wounded. At the end of the attack however the only vehicles in action were two jeeps, and one 30-cwt truck; the others were completely burnt out. This left the party very short of supplies, apart from the fact that there were many more men than the available transport could carry. The M.O. and a navigator were sent on with the wounded men, now six in all, in the 30-cwt truck and a jeep which was in rather a bad way. The remaining 24 men continued their march in two parties on foot, the small supply left of food, water and ammunition being carried in the other jeep.

On the 15th the M.O's party pushed on and less its jeep which had to be abandoned on the way, reached landing ground 125 ((X)E6884 – 90 miles S.E. of Bir ken Gania) on the 16th, where they were found by Y.1 patrol on its way back from Tobruk. The R.A.F. then came to the rescue with a "Bombay" aeroplane, and took the whole of the M.O's party of wounded to Kufra, and thence to Cairo.

The two "walking parties" were pursued by hostile aircraft throughout the 15th, and the Charruba district through which they had to pass is very deficient in cover. That night they were given food and milk in a Bedouin encampment. On the 16th, a well of good water was found at the Wadi Sammalus ((S)T.2578). On the 17th the "walking party" under Major Easonsmith reached the Bir el Gerrari area, and met S.2 patrol under Capt. Olivey which was on its way back from Bengasi. In the afternoon of the same day they moved 11 miles east from Bir el Gerrari to Point (S)T.6241 where they had hidden the 30-cwt lorry during the outward march, and known to them as "rendezvous G.5" (see page 170 above). The other walking party however had not arrived there, and Major Easonsmith and Capt. Olivey therefore decided to wait with three of S.2's trucks in the hope of finding them. A search was made N.W. towards Cheda bu Maun; and at Zauiet Umm el Ghizlan (about 45 miles N.W. of Rendezvous G.5) Arabs informed Major Easonsmith that the men had been there two days before (16 September), and the direction in which they had gone showed that they were heading for the rendezvous. The patrol moved back in that direction, and on the way received a message to the effect that Lieut.Colonel Stirling was stranded on his way back from Bengasi and required 50 gallons of petrol at a point 45 miles away. Capt. Olivey with one truck went to his assistance while the search for the missing men was continued with a jeep and a 30-cwt truck. On the 19th eight of them were found of whom two were wounded. The search for the remaining two was continued for two days and was then abandoned; food, water and money having been left at rendezvous G.5. The rest of the party arrived at Kufra on 25th September.

Escape of Guardsmen Duncalfe and McNobola.

The two men who were not found but eventually escaped were Guardsmen R. Duncalfe and P. McNobola of G.1 patrol. They had a great deal of help from the local Senussi tribesmen, including a man who was in the employment of Capt. Grandguillot of I.S.L.D. On 16 November, two months after the Barce operation, when near Bir el Gerrari they saw a great number of British planes in the sky, and came to the correct conclusion that we had taken the offensive.

On 19 November they heard transport moving near Garet Tecasis

(S)T.2090, and found a column consisting of a battalion of the K.R.R. and 'M' Battery R.H.A. which picked them up and took them into Barce. Next morning they were sent back with 'B' Echelon vehicles along the L. of C. and eventually reached the Transit Camp at Mersa Matruh on the 24th. Their arrival was reported to the L.R.D.G., but it was not until 15 December that they were able to rejoin their patrol at Abbasia.

As stated earlier Y.2 patrol (Capt. Hunter) was detailed to take part in the projected operation against Jalo (known as "Nicety"), which was to be carried out in connection with the S.A.S. raid on Bengasi by troops of the Sudan Defence Force garrison at Kufra; and their principal task was to provide guides. The troops who were to carry out the attack were known as 'Z' Force, and commanded by El Miralai Brown Bey.

The force left Kufra on 11 September and the approach march was made on foot in three columns from a point about 15 miles west of Jalo. Each column had its own objective and had two L.R.D.G., guides. The enemy however were on their guard and for this reason and on account of numerous minefields, the attack failed. The force was withdrawn, and for the next four days Y.2 was employed in making reconnaissances as far as intense air activity on the enemy's part allowed.

Early on the 20th 'Z' Force retired to a Wadi at N.6742 covered by a rearguard composed of one company of infantry, one 3.7 Howitzer and Y.2 patrol.

In the afternoon of the same day the rearguard was joined by 86 men of Lieut.Colonel Stirling's 'X' Force which had retired from Bengasi and had had orders to assist the attack on Jalo if possible. Next day the retirement was continued through Zighen and the force reached Kufra on the evening of 22 September. There was little if any doubt that the enemy knew that the attack was impending, and the darkness of the night made it difficult for the guides to locate the objectives until they were very close to them.

In connection with this operation R.2 (Lieut. Talbot) patrolled the area between (X)H.3240 and (X)C.7030, a distance of about 70 miles, daily until 18 September, when a message was received from Y.2 with 'Z' Force asking them to come to Jalo for a closer reconnaissance. On 19 September while on the way the patrol was heavily attacked from the air, and had to scatter and take "avoiding action". Air attacks continued and the trucks remained dispersed for four days; but all eventually returned to Kufra with seven men wounded.

Other journeys were made by patrols during this period. One was a detailed reconnaissance by S.2 of the salt marsh area near El Agheila, of the wire and minefields on the Marada-El Agheila road and of M.T. routes through the Harudj Hills about 70 miles S.W. of Marada, with a view to future operations. The remainder were routine journeys for transporting parties of the I.S.L.D. and in one case a reconnoitring officer of the R.A.F., to areas behind the enemy lines.

Transport replacements.

The loss of ten Chevrolet trucks at Barce in the middle of October was a serious matter, and they had to be replaced by the 30-cwt C.A.S. Fords, which had been used earlier and handed in to Ordnance when the Chevrolets were issued. They had had a "guaranteed" overhaul by the R.A.O.C., but their performance when reissued was not impressive.

The six 10-ton "Macks" of the Heavy Section were exchanged for ten 3-ton Chevrolets. These lighter vehicles were better in soft going, and more suitable for the formation of advanced dumps which was anticipated in the near future.

Capt. E.F. Spicer, Wiltshire Yeomanry, joined to replace Capt. Lloyd-Owen who had been badly wounded during an air raid on Kufra. Lieut. J. Henry replaced Capt. Olivey who went on leave to South Rhodesia. Lieuts. Denniff and McLauchlan also joined.

The remainder of the Indian Long Range Desert Squadron, ie. H.Q. and Nos. 3 and 4 Patrols, was put under command of the L.R.D.G. on 1 October 1942, but had not arrived at Kufra by the end of the "Eighth Phase" (23 October).

The Tripoli road watch was resumed, and Y.1 patrol under Capt. Spicer left Kufra on 23 October for the first period, which will be dealt with in the next section.

Section XXI

The next phase of the L.R.D.G. operations cover the period 24 October 1942 to 23 January 1943.

Eighth Army's final offensive 23 October to 23 January 1943.

During this period the Eighth Army which resumed the offensive on the night of 23/24 October 1942, and entered Tripoli on 23 January 1943, covered a distance of 950 miles as the crow flies. During the first stage of the attack which ended on 11 November the enemy was driven across the Egyptian Frontier. The second stage may be said to have ended with the capture of Derna on 15 November. The pursuit was then delayed by rain, but Bengasi was taken on 20 November, and after a halt for reorganization of a fortnight from 27 November, El Agheila was taken on 12 December, and Buerat el Hsun on the 26th. After another halt of twenty days the advance was resumed on 16 January, and Tripoli was taken a week later. H.Q. L.R.D.G. which came under command of the Eighth Army on 20 December moved parallel to the advance from Kufra by Zella to Hon.

Increase of S.A.S.

The strength and scope of what had previously been known as 'L' detachment S.A.S. Brigade (under Lieut.Colonel D. Stirling) had considerably increased, and towards the end of September 1942 it became known as the 1st S.A.S. Regiment. It was necessary to define the respective roles of L.R.D.G. and the S.A.S. and the definition was contained in G.H.Q. M.E.F. Operation Instruction No. 144, dated 22 September 1942. The essence of the decision then made was that the L.R.D.G. would normally carry out long range reconnaissance tasks under orders from G.H.Q., M.E.F., and that the S.A.S. would attack the enemy's communications and aerodromes at shorter range; a task for which their training and equipment made them specially suitable. It was left open to the L.R.D.G. to make similar attacks on long range targets, and the boundary between their activities in this respect and those of the S.A.S. was to be the 20th meridian

176

of longitude east, that is to say a north and south line running approximately through Jedabia. For various reasons however no such attacks were made, and until the Eighth Army took El Agheila in the second week of December the L.R.D.G. took little or no part in the actual fighting.

Tripoli Road Watch, 30 October – 22 December 1942.

The Tripoli Road Watch however which had been begun again by Y.1 on 30 October increased in importance; and as the enemy retreated it became more and more difficult to maintain. The L.R.D.G. patrols were therefore fully employed in this way until 22 December, when the watch was cancelled by H.Q. Eighth Army. They also continued to transport parties sent out by the I.S.L.D. and G(R), and of No. 1 Demolition Squadron as Major Peniakoff's Arab Force was now called. These varying missions will be dealt with in chronological order.

Dispositions 24 October 1942.

On 24 October Group H.Q. and H.Q. 'A' Squadron were at Kufra with G.2, R.1 and R.2 patrols. T.1, G.1 and Y.2 patrols had gone to Cairo to refit and had not yet returned. The Indian Long Range Squadron was also at Cairo. S.1 and S.2 patrols were out doing transport duties, or "taxi service" as it was called. Y.1 had left for the Tripoli road watch on 23 October; and S.2 as related earlier was carrying out a reconnaissance in the neighbourhood of El Agheila, one result of which was the discovery of a new east to west route through the Harudj Hills at latitude 27°N which later proved very useful.

Y.1's road watch 23 October to 8 November 1942.

Y.1 patrol left Kufra on 23 October to watch the Tripoli road from the usual spot in the neighbourhood of the "Marble Arch". It reached the area without incident, concealed the vehicles in the Wadi Hatema (X)A.6077, and observed the road from 1900 hrs (local time) on the 30th until relieved by R.2 at 1900 hrs on 8 November. The total number of vehicles in both directions averaged less than 100 daily during Y.1's watch, but two days later the effects of the battle of El Alamein were beginning to show, and enemy transport streamed westward at the rate of 3,500 vehicles a day. These figures combined with the absence of any eastward movement of fighting troops, confirmed the belief that Rommel intended to evacuate Cyrenaica.

R.2's road watch to 15 November 1942.

R.2 patrol continued to take a traffic census until the night of 15 November from the flat ground between the escarpment and the road ((X)A.8380). During daylight on the 14th, small parties of Germans with two trucks reconnoitred the ground on both sides of the road and appeared to be marking it out. Some of them came within 150 yards of the bush in which the two observers were concealed. Later a reconnaissance plane circled round the mouth of the Wadi Hatema in which the patrol's trucks were concealed, and then followed the many tracks of the observers on their way to and from the watch site, passing only about 20 ft. above the bush. The Patrol Commander therefore decided that on the 15th the road should be watched from the escarpment. On that day, apart from road traffic, there was a great deal of activity on the enemy's part. Working parties were seen near the "Marble Arch" landing ground, over a thousand vehicles were dispersed in the area, mainly round the landing ground, and tents were erected. A cruiser lay off shore until 1600 hrs when it put out to sea after being bombed by six aircraft, and set on fire. The neighbouring Wadis were being occupied and it seemed likely that the enemy would also want to occupy the Wadi Hatema. Lieut Talbot therefore withdrew during the night 15/16th towards Hofra ((X)F.5545) where he intended to lie up and ask Group H.Q. for instructions. When about 15 miles N.E. of Hofra an enemy force of at least seven vehicles including two A.F.Vs was seen approaching. In order to avoid an unequal fight, the patrol withdrew west and then south. The enemy started to pursue, but did not continue to do so. Orders were then received to return to Kufra, and during its homeward march the patrol passed T.1, and later G.1 on their way to take over the road watch.

Indian (3) Patrol to Regima 30 October 1942.

The 3rd Indian Patrol under Capt. Rand left Kufra on 30 October with the task of picking up Major Chapman, M.C., and a small Intelligence party near Regima on the Bengasi escarpment; but owing to the inexperience of his Indian drivers much time was lost in the Sand Sea and he had to abandon his mission. On the way home however when on the north edge of the Sand Sea the attention of the patrol was attracted by the sound of moving vehicles, and a continuous stream of traffic was seen moving from east to west along the Jarabub-Jalo track, which continued throughout the day (11 November) and the following night.

The enemy evacuates Siwa and Jarabub 11-13 November 1942.

On the 13th the patrol was given orders to reconnoitre Jarabub and Siwa, and it was able to confirm that both places, which had been occupied by the enemy during Rommel's advance to El Alamein, had been evacuated. The 2nd Indian Patrol (Capt. T.J.D. Birdwood) was then sent to pick up Major Chapman, and brought back two escaped prisoners.

G.2 to Tripoli road watch 10 November 1942.

G.2 left Kufra for the Tripoli road watch on 10 November. On the 16th it received orders to occupy a new observation area at (S)V.1524, some 40 miles west of the Marble Arch, and reached this point on 19 November. The watch was continued until the 27th, and as there was no sign of the relieving patrol, and his wireless was not working, Lieut. Sweeting decided to start his return journey. On the 29th he received a message informing him that the relieving patrol (G.1) had been attacked, and that he was to await orders. He was then told to return to Kufra, and on his way to reconnoitre the going in the area Tagrifet (W)K.3751 – Zella (W)P.5978 – Hon. In his report Lieut. Sweeting stated that about 30% of the vehicles seen were British, and that a larger proportion of German troops were going west than east. Those going west seemed to be "in much better form than those going east, judging by the shouts they gave each other when they passed!"

R.1 and Y.2 to Bir Tala and Buerat 12 November 1942.

On 12 November R.1 patrol (Capt. L.H. Browne) and Y.2 patrol (Capt. Hunter) were sent to carry I.S.L.D. personnel to Bir Tala (R)R.0541, about 60 miles S.W. by south of Misurata, and to the Buerat-el-Hsun area respectively.

It was originally intended that the two patrols should also carry out an attack on traffic along the coastal road, but this order was cancelled during the outward march. Capt. M. Pilkington (Life Guards) who was attached from the Arab Legion in Trans-Jordan, accompanied R.1.

The two patrols met on 17 November at (W)E.6449 in the neighbourhood of Hofra, and again in the Wadi Tamet (about 40 miles S.W. of Sirte) on the 18th.

Death of Capt. Pilkington 18 November 1942.

About midday on 18 November, shortly before it reached the Wadi Tamet, R.1 patrol was attacked by Italian fighters which were driven off. Capt. Pilkington and L/Corporal O'Malley (N.Z.E.F.) were mortally wounded and died soon afterwards. Private Fogden (N.Z.E.F.) was shot in both legs; and the patrol Commander's truck and the W/T truck were damaged beyond repair. The patrol had therefore to divide into two parties, one of which took Private Fogden back to Taiserbo where he was picked up by an aeroplane.

The I.S.L.D. men were deposited at Bir Tala at sunset on the 20th, and the patrol started next day for Kufra which it reached on 30 November.

Special Forces in the Desert War 1940–1943

Y.2 also attacked 18 November 1942.

Y.2 patrol could see the attack made on R.1 on 18 November and was itself attacked later. Two trucks were destroyed but their occupants escaped. The I.S.L.D. were dropped in the Wadi Tamet some 35 miles from Buerat-el-Hsun, and the patrol returned to Kufra. They had much mechanical trouble, but there was no further incident.

Capt. Hunter's report states that the Wadi Tamet appeared to be patrolled daily by aircraft, and that there was probably a chain of posts connected by patrols on the line Marada-Tagrifet-Zella. These precautions indicated that the enemy was nervous about his southern flank.

A detachment of the Heavy Section (one jeep and six 3-tonners) under 2/Lieut. Denniff was sent with 2000 gallons of petrol, by a separate route to a rendezvous about 120 miles N.W. of Marada, at which R.1 and Y.2 patrols were able to refuel.

S.1 and T.2 to Jalo 13 November 1942.

On 13 November S.1 patrol (Lieut. Lazurus) left Kufra with orders –
(a) to report whether Jalo was still occupied, and if so, on enemy movement from it,
(b) to find out the strength of the enemy garrison at Marada by obtaining prisoners on the Marada-El Agheila road.

T.2 patrol (Lieut. Cramond) left on the same day with similar orders but by a different route.

The two patrols met at Taiserbo on 16 November and then went north together. On the 17th they arrived at Ain Sidi Mohammed half way between Jalo and Marada, and then operated independently but kept in W/T touch, and met more than once. During the next few days some traffic was seen going north from Jalo, and on the 19th S.1 met Arabs who confirmed that there was still a small Italian Force there. On 22 November a Lancia truck was destroyed on the Marada-El Agheila road, five Italians were captured and the patrol then returned to Kufra.

Jalo evacuated 20 November 1942.

T.2 remained in the neighbourhood of the Jalo-Marada road, and on the 20th were told by Arabs that the Italians had evacuated Jalo on the previous day. They entered the Oasis on the 22nd, and captured two Italian motor cyclists who were on the point of leaving for El Agheila. The place had evidently been abandoned in haste for personal belongings and stores had been left behind, and dumps were intact. The patrol remained in Jalo making reconnaissances and destroying "booby traps" until the 29th, when it was replaced by a party of I.L.R.S., and returned to Kufra.

Tripoli Road Watch doubled.

When the enemy began to evacuate Cyrenaica the importance of the Tripoli road watch increased, and it was decided to use two patrols at a time so as to ensure continuity. The routes to the coast of the Gulf of Sirte crossed the Zella-Marada "Gap", and the enemy was fully aware of the extent to which they were used both by the L.R.D.G. and the S.A.S. Regiment. They therefore laid mines in the Gap towards the end of November and maintained patrols across it.

T.1 and G.1 to relieve G.2.

T.1 and G.1 patrols both left Kufra on 20 November to continue the road watch in relief of G.2 patrol. T.1 lost a truck on a mine and one of its men broke a leg, another truck broke down and had to be abandoned, and the patrol was then recalled.

G.1 accomplished the first five days of the march with no trouble, but on the 25th, when moving S.W. along an escarpment near Hofra (X)F.0546, it encountered a force of eight enemy vehicles, two of which were armoured cars. As his object was to get to the coast road, Capt. Timpson did his best to avoid a fight and turned north, only to find that he was confronted by five more enemy vehicles, and an engagement was thus unavoidable. The enemy's armament was superior and after a hard fight, in which he lost four of his seven vehicles and the men in them, Capt. Timpson got away with the other three.

The patrol then continued its journey to the coast road, but owing to bad weather navigation was difficult and progress slow. They reached G.2's camp on the 28th and found that it had been evacuated though only quite recently. Not knowing whether the road watch was still being maintained or not, Capt. Timpson tried to get information by W/T from Group H.Q.; but it was not until the 29th that he got into communication and heard that G.2 had moved south, and that the road was no longer under observation. The watch was, however, re-established by 0400 hrs on the 30th from the top of a hill overlooking the road, about half a mile west of Wadi Zebaui about (S)V.2020.

By this time the strength of the patrol was reduced to two officers (Capt. Timpson, and Lieut. Hon. B. Bruce, Scots Guards) and 8 O.Rs including a signaller. They had one jeep which never went wrong, and two 30-cwt Fords, one with unsound steering and the other with a doubtful big end bearing. They had petrol for 550 miles, hardly enough to get them back to Taiserbo. There were rations for 24 days but these did not include tea, sugar or oatmeal; and there was but little milk for most of it had been kept in the lost cook's truck. There was some difficulty in finding a suitable place for a "base camp" but finally a site was selected at (X)A.1687. It was in stony ground and tracks were not conspicuous, but it was thirty miles inland from the point at which the observers were stationed. The watch party was driven in a jeep to within about three miles of the road at (S)V.1718. Moves from the camp to the observation post were hampered by the enemy who pitched camps in various places and to an increasing extent as they moved west; and this led to difficulties in the relief of the road watch. On 7 December Lieut. Bruce poisoned a hand as the result of being pricked by a thorn and developed a temperature of 103°, but after treatment was better next day. The watch party on 10 December was lost, and was presumably captured through walking into one of the enemy's camps.

On 13 December when Capt. Timpson and Guardsman Welsh were on watch, the enemy pitched a camp all round them except in the space between them and the road. They were all speaking German, and Capt. Timpson describes them as "well disciplined and quite cheerful, though a bit rattled when a British night-fighter straffed the area by moonlight at 8 p.m. They apparently fed well, macaroni and goulash for lunch!" Capt. Timpson decided to leave the observation post early so as to stop the next party coming to the same place. While getting away they were seen and fired at as the answer "freund" when they were challenged, did not satisfy the sentry, and they had to take to their heels. Eventually they evaded the pursuit but got separated while doing so. The enemy searched all round them, and Capt. Timpson heard one of them say "I think they were only food thieves". After searching for Welsh for three quarters of an hour Capt. Timpson reached the rendezvous where he found the relieving party and the jeep. Having heard the firing they had prudently waited there.

Guardsman Welsh had also waited for an hour in the hope of rejoining Capt. Timpson, and then had a series of adventures. He walked into four camps, and was shot at in three of them, but got away and arrived at the rendezvous at 0400 hrs on the 14th. By this time Capt. Timpson had left it, for at 0300 hrs he had had a signal from H.Q. to say that S.1 (Capt. Lazurus) the relieving patrol had already established its road watch. Later in the morning he found Welsh who was within two miles of the camp, and had walked some 20 miles after a very strenuous night. Later he met T.2 (Lieut. Tinker) and the remainder of his own patrol, whom he sent to a camp established by No.1 Indian Patrol whose whereabouts he knew.

Orders to return home were then received and G.1 and the Indian Patrol started together on 15 December. On the 18th they were told to go to Zella, and while approaching it from the N.E. on the 20th found and exploded mines laid by the enemy on the track. They reached their destination at noon the same day.

S.1's Reconnaissance and road watch 28 November 1942.

The Tripoli road watch was to be continued by S.1 patrol (Capt. Lazarus) and "Indian (1)" patrol (Capt. Cantlay) which left Kufra on 28 November and 1st December respectively. S.1 had the secondary task of finding a new way to the coast with the object of avoiding the mined "Gap" between Marada and Zella. A suggested new route was to be given to the patrol commander by the Intelligence Officer, but if it proved unpracticable, he was to go by the usual one.

The new route followed by S.1 was by the Harudj Hills, (long. 18°E. lat. 27°N), thence down the Wadi Agheib from (W)O.5032, and across the Hon-Zella road, halfway between those places. On 5 December the patrol reached the Wadi Chalifa at (W)K.1075, marched down it to (W)K.4083 (where the map was reported to be inaccurate) and camped on the edge of the Dor el Muelah Hills at (W)K.4688. Here they received instructions to watch the road from about Point (R)S.3040 in the Gheddahia area. They then travelled N.W. by (W)J.6071 to (W)D.1201 through country inter-sected by many wadis, thence along the eastern edge of the Ramlet Agareb to (W)C.7930 where they encamped on 9 December, close to the Hon-Misurata road, and about 50 miles north of Hon. They reached the neigh-bourhood of the coast at (R)W.9072 on 11 December and the watch began at 1700 hrs on the 13th, from (R)S.2638. This position is only 25 miles south of Misurata and was much further west than the area from which previous watches had been carried out. Owing to the numerous camps on both sides of the road, it was difficult to maintain an accurate record of traffic, for watchers in the daytime could not get within about half a mile of the road, and on four occasions they were hindered by convoys stop-ping for meals or bivouacking near, or even round them. Moreover, the S.A.S. were active in the neighbourhood which attracted the attention of aircraft and of hostile patrols, though it had been more than once pointed out to G.H.Q. that road watching and "beating up" the enemy could not be done satisfactorily in the same area. S.1 was relieved by T.2 on 20 December.

Indian (1) Patrol 1 December 1942.

No. 1 Indian Patrol under Capt. J.E. Cantlay left Kufra on 1 December 1942, to duplicate S.1 on the Tripoli road watch. It included three British officers, two British O.Rs and eleven Indian O.Rs in five trucks. It had orders to watch the road between El Agheila and Sirte in relief of G.1, and marched by the Marada-Zella gap, crossing the road between those places at Abu Naim about 30 miles S.W. of Marada. On 6 December the road watch orders were cancelled and they were told to assist G.1 which as already related, had not only lost trucks and men on its way to the coast, but was also short of rations. In accordance with this order they moved to "Denniff's Dump" ((W)E.7449), about 55 miles south of Nofilia on the road from that place to Zella, and arrived there on 9 December. The weather was bad and they had difficulty in finding G.1's camp, but located it on 13 December in (X)A.18 about 12 miles west of Bir el Merduma ((X)A.3587). After the survivors of G.1 had been supplied with the necessary rations, the two patrols started for Kufra, but on the way there were directed to Zella and arrived on 20 December. On the 21st the Indian Patrol went out again along the road towards Marada, and completed the destruction of a minefield they had come across the day before.

T.2 8 December 1942.

In continuation of the Tripoli road watch T.2 patrol (Lieut. R.A. Tinker, M.M.) left Kufra on 8 December to relieve S.1 patrol in the Gheddahia area. T.2 arrived at S.1's camp in the Wadi Masna (R)W.9072 on the morning of the 19th, and established a "rear base" there with three trucks. The road watch was taken over in the afternoon of 20 December. Camps again made watching very difficult, and on the 22nd the forward echelon of the patrol was discovered near the road by German armoured cars. The patrol commander and three O.Rs managed to escape to the Wadi Masna, but six men were missing. More armoured cars were seen next day, and as petrol was short the patrol had no choice but to abandon the watch and it returned to H.Q. at Zella on the 29th. By this time the Eighth Army had attacked at El Agheila, and for that reason as well as the difficulty of maintaining it, the road watch was cancelled.

French advance into Fezzan.

Early in November it was arranged that General Leclerc's force should invade the Fezzan to cooperate with the advance of the Eighth Army. The first stage of the advance was to be the establishment of a base at Uigh el Kebir (long. 15°4'E. lat. 24°8'N.), the next an advance north along the road to Tripoli against Umm el Araheb and Sebha.

G.H.Q. Instruction No. 151 dated 15 November 1942 allotted tasks to the L.R.D.G. for cooperation with General Leclerc, on the assumption that without prejudicing the Tripoli road watch, five patrols would be available. The L.R.D.G. were told to attack the enemy's L. of C., to harass his garrisons and to destroy aircraft on the ground, and they were to give General Leclerc all possible information of the enemy's disposition and movements.

The boundaries for L.R.D.G. operations were –
on the north – lat. 30°N
on the east – long. 18°E
on the south – long. 27°N.

It was anticipated that as the advance of the French and of the Eighth Army progressed, H.Q. L.R.D.G. would have to move to Zella or Hon whence patrols would attack the enemy's southern flank; and also that in the later stages of the operations the L.R.D.G. would be placed under command of the Eighth Army.

S.2 patrol joins the French 20 November 1942.

These were the opening moves of General Leclerc's now famous march to Tunisia in which the L.R.D.G. had its share. The first patrol selected to join the French force was S.2 under Lieut. J. Henry. He took with him 18 O.Rs and six 30-cwt Chevrolet trucks two of which were equipped with No. 11 W/T sets.

The patrol left Kufra on 20 November 1942 and marching S.W. by Ounianga Kebir and Faya where there were French garrisons, they arrived at Zouar (long.16°35'E. lat. 20°25'N) on 2 December, and were ordered to go on to Zouarke about thirty miles further west; but on the 5th they returned to Zouar. One of the W/T operators, Private Jordan, had had a bad accident on the way, and was flown to hospital at Fort Lamy where he died a few days later. On 14 December news arrived that the Eighth Army had attacked at El Agheila, and General Leclerc came to Zouar.

On 29 November a message had been sent to Colonel Prendergast by G.H.Q. M.E.F. to the effect that D day i.e the day on which the French column was due to arrive at Uigh el Kebir, would be 14 December. In actual fact the French did not leave Zouar until the 18th and reached Uigh el Kebir on the 23rd. In his report Lieut. Henry describes the advance as being slowed down by the inexperienced drivers of the French trucks. On 25 December the column again moved forward, S.2 patrol leading the advance guard under Colonel Dio. They marched all night and at daybreak arrived within sight of Gatrun (long.15°4'E. lat. 24°8'N) about 140 miles south of Umm el Araneb. S.2 went forward with two French trucks and they were fired on by "Field Artillery and Bredas of various calibres". They were then withdrawn out of range and in Lieut. Henry's words, "held a council of war". He goes on to say, "The original plan was to shell Gatrun sufficiently to shake up the garrison and then by-pass it, leaving the main body (groupe "M") to capture it. Just before lunch S.2 patrol with a French patrol was sent out with the idea of doing a reconnaissance of the northern part of the Oasis, just out of artillery range, to lure out any Saharan Companies, and to lead them into range of the French 75 mm's in position near the hills. We got to within a couple of miles of the oasis, when we were attacked by six fighters and two bombers with machine gun fire and bombs. The desert was good going, so we fought back, gradually easing off towards the hills and dodging bombs during our spare moments". It appears that one of the enemy's aircraft crashed and the patrol was credited with having shot it down. Lieut. Henry reported that he saw two planes hit and adds "The personnel of S.2 behaved exceedingly well during the show".

Late in the afternoon the column continued its march northwards and again travelled all night. Early on the 27th the patrol was sent to reconnoitre the Magedul Oasis.

The patrol was then again attacked from the air by a single fighter which was driven off. Other aircraft (2 Savoia Bombers and 5 C.R.42 fighters) attacked the main body for an hour and destroyed one of the patrol's W/T trucks which was with column H.Q. Capt. Carter, a British liaison officer who was with the wireless trucks, sent in a report on the courageous behaviour of Sergeant Jackson and Signaller du Toit who engaged the aircraft with a machine gun, and were both wounded. The column again moved forward at 0230 hrs on 28 December towards Umm el Araneb and camped at daylight in a palm grove about 15 miles from it. There they were once more attacked by aircraft, and later rather half heartedly by 12 trucks of an Italian "Auto Saharan" Company, who were driven off by the French guns with the loss of two trucks and some men. Before sunrise on the 29th a short move was made to the west, to the edge of the oasis. At 0700 hrs the enemy aircraft attacked the area the column had just left, but did no damage to the position it was actually occupying; and again on the 30th "two bombers and several fighters religiously straffed the wrong places!" When the moon rose in the early morning of 31 December the column moved on through the village of El Bder and camped in an oasis about three quarters of a mile west of it. The enemy's aircraft continued to attack other areas and at 1545 hrs the column moved off to try another route to Umm el Araneb.

General Leclerc arrived in the evening of 31 December from Uigh el Kebir and one of S.2's trucks, which had been detached, rejoined the patrol. The column camped in the desert and moved on at 0500 hrs on 1 January 1943. At 0640 hrs two French planes bombed the enemy and the French guns opened fire soon afterwards. The bombardment continued on the 2nd and 3rd in the hope of inducing the Italians to surrender, and at 1230 hrs on the 4th they did so.

Capture of Umm el Areneb, 4 January 1943 and of Gatrun 6 January 1943.

On the same day a message from Group H.Q. informed the patrol that they were to be relieved by Capt. Cantlay's Indian Patrol, though Colonel Ingold of the British Mission with General Leclerc, expressed the wish that S.2 should remain with him till the conclusion of operations.

Gatrun, which had been "by passed" surrendered on 6 January, Brach was evacuated by the Italians on the 7th, and Murzuk on the 8th. The

Indian patrol arrived at Umm el Araneb at 1730 hrs on the 9th and took over communications next day. A French patrol took Esc-Sciueref[1] on the 11th, and on the 12th news came that the enemy had left Hon (200 miles N.N.E. of Umm el Araneb) and S.2 patrol was ordered to go there.

They marched on 13 January and arrived on the 15th "after lunch". The Eighth Army were at this time at Buerat el Hsun which they had occupied on 26 December.

H.Q. L.R.D.G. Zella to Hon, 16 January 1943.

The final stage of the march to Tripoli was begun on 16 January and on the same day H.Q. L.R.D.G., which had left Kufra for Zella on 28 December, arrived at Hon.

Action of other patrols. December 1942.

It is now necessary to go back about six weeks and describe the operations of the other patrols, which in several cases, were connected with General Leclerc's attack on the Fezzan. General Leclerc had been told that he could not have any air support for his operations, but it was hoped that the L.R.D.G. could help to some extent by destroying aircraft on the ground a day or two before the advance began. For this purpose Y.1 (Capt. Spicer)[*] and "Indian (4)" (Lieut. Nangle) under Capt. Spicer's command left Kufra on 1 December to attack the landing ground at Hon. Owing however to bad going and heavy rain neither patrol reached its objective.

On 2 December R.2 (Lieut. R.J. Talbot) left Kufra with a similar mission, its objective being the landing ground at Sebha, about 60 miles N.N.W. of Umm el Araneb. This raid also failed owing to the weather and the patrol rejoined H.Q. at Zella on 22 December.

Y.2 to Northern Fezzan, 6 December 1942.

To give additional support to General Leclerc's column patrols were sent out to attack the enemy's L. of C. in the northern Fezzan. With this object in view Y.2 patrol (Capt. Hunter) left Kufra on 6 December to attack the roads Hon-Sebha, Hon-Gheddahia and Brach-Esc Sciueref.[2]

The patrol reached the Harudj Hills at Ploint 686, (M)W.9334, on 9 December. For the next four days it poured with rain and the boggy area west of the hills could not be crossed until the 15th. The patrol then went to the Hon-Sebha road at (W)N.5393 and mined it. On the 17th the mines were heard to explode. By the time the patrol reached the road the convoy

---

1 At (W)B.4043 and about 200 miles from Tripoli on the road running south from that place.
2 Also written Brak-Ech-Choueref ((W)B.4043).
* Wiltshire Yeomanry

had passed, but debris was strewn about. On the 18th the patrol received instructions to attack the Brak-Esc Sciuref road[1] and before leaving again mined the Hon-Sebha road.

On 19 December they took up a position at (W)M.8873, about 65 miles N.E. of Brak, and on the 20th destroyed a Diesel truck, killing an Italian and taking two prisoners. On 22 December they received orders to go to Zella which had become the H.Q. of the Group, and
arrived there on the 26th.

R.1 guides 2 N.Z. Div. 4 December 1942.

At the beginning of December H.Q. Eighth Army asked for a patrol to guide a force in a movement to outflank the El Agheila position which was still held by Rommel. R.1 patrol under Capt. L.H. Browne, D.C.M., was detailed for this duty. The account of this mission is incomplete as on 22 December the jeep in which Capt. Browne was travelling struck a mine, and he was obliged to go to hospital. He was succeeded by 2/Lieut. V.F. MacLauchlan, who points out in his report that he had no knowledge of information given verbally by his predecessor to H.Q. Eighth Army.

The first task of the patrol was to guide the 2nd N.Z. Division round the enemy's right flank at the Wadi er Rigel ((X)A.28) and later to the Wadi el Nizam ((R)Z.63) west of Nofilia. It was also required to supply local knowledge of the country in the El Agheila sector, and to make certain reconnaissances. The patrol, less Capt. Browne who flew to Bengasi on the 6th, left Kufra on 4 December, and reported on the 7th to H.Q. 4th Light Armoured Brigade at El Haseiat, 35 miles S.E. of Jedabia. Capt. Browne rejoined it next day and the patrol marched to H.Q. XXX Corps at Mulch en Nogra about 20 miles S.W. of Jedabia. Here Capt. Browne had conferences with Lieut.General Freyberg, General Montgomery and H.Q. 51st Division. On the 11th Generals Montgomery and Freyberg inspected the patrol, and on the same day it moved to H.Q. 2nd N.Z. Division near Bir Gwetin (long. 20°40' lat. 29°55'). The Division marched on the 14th, the patrol moving with the Divisional Cavalry along the axis of the advance. It crossed the road running N.E. from Marada at El Hagfa at noon that day, and reached Bu Grea ((X)A.9136) the same night. On the 15th the Division continued its advance though the patrol was not now leading it, and arrived that evening just west of Wadi er Rigel (X)A.2087, about 20 miles S.W. of the "Marble Arch". The 4th Light Armoured Brigade, and the 5th and 6th Infantry Brigades prepared to attack but the enemy slipped away during the night. On the 16th the patrol guided the 6th N.Z. Field Company to the landing ground at Bir el Merduma (X)A.3587; and on the 17th it again guided the 2nd N.Z. Division round the southern flank of Nofilia

---

1   See Note 2 on previous page.

to about (R)Z.7434 (Trig Point 121). From this point the 5th Infantry Brigade fought its way northwards for five miles to Point (R)Z.6839 where the coast road is crossed by the Wadi el Nizam; but the enemy once more slipped away. Capt. Browne again saw the B.G.S. Eighth Army at the "Marble Arch" on the 19th, and was told to reconnoitre the "going" through the Wadi Tamet,[1] the Wadi el Chebir[1] and the Wadi Zem Zem;[1] to report on the suitability of the Zem Zem area for tank action; and to take "astrofixes" in the Chebir and Zem Zem Wadis, which would help in the interpretation of air photographs. These tasks were entrusted to Sergeant Gorringe with 9 O.Rs in two trucks, who acted under the orders of the 2nd N.Z. Division. This party moved to Nofilia and left there on 22 December. Two S. African officers went with them to take the "astrofixes". Capt. Browne marched approximately due west with the rest of the patrol, and after covering about 80 miles arrived at El Machina, (R)Y.5017. It was here that he was injured and Capt. le Rou who was with him died of his injuries not long afterwards. 2/Lieut. MacLauchlan then took command and was ordered to make an additional reconnaissance further south in the direction of Bu Njem at (R)X.5005 on the Hon-Misurata road. He had with him Lieut.Colonel Pyman (from 7th Armoured Division) and Capt. Alexander of the S. African forces with 10 O.Rs; and the vehicles were one jeep and three 30-cwt Chevrolet trucks, one of which carried W/T.

R.1's reconnaissances to Bu Njem.

Lieut. MacLauchlan's party marched on 25 December and moving by the Wadi Tamet (R)Y.1525 reached Point (R)X.7820, 20 miles N.E. of Bu Njem. He intended to get on to a safe base, either with T.2 patrol (Lieut. Tinker) which as described earlier was on road watch near Gheddahia with a camp in the Wadi Masna (R)X.9060; or at the old Roman reservoir of El Faschia (R)W.9957 in the same area. On the 27th he reconnoitred Bu Njem in a jeep and on returning to camp heard that Lieut. Tinker was missing, which for some hours was in fact the case, and that El Faschia was in the enemy's hands which was probably true. He then decided to go north next day to the Wadi el Chebir, and to get in contact with patrols of the 7th Armoured Division from the Wadi Tamet. During its move to the north on 28 December the patrol met a squadron of the K.D.Gs at the landing ground of Bir el Zidan (R)X.6953, and was told the position of the squadron's patrols and that the area between them was clear of the enemy. The patrol made for Fortino, (R)X.4355, which is on the

---

1 The Wadi Tamet runs into the sea about 30 miles west of Sirte; the Wadi el Chebir 35 miles west of Sirte: and the Wadi Zem Zem at Buerat el Hsun (R)X.8496 20 miles further on.

Hon-Misurata road and about half way between Bu Njem and Gheddahia. When about three miles from Fortino an armoured car came from the rear through the patrol which was spread out in "desert formation", and in Lieut. MacLauchlan's own words "the commander had no hat on, he was smiling and I wrongly assumed that he was from the K.D.Gs. As he drew alongside he picked up a rifle and covered the three of us; and ordered us in English to put up our hands. For a moment I thought it was a joke, but then realized that the armoured car was hostile". Lieut. MacLauchlan goes on "the ambush was well planned, but as far as R.1 truck (his own) was concerned was not well done. The armoured car had drawn up about five feet away on the same axis (this no doubt means that it was parallel and facing the same way); I concluded that we had a reasonable chance of getting away and instructed the driver to drive on. This he did admirably and the armoured car manoeuvred to bring its "fixed line" 20 mm gun to bear on us – the commander with his rifle was loth (sic) to pull the trigger on us until we moved some five yards. The car turned left to head us, we turned right and then turned 180° to make for safe territory; as we turned we saw a similar armoured car alongside the W/T truck and the entire personnel (sic) had surrendered".

The enemy pursued for two miles, hitting the truck twice and then "we crossed a Wadi at 30 miles an hour, and the enemy called it a day, contenting himself with having pot shots at us as we crossed the skyline!"

Half an hour later Lieut. MacLauchlan got back to the K.D.Gs at Bir el Zidan, and Lieut.Colonel Hermon commanding the regiment, wirelessed to the K.D.G. patrols to close in on the area where the ambush had taken place. He then went on to H.Q. 4th Light Armoured Brigade in order to report to Eighth Army, and thence to H.Q. 7th Armoured Division to communicate with Group H.Q. On 30 December Lieut.Colonel Pyman returned with the fitter's truck and told the rest of the story. He also had been attacked and had retired on the K.D.Gs, eventually reaching them, with six men, on foot as his truck had got stuck in a Wadi.

The total losses were Capt. Alexander, one South African driver and four men of the L.R.D.G. with a jeep and a 30-cwt (W/T) truck which contained all the signal instructions and ciphers. The surviving men and trucks went back to Nofilia, whence Lieut. MacLauchlan went to report to H.Q. Eighth Army. There he met Lieut.Colonel Prendergast and was given orders to go to Zella. The patrol arrived there on 5 January, by which time it had covered 2,540 miles.

T.1 to Hon-Sebha road, 6 December 1942.

The harassing of the enemy's L. of C. to the Fezzan was continued by T.1 patrol (Capt. Wilder). The patrol left Kufra on 6 December 1942, with orders to attack traffic on the Hon-Sebha road between points (W)N.4050 and Umm el Abid, and on the Esc-Sciuref-Brach road between (W)M.9550 and Brach. The route taken was by Taiserbo and on the western side of the Harudj Hills they encountered Y.2 patrol which as related earlier had a similar task. Both patrols were held up by rain and floods for three days. They moved on 15 December, and on the 16th T.1 reached the Hon-Sebha road. No traffic was seen, but mines were laid that day and on the 18th. Capt. Wilder then moved northwards for 17 miles along the road and on the 20th again met Y.2 patrol on the Esc-Sciuref-Brach road. The patrols remained in the same area for four days, destroyed a Fiat truck and captured prisoners which Y.2 took back to Zella on the 24th. On that day T.1 laid more mines, and on Christmas Day destroyed two 10-ton trucks with trailers and captured three Italians, on the Esc-Sciuref road about 60 miles N.E. of Brach. It was then ordered to Zella and arrived there on the 27th.

Eighth Army Instructions to L.R.D.G. 21 December 1942.

Eighth Army Operation Instruction No. 5 dated 21 December 1942 allotted the following tasks to the L.R.D.G. in order of priority:-
"(a) Topographical Reconnaissance.
 (b) Sabotage by the 1st Special Demolition Squadron
 (c) Transporting personnel of Adv. H.Q. 'A' Force[1] and I.S.L.D.
 (d) Liaison patrol with General Leclerc until his operations are completed."
The object of the reconnaissance was to obtain information of topography generally and of water supplies and possible landing grounds in particular, with a view of further operations. The area to be covered was marked on a map and extended north of 1at 31°30'N and west of long. 15°E to Gabes (in Tunisia, and 100 miles west of Tripoli). A report was also required on the best approaches for a force of all arms moving from the Gheddahia area (inland from Bouerat-el-Hsun):-
1. To Homs (on the coast, 60 miles east of Tripoli).
2. West of Tripoli by the Jebel Nefusa a range of hills extending from east to west for about 100 miles from Garian[2] 50 miles south of Tripoli, and then north to Matmata.
'L' detachment S.A.S. were to confine their activities to the coast road east of Tripoli and were to give the coordinates of any area they had mined.

No. 1 Special Demolition Squadron, under Major Peniakoff, otherwise known as "P.P.A", came under command of the L.R.D.G. on 10 December 1942. Its war establishment was 5 British officers, 18 British O.Rs and 24 Arab O.Rs; and it had 8 jeeps and four 3-ton trucks. When it joined the L.R.D.G. it had not as yet been actively engaged, but later it performed

---

1 The "covername" of an organization for helping P.O.W. and "baled out" airmen.
2 Or "Kasr Rhariane".

some remarkable feats. It inflicted considerable loss on the enemy by inserting its trucks into hostile convoys by night, and moving with them until the some point was reached where movement off the road was easy. On reaching such a place it would fire on the enemy's trucks, and then leave the road and escape into the darkness.

Y.1 and G.2 patrols' reconnaissances 25 December 1942.

Y.1 patrol (Capt. E. Spicer) and G.2 patrol (Lieut. Hon. B. Bruce) left Zella on 25 December to make a topographical reconnaissance in accordance with Eighth Army's orders. Their respective areas were as follows:-

Y.1 Patrol			*G.2 Patrol.*
North	–	Coastal Road	Coastal Road
East	–	Long. 14°E.	Coastal Road
South	–	Lat. 31°20'N.	Lat. 31°20'N.
West	–	Long. 13°E.	Long. 14°E.

The two areas were included approximately by Misurata, El Gheddahia, Mizda (long. 13°E. lat. 31°27'N) and Tripoli.

Y.1 while reconnoitring the western area ran into considerable numbers of Italian vehicles and men at (R)Q.8386 on 6 January, who appeared to be occupying a defended locality. On 16 January they heard from Group H.Q. that Lieut. Talbot of R.2 patrol which had left Zella on 27 December to act as a reserve to Y.1 and G.2, was missing in Esc-Sciuref; and later in the day they met R.2 at (W)B.9721, who said that the enemy was occupying that place. On the 7th Y.1 and R.2 started to return to Group H.Q. now at Hon, and arrived there on 22 January.

Lieut. Bruce (G.2) had with him Major J.D. Player of the Sherwood Rangers (Yeomanry), lent by H.Q. 8th Armoured Brigade. The patrol was split into two parties, 'B' (Bruce) Patrol and 'P' (Player) Patrol. El Faschia was found to be occupied by the enemy and the patrol had to cross a mine-field on the eastern side of it with Italian A.F.Vs giving chase. The report sent in by Lieut. Bruce was very complete and the area had been thoroughly covered. He remained at Army H.Q. to advise on the going during the advance from Buerat el Hsun to Tripoli during the latter half of January. His patrol reached Hon on 23 January.

R.2 patrol left Zella on 27 December to act as reserve to Y.1 and G.2. It was given four possible areas which it might be required to reconnoitre and on the evening of 1 January 1943 it arrived at (W)C.3807 about 60 miles N.W. of Hon. It then received orders to go to the western end of the Wadi Zem Zem (30 miles N.W. of Esc-Sciuref) and act as reserve to G.2 patrol. On 9 January it was ordered to meet G.2 patrol at Bir Cau (R)W.7992; but orders were again changed, and on the 14th the patrol was told to join the French at Esc-Sciuref and wait for Y.1. On the 15th it arrived at a point about 4 miles from the Fort, and some men were seen on a sandhill. The recognition signal was not acknowledged and when Lieut. Talbot went towards them on foot they scattered and ran away. Thinking they were natives he took Lieut. Kinsman with him to reconnoitre the fort and disappeared from view. After this firing was heard and Sergeant Waiteford, who was left in command of the trucks went forward to look at the dead ground between the fort and the truck's position. He soon realized that the fort must be occupied by the enemy, and this was confirmed by natives next day. The French had taken the fort on 11 January but had been driven out again. In the afternoon of the 16th Y.1 patrol arrived and being unable to communicate with H.Q. by wireless, both patrols moved towards Hon, which R.2 reached after a good deal of mechanical trouble on 20 January. Lieuts. Talbot and Kinsman were missing.

Indian (4) Patrol to Uaddan and Hon. 24 December 1942.

"Indian (4)" Patrol (Lieut. Nangle) was sent out from Zella on 24 December 1942, to ascertain whether the enemy were in occupation of Uaddan and Hon, and if so in what strength; and also whether they intended to evacuate either or both of those two places, and if so when.

At 0800 hrs on the 25th the patrol came under fire from a sandhill east of the road at about (W)J.3932, 17 miles short of Uaddan. It wheeled into line to the right and attacked, but unfortunately ran into soft sand. Half the men then continued the attack on foot while the remainder started to get the trucks out of the sand. The enemy took advantage of this opportunity to retire in their four trucks towards Uaddan, and by the time the patrol was on firmer ground were out of sight. The patrol then took cover at (W)J.4141 in the foothills to the north; and aircraft came over but failed to discover it. At dusk the patrol moved into the mouth of the Wadi Tescena at (W)J.3846, 4 miles to the N.W. Next day two Arabs who had accompanied them were asked to go into Uaddan and make enquiries, but having been badly demoralized by the shooting on the previous day they refused to do so. A reconnaissance made on the 27th showed that the enemy was still in occupation of the place, but on 2 January 1943 it was discovered that they had evacuated it and they left Hon shortly afterwards.

Indian (2) Patrol to Brach-Mizda road 31 December 1942.

On 31 December 1942 Indian (2) Patrol (Capt. Birdwood) left Zella with orders to engage enemy vehicles on the Brach-Mizda-Tripoli road, between lat. 29°N and Esc-Sciuref (W)B.4040. At this time General Leclerc's force had its H.Q. at Umm el Araneb, but had occupied Brach about 160 miles south of Esc-Sciuref. S.2 patrol was with the French, but was relieved by "Indian (1)" patrol at Umm el Araneb on 9 January 1943.

On 4 January Indian (2) patrol had reached a point from which an attack on the road could be made at (W)G.4140, about 90 miles south of Esc-Sciuref, and four miles off the road to the S.W. On the 6th a column of some thirty lorries passed along the road led by two A.F.Vs. Fifteen were allowed to pass and the patrol then moved forward in "line ahead". The leading truck opened fire at 400 yards setting one vehicle on fire, and for a short distance the two columns moved parallel. The enemy's lorries, however, were full of infantry who jumped out and opened fire with all their weapons. The fire then became too hot for the patrol's trucks which withdrew. The patrol remained in the same area for the next five days, that is until 16 January, and mined the road. On the 8th, however, the mines had to be removed as information was received that a French patrol was moving from the south of attack Esc-Sciuref, though the number and description of the vehicles were not given. On 11 January at 0900 hrs a small column passed moving north, which consisted of two light trucks followed by an armoured car carrying the French flag, six large lorries full of infantry and another armoured car. The patrol was in an excellent ambush position, and after the leading armoured car had passed a recognition signal was made. This was not acknowledged and the column went on for about a mile and halted. The armoured cars then came back, and while the patrol withdrew 500 yards without being observed opened fire on the hillside and all the patrol's trucks replied. A running fight took place for about five miles after which the armoured cars stopped; but petrol was now getting short and the patrol was ordered home. On the way back they met a small French Force and were told that the French patrol which was expected to come by the road had moved across country, and that the force the patrol had engaged were, as was supposed, Italians. The patrol arrived at Hon on 17 January, having been refuelled by the Heavy Section en route.

Y.2 and T.1 reconnoitre across Tunisian border 3 January 1943.

Y.2 (Capt. Hunter) left Zella on 3 January 1943 to carry out a topographical reconnaissance in the area on the border of Tunisia, bounded on the north by the coastal road, on the east by the 12th Meridian E., on the south by lat. 31°30'N and on the west by the 11th Meridian E. The instructions included information that an "escape dump" had been formed for stragglers.

T.1 patrol (Capt. Wilder) marched on the same day to reconnoitre an area further west, and the two patrols travelled together for about a week. The going over the Hammada el Hamra, west of Esc-Sciuref was good but it had a steep escarpment on its N.W. edge and after that going deteriorated. The patrols parted at (Q)U.8635 and Y.2 went north to (Q)U.8944 about 30 miles N.W.of Mizda and near the Jebel Nefusa. In an attempt to get down an escarpment one of the jeeps overturned and rolled down the cliff, which "aroused the curiosity of some Tripolitanian soldiers". No way down the escarpment was found and on 16 January the patrol was attacked by men on foot and had to withdraw. It was then ordered to return to a rendezvous near the Esc-Sciuref-Mizda road. A certain amount of topographical information had been obtained.

T.1 patrol had orders to reconnoitre an area bounded on the north by the coast, on the east by long. 11°E, on the south by lat. 31°20', and on the west by long. 10°. This area covers most of the S.E. of Tunisia from the coast at Gabes southwards and includes the northern arm of the Jebel Nefusa hills running south from Gabes through Matmata and Foum Tatahouine, which covered the right flank of the German position, known later as the "Mareth Line". On the 12th T.1 crossed the border into Tunisia at (Y)P.7080, 45 miles N.W. of Sinauen; and on the 14th travelled over broken country between (Y)K.2357 and (Y)E.3133, 20 to 30 miles west of Foum Tatahouine, which caused many breakdowns. At midday they received a message from Group H.Q. instructing them to find a route through the range of hills running south from Matmata on to the plain lying west of them. On the night 15/16th the reconnaissance was continued on foot, and the country was found unsuitable for a force to move, even on a very narrow front. On the 19th a way on to the plain was found between (Y)K.5093 and (Y)K.5095, where there is a break in the hills east of Ghermessa (long. 10°17'E, lat. 32°59'N), and about 25 miles S.W. of Foum Tatahouine, which is wide but not otherwise suitable for a large force as there is much rough going. Owing to the shortage of petrol and the bad condition of the trucks, it was then decided to return home; and the patrol reached Hon on 27 January. On the way back H.3, a Troop of the Heavy Section, supplied it with petrol from the dump at (Q)T.4523.

The patrol's report contained much topographical information of interest, especially in regard to the difficulties of crossing the escarpments.

S.1 6 January 1943.

Reconnaissance was continued by S.1 patrol which left Zella on 6 January with 16 of all ranks of the L.R.D.G. and 6 of the "P.P.A" (1st Demolition Squadron). The area allotted to it was to the N.W. of those reconnoitred hitherto and embraced roughly the southern half of Tunisia between long. 10°E and the Algerian border. Its N.E. corner was just short of the coast at Gabes, and it included the town of Tozeur (8°E, 34'N) the salt lake of Shott Djerid just south of it and Ksar Rhilane (9°35'E. 33°N). It is behind i.e. N.W. and W., of the position known later as the Mareth Line. Information was asked for from the point of view of a force of all arms advancing on a wide front.

The patrol camped at (W)C.3758 about 30 miles S.S.W. of Bu Njem and spent the next three days negotiating the hilly and stony country to the

N.W. which leads to the Wadi Zem Zem. On the 15th when in the Wadi Zem Zem about (R)V.8018, a hostile convoy was seen travelling north along the road from Esc-Sciuref to Mizda, and it was watched by Major Peniakoff and the men of the P.P.A. Capt. Lazurus who had first located the convoy, had gone ahead of his trucks. He heard firing in their direction and realized that they had been engaged by the enemy who had two German armoured cars and six or seven heavy open cars, probably "Opels", armed with light M.Gs. Four of the patrol's trucks which had stuck in the sand were captured, and the only one saved was the W/T truck, skillfully driven by Private Brannigan who got it away into the hills. The enemy moved north and the patrol, now reduced to the W/T truck and two jeeps, camped at (R)V.9128. It waited there two days for three men who were missing and then as they did not appear returned to Hon, arriving on 22 January, less Major Peniakoff's party which remained out in the vicinity of Esc-Sciuref. One other man known to have been wounded was left behind. The three men missing were later brought into Hon by Arabs.

Indian (1) joins the French 6 January 1943.

"Indian (1)" patrol (Capt. Cantlay) left Zella on 6 January and relieved S.2 (Lieut. Henry) which was with General Leclerc's force of Fighting French at Umm el Araneb on the 9th. Its principal duty was to provide a W/T link between the French and G.H.Q. Middle East, through H.Q. L.R.D.G.: but it was also to assist the French in operations as far as lay in its power.

The patrol accompanied the French Force during its unopposed march to Nalut (Z)F.3515, which was reached on 21 February, and rejoined H.Q. L.R.D.G. at El Azizia, 27 miles S.W. of Tripoli on the 26th.

T.2 16 January 1943.

On 16 January T.2 left Hon with three tasks -
(a) To escort three 3-ton lorries of the Heavy Section which were to form a fuel dump in the vicinity of the Esc-Sciuref – Mizda road about lat. 30°30' (Square (R)V.70).
(b) To escort a party of the Demolition Squadron ("P.P.A.") to a rendezvous with Major Peniakoff, the position of which was to be signalled.
(c) Topographical reconnaissance.

During the first day's march they met Indian 2 patrol returning to Hon, and a party of Free French. On 17 January they were ordered not to move north of lat. 29°N on account of enemy activity near Esc-Sciuref, but on the 18th further orders were received that they were to go to lat. 29°30' on the Brach-Mizda road (about 40 miles south of Esc Sciuref), and await the arrival of R.2, Y.1, Y.2 and S.1 patrols, and of Major Peniakoff. In the morning of the 19th R.2, Y.1 and Y.2 and a party of the Heavy Section reached the rendezvous; and Lieut.Colonel Prendergast arrived by air in the afternoon. R.2 left for Hon shortly afterwards. On the 20th S.1 and Major Peniakoff arrived. Next day T.2 with "P.P.A." and the Heavy Section Detachment established a fuel dump at (W)B.0848, close to Esc-Sciuref which was now occupied by the French; and T.2 with the P.P.A. party continued their march N.W. At Wilder's dump at (Q)T.4522 on 23 January they met T.1 patrol and were given information about the going; and on the 24th they moved westward across the Gadames-Nalut and Gadames-Geneien roads to (Y)P.2571 (long. 9°45'E. lat. 31°30') which is 10 miles across the Tunisian border. Here orders were received for topographical reconnaissance of an area bounded on the north by the line Matmata-Kebili, on the east by long. 10°E, on the south by lat. 33°N and on the west by long. 9°E. This area of some 2,500 square miles, is in the centre of Tunisia, S.E. of the Shott Djerid. The reconnaissance begun on the 26th continued until the 30th, and terminated at Kasr Rhilane on the southern boundary. It was carried out by the patrol commander and a small party in two jeeps and was very comprehensive, in spite of patrolling by hostile aircraft, and the presence in places of the enemy's ground troops. When he arrived at Kasr Rhilane Lieut. Tinker found men of his own patrol and of Major Peniakoff's reconnaissance party, six Free French parachutists and two stranded men of the S.A.S., thirty seven men in all. It appeared that the base camps of both T.2 patrol and the P.P.A. at (Y)D.9404 (55 miles W.S.W. of Foum Tatahouine) had been attacked by hostile aircraft on the 27th. Six 30-cwt trucks and a jeep had been set on fire, and two of T.2's men had been wounded. Sergeant Garvin of T.2, with Capt. Yunnie and two Arabs of "P.P.A" had remained at the base to meet S.2 patrol which was on its way out. Five jeeps only were now available of which two belonged to T.2. In the afternoon of the 30th Lieut. Tinker left for Sabria nearly 60 miles to the N.W., which was believed to be held by the French, taking with him 11 men including the two wounded, and three jeeps. The remainder of the party, with two jeeps carrying provisions, were to walk, following the tracks made by the three jeeps that went ahead. It was found, however, that the French had moved on from Sabria, and on 1 February Lieut. Tinker and his party marched along the S.W. edge of the Shott Djerid by a camel track to Nefta, and thence to Tozeur near the Algerian border, arriving there in the evening of the same day. On 2 February he went by Gafsa to Tebessa, 100 miles to the north in the First Army area, and was able to make arrangements there to borrow additional transport, and to signal information to H.Q. Eighth Army. On the 3rd he returned to Tozeur and then started to pick up the walking party, whom he found at (Y)D.1559 in the afternoon of 4 February. On the 6th Capt. Yunnie and Sergeant Garvin who, as already related, had waited at T.2's original base camp to meet S.2, were brought to Tozeur on the 6th by Lieut. Henry who commanded that patrol, the main body of which had arrived at Sabria.

On 7 February T.2 patrol and the P.P.A. party moved on to Tebessa, and Lieut. Tinker went from there to H.Q. Eighth Army at Tripoli, travelling part of the way by air. He arrived there on the 14th and reported to the Commander, L.R.D.G. In his report Lieut. Tinker states that the attitude of the natives (in southern Tunisia) was "generally unfriendly".[1]

Major Easonsmith's visit to Algiers January 1943.

At the beginning of January Major Easonsmith, second in command of the L.R.D.G., visited Allied Headquarters in Algiers to examine the possibility of sending part of the L.R.D.G. to operate from a base in Tunisia. It was decided that this was not desirable, but arrangements were made for reserves of P.O.L. and rations to be available at Tozeur for the use of patrols in that area; and, as already described, T.2 went there on 1 February 1943 to obtain supplies. Capt. Easonsmith wrote, on his return, an interesting report dated 18 January 1943. In it he gave first an account of the Allied dispositions in Algeria and on the border of Tunisia. At that time the front as far south as latitude 36°N was held by the British First Army with H.Q. at Constantine, next to the south was the V. American Corps under General Friedenall, and further south again was the French XIX Corps with H.Q. at El Kuif (T)S.5497. Being badly equipped for mobile operations the French had been strengthened by an American force approximating to a brigade group, which had its H.Q. at Feriana (T)S.8237, and elements as far south as Gafsa, about 75 miles W.N.W. of Gabes. The French also had some semi-fortified positions at Gafsa. Further south the troops were all "Goumiers" i.e. native troops under French officers, who were badly equipped, having no M.T. and no heavier weapons than machine guns. They had small garrisons at Metlaoui, Kriz, Tozeur, Nefta and El Oued near the Shott Djerid, and at Tuggurt about 100 miles S.W. of it, but these garrisons had to rely on horses and camels for reconnaissances. The enemy were at Gabes in some force, and were organizing and strengthening the Mareth Line (running roughly S.W. from the southern coast of the Gulf of Gabes through Arram (T)Z.5602). They also were reported to have troops at Kebili on the eastern edge of the Shott Djerid, Foum Tatahouine, Nalut, Sinaouen, Ksar Rhilane, Gadames and elsewhere; but from the report of T.2 patrol's reconnaissance at the end of January it appears that Ksar Rhilane was not occupied at that time.

The report continued by giving details of the going and of communica-

---

1 The Germans by efficient propaganda and lavish use of money had turned the Arabs' longstanding dislike of the French into pro-Axis feeling.

tions generally, and of the steps taken to form a supply base for the L.R.D.G. at Tozeur; noting that the French Chief of Administration there spoke good English. Finally, Major Easonsmith pointed out that it was possible for the L.R.D.G. to operate in aid of the Allied forces in Tunisia from Eighth Army bases, and that a request had in fact been made by H.Q. First Army for two patrols to carry out protective reconnaissance on the southern flank of the Allied forces, which was very weakly guarded.

He recommended that if the L.R.D.G.'s commitments with Eighth Army allowed of it, the task should be accepted. In northern Tunisia on the other hand, there was no scope for the L.R.D.G., which had been specially trained for long distance work.

R.1 joins General Leclerc 25 January 1943.

R.1 patrol left Hon on 25 January to remove mines from the Socna-Esc Sciuref road, and then to join General Leclerc's column. They had the further task of reconnoitring an area west of Garian (Ksar Rhilane) the exact locality of which was to be indicated later.

The patrol joined the French at Mizda, which had been occupied about 22 January. On the 26th they received instructions to report to the O.C. at H.Q. Eighth Army at El Azizia for orders in regard to their reconnaissance task; and arrived there on 27 January, only to be told that the reconnaissance was cancelled as far as they were concerned since it was thought necessary to use armoured cars for the purpose. Three days later the patrol returned to Hon and arrived there on 2 February.

Indian (3) to Southern Tunisia 21 January 1943.

"Indian (3)" patrol (Capt. Rand) left Hon on 21 January for topographical reconnaissance of an area bounded on the north by lat. 33°N, on the east by long. 10°E, on the south by lat. 32°. and on the west by the Sand Sea known as the "Erg Oriental". This area about 70 miles from north to south and 10 miles from east to west extends south from the line Ghermessa-Ksar Rhilane, and is in the most southerly part of Tunisia. The Erg Oriental lies for the most part in southern Algeria, but its eastern edge crosses the Tunisian border. They were also told to find a route suitable for the passage of a force of all arms on a north and south axis. They camped on the night 21/22nd at (W)G.8892 about 43 miles S.E. of Esc Sciuref having met R.1 patrol at midday. They reached Esc Sciuref with R.1 at midday on 22 January, and moving north west camped in the neighbourhood of Allagh, (Q)Z.0576, on the night 24/25th. The going was good and continued so until they reached (Q)T.6002 where they came into a wide dune belt made up of closely packed dunes varying from three to six feet in height. The jeeps crossed them easily, but they put a considerable strain on the 30-cwt trucks. They encamped on the 25th at "Wilder's Dump" (Q)T.5010 and refuelled there; and next day met Capt. Wilder (T.1) before starting. They moved at midday, crossed the Sinsuen-Nalut road at (Z)L.2384 and camped at (Y)P.8989 (long. 10°27'E. lat. 31°37'N), having covered about 45 miles in a north westerly direction. This point is near the border between Tripolitania and Tunisia, 38 miles W.S.W. of Nalut. On the 28th, having been forced to leave a jeep behind with a burnt-out clutch, they crossed the Ghadames-Geneien track at Bir Zar and encamped at (Y)P.0898 about 25 miles west by south of Bir Zar and on the edge of the "Erg". On the 29th they moved north over more bad going. On the 30th they encamped at (Y)K.0348, also on the east edge of the "Erg" and 40 miles south of Ksar Rhilane. Here a base camp was formed and Capt. Rand decided to reconnoitre his area with a jeep and two 30-cwt trucks, one carrying wireless. At midday on 2 February the patrol received a W/T message ordering it to look for T.2 patrol from which nothing had been heard for several days, at (Y)D.9404. As already described T.2's base at this point had been attacked from the air on 27 January, and Capt. Rand found only the burnt-out remains of its trucks, T.2's commander being at that time on his way from Gafsa to Tebessa to get into communication with the H.Q. L.R.D.G. Capt. Rand made a further investigation of T.2's camp next day and found two written messages, one from Sergeant Garvin, and the other from Capt. Yunnie of the P.P.A. Both contained warnings against local Arab spies, and stated that they had been attacked from the air without any previous reconnaissance by hostile aircraft. The reconnaissance continued and when he returned to his own base on 5 February Capt. Rand found "Indian (2)" Patrol there; and "Indian (4)" Patrol arrived next day. Orders were then received for the patrol to return to Mizda, whence its commander was to be taken by air to H.Q. Eighth Army, then at Tripoli. Marching along the southern edge of the Djebel Nefusa, by Nalut and Djado, over bad going and having to tow two jeeps (including the one left behind on the outward journey), the patrol did not reach Mizda till 12 February. Capt. Rand flew next day to Tripoli, and the patrol returned to Hon, arriving on the 15th. At Tripoli Capt. Rand and the Commanders of T.2, R.2 and S.2 patrols were interviewed by General Freyberg.

In his report Capt. Rand stated that time did not allow for reconnaissance north of latitude 32°45'N, but he was able to recommend a suitable route from south to north through the area he had covered, which led past the right flank of the enemy's position on the Mareth Line.

Changes among Officers.

During phase IX Capt. Timpson, Grenadier Guards, and Lieut. A.R. Cramond left the unit. Lieuts. Hon. B. Bruce, Scots Guards, A.H. Kinsman, Grenadier Guards joined and R.A. Tinker, M.M., returned from O.C.T.U.

Lieuts. J.R. Talbot and Kinsman, as already related, were taken prisoner at Esc-Sciuref in the middle of January.

In December 1942 the D.M.I. at G.H.Q. in a note to the D.M.O. on the Intelligence value of the L.R.D.G. wrote as follows:-

"LRDG road watch provides the only trained road traffic observers. Not only is the standard of accuracy and observation exceptionally high, but the patrols are familiar with the most recent illustrations of enemy vehicles and weapons.

During periods of withdrawal or reinforcement of the enemy the LRDG road watch has provided and still provides, an indispensable basis of certain facts on which calculation of enemy strength can be based. Without their reports we should frequently have been in doubt as to the enemy's intentions, when knowledge of them was all important; and our estimate of enemy strength would have been far less accurate and accepted with far less confidence.

The road watch immediately in rear of the EL AGHEILA position been of quite exceptional importance and the information which it has provided, in spite of interruptions due to a difficult and dangerous situation, has been invaluable. From the point of view of military intelligence the risks and casualties which the patrols have accepted and are accepting have been more than justified."

The establishment of the 'B' Echelon (the "Heavy Section") had been increased to a total of twenty 3-ton Chevrolets and six 10-ton Macks; and it was now organized in four detachments known as H.S. 1, 2, 3 and 4. Its work during phase IX included journeys to Cairo and Tobruk from Kufra, and forward dumping from Hon to points nearly as far west as the Tunisian Frontier. A severe loss was suffered by the L.R.D.G. when the Heavy Section Commander, Lieut. Arnold, was killed by a land mine in Hon on 15 January. He was succeeded by Lieut. A.S. Denniff.

The reconditioned 30-cwt Fords, to which reference has already been made, proved most unsatisfactory, and 30-cwt Chevrolets, which continued to be lost, could not be replaced by similar vehicles. At the end of January therefore patrols were reorganized so as to have two jeeps and four 30-cwt Chevrolets each.

Section XXII

Tenth Phase January 1943 to March 1943.

The tenth and last phase of the Long Range Desert Group's cooperation with the Eighth Army in North Africa covers the period from 24 January to 29 March 1943. It begins on the day after the Eighth Army's entry into Tripoli, and ends on the day it entered Gabes. Throughout this period the L.R.D.G. was actively employed on the left flank of the Army. In the subsequent fighting, which ended with the surrender of the Germans under General Sixt von Arnim at Cape Bon, the First and Eighth Armies with their French and American allies, fought as a whole and from positions which formed a continuous front. There was no uncovered flank round which the L.R.D.G. could carry out the long distance work for which it had been trained.

Operations of Eighth Army.

The general course of the Eighth Army's operations during this period was briefly as follows. After the capture of Tripoli the advance continued, and by 2 February Zuara on the coast and 30 miles from the Tunisian border, and Zelten, 10 miles west of it were in our hands. By 8 February the enemy had been completely driven from Cyrenaica and Tripolitania, and on the 20th Sir H. Alexander took command of all the Allied troops in Algeria, Tunisia and Tripolitania. At that time the First Army held a line running for 100 miles due south of Cape Serrat. Thence for 150 miles further south, that is to say as far as Gafsa, the line was continued by the French in the centre and the Americans on the right. The southern half of the line was by no means strong, and the enemy who had begun to counter attack westwards in Southern Tunisia at the end of January, captured Gafsa on 15 February which forced us to evacuate Sbeitla, Kasserine, Feriana and Tozeur; and we lost the use of the neighbouring airfields. The attack was continued on 20 February, but the enemy was eventually held at the Kasserine Gap, and fell back on the 26th. Tozeur was re-occupied on 8 March, and Gafsa on the 15th; while Sabria and Douz were occupied by the French Camel Corps on the 21st.

Meanwhile the Eighth Army had pushed forward during the latter half of February along the coast through Medenine, and on the left by Foum Tatahouine to Ghermessa (30 miles east of Ksar Rhilane). It had thus established itself before Rommel's position known to history as the Mareth Line. Mareth itself is a small village at about (T)Z.5306 just behind the left of the enemy's position, and about 7 miles from the coast of the Gulf of Gabes.

The forward localities of the position were protected by the Wadi Zig Zaou and extended N.E. to S.W. from El Mers on the coast at long. 10°25'E, lat. 33°40'N, through Arram, (T)Z.5502, thence for about 15 miles in a south westerly direction to the neighbourhood of Tugian (Toujane) about (Y)E.4185, which is situated in the north to south arm of the Jebel Nefusa, sometimes referred to as the "Matmata Hills". The attack on the Mareth Line began on 22 March, and the enemy was finally driven out of it on the 29th.

On 24 January patrols were disposed as follows:-

Indian (1) and R.1 patrols were with General Leclerc's column near Nalut.
Indian (3) was on its way to reconnoitre the eastern edge of the "Erg Oriental" in Southern Tunisia. T.1 was on its way back to Hon from Southern Tunisia. T.2 was at Wilder's Dump on its way to Southern Tunisia. H.2 Troop of the Heavy Section, having formed a forward dump, was returning to Hon. H.3 was at another dump at (Q)T.4523. The remaining patrols were at Hon. G.1 and G.2, however, owing to losses sustained on the Tripoli road watch at the end of November, had been amalgamated and during the Tenth Phase operated as 'G' Patrol. Group H.Q. remained at Hon, but in the middle of February Colonel Prendergast established an Advanced H.Q. with H.Q. Eighth Army at El Azizia.

Eighth Army Instructions.

After the capture of Tripoli, the commander L.R.D.G. was instructed by General Montgomery to make a careful and detailed reconnaissance of the area bounded on the north by the sea, on the east by long. 13°E, on the south by lat. 32° and on the west by long. 7°. The expression "the sea" is vague, and could be misinterpreted as including the north coast of Tunisia from Cape Bon to Philippeville, but the northernmost edge of any reconnaissance area allotted to a patrol was lat. 34°N, which is just north of the line Gabes-Tozeur. Thus the western boundary extended for about 140 miles along the western edge of the Erg Oriental, and the southern boundary 350 miles west from (approximately) Ksar Rhariane (Garian). The area as a whole represented "No man's land" in front of the Eighth Army's left flank, and on the right and right front of the forces in Algeria and Tunisia under General Alexander's command.

The object of the reconnaissance was to supply detailed information for the production of "going maps", for use if the Eighth Army found it necessary to make an outflanking movement round the right of Rommel's Mareth Line, as was eventually the case. It is to be remembered, however, that reconnaissance on much the same lines had been going on for some time, and that those which took place in the Tenth Phase were merely a continuation of them.

S.2 Patrol January and February 1943.

The first reconnaissance which was undertaken by Lieut. Henry with S.2 patrol was marred by the accidental wounding of the patrol commander (who died later) and the death of his driver, Rezin. The Operation Report was written by Lance Sergeant Calder-Potts who was second in command. The patrol left Hon on 25 January with two tasks.
(a) to convey a party of Advanced 'A' Force, consisting of Capt. Grandguillot, Capt. McKee, a W/T operator and four Arabs, with their rations and signalling equipment, to Tozeur; and thence to any area in which they might wish to operate,
(b) to reconnoitre a route from Hon to Tozeur, and an area bounded on the north by lat. 34°, on the east by long. 9°, on the south by lat. 33° and on the west by lat 7°30'. These limits include the Shott Djerid, and a stretch of country to the south of it.

Their first march took them to Socna; thence avoiding Esc Sciuref, they followed the Mizda road to (W)B.2947 and camped on the night 27/28th at (W)A.7462. They then moved N.W. across the Hamada el Homra, and arrived at (Y)P.1993 on the edge of the Erg and about 100 miles north of Ghadames, on 30 January. As they were carrying spares for T.2 and for Major Peniakoff's Demolition Squadron, the patrol commander went on the 31st with a small party to T.2's base camp at (Y)D.9404, but found only the trucks burnt out in the air attack made four days earlier. He could obtain no information from local Arabs of what had happened to T.2's men; but he was able to get sufficient spares from a burnt out truck to repair a truck of his own whose steering column had broken.

On 1 February the patrol searched without success for a route across the dunes on the east edge of the Erg to the western part of their area. On 2 February they reached (Y)D.9404 and met Capt. Rand's Indian (3) patrol searching for men of T.2. Later, having made their way over the dunes, they found Sergeant Garvin of that patrol with Capt. Yunnie and two Arabs and picked them up, less the Arabs who were paid off. They halted for the night at (Y)J.9278 and on the 3rd, after moving N.W. over about 23 miles of dune country, they arrived at (Y)D.6323, near the northern limit of it. The 30-cwt trucks were doing only some three miles to the gallon, and the jeeps about eight; moveover, the steering pillar of one truck kept on getting bent. On the 5th the patrol commander went with three jeeps to Tozeur to get petrol, taking Capt. Yunnie and Sergeant Garvin with him, and there met Lieut. Tinker with what was left of T.2 patrol. The remainder of S.2 followed next day as far as Shott Elcharbe in the low ground north of the dunes. Sergeant Calder-Potts reconnoitred this area on 7 February, and found an excellent landing ground that had been marked out by the French. On 9 February Lieut. Henry returned with a supply of petrol, and the patrol moved further west to (Y)C.7455.

On 9 February it arrived at Tozeur, and on the 10th the patrol commander left for Tebessa with a jeep and the W/T truck, to try and obtain a new swivel arm. About 13 miles out the W/T car ran over a mine and was badly damaged. Two men were wounded and had to be taken back to the French hospital at Tozeur where they were well looked after. On the morning of the 11th arrangements were made to transfer them to an American hospital at Tebessa. At 1730 hrs the patrol, short of a truck, moved on, and for the next three days continued its reconnaissance round the west and south edge of the Shott Djerid. On the 15th they arrived at (Y)D.1543, the "escape rendezvous" at which Capts. Grandguillot and McKee and their 'A' force party were to be dropped. Here they received a W/T message saying that further reconnaissance was not required, that the patrol commander was to go to Eighth Army H.Q. and the patrol to return to Hon. Next day a detachment of the French Camel Corps arrived to joint Capt. Grandguillot's party and reported that we had lost Tozeur. The patrol moved east that afternoon and continued in the same direction on the 17th, along the north edge of the Erg. During the day they met an Arab soldier of the French Army who told them they were heading straight for a detachment of the Italian Camel Corps, about 100 strong and only six miles away. They therefore turned south across the dunes, and for the second time in two days lost time in straightening a steering column.

Lieut. Henry wounded 20 February 1943.

On 18 February the sand was so deep that only 7 miles were covered. On the 19th they reached (Y)K.1342, about 60 miles S.S.W. of Foum Tatahouine, and near the road from that place to Ghadames, having travelled part of the previous night. It was on the next day that Lieut. Henry was mortally wounded, and the account of the incident is contained in Lance Sergeant Calder-Potts' report. About fifteen trucks were seen and thought to be French; and later at (Y)K.4113, close to the Ghadames road, they were challenged by a Camel Corps detachment also thought to be French, with whom signals were exchanged. In Sergeant Potts' words, "They were on the top of a knoll ... about 1,500 yards away; one of them came running down the knoll, and the O.C. patrol went up in his jeep to meet him. The man came up to the jeep, and then ran back about 10 yards waving his hand. I saw two puffs of dust near him as he was running back. They then opened fire on the jeep with one M.G. and two rifles ... there were about 30 to 40 men with 50 camels. We uncovered our guns (we had come through a sand storm the day before) and the only gun that worked was the 20 mm Breda. After the Breda had moved them from the top of the knoll and we had moved behind cover, it was decided that the O.C. and Private Rezin had been killed and the enemy held the advantage, so it would not pay us to continue the fight." The patrol then continued its march towards Wilder's Dump, and arrived there on 21 February. Here they found three trucks of Indian (1) patrol which had been sent to meet them with petrol, and they then went on to Nalut, which they reached on the same day. Here they learned that the engagement they had had was not with enemy but with the French, and that the patrol commander who was wounded, had been brought to Nalut in an ambulance. Private Rezin had been killed.

Sergeant Calder-Potts saw his commanding officer on 22 February just before he left in an ambulance for Tripoli. It appeared that the latter had himself mistaken the French "Méharistes" for Italians. Colonel Prendergast in recording the incident, explains that owing to the failure of S.2's wireless set he had been unable to warn Lieut. Henry of their presence in the area.

The patrol continued its march on 22 February, and reported to the Group Commander at El Azizia on the 23rd. On the 25th they left for Hon, and marching by Tripoli and Misurata arrived there on the 27th.

Reconnaissance Areas Indian (2) and Indian (4) Patrols January and February 1943.

The country to be reconnoitred in accordance with General Montgomery's orders had been divided by Lieut.Colonel Prendergast into four areas. On 24 January 1943 orders were issued by Major S.V. McCoy, commanding the Indian Long Range Squadron, for the reconnaissance of Area 4 by the 2nd and 4th Indian patrols, under command of Capt. Birdwood. About 10 days later, however, while the patrols were on the march, this order was cancelled and the final instructions were -

(1) To reconnoitre and report on the going in the following area, with a view to the passage of a force of all arms through it.

Boundaries   North Line Bir Negoua (Y)D.8397 – Kebili (T)Y.3002.
East Long. 9°30'E.
South Lat. 33°N.
West Long. 9°E.

(2) To get an idea of the going in the Jebel Tebaga (T.Y.40 - T.Y.93).

The centre of this area is about 30 miles S.E. of the eastern edge of the Shott Djerid, and the Jebel Tebaga lies along its northern edge.

Indian (2) Patrol left Hon on 27 January and reached Wilder's Dump at (Q)T.4522 on 1 February, having been forced to abandon a 30-cwt truck on the way, on account of a leaking radiator and worn steering. On the 2nd the patrol reached (Y)X.1040 where it found Indian (3) Patrol, and it was joined there by Indian (4) on the 6th. The latter patrol had left Hon two days earlier and marched by a different route. It too had had to abandon one 30-cwt truck, and had had trouble with the steering of another which retarded progress.

The reconnaissance was made by a composite patrol consisting of four jeeps and four 30-cwt Chevrolets. Two "rear bases" each of two 30-cwt trucks were formed at (Y)J.8856 and (Y)K.1257, and in order to guard against the danger of the trucks being destroyed by fire, as had happened to T.2 not long before, the petrol was taken out of them and hidden elsewhere. The reconnaissance was completed by the evening of 10 February.

A detailed "going report" was compiled in which the most important point was that the Jebel Tebaga appeared to be impassable, but the plain to the south of it could be crossed by any form of M.T. Arabs were numerous, but no enemy were met on the ground, and possibly owing to the weather, few aircraft were seen in the air. The patrol reached Hon on 18 February.

Y.2 Patrol February 1943.

Y.2 patrol (Capt. Spicer) left Hon on 31 January with orders to reconnoitre an area bounded on the north by lat. 32°N, on the east by long. 11°E, on the south by the line Wilder's Dump (Q)T.4522 – (Y)P.5080, and on the west by the line (Y)P.5080 – (Y)K.5030. Nalut is at the north east corner of this area, which includes the track junction of El Geneien, about 50 miles west by south of Nalut. Special attention was to be paid to a possible route from, approximately, (Y)P.5080 to Dehibat (Z)F.0733, and to finding a way for M.T. over the escarpment from the Tripoli plain N.E. of El Geneien to the Dehibat area, which was near the right flank of the Mareth Line.

On leaving the reconnaissance area the patrol was to move north towards the Matmata area about 20 miles south of Gabes. The nearest posts believed to be occupied by the enemy at that time were Nalut (which was not), Dehibat and Foum Tatahouine; and it was thought probable too that Bourg le Boeuf, 80 miles S.W. of Foum Tatahouine, and Ksar Rhilane, 80 miles west by north of it were also occupied.

The patrol was accompanied by an officer of the 7th Armoured Division (Lieut. Bristowe) to decide whether the ground was suitable for a mixed armoured force. It marched by Socna and Esc Sciuref, and was joined on 2 February by R.2 patrol (Capt. Lazarus). On 4 February the two patrols arrived at (Z)L.0068, about 30 miles S.W. of Nalut where a dump was made, and on the 5th Y.2 went on alone and started to send in route reports from its "lunch position" at (Y)K.1979. At (Y)K.2256 they met a patrol of the S.A.S.; and encamped at (Y)K.3987, four miles west of what became known as "Wilder's Gap", about 30 miles S.W. of Foum Tatahouine. Next morning while making a local reconnaissance they saw a patrol of four German 8-wheeled armoured cars going south down the road from Foum Tatahouine to Bourg le Boeuf, which stopped opposite them, examined their tracks and then went on.

On 8 February orders were received to reconnoitre Bourg le Boeuf, and later more details of Wilder's Gap were asked for. The patrol commander was also told to report to Nalut on the 17th to give information. Having carried out these two reconnaissances, he started on 12 February for Nalut and arrived there on the 13th, when he received further orders to be at Jiado, 60 miles east of Nalut on the 17th. Capt. Lazarus, with R.2, arrived at Nalut next day. At 1400 hrs orders came that both patrols were to go to H.Q. N.Z. Division at Castel Benito, 15 miles south of Tripoli. The 15th, 16th and 17th were spent in collating information, and in interviews with General Freyberg. Y.2 patrol under Sergeant Springford was sent on to Hon on the 16th and arrived there on 20 February; Capt. Lazarus and Capt. Spicer arrived there on the 21st.

A route had been mapped within the area reconnoitred which was suitable for all arms including laden transporters, and had an average frontage of one to three miles.

R.2 Patrol February 1943.

R.2 patrol (Capt. Lazarus) had orders to make a topographical reconnaissance from Wilder's Gap (Y)E.4389 to (Y)E.1030, a point about 7 miles east of Ksar Rhilane.

It was also to form a reserve of petrol carried in three 3-ton Chevrolets of the Heavy Section, at Wilder's Dump (Q)T.4523.

The patrol left Hon on 1 February and travelled with Y.2 as far as (Z)L.0168 on 4 February. The patrols then parted and on the 7th R.2 lay up at (Y)J.9265 on the edge of the Erg Oriental, and awaited instructions. As there were many Arabs about the patrol moved next day to (Y)K.0887, 17 miles to the N.E. There instructions were received to find the best route to the area about point (Y)E.1333, some 30 miles further north, and 8 miles east of Ksar Rhilane; and afterwards to go to the latter place and pick up two men of the S.A.S. who were reported to be there. A search for the men in question was made on the 9th, but was unsuccessful. Ksar Rhilane was not occupied and was thoroughly investigated, good water being found.

Further reconnaissance was carried out during the 11th and 12th, for a route westward from Wilder's Gap to (Y)E.0500 and thence northward as far as lat. 33°N.

The patrol then moved to Castel Benito and reached Hon on 20 February.

Capt. Lazarus' report showed that the route reconnoitred was passable by a force of all arms and that except at Wadi crossings, movement would be possible on a fairly wide front.

G Patrol February 1943.

The last reconnaissance of the country on the right, and to the right rear of Rommel's positions was done by 'G' Patrol (Lieut. Hon B. Bruce) which left Hon on 3 February taking with it Lieut. Lee of the Royal Dragoons (7th Armd. Div.) to advise on going. The area to be covered was bounded on the north by lat. 33°30'N, on the east by long. 9°E, on the south by lat. 33°15'N, and on the west by long. 7°30'E. This area is in the form of a parallelogram, about 85 miles from east to west and 20 miles from north to south. It lies mainly in the low, salty ground south of the Shott Djerid, but includes a strip of dune country on the north edge of the "Erg"; and its N.E. corner is at Douz, about 25 miles south of Ksar Rhilane. In his report Lieut. Bruce stated that "none of the area that was covered could be recommended as passable for any force … in the patrol of six vehicles, three steering assemblies and six springs were broken, and it was only owing to the exceptional desert worthiness of the vehicles that it was possible to cover the area." He said also that much sand must have blown over the area since the French 1:200,000 maps were made in 1932, for the roads and tracks marked seemed barely to exist. The patrol was attacked by Arabs near Rhidma on the S.E. edge of the Shott Djerid, in the early morning of the 13th and two men were wounded. They were taken to Tozeur, but as an attack was expected there, the patrol went to the oasis of El Oued, 80 miles to the S.W., and the wounded were evacuated by air to Touggourt.[1]

The patrol followed them to Touggourt and arrived there on the 18th. On the 19th Lieuts. Bruce and Lee with seven O.Rs, started for First Army H.Q. to obtain supplies and spare parts, and if possible to enable Lieut. Lee to go direct to Eighth Army H.Q. After spending a night at Biskra, where they were warmly welcomed by a wing of the 12th U.S. Air Force, they reached Constantine on the 20th, where they found the H.Q. of Sir H. Alexander's 18th Army Group, and not the First Army as they had expected. Lieut. Lee was able to fly to Tripoli with the reconnaissance

---

1 Tozeur was evacuated on 16 February as a result of the enemy's capture of Gafsa (60 miles to the N.E.) the day before.

report within two days, and arrangements were made for three steering assemblies to be flown from H.Q. Eighth Army as there were no Canadian built Chevrolets with the First Army. Arrangements were also made for the evacuation of the two wounded guardsmen. The party started back to Touggourt on the 27th, and arrived on the 28th to find that, in Lieut. Bruce's words, "a pleasant time had been had by all, despite the fact that there was no one in the small town who could speak a word of English!" The return journey was made by Ouargla, Fort Lallemand and Fort Flatters, where Lieut. Bruce emphasises the great hospitality shown by the French garrison, and says that "among the souvenirs of the Foreign Legion battery stationed there that the patrol took back were three small puppies!" On the 9th the patrol arrived at El Azizia, where it joined Y.1 and reached Hon on the 11th and 12th having covered 3,515 miles. In addition to the report called for in the original orders, Lieut. Bruce reported very fully on the going from El Oued to Touggourt, and on the route followed during the return journey, from Touggourt along the "formidable southern edge of the Erg Oriental" to Sinauen.

T.2 Patrol March 1943.

The last task in connection with the advance of the Eighth Army into Tunisia was allotted to a detachment of T.2 patrol (Lieut. R. Tinker, M.C., M.M.), which was sent to guide the New Zealand Division and attached troops during their outflanking movement round the enemy's right during the attack on the Mareth Line. The detachment, consisting of the patrol commander with three O.Rs and two jeeps, left Hon on 2 March 1943, arrived at El Azizia on the 3rd and remained there for five days.

On 6 March Rommel counter attacked unsuccessfully from Toujane in the Matmata Hills and lost 52 tanks from anti-tank gunfire and air attack. Three days later he attacked Ksar Rhilane, 40 miles south west of his right flank, also without success; and the air bombardment in preparation for the Eighth Army's attack on his position then began. On 9 March T.2 patrol's detachment marched to join H.Q. N.Z. Division at Medenine, (Y)E.7777. On the 12th the Division moved east to Ben Gardane and then S.W. by Foum Tatahouine to (Y)K.3293, in the Jebel Nefusa hills near Wilder's Gap. Here a halt was made for seven days during which Lieut. Tinker's party made several reconnaissances to the north and north west. The first of these was to Ksar Rhilane now held by the French, the second to the Wadi Mahabes, which runs north from (Y)E.1015 to Ksar Rhilane. The third made by Lieut. Tinker and an officer of the N.Z. Engineers was to the Wadi el Aredj (described on the 1:500,000 map as Wadi el Midjend). A possible crossing was found at (Y)E.1238, but it was commanded by the hill of El Outid (Y)E.1545. This feature was held by the enemy, but on 18 March they were driven off it by the French. Meanwhile on 16 March

Corporal Bassett of T.2 patrol, and the provost personnel marked a track for the axis of advance of the Division as far as Wadi Mahabes, and on the 18th and 19th the marking was continued as far as the Wadi el Aredj at (Y)E.1238. On the 18th a reconnaissance was made north of the Wadi el Aredj and a proposed route to the Jebel[1] Tebaga was plotted. Late on 19 March the Division moved forward to the Wadi el Aredj, and on the 20th the advance was continued as far as point (Y)D.9696, 35 miles S.W. of Gabes. Some opposition was encountered at Kasr Tarcine (Y)E.15, and Bir Soltane (Y)E.06; and later from the foothills of the Jebel Tebaga just north of (Y)D.9696. During the 20th Lieut. Tinker's party was attached to the Staffordshire Yeomanry. On the 21st it marched with the 3rd Bn. R.T.R., when the advance was continued to point 201 at (T)Y.8909, 30 miles W.S.W. of Gabes and at the foot of the S.E. end of the Jebel Tebaga. On 22 March the party was with H.Q. 8th Armoured Brigade, and on the 23rd they returned to H.Q. N.Z. Division, with which they remained until Gabes was occupied on the 29th.

Eighth Army Attack on Mareth Line.

General Montgomery's frontal attack which had begun on 20 March but was checked next day, was resumed when General Freyberg's column captured El Hamma, 18 miles west of Gabes, on the 28th. During the night 27/28th the enemy slipped away from the Mareth Line and fell back to prepared positions on the Wadi Akarit. Lieut. Tinker's detachment left Gabes on the 20th and went to Alexandria, arriving there on 3 April.

During the previous weeks Colonel Prendergast had paid several flying visits (in the "Waco") to G.H.Q. Middle East to discuss the future of the L.R.D.G. After much discussion it was decided that the unit should not be disbanded, but should continue to operate in Europe on much the same lines as before; and a revised establishment was drawn up.

L.R.D.G. withdrawn to Egypt.

During the last week of March and the first week of April the Group moved from Hon to Alexandria. While en route to Egypt R.2 patrol, under Lieut. J.M. Sutherland, who had recently joined, carried out a task for H.Q. Cyrenaica District by transporting Administrative officers to Kufra and "showing the flag" at Jalo and Jarabub. One of its trucks was destroyed by a mine 1,000 miles east of the area of active operations, which in Colonel Prendergast's words, "made a fitting curtain to the Desert activities of the Unit".

The Indian Long Range Squadron was moved up from Hon to

1   The long range of hills running from east to west between Gabes and the Shott Djerid.

the Tunisian front early in March, and was employed for a time in road reconnaissance, in providing protective patrols for aerodromes, and similar work; but on 3 April it too was sent back to Egypt.

In a letter to Colonel Prendergast, dated 2 April 1943, General Montgomery writes "I would like you to know how much I appreciate the excellent work done by your patrols and by the S.A.S. in reconnoitring the country up to the Gabes Gap. Without your careful and reliable reports the launching of the "left hook" by the N.Z. Division would have been a leap in the dark: with the information they produced the operations could be planned with some certainty, and as you know, went off without a hitch."

Appendix 1

L.R.D.G. Signals.

At the beginning of December 1940, about five months after the formation of the L.R.D.G., Lieut. G.B. Heywood, Middlesex Yeomanry, joined it as signal officer, and remained so throughout the unit's operations in North Africa. The "Signal Troop" at the end of 1940 consisted of one officer and four O.Rs, who were on loan from the signal pool. By April 1943 it had two officers and fifty-one O.Rs, most of whom had been with the unit for eighteen months and had accumulated much experience. Both signallers and technicians were "hand picked", and as the break down of a set usually involved the abandonment of a mission, a high standard of maintenance was of the utmost importance. There is no need to emphasize the obvious importance of effective inter-communication in the type of work the L.R.D.G. was called upon to perform, nor should the difficulties of ensuring it be under-estimated. At the end of the "Desert Phase" Lieut. Heywood wrote a full report on the work of the L.R.D.G. Signals from which certain extracts have been taken in order to point out the difficulties that had to be overcome, without going deeply into technicalities.

The general policy was that W/T communications should be provided for all patrols, sections or parties moving far from Headquarters. The distances between stations naturally varied, but patrols required communications over distances which might be 1,000 miles or more. The next higher formation, G.H.Q. Middle East, or H.Q. Eighth Army as the case might be, was usually from 200 to 600 miles away. Except for the times when Group H.Q. was at Siwa, at Alexandria or in the Fayoum, no alternative means of communication was available, and at Siwa the telephone was most unreliable.

When patrols were out W/T Control Stations at Headquarters had to be on continuous watch. In order to simplify matters patrols were at first allotted three daily signalling periods, in the early morning, during the mid-day halt and in the evening, but it was also necessary that they should be able to call H.Q. at any time in the event of emergency. The schedule system was however never really satisfactory, and eventually patrols were allowed to call Group H.Q. at any time that was convenient, so long as at least one call was made every day. It has to be remembered that the patrol commander could not use his wireless on the move, and that the periods during which he could halt to do so varied with circumstances throughout the journey. When close to his base be could not use his W/T before dawn since the type of set used would not work on a low enough frequency for communication over short distances at that time of day. Communication was at its

213

best at mid-day; but when several patrols were out the time available for any one patrol was short, as each had to have its turn. Near the area of operations there was always the danger of being spotted by hostile aircraft which were in the habit of reconnoitring in the early morning. After the morning reconnaissance the wireless could be used freely if care was taken to drop the mast when an aircraft was heard. Owing the to variation due to changes in longitude G.M.T. was always used as signal time.

The W/T set used by patrols and squadron H.Q. was the No. 11 set H.P. Other types were tried but for one reason or another were found unsuitable. The disadvantage of the No. 11 set lay in its frequency range, for after dark it would not cover a frequency low enough for satisfactory communications over distances of less than about 200 miles, especially in winter and early spring. Breakdowns were rare and for the most part occurred in sets that had seen 18 months service or more. One set was for 24 hours under water in a flooded Wadi, and after being taken out of the vehicle, was found to be full of sand, but when cleaned it worked as well as ever.

Power was obtained from the vehicle generator and battery with the addition of another six volt battery and 4 pole switch, and an ammeter.

In addition to the No. 11 set patrols carried a broadcast receiver in order to obtain time signals for navigation purposes. Efforts were made to obtain a more powerful set for Headquarters use, and since no British equipment was available, a captured Italian set was eventually used. No trouble was experienced with charging, or with line and other equipment; but owing to the remoteness of Group H.Q. from L. of C. supply centres, three months supply of consumable stores and spares was always carried by the unit.

A high standard of security had of course to be maintained, and the isolation of the Group facilitated it. Among other precautions, international commercial procedure was used when possible. No word of plain language in any tongue was used except in emergency, and speech was never used during an operation except in emergency. The forms of cipher employed gradually increased in security, and high grade cipher was always used for communication between Group H.Q. and higher formations. As most signal traffic passed during short but busy periods the cipher staff had to be large. The greatest distance achieved was 1,400 miles, and it was only when a patrol was so close to H.Q. that a breakdown was not a serious matter, that communication was unreliable.

Appendix 2

The Fezzan Operation – December 1940 to February 1941.

(See Section VII)

This Appendix contains extracts from an account written by Capt. M.D.D. Crichton-Stuart, Scots Guards, of the expedition of two patrols of the L.R.D.G. and a Free French party under Lieut.Colonel Comte d'Ornano to the Fezzan. Capt. Crichton-Stuart was then in command of 'G' (Guards) Patrol, the first patrol to be recruited from British Troops.

The original is a complete and well written narrative of the whole expedition, which began on 27 December 1940 and ended when the patrols reached Cairo on 9 February 1941, after covering about 4,300 miles, and it is profusely illustrated with photographs taken by Capt. Crichton-Stuart and his second-in-command, Lieut. M.A. Gibbs, Coldstream Guards. The extracts that have been taken from it give a very good idea of the early organization of a L.R.D.G. patrol, and of the country that patrols had to cross; and the account of the attack on Murzuk exemplifies their habitual boldness and initiative.

> "Briefly, the Patrol was made up as follows: One light scout car and ten 30-cwt lorries, specially fitted but unarmoured; the principle was three men per truck, commander, driver and gunner. Besides the Patrol Commander and Second-in-Command, we carried as navigator Lt. W. Kennedy Shaw, who has done as much desert travelling by car and camel as anyone alive, and who came from a Government Archaeological job in Palestine. Other specialists were a R.A.M.C. Orderly, a R.C.S. Signaller for the wireless, and a R.A.O.C. Fitter. Excluding Easton and Winchester, there were 29 N.C.Os and Guardsmen to make up the number to 35, the two extra being carried as immediate reserves. Our armament consisted of a 37 mm Bofors Anti-Tank gun, portée, on a fixed mounting, four Anti-Tank Rifles, four Vickers and seven Lewis Guns all mountable for Anti-aircraft. The usual revolvers, rifles, etc. per man: and as a final – and most fortunate – afterthought, a 2" Mortar. The other Patrol was similarly equipped: petrol, water, rations and ammunition made up the loads."

****

> "We also carried with us a famous old Senussi chieftain, Sheik Abd El Gelil Sief Al Nasr, one of the last to hold out against the Italians in Libya together with his personal slave, a coal black gentleman who was immediately and affection-

ately christened "Midnight" by the Patrol. After having been defeated by the Italians at Kufra, the last Senussi stronghold in Libya, in 1931, these two had escaped with others to the Nile Valley on foot, a distance of rather over 500 miles with only one watering-point, Uweinat, on the way. The old man had welcomed this opportunity of a trip to his old tribal lands, so long as he got a chance to shoot an Italian or two."

****

"This vast sand barrier, The Egyptian or "Great" Sand Sea, in area about the size of Ireland, stretched from Siwa Oasis in the North, almost down to the Sudan, along the Libyan frontier. Since the great disaster to Cambyses' army of 40,000 men, which attempted to invade Siwa from Luxor and disappeared to a man in the sand, it has been rather avoided by military bodies, and by all but the fewest travellers. The Italians felt safe behind its impenetrability, but previous Patrols had probed a way across, and we were now taking advantage of this secret to cross it, and after, to surprise them with the largest practical force."

****

"The parallel lines of dunes run almost North and South, with a slight North-West and South-East tendency, rising to some 500 feet above the desert floor in the centre of the Sand Sea. Here and there the great, smooth "whale-back" dunes break into sharp, twisting crests and ridges, falling almost sheer on one side, utterly impassable except with the greatest labour on foot. Packed and shaped by the prevailing wind over thousands of years, this Sand Sea compares in shape and form with a great Atlantic swell, of long rollers, crested here and there, with great troughs between; and as you may notice in such a sea occasional whirlpools and disturbances, so in the Sand Sea are sudden, unexpected and invisible soft patches. Withal it is utterly lifeless and dead, without a blade of grass or a stone to break the monotony of sky and sand."

****

"Gathering speed on the downward slope into the trough, the trucks soared up the next dune with their impetus, their desert tyres, partly deflated, making the shallowest impression in the minutely rippled sand. Sometimes their impetus carried them through a soft patch, but more often they had to be manhandled, one at a time, on to harder going, the two Patrol Commanders, in their light scout cars, trying to avoid soft patches and altering course to avoid crested dunes. The unfortunate Seconds-in-Command brought up the rear, shepherding and pushing the chronic "stickers" in front of them."

****

"After replenishing from various dumps next morning we set off after our New Year's dinners, about 2.30 and ran very soon out of the sand into Libya, on to a wonderful smooth level plain. This "Serir" as it is called, is the best going in the world, hard sand and small gravel, stretching smooth and featureless for nearly 100 miles. At sunset we began to run into sand again, and once more camped by a dune, this time on the edge of the Libyan Sand Sea. This is but a continuation of the Egyptian Sand Sea, which from Siwa sweeps west into Libya, and South again where we now reached it. In shape it resembles an irregular horse-shoe, with its West tip North of Kufra, and its East tip in South-Western Egypt, and the oases of Jalo and Siwa respectively, at the North-West and North-East corners of the curve. We struggled right across the Libyan range of dunes on the 2nd, not so large, but more treacherous, than the Egyptian, and about 100 miles in width."

****

"We crossed the road consisting of thousands of vehicle tracks spread over half a mile in wide formation, and ran on fast for many miles. With no windshields, at high speed, and in the bitter cold, conditions were almost "arctic". This day, 3 January, we went nearly 200 miles in all, roughly West South-West, over mostly good "Serir", to camp in yet another sand-sea West of Taiserbo, the Northern-most of the Kufra group of oases. This Sand Sea also, the Italians considered impassable; we had slipped them alright.

After the fifth successive freezing night we continued South-West for a further 150 miles, first through sand, then over serir, then rock, then thick floury dust through which we ploughed and pushed and boiled. The country was as featureless and barren as could be, but when we stopped on rock once, to pump up our tyres again after deflating for the soft sand, Shaw discovered flint instruments of some bygone civilization. In the late afternoon we came on to serir broken up by small, shallow wadis, and folds in the ground. Here, in the middle of nothingness, we made a standing camp, on 4 January. Short of following our tracks, we would not be seen or suspected where we were in a hundred years. We had travelled some 1,100 miles in 9 days running."

****

"Clayton left Southwards with four trucks next morning, for Kayugi, in the North fringe of the Tibesti Mountain mass, to contact the French, while Shaw and Gibbs went off with three trucks South-East to explore, (or more militarily, "reconnoitre") an unknown but believed passable route called the Terenegi Pass, to the North-East of the Tibesti massif.

About midday on the 7th Clayton returned with his trucks laden with French and petrol. The leader of the former, Colonel d'Ornano, was a magnificent figure of a man, very tall, in native uniform, complete with burnous and a monocle. With him as a "Capitaine", a Lieutenant, two French Sergeants and five "Indigènes" or native irregulars, making ten in all – the representatives of the Chad Province, the first to declare for General de Gaulle. That evening there was an international council of war, at which representatives of England, Scotland, New Zealand, France and Libya attended."

****

"There were two high spots in it (i.e. the Conference). First, the arrival of a long wireless message from Cairo giving fearsome and rather incredible details of the defences of Murzuk, from a document captured at Sidi Barrani. The other was when the old chieftain, on being referred to about the way to attack Murzuk, admitted that some years ago he himself had successfully besieged the place for two months. The result of the conference was a unanimous decision to make straight for Murzuk, missing a smaller Italian outpost called Wau-el-Kebir, which might give our presence away, by wireless.

We set off next morning, the 8th, now North-West, over the same featureless plain. This at last gave way to more broken country, with rocky flat-topped hills and uneven going between. Sand gave way to dark basalt and volcanic rocks, and once, when we attempted to cut across a rocky plateau which stood across our compass bearing, we ran on to the most terrible going. Great sharp-cornered boulders, half buried in the ground, forced us to go down and around. However, we managed 100 miles of tortuous going, and that evening stopped short of an escarpment which dropped down to a plain in the West."

****

"Our objective, Murzuk, we knew a certain amount about. The greater part of the population of Fezzan lives in a string of small oases around the North and East sides of a huge mass of sand, called the Edeye of Murzuk. Murzuk itself, the largest and most westerly village, the Capital", sported an aerodrome and a large, modern stone fort, with a considerable garrison and a wireless station. There had been stationed there an "Auto-Saharan Company" the Italian equiv-alent of our Long Range Patrol, well equipped but absurdly used: for this one and two others had been captured intact at Sidi Barrani. Our intelligence about the place was naturally scanty, though we knew the aerodrome to be defended by a couple of machine-gun posts. The general plan was to make a reconnais-sance from the Northern ridge overlooking the place, prior to surrounding the fort and destroying the aerodrome; with no gun which could knock holes in the walls of the fort, we could hardly hope to take it. On the other hand, if we could frighten or surprise the garrison into doing the incredible, propaganda would be a mild word for the stir we would spread in Murzuk town after the surrender. Our danger was from the fort wirelessing to Hon, the main Italian army and air base in the Fezzan some 250 miles North.

In the early morning of 11 January, the two Patrol Commanders, Colonel d'Ornano, the "Capitaine", and Shaw, went ahead in the three light cars, West-wards, the rest following well behind. The main road from Murzuk North to Hon, an engineered affair, was struck about 9 o'clock, some 10 miles North of Murzuk. A trap was immediately set to put any visitors from Hon in the bag, and we drove South to the ridge overlooking Murzuk, nearly 5 miles to the North of it, and by 9.30 the Reconnaissance party was studying the objective."

****

"With no possibility of closer reconnaissance Clayton decided to attack at once. The New Zealand Patrol, less one troop, under Lieut. Ballantyne, the second-in-command, was to go straight for the aerodrome while 'G' Patrol with a New Zealand troop of three trucks and both 2" mortars were to "contain" the fort. Orders were issued and a quick meal eaten preparatory to starting at midday. The start was delayed owing to an aeroplane which was sighted over the fort, but when this had disappeared we started at 12.30 in close convoy down the road, the New Zealand Patrol leading, to pay our 1,440 mile call.

As the column entered the belt of palms, a solitary cyclist met it: this gentle-man, who proved to be the Postmaster, was added to the party with his bicycle.

Then as the convoy approached the fort, above the main central tower of which the Italian flag flew proudly, the Guard turned out. We were rather sorry for them, but they probably never knew what hit them.

All positions were from 250 yards – 500 yards from the fort, the broken ground, scrub, and a few native huts affording considerable cover. After the first few minutes, during which the Bofors hit a car and a truck trying to get into the fort, and a number of Italians were caught by small arms fire in the same act, few targets presented themselves. The Bofors was ineffective against the bases of the wireless masts, and saved its fire, while the effect of heavy Anti-Tank rifle and Machine Gun fire on windows and slits could not be observed: there was heavy sniping fire on both sides, and some from the town itself. But Gibbs with the two 2″ mortars, who had been ordered to work his way in as close as possible on the West, scored a success. Working his way to within 300 to 400 yards of the fort, one of the first bombs started a column of black smoke on the roof of the main tower, which was soon followed by flames, and in a quarter of an hour the roof was blazing, and the Italian flag was no more. For half an hour the fire increased in intensity, being confined to the main central block which appeared to be completely gutted; but it eventually died down, while intermittent firing continued.

While the fire in the fort was raging, a huge column of black smoke from the direction of the aerodrome told us the New Zealanders had been successful. On reaching the aerodrome they had found the Italians running to man their posts: they had forestalled one lot, and knocked another post out after a little trouble, with their Bofors gun. Unfortunately the latter machine gun post killed Colonel d'Ornano, who was on the back of Clayton's truck when he ran on it unexpectedly. When the remaining forty odd Italians had been rounded up, the hangar was burnt, together with three fully loaded reconnaissance Bombers, petrol, oil, bombs and other equipment. Finally four prisoners were selected from the rest, and Clayton fired a white flare as a signal for withdrawal.

We never saw the signal, for sand had begun to blow and the Italians had brought all their machine guns to bear on us. Any movement brought down heavy fire, and "Midnight", the old Chieftain's slave, was making himself unpopular with one post where he would fire his rifle (he had knocked off the sights for getting in his line of view) and then stand up and shout abuse at his enemies. When the signal for withdrawal finally arrived at about 4 o'clock, by hand, the Patrol Commander had to run the gauntlet to get round the various posts. It seemed as if we must get considerable casualties in getting trucks and crews out and away from the soft sand, but God most opportunely sent the wind, as with the Armada, and the whole Patrol withdrew in a thick sandstorm to the aerodrome, while the enemy continued firing blindly in all directions."

****

"Now we entered them [the Tibesti foothills] and came into the worst country we ever experienced. From broken rocky plateaux we dropped steeply into rock bound valleys, only finding a way out with great difficulty, by putting flat stones over the soft sandy patches between the stony going, and charging the trucks up the escarpments one by one. Somehow the tow kept up, by masterly driving, even over giant sand-dunes which checked the way between great black crags with vertical cliffs. We had to go round these, struggling through the soft dunes, and down steep sand slopes. The country was wild and magnificent, but not exactly ideal motoring: springs, tyres and drivers were hard tested.

At last we wound our way, with great difficulty, down several broken black escarpments – in one of which Gibbs found caves full of rock paintings and carvings of animals – to come quite suddenly on a narrow plain through which a track ran East and West. We had struck the track from Tibesti to French West Africa – the road to Timbuctoo! – but had covered only 9 miles in the whole morning.

After some miles the deeply rutted dust began to give way to sand once more, and an enormous mass of sand stretched away to the South. This new sand-sea was laconically named the "Grand-Erg (Sand-Sea) Bilma-Eochimi-Agadem", covering a vast and unknown area to the South West of Tibesti and rising into great twisted dune masses, unexplored and probably impassable to any vehicle. Our way was difficult to follow, as the tracks disappeared time and again in the blown sand of the North East corner of the Sand Sea. Huge fantastic rocks rose out of the sand about the French Equatorial Frontier, grim and desolate and magnificent. Then odd patches of grass began to appear, and we ran steadily down-hill through more grass and a few trees. Quite suddenly we saw a green valley before us, a wadi thick with trees, and beyond it rocky grey-black hills, and gazelle grazing in twos and threes. This was the beginning of the Capitaine's "beau pays" he had told us of, and tomorrow we would reach his own fort of Zouar, right in the mountains themselves."

****

Appendix 3

A.

The following officers whose names are given in the Unit Casualty Returns (A.F.3010) served in the L.R.D.G. during 1940, 1941, 1942 and the first four months of 1943. Ranks are those held at the end of the period or when they left the unit.

Date of Joining.	Name.	Regiment or Corps.
July 1940.	Lt. Col. R.A. Bagnold, O.B.E.	R. of O. Royal Signals.
" "	Capt. P.A. Clayton, D.S.O.[1]	General List.
July 1940.	Maj. E.C. Mitford, M.C.	R.T.R.
August 1940.	Capt. L.B. Ballantyne.	N.Z.E.F.
" "	Lieut. F.B. Edmundson, (M.O.)	N.Z.E.F.
" "	Lieut. R.B. McQueen.	N.Z.E.F.
" "	Capt. D.G. Steele. O.B.E.	N.Z.E.F.
" "	Lieut. J.H. Sutherland, M.C.	N.Z.E.F.
September 1940.	Capt. C.A. Holliman, M.C.	R.T.R.
July 1940.	Capt. W.B.K. Shaw, O.B.E.[2]	Intelligence Corps.
December 1940.	Capt. G.B. Heywood,[3] M.B.E.	Middlesex Yeomanry.
December 1940.	Capt. M.D.D. Crichton-Stuart.	Scots Guards.
" "	Lieut. M.A. Gibbs.	Coldstream Guards.
" "	Lieut. C.H. Croucher.	General List.
January 1941.	Capt. P.J.D. McCraith.	Notts Yeomanry.
" "	Capt. J.R. Olivey, M.C.	S. Rhodesia Force.
" "	2/Lieut. W.P. Pulzer.	N. Somerset Yeomanry.
" "	Lieut. (Q.M.) H.A. Cox.	General List.
February "	Lt.Col. G.L. Prendergast, D.S.O.	R.T.R.
March "	Capt. J.R. Easonsmith, D.S.O., M.C	R.T.R.
May "	Maj. E.C.T. Wilson, V.C.	E. Surrey Regiment.

1 P.O.W. 1.2.41.
2 Intelligence Officer.
3 Signal Officer.

Date of Joining.	Name.	Regiment or Corps.
July "	Capt. A.M. Hay.[4]	Coldstream Guards
July 1941.	Capt. K.H. Lazarus.	E.A. Engineers.
September 1941.	Capt. P. Arnold.	General List.
" "	Capt. J.A.L. Timpson. M.C.	Scots Guards.
" "	Capt. R.P. Carr, M.C.[5]	R.A.
September 1941.	Lieut. D.I. Ross.	N.Z.E.F.
" "	Lieut. D. Barrett.	N.Z.E.F. (Q.M. and in Feb. 1943. Adjt.)
September 1941.	Capt. D.L. Lloyd-Owen, M.C.	The Queens.
October "	Capt. T.W. Ashdown.[6]	R.A.O.C.
October 1941.	Capt. F.C. Simms,[7] M.C.	R. Warwickshire Regiment.
October 1941.	Capt. A.D.N. Hunter.	R. Scots Fusiliers.
December 1941.	Capt. R.P. Lawson.[8] M.C.	R.A.M.C.
January 1942.	2/Lieut. H.P. Eitzen.	R.A.
February 1942.	Lieut. E.M. Tobin.	R.A.C.
" "	Lieut. Hon. R.B. Gurdon.[9]	Coldstream Guards.
March 1942.	Capt. L.S.W. Cranfield.	H.A.C.
April "	Capt. C.S. Morris, M.C.	N.Z.E.F.
" "	Capt. N.P. Wilder, D.S.O.	N.Z.E.F.
" "	Capt. A.I. Guild.	N.Z.E.F.
" "	Lieut. J.E. Crisp.	N.Z.E.F.
July "	Lieut. K. Sweeting.	Coldstream Guards.
" "	Capt. J.R. Talbot.[10]	N.Z.E.F.
July 1942.	Lieut. A.R. Cramond.	N.Z.E.F.
August 1942.	Lieut. V.F. McLauchlan.	N.Z.E.F.
" "	Capt. O.R.S. Poole.[11]	Warwickshire Yeomanry.
August 1942.	Lieut. J.D. Henry.	E.A. Engineers.
" "	2/Lieut. A.S. Denniff.	R.T.R.
October "	Capt. E.F. Spicer.	Wiltshire Yeomanry.
" "	Lieut. Hon. B. Bruce, M.C.	Scots Guards.
" "	Capt. L.H. Browne, D.C.M. M.C.	N.Z.E.F.
" "	Lieut. R.A. Tinker, M.C., M.M.	N.Z.E.F.
" "	Lieut. A.H. Kinsman.[12]	Grenadier Guards.
March 1943.	Lieut. J.M. Sutherland.	N.Z.E.F.

4 P.O.W. 18.12.41.
5 P.O.W. 26.1.42. (Adjutant.)
6 Equipment Officer.
7 P.O.W. January 1942.
8 Medical Officer.
9 Killed in action 13.7.42
10 P.O.W. 15.1.43.
11 Adjutant.
12 P.O.W. 15.1.43.

B.

The following officers of the Indian Army served with the Indian Long Range Squadron which was under Command of the O.C. Long Range Desert Group from 1 October 1942 to April 1943.

Squadron Leader.	Major S.V. McCoy.
Commander No. 1 Patrol.	Capt. J. Cantlay.
" No. 2 "	Capt. T.J. Birdwood.
" No. 3 "	Capt. A.B. Rand.
" No. 4 "	Lieut. F.E. Nangle.

Appendix 4

Long Range Desert Group.
Establishment Authorized
on 22nd November 1940.

Consisting of H.Q. and Two Squadrons
each of Three Fighting Patrols.

Summary of Ranks.

Detail	Officers.	W.Os.	S/Sgts & Sergts.	Rank & File.	Total.
Group Headquarters.	5	–	4	33	42
Attached Headquarters.	2	–	2	23	27
Two Squadrons.	14	2	8	178	202
Total Desert Group.	21	2	14	234	271

Personnel.

Group Headquarters.

	Officers.		S/Sgts & Sergts.	Rank & File.	Total.
Commander (Lieut-Colonel).	1				1
2nd-in-command (Major).	1				1
Adjt. & Q.M. (Captain).	1				1
I.O. and Topographical Officer (Capt. or Lieut.)	1				1
Transport Officer (Subaltern).	1				1
Total Officers.	5				5
S.Q.M.S.			1		1
Sergeants.			3		3
Total S/Sgts and Sergeants.			4		4
Corporals.				3	3
Privates.				(a)30	30
Total Rank and File.				33	33
Total Other Ranks.			4	33	37
Total, All Ranks.	5	–	4	33	42

Detail	Officers.	W.Os.	S/Sgts & Sergts.	Rank & File.	Total.
Attached –					
R. Signals. Subaltern.	1				1
Sergeant.		1			1
Corporals. (Operators).				2	2
Inst. Mechanic.				1	1
Signalmen. (Operators).				14	14
R.A.O.C.Armourer.			1		1
R.A.M.C.Medical Officer.	1				1
Nursing Orderlies.				6	6
Total Attached.	2	–	2	23	27
Total Desert Group/incl H.Q. attached.	7	–	6	56	69
Two Squadrons (each)					
Squadron Headquarters./					
Commander (Major or Capt).(b)	1				1
Squadron Sergeant-Major.		1			1
Sergeant Fitter.			1		1
Corporals.				1	1
Privates.				(c)7	7
Total Squadron Headquarters.	1	1	1	8	11
Three Fighting Patrols (each)					
Captain.	1				1
Subaltern.	1				1
Sergeant.			1		1
Corporals.				3	3
Privates.				(a)24	24
Total Fighting Patrol.	2		1	27	30
Total Three Fighting Patrols.	6		3	81	90
Total Squadron.	7	1	4	89	101

Distribution of Rank and File by Trades and Duties

Detail.	H.Q.	Sqn H.Q.	3 Ft. Ptls (each)	Total Sqn.	2 Sqns.	Total
Tradesmen.						
Fitters (R.A.O.C.)	3	1	1	4	8	11
Draughtsmen (R.E.)	1					1
Driver Mechanics.	3		1	3	6	9
Clerks R.A.S.C.	2					2
Total Tradesmen.	9	1	2	7	14	22
Non-Tradesmen.						
Navigators.			2	6	12	12
Gun Numbers.			2	6	12	12
Cooks.		1		1	2	2
Storemen.	3	1		1	2	5
Drivers I.C.	21	5	14	47	94	115
General Duty.			7	21	42	42
Total Non-Tradesmen.	24	7	25	82	164	189
Total Rank and File.	33	8	27	89	178	211

Transport.

Detail.	H.Q.	Sqn H.Q.	3 Ft. Ptls (each)	Total Sqn.	2 Sqns.	Total.
Cars, 4-seater.	1	2 Sqns each				1
Motor cycles.	1					1
Trucks, 15-cwt.	1	2	1	5	10	11
Lorries, 30-cwt.	4	3	10	33	66	70
Lorries, heavy.	8					8

Table of Weapons and Ammunition.
Ammunition – rounds.

Detail.	Number.	On man or with gun.	Reserve.	Total.
Guns .37 mm Bofors or 2-pr (truck mounting)	6	90*	540*	1080*
Mortars 2-inch.	6	120@	720@	1440@
L.M.Gs. .303 inch.	61	1000%	61000%	122000%
Vickers M.Gs.303 inch.	6	3500	21000	42000
Rifles A.Tk .55 inch.	24	100	2400	4800
Rifles .303 inch.	220	100	2200	4400
Revolvers .38 inch.	51	18	–	918
Thompson Guns.	12	1000	12000	24000
Grenades	–	586	–	586

* 50% H.E. and 50% A.P.
@ All H.E.
% 20% Tracer.

Notes:- (a) Includes 3 Lance Corporals.
(b) Squadron Commanders one Major one Captain.
(c) Includes one Lance Corporal.

Appendix 5

War Establishment Long Range Desert Group.
February 1942.

Personnel

		H.Q. Sqn				Detachable Sqn.				
	Group H.Q.	3 patrols each	3 patrols each	Sabotage Pl	Total Sqn	Sqn H.Q.	2 patrols each	2 patrols each	Total Sqn	Total LRDG
Comdr Lt-Col	1									1
2 i/c & OC HQ Sqn Major	1									1
OC Detachable Sqn Major	1								1	1
Capts or Subalterns		1	1	2	8		1	1	4	12
Adjutant Capt	1									1
Intell & Topo Offr Capt	1									1
Survey Offr RE Subaltern	1									1
O.C S & T Section Subaltern	1									1
Subaltern (Air Duties)	1									1
Subalterns				2	2					2
Q.M.	1									1
Total Officers	8	1	1	4	10	1	1	1	5	23
Sqn Sgt Major	1					1			1	2
Sqn Q.M. Sgt.	1									1
Sgt. Clerk	1									1
Sgt. (Air Duties)	1									1
Sgts.	3	1		1	4	1	1		3	10
Total W.O. S/Sgts & Sgts	7	1		1	4	2	1		4	15
L/Sgts	1		1		3			1	2	6
Cpls	5	1	1	3	9	1	1	1	5	19
L/Cpls	6	2	2	4	16	1	2	2	9	31
Ptes	28	10	10	12	72	6	10	10	46	146
Total R & F	40	13	14	19	100	8	13	14	62	202
Total O.Rs.	47	14	14	20	104	10	14	14	66	217
Total all ranks (any arm)	55	15	15	24	114	11	15	15	71	240

	H.Q. Sqn					Detachable Sqn.				
	Group H.Q.	3 patrols each	3 patrols each	Sabotage Pl	Total Sqn	Sqn H.Q.	2 patrols each	2 patrols each	Total Sqn	Total LRDG
Attached										
R.E. Draughtsman Topo	1									1
RAMC Medical Officer	1									1
Nursing Orderlies L/Cpl	2									2
Ptes	4									4
A.C.C. Cooks (Incl a Cpl)	3					1			1	4
Total incl attached	66	15	15	24	114	12	15	15	72	252

Distribution of Rank and File by trades and duties.

	Group H.Q.	3 patrols each	3 patrols each	Sabotage Pl	Total Sqn	Sqn H.Q.	2 patrols each	2 patrols each	Total Sqn	Total LRDG
Tradesmen										
Driver Mechanics	5	1	1		6		1		4	15
Clerks	1					1			1	2
Total Tradesmen	6	1	1		6	1	1		5	17
Non-Tradesmen										
Navigators	3	1	1		6		1	1	4	13
Gun Numbers		2	2		12		2	2	8	20
Drivers I.C.	26	7	7		42	5	7	7	33	101
Storemen	3					1			1	4
Personnel for Low Grade Ciphers	1					1			1	2
Officers Mess Servants	1									1
General Duty Men		2	3	19	34		2	3	10	44
Total Non-Tradesmen	34	12	13	19	94	7	12	13	57	185
Total Rank and File	40	13	14	19	100	8	13	14	62	202
Transport.										
M/Cycles	1									1
Car 4 seater	1									1
Truck 15 cwt	7					1			1	8
Lorry 30 cwt	7	6	6		36	5	6	6	29	73
Lorry 3 ton	6									6
Lorry 10 ton	6									6
Aircraft	2									2

Table of arms and ammunition (incl attached)

| | Number | Ammunition – rounds | | |
		On man or with gun	Reserve	Total
Pistols .38	66	12	396	1188
Rifles .303	180	50	9000	16000
L.M.Gs.	93	1000	93000	186000
Medium M.Gs.	13	1000	13000	26000
Heavy M.Gs. .5"	26	1000	26000	52000
Guns 20 mm Breda (Truck Mounting)	12	200	2400	4800
T.S.M.Gs.	30	1000	30000	60000
Mortars 3" H.E	3			

L.R.D.G. Light Repair Squadron R.A.O.C.
Personnel

Detail	Group HQ	"A" Troop	"B" Troop	Total
OME 3rd Cl Capt or Subaltern	1			1
Armament Artificer QMS WO II	1			1
" " S/Sgt.	1		1	2
Armourer Sgt	1			1
Sgt		1		1
Cpls	1		1	2
Ptes (Total incl 6 L/Cpls)	15	4	9	28
Total	20	5	11	36

Distribution of Rank and File by Trades and Duties

Storeman (also acts as clerk)	1			1
Electrician	1			1
Fitters	2		1	3
Fitters M.V. (incl 1 Cpl 1 L/Cpl)	4	4	7	15
Motor Mechanic	1			1
Blacksmith	1			1
Tinsmith	1			1
Welder (Trained in electric and acetylene welding)	1		1	2
Carpenter and Wheelwright	1			1
Cobbler	1			1
Instrument Mechanic (Watchmaker)	1			1
Turner (for W/Shop Lorry)	1		1	2
Total	16	4	10	30

Transport.

Lorry 30-cwt	3		3
3 ton binned store lorry	1		1
3 ton W/Shop lorry	1	1	2

Table of weapons and Ammunition.

		Ammunition – rounds		
	Number	On man	Reserve	Total
Revolvers .38 inch	2	12	12	36
Rifles .303 inch	34	50	1700	3400
L.M.G.	1	1000	500	1500

Provision War Establishment
Signal Troop for L.R.D.G.

Personnel.

Detail		Remarks
Captain or Subaltern	1	
Sgt	1	
Cpls	3	
Signalmen	29	Includes 3 L/Cpls.
Total all Ranks	34	

Distribution of Rank and File by trades.

Operators W and L	27	
Storeman	1	Also to act as clerk.
Instrument Mech.	2	
Electrician	2	
Total	32	

Attached
Cipher Personnel

Sgt.	2	From Intelligence Corps.
Cpls.	1 (a)	
L/Cpls.	1 (a)	
Total4		

Armament.

Ammunition – rounds Detail	Number	On man	Reserve	Total
Revolvers .38 inch	1	12	6	18
Rifles .303 inch	33	50		1600

Note
(a) For Low Grade Cipher. Found from personnel within L.R.D.G.

Appendix 6

The following honours and awards were won by N.C.Os and men of the L.R.D.G.:

D.C.M.

Bassett, Pte. D.M.	N.Z.E.F.
Browne, Cpl. L.H.[1]	N.Z.E.F.
Moore, Tpr. R.J.	N.Z.E.F.

M.M.

Brown, Tpr.	N.Z.E.F.
Cave, Tpr. A.H.R.	Wilts Yeomanry
Craw, Cpl. M.	N.Z.E.F.
Crossley, Cpl. J.	Coldstream Guards.
Dennis, Cpl. J.	Coldstream Guards.
Dobson, Trp. T.B.	N.Z.E.F.
Dornbush, Tpr. C.	N.Z.E.F.
Duncalfe, Gdsman R.	Coldstream Guards.
Ellis, Tpr. E.	N.Z.E.F.
Fraser, Cpl. M.B.P.	Scots Guards.
Garwen, Cpl. G.C.	N.Z.E.F.
Gibson, Cpl. L	Scots Guards.
Gunn, Pte. D.	Seaforth Highlanders.
Hutchins, Sergt. D.N.	Somerset Yeomanry.
Jackson, Sergt. C.	Rhodesia.
Lewis, L./Cpl.T.J.	N.Z.E.F.
Low, Pte. K.T.	Rhodesia.
McInnes, Cpl. I.H.	N.Z.E.F.
Sadler, Cpl. W.M.	Rhodesia.
Sanders, Gnr. E.	N.Z.E.F.
Sturrock, Pte. E.C.	N.Z.E.F.
Tighe, Pte. A.	R.A.O.C.
Tinker, Cpl. R.A.[2]	N.Z.E.F.
Tippett, Tpr. K.E.	N.Z.E.F.
Waetford, Cpl. G.	N.Z.E.F.
Welsh, Gdsman M.A.	Scots Guards.
Wilcox, Tpr. L.A.	N.Z.E.F.
Wilson, Sergt.	Scots Guards.

1 Later Captain.
2 Later Captain.

The History of Commandos and Special Service Troops in the Middle East and North Africa

January 1941 to April 1943

Brigadier H. W. Wynter, D.S.O.

PREPARED BY THE HISTORICAL SECTION
OF THE WAR CABINET

Contents

Commandos and Special Service Troops in the Middle East
and North Africa

(January 1941 – April 1943)

All operations described took place on the mainland of Asia or Africa, except those of "A" and "D" Commandos in Crete, and by the Special Boat Section in the Aegean.

Maps and Sketches

Section II	Bardia 1:50,000	WDR 1003/2595 – Bardia
Section III	Tobruch 1:100,000	DR 44 – Tobruch (with certain additions) HS/MEF/4
Section IV	Litani River Area (Syria) 1:200,000	GSGS 4195 – Beyrouth NI-36-XII
	Litani River Operation 9 June 1941	HS/MEF/3 (Sketch 1:50,000)
Section V	Kassala Area 1:2M	GSGS 2871 Sudan
Section VII	North East Africa (Area covered by L.R.D.G. Patrols)	Map A 1:4M HS/MEF/1
	Western Desert and Cyrenaica L.R.D.G.	Map B HS/MEF/2
Section VIII	Gabes Area (Southern Tunisia) 1:1M – gridded	GSGS 2465 – NI-32 and pt of NJ-32
Section IX and X	North Africa 1:2M	OR 5404 and OR 5379
	Tabarka – Beja Area 1:200,000	GSGS 4227 – 1, 2, 4 and 5
	Algiers Area 1:200,000	GSGS 4180 – 5 and 14.

Introduction

This narrative gives the history as far as information is available:-

(a) Of Nos. 7, 8 and 11 British Commandos (afterwards re-named "A", "B" and "C" Battalions "Layforce") which, were sent from Great Britain to Egypt at the beginning of 1941; and part of which after incurring heavy losses, were re-organized in the Autumn of that year, first as "L" Detachment Special Air Service, and later as the 1st S.A.S. Regiment, under Lieut. Col. D. Stirling, Scots Guards.

(b) Of Nos. 50 and 52 Middle East Commandos which were raised in Egypt, took part in the early stages of the invasion of Abyssinia from the Sudan, and were then amalgamated to operate as "D" Battalion of the group known as "Layforce", of which Nos. 7, 8 and 11 British Commandos already formed part. Some men of these two Commandos were also absorbed eventually into "L" Detachment S.A.S. Others were to form the "Middle East Commando" (later 1st S.S. Regiment) disbanded in October 1942.

(c) Of Nos. 1 and 6 British Commandos which took part in the Anglo-American landing in Algeria in the Autumn of 1942 and in the subsequent campaign in Tunisia.

The narrative deals with operations, whether "Combined" or otherwise, which, with the exceptions noted below, took place in "North Africa", i.e. Egypt, Cyrenaica, Tripoli, Tunisia and Algeria. Outside North Africa the narrative includes:-

(a) An account of the part played by No. 11 Commando in the invasion of Syria from Palestine in June 1941.

(b) A short account of the work of No. 52 M.E. Commando in the early stages of the invasion of Abyssinia from the Sudan.

(c) An account of the action of "A" and "D" Battalions "Layforce" during the withdrawal from Crete, May 1941.

(d) A brief reference to the history of the "Special Boat Section" which later became part of the 1st S.A.S. Regiment, and an account of three raids in the Aegean in 1942.

The operations of the Commandos as such in the Spring and early Summer of 1941 were not as numerous as had been hoped; this was due to various circumstances over which the Commandos themselves had no control. Nor were the operations undertaken at that time or later, invariably successful.

The extensive re-organization which began in July 1941 was necessitated by the heavy and irreplaceable casualties incurred in the withdrawal from Crete when two Commandos were used in rearguard fighting for which they were not suitably armed; and in a smaller degree by the losses sustained by No. 11 Commando in the action on the Litani River at the beginning of the invasion of Syria, which was a typical, and to a great extent successful "Combined Operation".

When the re-organization of raiding forces on a smaller scale began the intention, as will be seen, was that one raiding force should be a parachute detachment, and it was for this reason that the expression "S.A.S." was used; but facilities for parachute training in Egypt were inadequate. The only airborne raid attempted was not a success, and training for airborne attacks was postponed until after the conquest of North Africa.

The operations of "L" Detachment were, for the most part, carried out in concert with the Long Range Desert Group, and accounts of them were unavoidably duplicated in the narrative of that unit. When the 1st S.A.S. regiment was formed it was supplied with its own transport (of which "L" Detachment had but little), and enough navigators had by that time been trained to make it independent of outside help in reaching its objectives; and it was also able to maintain itself. As in the case of the distant activities of the Long Range Desert Group, there can be no doubt that the short range operations of the S.A.S. parties against the enemy's exposed Southern flank and long lines of communication, were of the greatest assistance to our main Army; and were particularly valuable immediately before and during the last battles on the El Alamein position in the Autumn of 1942. Success was due to the enterprise, energy and daring of all concerned; and the frequent raids that were made not only inflicted heavy losses on the enemy's supplies of all sorts, but also reduced the strength of his Air Force, and caused him to withdraw troops from the front to strengthen the defence of landing grounds, roads and tracks.

Lastly, it is important to remember that a considerable proportion of the Officers and Other Ranks of "L" Detachment and of the 1st S.A.S. Regiment were Frenchmen, from Syria and elsewhere, whose exploits were in no way less remarkable than those of their British comrades; and accounts written by two of them have been used in compiling this narrative.

Section I

Origins.

Independent Companies.

The formation of "Commandos" for amphibious operations, which began after the evacuation of Dunkirk, was in the first place the idea of Lt. Colonel Dudley Clarke R.A., then head of M.O.9 at the War Office; but the prototype of the Commando was the "Independent Company". These Companies were recruited in the Spring of 1940 from volunteers from various regiments under the auspices of the M.I. branch, and five took part in operations in Norway.

C.O.H.Q. June 1940.

On the 6th June 1940, the Prime Minister appointed Lieut. General Bourne, Adjutant General Royal Marines to organize raiding operations on the enemy's coast from Norway to Spain, with Lt. Colonel A.H. Hornby M.C., R.A. as his staff officer. This was the origin of Combined Operations Headquarters. The staff was soon afterwards increased by the addition of an Intelligence Staff of which Captain Maund R.N. was Chief. It was located at the Admiralty, because accommodation was available there, and tended to come under the orders of the First Sea Lord, though the intention was that it should co-operate with all three Services.

At first little raiding was carried out, but in October Admiral of the Fleet Sir Roger Keyes succeeded Lieut. General Bourne and Combined Operations H.Q. was moved to new offices. A branch of it under Captain Garnons-Williams R.N. remained at the Admiralty, and Lieut. Colonel D. Clarke at M.O.9 represented it at the War Office. With the Air Staff there was at first not much contact.

In November 1940, training centres were established in Scotland.

Commando establishments November 1940.

The original "Commando" had a headquarters of thirty-six of all ranks, and ten troops, each having a captain, two subalterns and forty-seven O.R.

The total strength of all ranks in a Commando was therefore 536. Each Command in the U.K. was asked to find two Commandos. The response varied, but eventually ten Commandos were formed, and by July 1940 one of them raised by Lt. Col. R.E. Laycock R.H.G. in the Eastern Command, was already training for small scale raids, at Burnham-on-Crouch.

In November 1940 the War Office decided to reorganize the Commandos as five "Special Service Battalions", each consisting of a Headquarters and two Commandos. The strength of a battalion was 72 Officers and 1,000 O.R.; it had twenty sub-units and was too unwieldy for the type of operation it had to carry out. Shortly after this reorganization, it was decided to send a force of Special Service Troops to the Middle East, and the battalion organization was abandoned. Independent Commandos were restored to life and on the 1st February 1941, Nos. 7, 8 and 11 were sent to Egypt. Later Nos. 1 and 6 took part in the landing in Algeria and the subsequent operations in Algeria and Tunisia.

Commandos go to M.E. February 1941

There were several good reasons for this decision. It was in the first place considered that a properly constituted raiding force of this kind would be of strategic and tactical value, if it were to operate not only in conjunction with a large scale offensive which was within our power in the Middle East though not in Europe, but also at frequent intervals during "static" periods. Moreover, raids carried out on the enemy's long and vulnerable lines of communication along the coasts of North Africa, in Italy or in the Balkans would in effect be "flank attacks", whereas a raid on the Western Coasts of Europe was purely "frontal". Objectives in the Mediterranean were more accessible and less well defended than those in Europe, which could be dealt with more effectively by Bomber Command.

In order to suit the landing craft then in use (A.L.Cs) the establishment was somewhat altered, and the new British Commando had a Headquarters, and six troops, each of sixty-five of all ranks (instead of ten troops of forty-seven), a number which enabled a troop to fit exactly into two A.L.Cs.

M.E.Commandos.

Soon after the three British Commandos arrived in the Middle East at the beginning of March 1941, two of the three Middle East Commandos, Nos. 50 and 52, were added to the Special Service Force. They had been locally raised with a smaller establishment, and included a number of Palestinians and volunteers from the Spanish Foreign Legion. For security reasons the Commandos were called battalions, Nos. 7, 8 and 11 becoming "A", "B" and "C" battalions respectively, while Nos. 50 and 52 were amalgamated to form "D" battalion. The force was put under command of Lt. Col.

Laycock who was given a Bde H.Q. and the rank of Colonel, and called "Layforce".

"Layforce".

After rehearsing an operation which was cancelled, "Layforce" came into G.H.Q. Reserve, but was later distributed between Mersa Matruh, Alexandria, Cyprus, and Geneifa, which is on the Suez Canal, and was also used as a depot and training camp.

Crete.

The Battalions took part in certain operations which are dealt with later; the most important being the evacuation of Crete in May 1941 in which "A" and "D" Battalions were engaged under Colonel Laycock's command, and the advance into Syria in June 1941, when "C" Battalion was with the invading force. Of 1200 men who were sent to Crete, about 800 were lost.

Sections II, III and IV which follow, contain accounts of "A", "B" and "C" Battalions of "Layforce". Section V contains the early history of No. 52 Middle East Commando which was amalgamated with No. 50 Middle East Commando to form "D" Battalion of "Layforce"; and an account of the doings of "D" Battalion during the withdrawal of Crete, as far as they are known.

In the Summer of 1941 the battalions which originally formed part of Middle East Forces ceased to exist. Subsequent raiding and special service organisations which took part in operations based on Egypt are dealt with in Sections VI, VII and VIII. Operations in Algeria and Tunisia by the two Commandos which formed part of the First Army are described in Sections IX and X.

Section II

"A" Bn. "Layforce"
(formally No. 7 Commando).

March 1941 – May 1941.

No. 7 Commando (Lieut. Col. F.B. Colvin, Dorsetshire Regiment) arrived in the Middle East at the beginning of March 1941 and for a month or so continued its training for Combined Operations on the banks of the Suez Canal. Towards the end of the month it was re-named and became "A" Battalion "Layforce". On the 14th April 1941, it was transferred to Alexandria, and "Layforce" at the same time came under the orders of the Western Desert Force which was later expanded to form the Eighth Army.

General situation.

At this time the general situation in North Africa was as follows. Under pressure from the newly arrived German forces under Rommel Sir A. Wavell had been obliged to withdraw his troops from Cyrenaica. The retirement began on the 28th March, and Benghazi was evacuated on the 3rd April. The 9th Australian Division, with British artillery and Indian troops, was left in Tobruk which was held successfully for eight months; but Sollum was lost on the 28th April, and the Western Desert Force finally took up its position on the line Buq-Buq - Oasis of Siwa, some thirty miles or more inside the frontier of Egypt.

Raid on Bardia April 1941. Original plan.

On the 14th April the G.O.C. Western Desert Force intimated his desire for an immediate raid on Bardia and on the coast road near Bomba, and Col. R.E. Laycock commanding Layforce attended conferences in H.M.S. Warspite on the 14th and 15th April to discuss the naval aspects of the scheme and to make a plan. It was decided that the raid on Bardia should be carried out by "A" and "C" Bns. and the raid on Bomba by four troops (150 of all ranks) of "B" Bn. For security reasons speed was of the highest importance; and the four troops of "B" Bn. (under Major Lord Sudeley, R.H.G.) embarked in H.M.S. Decoy and Bde. H.Q. with "A" and "C"

Bns. in H.M. Ships Glengyle and Glenearn, in the evening of the 15th April. H.M.S. Decoy sailed at 2200 hrs that night and the Glengyle and Glenearn at 0400 hrs on the 16th.

The weather was calm until noon when the wind blowing from the East increased from force 2 to force 5, and there were frequent air raid warnings during the afternoon watch. By 1945 hrs. the swell was such as to suggest that there would be surf on the beaches where it was proposed to land; and this was confirmed by signals from the submarine Commander (Lieut. Commander W.J.W. Woods, H.M.S. Triumph) who reported that "folbots" (folding boats) could not leave the submarine, and also from H.M.S. Decoy. The S.N.O., Capt. Petrie, R.N. of the Glengyle, therefore cancelled the Bardia landing and Capt. McGregor of the Decoy made the same decision in regard to the landing at Bomba. It was considered not only that landing would be difficult, but that re-embarkation would at best be extremely hazardous. The expedition then returned to Alexandria.

The second plan.

On the 18th April the Mediterranean Fleet went to sea. Colonel Laycock had been informed by G.H.Q. Middle East that it was their desire that the raid on Bardia should take place at the earliest opportunity, and he went to a conference which was attended by the Captain S.N.O.2 (Captain H.M.S. Coventry) and the Captain D.10. Col. Laycock produced a meteorological report indicating the probability of four days fine weather, but the two naval officers asked for a 24-hour postponement. They were however overruled, and it was proved later that if the operation had been so postponed it could not have taken place, for the report was untrustworthy and the weather deteriorated sooner than had been anticipated. It was decided, however, that operations should be carried out by Bde. H.Q. and "A" Battalion only, working from H.M.S. Glengyle. 1 Officer and 19 O.R. of the Royal Tank Regt were attached, to assist in the use of captured A.F.Vs, and in their eventual destruction.

Operation Order 19 April 1941.

The Glengyle weighed anchor and sailed for Bardia at 0230 hrs. on the 19th April; and the Operation Order was issued at 1530 hrs. on the same day. The object was defined as "harassing the enemy's L. of C. and inflicting as much damage as possible on supplies and material".

The method adopted was to make landings on four selected beaches, "A", "B", "C" and "D". The battalion was divided into seven detachments, each including two or three men of the R.T.R. Nos. 1, 2, 3 and 4 detachments (200 men) were to land on "A" beach, No. 5 (70 men) on "B", No. 6 (70) on "C" and No. 7 (35) on "D". Their tasks differed and are given in detail later. Timings were laid down giving the hours at which

A.L.Cs. were to leave the ship and arrive at the beach, for arrival at and leaving the objective, and for arrival at and departure from the beach for re-embarkation. The Glengyle was expected to arrive at the rendezvous (30°49' North, 25°08' East) at 2205 hrs. on the 19th April. A.L.Cs were to leave the ship between 2215 and 2220 hrs. The last A.L.C. was to leave the beaches for re-embarkation at 0230 hrs. on the 20th April, and the Glengyle was due to leave the rendezvous at 0400 hrs.

The plan was timed so as to avoid exposing the ships to air attack during daylight in areas beyond the reach of fighter cover. Navigational aid in fixing the rendezvous was given by H.M. submarine Triumph which was also to report on the practicability of landing; and she carried Major R.J. Courtney, M.C. the originator of the S.B.S., who was to superintend the landing of a "Folbot" detachment. On arrival at a point bearing 13° and $2^1/2$ miles from Bardia the Triumph was to show a fixed white light to seaward in a sector between the bearings 350° through North to 110° (an arc of 120 degrees). As she approached Bardia, just before sunset on the 19th the wind veered to the N.E. and freshened, and her Commander decided to close the coast submerged. At sunset the wind decreased and it could be seen that conditions on the beach were favourable for landing. There was doubt, however, whether a "Folbot" could be launched. An effort was made to establish a light on an islet and one canoe was lost. Some delay was caused, but the "flashing position" was reached at 2145 hrs., only fifteen minutes late.

H.M.S. Glengyle was escorted from Alexandria by the A.A. cruiser Coventry and the destroyers Stuart, Voyager and Waterhen. During the passage air raid warnings were passed by H.M.S. Coventry but no attack developed. The Glengyle arrived at the rendezvous up to time, but as already described had to wait 15 minutes for the light from H.M.S. Triumph. Some difficulty was experienced in lowering the M.L.C. and one A.L.C. was unable to leave the ship; but time was made up during the passage to the beach and detachments were not unduly late, except in one case where troops were landed on the wrong beach and in one or two others where delay was caused by breakdowns. Two A.L.Cs. were to have landed on "B" Beach, but one of them was unable to leave the Glengyle, and the other went by mistake to "A" Beach. At "D" Beach the landing was 10 minutes late, as the approach to it was difficult and the detachment had to wade through water waist deep.

The operations of the various detachments from their respective beaches are dealt with in order.

Tasks of Detachments.

No. 1 detachment whose task was to secure and hold "A" Beach got into position without delay. It held its position and covered the withdrawal of

Nos. 2, 3 and 4 detachments from "A" beach without incident, except that one officer who unfortunately failed to answer a sentry's challenge was shot and mortally wounded. It was believed that he thought the sentry was challenging someone coming from another direction.

No. 2 detachment was to establish a block on the road triangle at Pt. 515397 in the hope that hostile M.T. might be intercepted. None, however, appeared and the detachment returned empty handed.

No. 3 detachment's task was to attack the "Square camp" and destroy enemy material. The camp was unoccupied and only a dump of motor tyres, mostly new, was found. This was set on fire with incendiary bombs and was still burning fiercely two hours later. One party of this detachment returned to "A" Beach without incident. The other lost its way and, having realized that this was the case, its Commander made for "B" Beach. As already related no A.L.C. had landed at this spot and the troop was ordered to make for Sollum. 20 men were eventually picked up by an A.L.C. from "C" Beach, and the Italian wireless claimed that the remainder were made prisoners.

No. 4 detachment's task was to raid Bardia from the South. It reached the Southern end of the town, which was unoccupied, but it was then too late to go any further and the detachment re-embarked from "A" Beach without incident.

No. 5 detachment, which was landed by mistake at "A" Beach, was unable to carry out its task, which was to attack Bardia from the North.

No. 6 detachment was to land on "C" Beach in two A.L.Cs. and its task was to demolish the road bridge at Point 51853959, the pumping station and the reservoir, and to crater roads. The landing was to be made at 2330 hrs. but as by 2350 hrs. only one A.L.C. had arrived, the detachment Commander modified his plan. He sent a small party to the pumping station and ordered the remainder to demolish the bridge and make one road crater.

Owing to difficulty in following the directions given by the Intelligence Branch, the first named party did not reach the pumping station till 0100 hrs. on the 20th, and it was then too late to effect any serious damage.

The second detachment, which was eventually reinforced by men from the missing A.L.C., attempted to crater the road on the escarpment at Point 51843957 but, owing to the hardness of the rock, only a small crater was blown. With a small force covering them, they then prepared the bridge for demolition. It consisted of from 2 to 3 inches of Macadam carried by 12" by 12" timber baulks supported on wooden trestles. The charge (72 lbs. of explosive) blew away a large part of the road and rendered the bridge impassable by M.T., though infantry could still have crossed. The detachment therefore returned to the bridge, soaked the trestles with petrol and set them on fire. There was no time to inspect results but the trestles were still burning when the detachment re-embarked from "C" Beach.

No. 7 detachment, which landed on "D" Beach, was ordered to put out of action any Coast Defence or A.A. guns on the peninsula about Point 52033960. No trace could be found of a mobile gun which had been reported in action several days before but four 5.9 inch naval guns were located. Their firing mechanisms had been removed and it was thought that they had not been in action since our evacuation of Bardia; but as this was no reason against their use in the future, their breeches were blown up with charges of gelignite.

Re-embarkation.

Some difficulty was experienced in re-embarking, as the wind had fresh-ened considerably during the raid, and the speed of several landing craft was reduced owing to sand which had clogged their cooling systems. One A.L.C. on "A" Beach became stranded and had to be destroyed; other craft were delayed owing to lack of compasses and the fact that the sky had obscured the stars. Another A.L.C., whose compass was faulty, was unable to find the Glengyle, which was lying 4 miles off shore, and therefore made for Tobruk which she reached, after a rough passage, at 1605 hrs. on the 20th April. There was also a case of engine breakdown and the last landing craft did not reach the Glengyle until 0500 hrs. on the 20th, one hour late.

Lieut. Col. Laycock's report.

Col. Laycock forwarded a report on the operation to the Naval Authori-ties and to H.Q. Western Desert Force. He stated that he was "not a little disappointed with the general conduct of the raid on Bardia", while admit-ting that he may have failed to appreciate "that many difficulties though foreseen during training, would make themselves even more apparent" in an actual operation. But the demolition of the Bardia bridge must have handicapped the enemy for some time at least. The report emphasized the importance of the time factor, and especially the necessity for reducing the interval between the arrival of the "parent ship" at the rendezvous and the arrival of the troops at their objective. As far as the Royal Navy was con-cerned he suggested that time could be saved by manning landing craft before the ship had stopped, so that they could be lowered and got away with the least possible delay when way was off the ship. Delay between landing on the beach and arrival at the objective was caused by inadequate knowledge of the ground, and failure to get full value from air photo-graphs; by crossing obstacles in single file instead of in line; and by a ten-dency to sacrifice speed for the sake of silence - which was no doubt necessary in a raid on a French coast town, but not in all circumstances. Col. Laycock also pointed out that the adoption of formations to avoid the danger of losing touch, though suitable when a raid was made on a dark night in the atmosphere of Northern Europe, was not desirable in the clear atmosphere of the Eastern night when it is always possible to see 50 or 100 yards. He also stressed the importance of finding the quickest way not only to the objective, but when withdrawing. This made it necessary for leaders to look back from time to time during an advance, to take back bearings, and if necessary to leave guides at selected points. Re-embarkation also required consideration. Accidents may and will probably always happen to landing craft, and Col. Laycock therefore suggested that reserve craft should be available to replace casualties and also to take off parties which had gone astray like the party belonging to No. 3 detachment which was left on "B" Beach during the withdrawal at Bardia. Lastly he drew attention to the difficulty of locating H.M.S. Glengyle which was experienced by landing craft returning to her from the beaches. This was partly due to the unreliability of compasses which made it difficult, if not impossible, to steer even an approximately correct course. This point was also commented on in the report made by Capt. Petrie, R.N., H.M.S. Glengyle, which contained several suggestions for technical improvements in naval equipment. Col. Laycock also suggested that the parent ship might have stood closer inshore during the re-embarkation period without being seen, and thus have been easier to find; but the appropriate distance off shore in such circumstances depends of course on the extent to which the coast is equipped with searchlights and coast defence guns. Though tactically an incomplete success, if not actually a failure, the raid on Bardia had certain strategical results; for it caused the enemy to divert the greater part of a German brigade from Sollum to Bardia, which relieved the pressure at Sollum. The enemy also seems to have been apprehensive of a repetition of the raid, and constructed boom defences in Bardia harbour.

"A" and "D" Battalions in Crete May 1941.

"A" and "D" Battalions of "Layforce" were sent to Crete to help in the evacuation of the island and in the withdrawal across it both battalions were used as rearguards. Being designed for offensive fighting at close quarters, they were not suitably organized or equipped for rearguard action, for they had no weapons capable of stopping the enemy at long ranges.

After a false start from Alexandria on the 24th March 1941, the Commandos were landed at Suda Bay on the night of the 26/27th. Before landing the impression had been formed that the situation was in hand except at Malemi, and in a lecture delivered later, Col. Laycock, who was in command of the force, said "We imagined that we were to carry out raids to restore the situation at Malemi ... when we landed, however, we found a very different state of affairs. Malemi had fallen, the Germans were

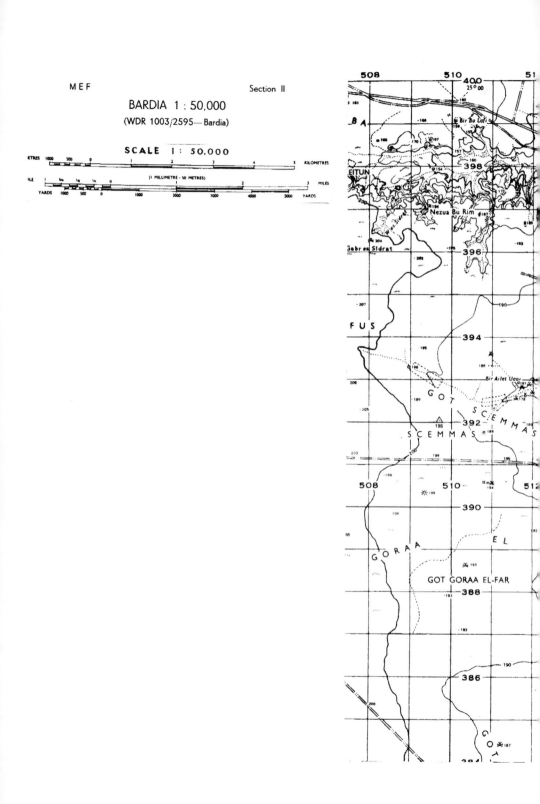

MEF   Section II

BARDIA 1 : 50,000
(WDR 1003/2595—Bardia)

SCALE 1 : 50,000

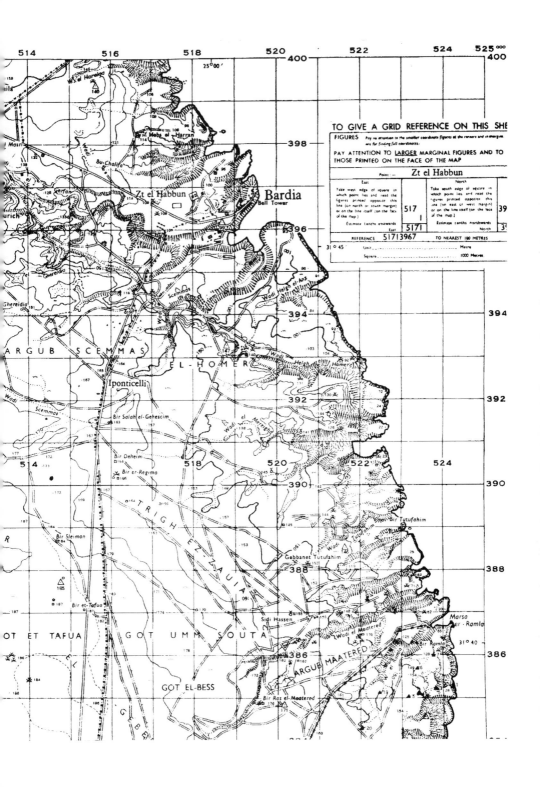

pouring airborne reinforcements into the island, and Creforce was in ... retreat. We were ordered to form a rearguard to cover the withdrawal of the main body to Sphakia some twenty miles across the mountains". Col. Laycock emphasized the necessity for Commando troops to train "so as to be prepared at all times to take on any form of action that may come to hand" and "to be soldiers as well as 'cat-burglars'". He also pointed out that most of the casualties (apart from men taken prisoner) were due to mortar fire, and not to dive bombing and low flying machine-gun attacks, though the effects of the latter on the morale of troops not accustomed to it are very great.

During the retirement "A" and "D" Battalions leapfrogged back from one rearguard position to another as far as Imbros which was reached on the 29th May. There a position was held until the 31st, when the remains of Brigade H.Q. and of the two battalions were embarked for Alexandria, arriving there on the 1st June.

Section III

"B" Bn. "Layforce"
(formally No. 8 Commando).

Siege of Tobruk begins 12th April 1941.

"B" Battalion "Layforce" was commanded by Lieut. Col. Dermot Daly, Scots Guards, and arrived in Egypt at the beginning of March 1941. Early in April it moved to Amiriya near Alexandria, and came under command of the Western Desert Force. Rommel's advance had carried him across the frontier of Egypt, and the siege of Tobruk, which was to last for eight months, began on the 12th April. The battalion remained at Amiriya for a fortnight and was then moved forward to Mersa Matruh. As it was intended that they should go to Tobruk, Lieut. Alston was sent there with an advance party and remained there for three weeks. In the meanwhile a party of 200 men was sent in the gunboat "Aphis" to raid the airfield at Gazala. On the way, however, they were attacked by a large force of "Stukas". Though there were only two casualties (both wounded) the ships engines were stopped, and she was forced to make her way back to Mersa Matruh. Later in May, a detachment of 100 men under Lord Sudeley R.H.G. was sent to Tobruk with orders to assist the garrison in the operation known as "Battleaxe", the intention of which was to relieve the Tobruk garrison. The principal task allotted to Lord Sudeley's detachment was to land behind the enemy's left rear about eighteen miles East of Tobruk. The Germans, however, attacked during the last week of May and the operation did not take place. The detachment then returned to Alexandria.

An advance party at Tobruk June-July-August 1941.

At the end of June an advance party of the Commando was again sent to Tobruk. It was commanded by Major M. Kealy (Devon Regiment), with Captain P. Dunne R.H.G. as second in command. There were three other officers, Lieuts. Lewis (Welsh Guards), Alston (R.A.) and Langton (Irish Guards), and 60 O.Rs.

Soon after their arrival in Tobruk the move was once more cancelled and orders were sent for the return of the advance party. The G.O.C. in

Tobruk, however, refused to let them go and they took part in three operations during July and August.

"Twin Pimples" Raid.

During the first weeks of their stay in Tobruk Major Kealy's detachment took part in various patrols carried out by the 18th Cavalry I.A. who "taught them a great deal"; and about ten days after their arrival they were ordered to raid an Italian strong point known as "Twin Pimples", which was close to and overlooked the forward localities held by an Indian Infantry battalion. It is situated at point 3995, 4395 (Map 1/50,000) near the N.W. corner of the Tobruk perimeter, and is about 2,000 yards from the sea.

Raid on "Twin Pimples" 17/18th July 1941.

Before the actual raid, which took place on the night 17/18th July, the detachment carried out reconnaissances of the enemy's position aided by Indian Officers and men, whom Captain Dunne in an account of the operation, describes as "very good indeed". The plan was to get through the enemy's position at a point South of "Twin Pimples", and reach the track along which his supplies were brought. It was then intended to move along the track and attack the enemy from the rear. At 0057 hrs. on the 18th, three minutes before the time at which the raiders were due to enter the enemy's position, the Indian battalion was to create a diversion by making a feint attack on some of his forward localities. The raiding party, which consisted of Major Kealey, Captain Dunne, Lieut. Lewis and forty men[1] and was guided by an Indian Officer, started at 2300 hrs. on the 17th July. Half the party were armed with Tommy guns and half with rifles and bayonets; every man carried a few grenades and every third man a ground sheet to be used for carrying wounded.

The party moved in single file through our forward localities which were about 1200 yards from those of the enemy. The three troops then split up, Major Kealey's being in the centre, Lieut. Lewis's on the right and Captain Dunne's on the left, with intervals of twenty yards between troops. With each detachment were two or three Australian sappers to carry out such demolitions as might be possible.

The night, though dark, was starlit and as the ground was well known, movement was quick, and silence unbroken. Captain Dunne writes "We went through the Italian forward positions, and then through their main defensive lines, consisting of a number of slit trenches. I shall never know if they were manned or not, because we heard nothing from them, and were very careful to make no noise. We eventually reached the track which

1 Nos. 4, 6 and 8 Troops commanded by Lewis, Dunne, and Kealey respectively.

we could recognize by the wheel marks of cars". They were a little ahead of time and waited five minutes before turning North along the track. As they approached the Western side of "Twin Pimples" the diversion started; and the enemy returned the Indians' fire, and sent up Verey lights. Two minutes later the raiders were challenged by a sentry about 30 yards away, and moved forward in line firing their Tommy guns and rifles. Captain Dunne relates that there were a lot of stone walls, which were probably some sort of "above ground rifle pits", and also slit trenches and dugouts quite impervious to fire. He goes on to say "The fight lasted about three or four minutes ... the Italians rushed into the dugouts, and we bombed them out of them ... then they rushed back again. They did not, however, surrender and most of them were killed by the bayonet and hand grenades". As soon as the sappers had completed their demolitions (and Captain Dunne relates that he saw an ammunition dump and at least one mortar dealt with) a whistle was blown which was the pre-arranged signal for withdrawal.

The plan was to move South for about a quarter of a mile and then to make straight for the British lines; and it had been arranged that an Indian Officer in one of our forward localities was a fire a white Verey light as a guide, every quarter of an hour. Each officer shouted for the men of his own troop, and in order to check their direction they "got the North Star over their left shoulders". As was expected, the enemy started to shell "Twin Pimples" about a quarter of an hour after the attack began; and when they opened fire with "everything they could, both at it and us", the raiders were only about a hundred yards away. Five men were wounded, all of whom were brought back, but one of them, Corporal Maynard, died later. Only one prisoner was taken, but he was mortally wounded and could not be interrogated. This, however, was rectified by Lieut. Lewis, who went out a couple of nights later and brought in an unwounded prisoner, "the only one to be found in one of the forward positions of the Italians".

Captain Dunne rightly attributed the success of the raid, in which heavy casualties were expected, to the careful preliminary reconnaissances, and also "to the skill of the Indians who taught us such a lot".

During its stay at Tobruk, Major Kealey's detachment took part in two other raids. Neither was successful, but it should be noted that one of them was carried out in spite of the fact that after his preliminary reconnaissance, Major Kealey advised against it.

The detachment left Tobruk during the night 31st August/1st September 1941 and arrived at Alexandria the following night.

"B" Battalion disbanded September 1941.

When it arrived in Egypt, the disbandment of the battalion, which had

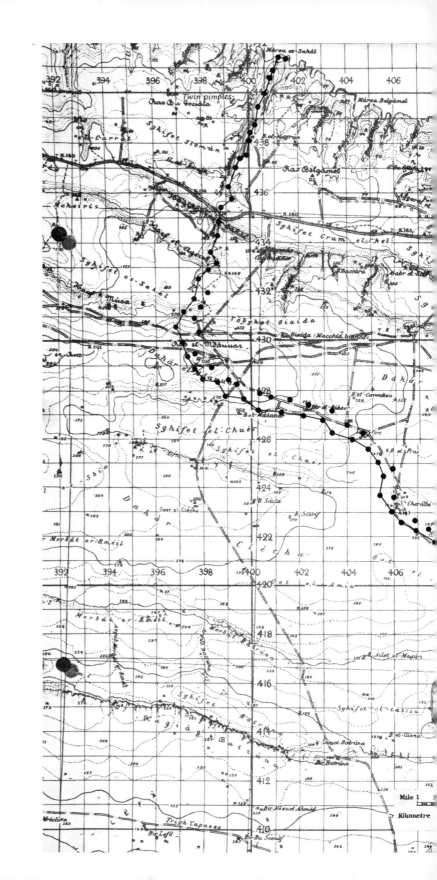

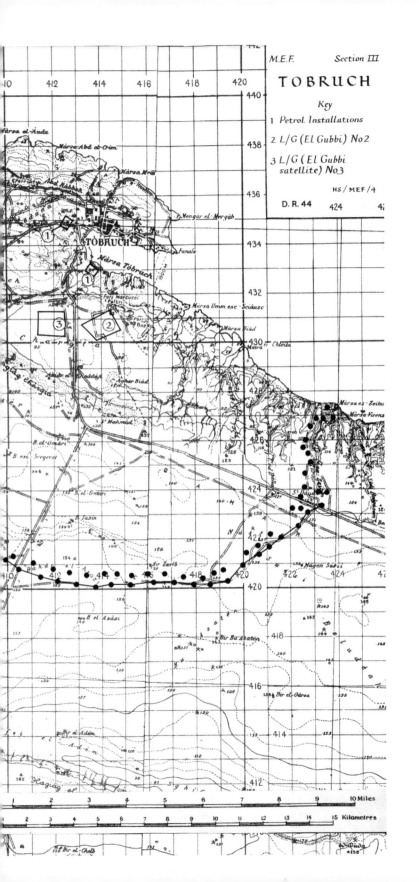

M.E.F.   Section III

TOBRUCH

Key

1 *Petrol Installations*

2 *L/G (El Gubbi) No2*

3 *L/G (El Gubbi*
   satellite) No3

HS / MEF / 4

D. R. 44   424   42

already begun, was completed. A number of the men belonging to the Scots Guards, were transferred to "L" detachment S.A.S. which was being formed by Captain D. Stirling; and Lieuts. Lewis, Welsh Guards, Langton, Irish Guards and Alston, R.A. went with them.

Section IV

"C" Bn. "Layforce"
(formally No. 11 Commando).
January 1941 – June 1941.

The 11 Commando left the West of Scotland on the 31st January 1941, as part of Force "Z" under command of Lieut. Col. R.E. Laycock, R.H.G. Its Commander was Lieut. Col. R.N.R. Pedder, H.L.I. and its strength (on 4th April 1941) was 33 officers and 513 O.Rs. It sailed round the Cape of Good Hope, and in due course arrived at Suez.

Commando moves to Geneifa 27th March 1941.

On the 27th March 1941, the Commando, which had become "C" Bn. "Layforce" and had been quartered in Cairo, went to Geneifa near Ismailia on the bank of the Suez Canal. At 1600 hrs. on the 7th April, orders were received that the Bn. was to embark (at Geneifa) on the 8th April in H.M.S. "Glenearn". The "Glenearn" sailed on the 9th April, arrived at Port Said the same evening and remained in port until the 13th April. At 1747 hrs. on the 13th the Bn. sailed for Alexandria, arriving at 0900 hrs. on the 14th. At midday on the 15th information was received that "A" and "C" Bns. "Layforce" were to raid Bardia, which had recently been occupied by the enemy.

An abortive operation 16th April 1941.

The "Glenearn" put to sea in the early hours of the 16th April, but in the evening the operation was postponed on account of bad weather; and the battalion returned to Alexandria, arriving just after midday on the 17th April. It was hoped that the operation might still be carried out, but it was finally cancelled as far as "C" Bn. was concerned at 1900 hrs. on the 18th April. In the evening of the 21st April the battalion disembarked and went into No. 3 Transit Camp at Amiriya.

Move to Cyprus 24th April 1941.

On the 24th Col. Laycock informed Lieut. Col. Pedder that the battalion was to be used independently for operations in Syria, and it was ordered to move by rail at 1400 hrs. on the 26th April. On the same day it resumed its original title - 11 Scottish Commando. The train left at 1510 hrs. and was seen off by Col. Laycock. The Commando was ferried across the Canal from Kantara to Kantara East, and having again entrained, crossed the frontier of Palestine at 0930 hrs. 27th April. It arrived at Lydda at 1330 hrs. and reached Haifa at 1740 hrs. where it went into bivouac. On the 28th April it embarked in the S.S. "Warzawa" and after a false start on the 28th, sailed eventually for Cyprus at 1600 hrs. on the 29th. At 1500 hrs. on the 29th April, the ship berthed at Famagusta and the Commando disembarked and marched to Salamis. The troops were distributed at various points in the area for the defence of which the Bn. was responsible.

Invasion of Syria June 1941.

On the 31st May, the Commanding Officer, the Adjutant (Capt. G.R. More, R.E.) and Capt. R.P. Carr, R.A. received orders to proceed by air to Palestine and report to Palestine Force H.Q. (MILPAL). They left Nicosia at 0710 hrs. on the 1st June, and arrived in Jerusalem at 1430 hrs. On the 3rd June, while the C.O. was still in Palestine, a code message was received by the Commando ordering them to be prepared to embark in two destroyers at Famagusta on the 4th June, at 0300 hrs. Detachments were brought in, civilian buses being commandeered for the purpose. The Commando (less rear party) 27 officers and 456 men in all, under Major Keyes, Royal Scots Greys, embarked in H.M. destroyers "Rex" and "Hotspur" at 0540 hrs. on the 4th June, sailed at 0625 hrs. for Port Said, and arrived there at 1700 hrs., having steamed at 25 knots. A rear party, consisting of details of the H.Q. staff and No. 5 troop under Major B.C.A. Napier, Gordon Highlanders, remained in Cyprus to strike the tents in detachment camps and re-erect them at Salamis. Meanwhile the Commanding Officer attended the G.O.C's Conference at Nazareth on the morning of the 4th June, and at 1700 hrs. left for Port Said by car. He arrived there with the Adjutant and Capt. Carr at 0500 hrs. on the 5th June.

Orders for the advance 5th June 1941.

The G.O.C's Conference was concerned with the decision to invade Syria, then still in the hands of the Vichy French, and already being used as a base by the German Air Force. The initial order issued by H.Q. Palestine Force for this operation was dated 5th June 1941. The force available for the invasion was divided into three groups which were to advance simultaneously. The left group consisted of the 7th Australian Div. under Maj. General Laverack, with attached troops including 11 Commando, described in Sir H.M. Wilson's report as "C" Bn. S.S. Bde.

Orders for 7th Australian Division 8/9th June 1941.

Maj. General Laverack was ordered to march by two main routes and subdivided his force into two further groups. With the action of the right group we are not concerned. The left group consisted of the 21st Australian Bde. with attached troops, including 11 Commando. The Group (less 11 Commando) was to move along the coast through the ancient sites of Tyre and Sidon, and its objective was the Beyrout aerodrome.

The enemy was known to be holding the line of the Litani River, which runs into the Mediterranean some twenty miles North of the Syrian frontier; and for the first day's operations the group was to cross the frontier soon after midnight 8/9th June in three columns, as follows:-

(a) *Right Column.* "DONCOL" composed of all arms, from El Malikiya (about 20 miles inland) and thence to move in a North-Westerly direction through Tibnine to Tyre.

(b) *Centre Column.* Cheshire Yeomanry (horsed) less one Squadron, to follow DONCOL to Tibnine and thence to strike North across country to Srifa and Kafr Sir, with the object of outflanking the Litani position from the East.

(c) *Left Column.*[1] "MOTCOL" composed of all arms, from Hanita, where the frontier meets the coast, and thence to move along the coastal road through Tyre, to the crossing over the Litani River.

Commando's task.

The Commando's task was to co-operate with MOTCOL's attack on the river line by effecting a landing from the sea. The original plan was for the Commando to land at 0430 hrs. on the 8th June, near the mouth of the Litani, and to prevent the demolition of the bridge over it.

The Commando embarked at Port Said in H.M.S. "Glengyle" on the 6th June, and sailed at 1200 hrs. on the 7th June.

Naval reconnaissance of beaches 7th June 1941.

No intelligence had been supplied as to the beaches in question, and they were not included in the R.A.F. photographs of the coast. The Senior Naval Officer concerned decided therefore to send his Senior Beach Master, Lieut. Potter, R.N. to Haifa in H.M.S. "Hero", to obtain information as to the possibility of landing; and a reconnaissance of the coast was made in the early hours of the 7th June, in the motor-boat "Gadwall" by Lieut. Potter and Sub-Lieut. Coldnott, R.N.R. The reconnaissance showed that heavy surf was running at an average distance of 300 yards from the beach as a result of ground swell, and that during the next two days the

---

1 For a full account of these operations see List A, Sec. 5, Chap. 6, The Campaign in Iraq and Syria

prospects of landing without considerable loss were not good. It was, however, decided to make an attempt on the following morning, 8th June.

Commando arrives off mouth of Litani River 8th June 1941.

The "Glengyle" with the destroyer escort (H.M.S. "Ilex", "Hero" and "Hotspur") arrived at a point four miles West of the mouth of the Litani River at 0038 hrs. on the 8th June. Eleven A.L.Cs. were lowered and the troops embarked in them. Just as this operation had finished Lieut. Potter arrived in the "Gadwall" with Sub-Lieut. Coldnott, and gave it as his opinion that the surf was so bad that the boats would be "rolled over" if they attempted to make a "beaching". In this opinion Lieut. Potter was supported by Sub-Lieut. Coldnott, an Inspector in the Palestine police (Sea Section) who, like Lieut. Potter, had considerable experience of the coast. The Senior N.O. (Captain D.2) had made Capt. Petrie, R.N. of the "Glengyle" responsible for deciding whether the boats could be beached or not, and had told him that the possible loss of a large number of landing craft must be accepted.

Landing postponed.

On hearing the opinions of Lieut. Potter and Sub-Lieut. Coldnott, Capt. Petrie decided that the operation could not be undertaken; not, as he explained in his report, because of the number of boats that might be lost on the beach, but because the A.L.Cs. to be used were unseaworthy in surf, and would have been capsized before reaching the beach. Lieut. Col. Pedder did not take this view, for he considered that in order to ensure surprise the risk was worth taking, and since the "Glengyle" was visible in the moonlight the enemy would be aware of her presence. The A.L.Cs. were re-hoisted with some difficulty, owing to the movement of the ship in the swell, and the Commando returned to Port Said, arriving there at 1500 hrs. on the 8th June. Lieut. Col. Pedder and the Adjutant then went on board H.M.S. "Rex" for a conference. They returned at 1600 hrs., and the "Glengyle" sailed once more for Syria at 1615 hrs.

Course of operations on land 8th June 1941.

Meanwhile the operations on land had not gone as well as had been hoped. "MOTCOL" (the left column) had been delayed by the effective demolition of the coast road South of the Iskanderoun Bridge, though the bridge itself was intact. The 2/14 Australian Inf. Bn., however, went forward on foot, and gained contact with "DONCOL" (the right column) at Tyre at 1700 hrs. on the same day.

At about the same time the Cheshire Yeomanry (Centre column) reached Tibnine and bivouacked for the night. On the 9th June, after encountering some opposition, they reached Kakiet-ej-Jisr at about

2000 hrs. the same evening after crossing very difficult country. This place is on the upper reaches of the Litani, but as it is some 11 miles from its mouth, the action of the Cheshire Yeomanry did not influence the situation in the area of the Commando's operations during the 9th June.

The Commando disembarks 9th June 1941.

H.M.S. "Glengyle" with her escorting destroyers H.M.S. "Ilex" and H.M.S. "Hero", arrived about 4 miles off shore near the mouth of the Litani at 0315 hrs. on the 9th June, which was as early as in the circumstances was possible. The weather was calm and no surf was observable. The moon which was full, was setting and the sun rose not long after the landing began. This of course was an advantage to the enemy, apart from the fact that the approach made from the sea in the morning of the previous day must have put them on the alert.

The landing craft (eleven A.L.Cs. and 1 S.L.C.) were lowered at once, and proceeded inshore led by Sub-Lieut. F.H. Coldnott. The "Glengyle" and her escort returned to Haifa as soon as the landing craft had been lowered. The landing craft returned there independently, arriving by 1125 hrs.

Lieut. Col. Pedder's orders to Commando.

Lieut. Col. Pedder had issued his orders for the landing of the "Glengyle" on the 8th June. His information was:-

(a) That approximately two Colonial battalions of the enemy were holding a position on the right bank of the Litani River facing South, with concrete posts along the hillside.
(b) That the bridge over the river had probably been demolished.
(c) That the 21st Australian Inf. Bde. with Artillery and a squadron of Armoured Cars, was to attack the enemy's position on the river (no time was given).

His intention was to seize the enemy's position, and to hold it long enough to enable the Australian Brigade to cross the river and pass through it.

For the attack the Commando was divided into three "fighting parties" organized as follows:-

"X" Party (Major G.C.T. Keyes) 4 A.L.Cs., Nos. 2, 3 and 9 Troops (8 officers and 136 O.Rs.)
"Y" Party (Lieut. Col. R.N.R. Pedder) 4 A.L.Cs., H.Q. and Nos. 1, 7 and 8 Troops (7 officers and 133 O.Rs., excluding H.Q. personnel).
"Z" Party (Capt. G.R.M.H. More) 3 A.L.Cs., Nos. 4 and 10 Troops (5 officers and 90 O.Rs.).

The strengths given are approximate. No. 6 Troop was left on board ship as the A.L.Cs. could only be lightly loaded. "X" Party was to lead the attack, with "Y" Party in reserve. "Z" Party's main task was to prevent reinforcements and supplies from reaching the enemy's position from the North. They were also to act as an additional reserve, if required and available.

"X" Party's objectives were the positions and barracks East of Aiteniye Farm.

Medical orderlies were attached to each party, and each party had one No. 18 W.T. set. "Z" Party had also a No. 11 set, to be used for intercommunication with the Australians. Unfortunately both "Z" Party's sets were rendered useless, as the A.L.C. in which they were struck a rock about 80 yards from the beach, and the men in her had to go ashore in deep water.

The beaches selected for each party are shown on the attached sketch. They are everywhere narrow, and the country beyond them rises quickly except along the narrow valley running East and West by Kafr Badda. It is covered with scrub and intersected by ravines, so that it was possible for one party of men to be near another without either being aware of it. The actions of "X", "Y" and "Z" Parties during the 9th June, will now be dealt with separately.

"X" Party lands South of the Litani.

"X" Party's landing craft were lowered and formed up by 0325 hrs. Lieut. Collar, R.N., who was in charge of the division, states in his report that no sign of the river mouth could be seen during the final approach; and it appears that the landing was actually made about half a mile to three-quarters of a mile South of the left bank of the Litani, that is to say more than a mile further South than was intended. It is not clear how the A.L.Cs. got so far out of their course, though it seems that a large house situated South of the river was mistaken for Aiteniye which lies North of it; but whatever its cause the error adversely affected the whole operation. The air photographs available did not include either the mouth of the river, nor any part of the beach to the South of a point about a mile North of Aiteniye, so that it was very difficult to recognize the coast line, and the difficulty was increased by the fact that the mouth of the river is hidden by a sand bank. First light was at 0500 hrs., and it was only after the party landed at about 0450 hrs. that it became possible to see the masts of feluccas lying in the river mouth; and Major Keyes then realised that he had been landed on the wrong bank of the river. The landing was effected without any opposition and Major Keyes gave orders for an advance Northwards with the river as the first objective. "A" Section of No. 2 Troop, under Lieut. T.I. Robinson (Gordon Highlanders), formed the advance guard.

Advanced Checked.

The party marched deployed along the beach and, shortly after moving off, passed through "C" Company of the 2/16 Australian Infantry Battalion which was waiting to support the expected Commando attack North of the river. The Company Commander was naturally surprised to see Major Keyes and his party; but volunteered to lend him some of the seven boats that he had brought with him. The advanced guard of the Commando party reached a point close to the left bank of the river at about 0510 hrs. and the enemy then sent up a red Verey light from a redoubt on the opposite bank. As a result of this "S.O.S." signal the whole beach, from the landing point to within 100 yards of the left bank of the river, came under the heavy and accurate fire of 75 mm. guns, heavy mortars, and heavy machine-guns from the direction of the main ridge to the North-East. The party was pinned to the ground, and several casualties were caused by sniping from a knoll on the opposite bank and due North. It was also fired at by two French vessels, but they were chased off by our own destroyers. No. 3 Troop under Captain Highland (Seaforth Highlanders) and Lieut. Garland (York and Lancaster Regt) succeeded in working forward on the right of the leading Troop (No. 2), but were then held up about 300 yards short of the river bank. Major Keyes sent back Lieut. G. Duncan (Black Watch) to bring up No. 9 Troop in support, using wireless if possible; but this could not be done, nor did the W.T. work. A little later four Australians, one of whom was killed on the way, brought up a boat.

Artillery support enables a party to cross the river.

Further movement was impossible until about 0930 hrs. when our artillery opened fire on the redoubt from which the Verey light had been fired some four hours earlier. Under cover of its fire Major Keyes, with Captain Highland, Lieut. Garland and about 20 men of Nos. 2 and 3 Troops, succeeded in getting the boat forward to the rushes on the South bank of the river, where they were out of sight of the enemy in the redoubt. There was a lull in the enemy's fire and at about 1000 hrs. Lieut. Garland, with six of his Troop (No. 3) and two Australians, crossed the river. The three remaining Australians, whose behaviour throughout the day was admirable, brought the boat back but the party was again pinned down, this time by the fire of a 75 mm. gun and of some M.Gs. on the high ground East of the coastal road. In the meantime Lieut. Garland and his men began to cut through the enemy's wire. Major Keyes sent back Lance Cpl. Dillworth, the Australian N.C.O. in charge of the boat party, to bring forward what was left of "X" Party and to ask his own Company Commander to move up in support, and bring more boats if possible. Lance Cpl. Dillworth, a most gallant man, returned about 20 minutes later, having been under fire both ways, with the following information:-

Withdrawal of No. 9 Troop.

Capt. Johnson (H.L.I.) commanding the remaining Troop (No. 9) had heard that Major Keyes and all the forward troops had been killed. He had therefore withdrawn his men and reformed them with the intention of attacking with the Australians and on their right. It transpired later that while doing this Capt. Johnson met Brig. Stevens (Australian Army) who ordered him to send his men to join "B" Echelon of the 21st Australian Brigade. Lance Cpl. Dillworth also told Major Keyes that his own Company Commander was re-organizing and would try to move up in support. The loss of No. 9 Troop, who did not rejoin till next day, was regrettable; and Major Keyes considered that with the additional 40 men he might have been able to capture Aiteniye during the evening of the 9th June.

The enemy's redoubt surrenders 1200 hrs. 9th June.

At about 1100 hrs. while Lieut. Garland, who had crossed the river with six men an hour earlier, was still engaged in cutting through the enemy's wire, Major Keyes and Capt. Highland, who were still on the left bank, noticed a white flag waving in the enemy's redoubt. With the aid of the same Australians as before Capt. Highland and six more men crossed the river at 1145 hrs., and after a short parley the enemy surrendered. One man of the Commando was killed while an isolated post was being cleared. Six of the enemy were killed, and thirty-five prisoners were taken. In view of the probability of counter-attack, Capt. Highland set to work to consolidate the position. In response to an urgent message, the Australian Company Commander came forward at 1300 hrs. with Capt. Johnson of No. 9 Troop, and Major Keyes asked him to move up in support, pointing out that as the redoubt was now in our hands it was possible for his men to come up along the beach out of sight of the enemy. This they began to do but, by neglecting to use the available cover, they drew heavy fire from the enemy who shot down the river from the rising ground to the east; and little progress was made.

Captured redoubt consolidated.

Major Keyes then took the remainder of his men across the river, using his prisoners to take the boat back. His losses had been considerable, and as most of his Bren Guns or their detachments had become casualties, full use was made of captured weapons for the defence of the redoubt which was very strongly fortified. The total of material captured was one 25 mm. A/Tk gun, one 37.5 mm Mountain gun, 2 Heavy Hotchkiss M.Gs., 5 light M.Gs., 45 rifles, and a great deal of ammunition. There were also three or four days' hard rations. About 20 Australians of C. Company 2/16 Battalion under Lieut. O'Keefe also crossed the river, but as the boats were fired on the Company Commander would not risk sending any more. At about 1330 hrs. Major Keyes located the position from which the enemy were firing down the river.

The enemy's fire silenced.

Lieut. Garland engaged it with the 25 mm. A/Tk gun, which had been found in the redoubt, and silenced the enemy's fire after 7 rounds. It was discovered next day that the position contained a 75 mm. gun and a heavy M.G. The post was defiladed from the South and the fire of our artillery had not been able to reach it. More of the Australian Company under Capt. Carron then crossed the river, but as they had orders not to move till nightfall Major Keyes decided to remain where he was, as he was too weak to attack Aiteniye. At 1800 hrs. he handed over the defence of the redoubt to the Australian Company, the whole of which was across the river by 1900 hrs. He had by this time been joined by some men of No. 1 Troop ("Y" Party).

Unsuccessful attack.

At 2100 hrs. the Australians moved off to attack Aiteniye, and "X" Party again took over the defence of the redoubt. The attack was unsuccessful and the Australians returned to the redoubt. The Australian artillery continued to fire on Aiteniye during the night and the French garrison surrendered early next morning to Capt. More commanding "Z" Party whom they had captured the previous evening!

"Y" Party (1, 7 and 8 Troops).

"Y" Party left H.M.S. "Glengyle" at about 0330 hrs. on the 9th June, and beached at about 0420 hrs. No. 1 Troop was landed on the right, No. 7 in the centre and No. 8 on the left. The enemy opened fire as soon as the troops began to disembark.

As already indicated, the task of "Y" Party was to act as reserve for "X" Party. The original orders, however, had been rendered nugatory by the fact that "X" Party had been landed South of the Litani River and so were completely out of touch with the rest of the Commando. The three Troops of "Y" Party therefore acted independently and their actions, as far as they are known, are dealt with in turn. Information about Commando H.Q. and No. 1 Troop (Commanded by Lieut. J. Bryant, R.E.) is scanty, and contact with Nos. 7 and 8 Troops seems to have been lost quite early. Sergt. Terry, with one sub-section of No. 1 Troop, had come ashore in a landing craft in which the majority of men belonged to No. 7 Troop. He went forward as far as the coastal road with No. 7 but then joined Capt. More, commanding "Z" Party, and remained with that party for the rest of the day. The remainder of No. 1 Troop went forward from the beach, with

Lieut. Col. Pedder and his Headquarters, into the hills to the north of the barracks, which they occupied. Using a 75 mm. gun which had fallen into their hands they made another attack and captured some more guns; but about two hours after landing, i.e. between 0630 and 0700 hrs., they were halted by fire from positions they could not locate, and were later forced to surrender.

H.Q. and No. 1 Troop captured.

Lieut. Col. Pedder, Capt. Farmiloe and Lieut. Goode had been killed by snipers and Lieut. Bryant was badly wounded. Towards nightfall they and their captors came under the fire of British destroyers and were forced to move to a safer place. Relations with the French were friendly, and as time went on a doubt seems to have arisen as to who were the captors and who the captives! Eventually the matter was settled by the arrival of Australian Troops between 0300 hrs. and 0400 hrs. on the 10th June.

No. 7 Troop and "B" Section No. 8 Troop.

No. 7 Troop (under Lieut. R.B. Mayne, Royal Ulster Rifles) which had landed under fire with the loss of one man killed, moved North along the beach for about 400 yards and then turned East, supported by "B" Section of No. 8 under Lieut. Fraser which from then onwards lost touch with the rest of its own troop. By 0520 hrs. No. 7 Troop had reached the coastal road in spite of fire from two machine guns; and about 40 French Colonial Troops surrendered to them. Lieut. Mayne sent a runner to find Lieut. Col. Pedder and report the capture of this objective, but the runner returned later having been unable to find Lieut. Col. Pedder's H.Q. The troop then continued its advance through the hills, passing North of the barracks; and then turned South-East towards Qasmiye. There was little opposition and they took several more prisoners. At 0630 hrs. they turned South towards the river, passing Lieut. Fraser's Section of No. 8 Troop which from now onwards acted independently. At 0730 hrs. No. 7 Troop arrived at an explosive store and 30 more prisoners were taken, but at 0800 hrs. they came under fire from Australians on the opposite side of the Litani.

No. 7 Troop under fire from Australians.

They displayed a white flag, but this had no effect and they were for a time unable to move. At about 0900 hrs. they managed to retire under cover and concentrated their prisoners at the explosive store. About two hours later they again moved East and by 1200 hrs. had captured more prisoners, chiefly mule drivers. At 1700 hrs., after a long detour, they arrived at the river but again came under fire from the Australians on the other side of it and one O.R. was killed. Just before dark they were able to cross the Litani by a pontoon bridge erected by the Australians near the bridge that had been blown up; and their prisoners, who were still with them, were taken next day to Tyre.

No. 8 Troop joins "Z" Party.

As previously stated, No. 8 Troop of "Y" Party, commanded by Capt. Glennie, lost touch with "B" Section of the Troop under Lieut. Fraser soon after landing; and Troop H.Q. with "A" Section acted with "Z" Party (under Capt. More) throughout the 9th June. They crossed the coastal road on the left of No. 7 Troop, and when about 200 yards from the beach came under "heavy but inaccurate" fire from A.F.Vs. on the coastal road about 200 yards South of the Kafr Badda bridge, and from a M.G. post situated under the bridge itself. An Armoured Car was set on fire by Lance Cpl. Tait with an anti-tank rifle and, with the co-operation of "Z" Party immediately to the North, the A.F.Vs. and the machine guns at the bridge were forced to cease firing. Captain Glennie then crossed the road with "A" Section and at about 0630 hrs. attacked a battery of French 155 mm. howitzers in the valley near Kafra Badda. The battery was also attacked at the same time by "Z" Party on the left, and surrendered without serious resistance. The sub-section of No. 1 Troop under Sergt. Terry, which had become detached from its own troop and had joined Capt. More, also took part in the capture of the battery. Capt. Glennie, having secured his prisoners, embussed his section in a captured lorry and at about 0900 hrs. moved South along the coastal road, in order to get in touch with the remainder of "Y" Party near the barracks. After going about 800 yards he met Capt. More commanding "Z" Party who, with Sergt. Hill, had moved along the hills with the same object. Capt. More told him that the road was under machine gun fire further along. Capt. Glennie dismounted his men and manoeuvred parallel to the road but he was checked by heavy fire from the neighbourhood of the barracks and could make no progress. At midday he was again joined by Capt. More and Sergt. Hill and, as several casualties had occurred, the party now numbered only about 12 men. Captains More and Glennie re-organized their available strength into two scratch sections and made two attacks which are described later, but without success. After the second attack the two sections became separated. Capt. Glennie retired to the road and heard heavy fire in the area of the Kafr Badda bridge. Several hostile A.F.Vs. were seen approaching the bridge and he decided to move North and reinforce No. 10 Troop of "Z" Party, to whom he thought his two anti-tank rifles would be useful. Before reaching No. 10 Troop, however, his party themselves came under fire from guns and machine guns and there were more casualties. No. 10 Troop was shortly afterwards forced to withdraw and Capt. Glennie's Troop fell back to the South, parallel to and East of the road, and in doing so lost touch with it.

"Z" Party forced to withdraw and surrender at Aiteniye.

Soon after the withdrawal began they were attacked by six A.F.Vs., two moving across country and the remainder along the road. The A.F.Vs. were successfully engaged and, after a fight at close range for ten minutes, retired in the direction from which they had come. Our troops suffered no casualties and the withdrawal continued. At about 1800 hrs. Capt. More re-appeared with Lieuts. McGonigal and Parnacott and the remnants of various troops, including No. 10, but the total number of officers and men was in all only about 24. It was decided to wait until night-fall and then to move West to the coast and thence South by Aiteniye (which they believed had been taken by Major Keyes' party) to the Litani. If Aiteniye was not in our hands they intended to swim the river and make their way to the Australian lines. Touch with No. 10 Troop was lost at about 1945 hrs. but it had been given orders to retire to the river. The rest of the party moved off at 0030 hrs. on the 10th June, and when it reached Aiteniye was fired at from two directions, including the M.G. post at Pt. S. Lieut. Parnacott and four O.Rs. were killed, three O.Rs. wounded and the party surrendered. They were well treated by the French, who attended to their wounded.

The French surrender to Capt. More 0830 hrs. 10th June.

At 0830 hrs. on the 10th A.F.Vs. of the Australians, which had crossed the river, came in sight and the French Officer commanding at Aiteniye surrendered to Capt. More. At 1015 hrs. the remains of "Y" and "Z" Parties joined Major Keyes' party.

Lieut. Fraser's Section.

"B" Section of No. 8 Troop (Lieut. Fraser, Gordon Highlanders) who had lost touch with the rest of their own Troop, supported No. 7 Troop's attack on the road at 0515 hrs. and remained in contact with them until about 0700 hrs. No. 7 Troop then turned South towards the river but Lieut. Fraser continued for a time to move East over the high ground. He was opposed by dismounted cavalry (Spahis) but overcame their resistance and captured about 30 prisoners. At about the same time he was joined by a Section of No. 4 Troop ("Z" Party) under Lieut. Richards, which had been sent by Capt. More to support "Y" Party, and remained with Lieut. Fraser for the rest of the day. They moved South along the crest of the hills without meeting any resistance but, on arrival at the ridge overlooking the Litani, they came under small arms fire apparently from the South side of the river. As the Australian artillery also opened fire on the ridge Lieut. Fraser withdrew his men to a covered position.

Enemy M.Gs. attacked.

A successful attack was then made from the North on enemy M.G. posts defending the river from positions on the rising ground North-East of the Litani bridge, and a number of prisoners were taken. It was then decided to move Northwards in the hope of gaining touch with "Z" Party and contact was made with Capt. More at 1730 hrs. At 2000 hrs. the party moved East, then South-East round the left of the French position, and eventually reached the river at 0300 hrs. on the 10th June. The river was crossed and at 0330 hrs. the march was resumed in a South-Westerly direction, contact being made with an Australian Battery at 1130 hrs. on the 10th June. During the afternoon Lieut. Fraser was hit by a bullet on the chin strap of his helmet. This caused slight concussion and, though he was able to remain with the party, he handed over command to Sergt. J. Cheyne.

"Z" Party (Nos. 4 and 10 Troops).

Capt. G.R.M.H. More, R.E., commanding "Z" Party, gave orders as follows:-

(a) No. 10 Troop (Capt. I.H. MacDonald, Cameron Highlanders) was to seize the Kafr Badda Bridge.
(b) No. 4 Troop (Lieut. J.C. McGonigal, Royal Ulster Rifles) was to support No. 10 Troop if necessary. Otherwise it was to manoeuvre so as to support "Y" Party, as laid down in Lieut. Col. Pedder's orders.
(c) Party H.Q. would be with No. 4.

The party landed safely at 0420 hrs. but two landing craft struck rocks before reaching the beach. The troops in them had to land through deep water and, as already described, the two available W.T. sets were rendered useless. A few stray shots were fired by the enemy but no damage was caused. By 0430 hrs. No. 4 Troop (less a section under Lieut. C.G. Richards, Wiltshire Regt.) was advancing towards Point "C" and No. 10 Troop, which had come under small arms fire for a few minutes after landing, towards the Kafr Badda Bridge.

Enemy attacked near Point "A".

Four enemy lorries were seen to halt at Point "A" and open fire with two Hotchkiss Heavy M.Gs. on "Y" Party, who had landed some hundreds of yards further South, but apparently they did not notice No. 4 Troop, which crossed the coastal road about 300 yards from them. Capt. More, with 2/Lieut. Richards' Section of No. 4 Troop, also crossed the road and engaged the Hotchkiss guns from their rear. Several of the enemy were killed and wounded and the remainder, about 40, surrendered. The rest of No. 4 Troop, who had reached high ground East of the coastal road, opened fire in support of Capt. More's attack and then moved North along the ridge towards Kafr Badda. At about the same time (0445 hrs.) No. 10 Troop, further to the North, came under heavy fire from a strong point, supported by Armoured Cars, just East of the Kafr Badda Bridge and from four M.G. positions on high ground near the bridge.

Attack near Kafr Badda Bridge.

Nos. 1 and 4 sub-sections were pinned to the ground but Capt. MacDonald, with Nos. 2 and 3, successfully attacked the enemy round both flanks. All the enemy's transport, including an Armoured Car manned by Germans, was put out of action and their position was captured. At about 0500 hrs. Capt. More sent 2/Lieut. Richards' Section of No. 4 Troop to support the left of "Y" Party and arranged for an escort to guard the prisoners and for a temporary R.A.P. for the wounded at Point "A". He also sent Sergt. Hill and Driver Foster, with the two captured Hotchkiss M.Gs. and 50,000 rounds of ammunition, to No. 10 Troop at the Kafr Badda Bridge. The Northward movement of Lieut. McGonigal's No. 4 Troop along the ridge towards the same area no doubt contributed to the success of No. 10 Troop's attack.

"Z" Party consolidates near Point "C" 0600 hrs. 9th June.

By 0600 hrs. Capt. More had concentrated the whole of his party, i.e. No. 4 Troop less 2nd Lieut. Richards' Section, No. 10 Troop and Sergt. Terry's sub-section of No. 1 Troop, in the neighbourhood of Point "C", and began to consolidate his position. He then (at 0630 hrs.) moved East along the valley with a sub-section of No. 4 Troop under Lieut. G.A. Parnacott (York and Lancashire Regt.) and Sergt. Terry's sub-section of No. 1 Troop and, with the help of part of No. 8 Troop of "Y" Party under Capt. Glennie, captured the battery of four 155 mm. Howitzers already referred to, with two French Officers and a number of Senegalese gunners. The battery was in a covered position facing South and one of its officers stated that he was unable to fire as the telephone wire to his O.P. had been cut. Capt. More decided to collect his prisoners at Point "D", the site of the Battery's wagon lines, and he was joined there at 0700 hrs. by Capt. Glennie with "A" Section of No. 8 Troop, which had moved along the hills from the South. Leaving Lieuts. McGonigal and Parnacott, with No. 4 Troop and Sergt. Terry's sub-section, to guard Point "D" he went on a motor cycle to bring in the wounded and prisoners left at Point "A".

"Z" Party's position reconnoitred by enemy's aircraft 0900 hrs.

For purposes of defence No. 10 Troop had occupied the high ground above and North-East of the Kafr Badda Bridge (Point "F") and No. 4 Troop was on high ground further East near Point "D". From about 0800 hrs. till about 0930 hrs. there was some reconnaissance by hostile aircraft. No. 10 Troop investigated the Kafr Badda Bridge and found that it was not mined. They also discovered a certain number of maps and documents in the captured vehicles, some of which were of value to the Australians next day. Capt. More, after making arrangements for the disposal of the wounded men and prisoners at Point "A", moved South to try and get in touch with the rest of the Commando. At 0830 hrs. he found that Aiteniye was being heavily shelled by our guns and after rounding a corner near that place, he came under M.G. fire also from the opposite bank of the river. His motor cycle was hit and he escaped with difficulty. Between 0900 hrs. and 1000 hrs. he returned to Point "D", and Capt. Glennie, with his Section of No. 8 Troop, left shortly afterwards to try and rejoin "Y" Party. At 1000 hrs. Capt. More and Sergt. Hill started Southwards along the hills with the same object in view. At 1100 hrs. they came under heavy machine gun fire at close range from the neighbourhood of the barracks and had great difficulty in withdrawing. At 1200 hrs. they were rejoined by Capt. Glennie who had lost nearly the whole of one sub-section.

Unsuccessful attack on the barracks 1230 hrs.

Although they had now only about 12 men in all, they decided to make an attack on the barracks in two detachments and at 1300 hrs. proceeded to do so. The first attack was a failure and, though in another attempt at 1500 hrs. they took 9 prisoners, they were eventually obliged to retire and, as already stated, the two detachments became separated.

Enemy recaptures Point "C".

Capt. More returned to Point "C" only to find that the enemy had recaptured it and released all the prisoners, and that Nos. 4 and 10 Troops had been forced out of their positions. He therefore withdrew to the next ridge to the South. The events that led to the retirement of what was left of "Z" Party were as follows. At 0930 hrs. three of the enemy's A.F.Vs. came down the road from the direction of Sidon but withdrew when fired on by No. 10 Troop from Point "F".

The enemy again attack 1140 hrs.

At 1140 hrs. A.F.Vs. again appeared on the road and made an attack. They approached by moving one vehicle at a time, supported by the fire of the others, until they were within 500 yards. No. 10 Troop then opened fire and the enemy retired in the same way. During the early afternoon the enemy brought several M.G. and light guns into action in the neighbourhood of the coastal road, which were out of range of No. 10 Troops's weapons and caused a lot of trouble.

The enemy reinforced and "Z" Party is forced to withdraw 1800 hrs.

By 1730 hrs. the enemy had been further reinforced by mortars and had in all eight armoured cars, one of which was put out of action and another damaged. Six more armoured cars then appeared, and the right flank of No. 10 Troop was uncovered by the retirement of a detachment of No. 4 Troop. It was then attacked from both flanks by A.F.Vs. and infantry and at 1810 hrs. was forced to retire "to the next ridge", which was presumably to the South.

Enemy's attack on No. 4 Troop 1600 hrs.

No. 4 Troop, defending the area about Point "D" where prisoners had been concentrated, was not interfered with until 1600 hrs. but they were reconnoitred by a hostile plane and could hear the sound of firing from No. 10 Troop's position. At about 1600 hrs. six armoured cars appeared about 1400 yds. to the East, along the road to Ed Douar, and engaged the area with 2-pdr. (or similar) guns and M.Gs. They inflicted heavy casualties on the prisoners and other prisoners were killed while attempting to disarm our men or to escape. The ground in the neighbourhood of the road was such as to make it impossible to block it and Lieut. McGonigal was forced to withdraw his main body, which included men of Nos. 1, 7 and 10 Troops as well as his own, leaving one sub-section of No. 4 Troop and two Anti-Tank rifles as rearguard.

No. 4 Troop has to retire.

The rearguard withdrew 15 minutes later and Lieut. McGonigal, having reformed his men in the hills to the South, moved West to support No. 10 Troop.

Capt. More takes command.

Leaving a sub-section to cover his rear, Lieut. McGonigal reported to Capt. MacDonald with the remainder of the Troop. At this juncture, and probably at about 1800 hrs., Capt. More arrived with Capt. Glennie and what was left of their party and took command. He ordered a further withdrawal Southwards, Nos. 4 and 10 Troops "leap-frogging" from ridge to ridge. His intention was that the party should retire to the mouth of the Litani and cross the river there, and with this object in view No. 10 Troop held their position until 1945 hrs. By this time they were being fired at by machine guns from in front and were being outflanked by A.F.Vs. on their left and by infantry on the high ground to their right. Accompanied by some of No. 4 Troop they again withdrew, this time up a gulley to the East, and lay up in a wood until it was dark. They then split into two parties and made their way back successfully to the Australian position. Captain

More, as described earlier, was obliged to surrender at Aiteniye, though his position was reversed next morning; and during the morning of the 10th the scattered detachments of "Y" and "Z" Parties made their way to the South bank of the Litani.

By 1200 hrs. on the 10th the 21st Australian Brigade had crossed the river in sufficient strength to advance through the position held by Major Keyes' "X" Party, between the river and Aiteniye, and by 2300 hrs. the Commando was concentrated in the transit camp at Haifa.

Major Keyes and Capt. More visit the C-in-C. 11th June 1941.

On the 11th June Major Keyes and Capt. More went to Jerusalem to see the Commander-in-Chief and returned on the 12th. The casualty return made out on the 13th June showed that the losses had been as follows: Officers 5 killed, 1 wounded, and 1 wounded and a prisoner.[1] O.R. 123 killed and wounded.

Commando returns to Cyprus.

At 1815 hrs. 14th June, the Commando completed embarkation in the S.S. "Rodi" which sailed for Cyprus at 1850 hrs. and Capt. Carr was sent to report at G.H.Q. Cairo. The S.S. "Rodi" berthed at Famagusta at 0700 hrs. on the 15th June, and at 0830 hrs. the Commando disembarked.

It was then re-organized as a Headquarters and three Companies of three Troops, each Troop having three Sections.

The gallant conduct of the following officers and other ranks was specially commended by their immediate Commanders.

Capt. A.G. Highland, Seaforth Highlanders.
Lieut. E.F. Garland, M.C. York and Lancaster Regt.
Lieut. G.A. Parnacott, Yorks and Lancaster Regt. (Killed)
No. 2888693 Lance Cpl. Robert Tait.
No. 2592099 Sergt. A. Reed, R.C. of Signals.
No. 2873369 Sergt. Charles Nichol.
No. 2876188 Sergt. Jack Cheyne.
No. 3530661 Lance Cpl. N. Sproule.
No. 4976786 Pte. G. Dove.
Lance Cpl. Jackson, R.A.M.C.
Lance Cpl. Dillworth, C. Coy 2/16 Bn. A.I.F.

1 Killed: Lieut. Col. R.N. Pedder, H.L.I.
                        Capt. W.A.R. Farmiloe, London Rifle Brigade.
                        Lieut. G.A. Parnacott, York and Lancaster Regt.
                        Lieut. D.A. Coode, R.E.
                        Lieut. C.G. Richards, Wiltshire Regt.

Wounded and prisoner: Lieut. J. Bryant, R.E.

On the 23rd June, Col. Laycock came to Cyprus from Egypt and inspected the Unit. For the remainder of the month the Commando was occupied in training and in the organization of its part in the Defence Scheme of Cyprus.

The attack on Rommel's H.Q.

The disbandment of "C" Battalion of "Layforce" during the Autumn of 1941, was delayed and part of it made the daring attack on General Rommel's H.Q. in the middle of November 1941, when their Commander, Lieut. Col. G.C.T. Keyes (Scots Greys), was killed and was posthumously awarded the Victoria Cross for his outstanding gallantry.

Primary objectives.

The four primary objectives of the raid are described by Lieut. Col. Laycock, who was still O.C. Middle East Commandos and took part in the operation, as:-

(1) To raid General Rommel's house and the German H.Q., believed to be at Beda Littoria (S.O.54, Sheet Bengasi 1/250,000).[1]
(2) To assault the Italian H.Q. at Cyrene.
(3) To assault the Italian Intelligence Centre at Apollonia.
(4) To sabotage telephone and telegraph communications at the cross roads at 632546 (four miles S.S.E. of Cyrene).

The operation was timed so as to synchronize if possible with General Auchinleck's offensive which opened on the night 17th/18th November 1941. As the objectives were some distance inland the landing was to be made on the night of 14th/15th November.

Capt. Haselden goes overland.

As a preliminary measure a small party was sent overland, to reconnoitre Chescem-el-Kelb (393688) the point on the Coast where it was intended that the raiders should land; and to co-operate with them after landing by "sabotaging" the H.Q. of the Trieste division on the main road near Slonta,[2] destroying M.T. camped in the area Slonta-Buerat-Gerdes, and cutting the main telephone on the Southern road (through the Jebel-el-Akhdar) near Slonta. The party was Commanded by Capt. Haselden, M.C., (G(R)) who had with him Capt. Chapman, Capt. R. Melot and 2/Lieut. Westall of the G(R) pool, and two Arabs of the 3rd Battalion Libyan Refugee Force.[3]

---

1 Subsequent references to map 1/100,000 Cyrene Sheet 2, unless otherwise stated.
2 Actually the H.Q. had left Slonta some time before; but this was not known.
3 In his report Capt. Haselden refers to Chescem-el-Kelb as Zauiet-el-Hammama. It is the same place.

They left Siwa on the 7th November with T.2 patrol of the L.R.D.G. under the Command of Capt. A.D.N. Hunter who carried them as far as the Southern extremity of the Wadi Heleigma (Bengasi 1/250,000 S.T. 68.) and arrived there in the afternoon of the 10th November. From this point Capt. Haselden and an Arab continued the journey on foot, and arrived at the beach at Chescem-el-Kelb in the morning of the 14th. They found the coast clear, and in the evening went down to signal to the submarines carrying the raiders, which was to be done every quarter of an hour and was begun at 1830 hrs. Some twenty minutes after the first signal an officer (Lieut. Inglis A & S.H.) and a Corporal arrived in a "folbot"; and disembarkation from H.M.S. "Torbay" began soon afterwards. Capt. Haselden remained with the raiding party until the morning of the 15th, and then left to rejoin his own party South of Slonta. An account of the landing by Commander A.C. Miers, V.C., D.S.O. (H.M.S. "Torbay") is given in the Appendix to this Section. The narrative which now follows is based on Col. Laycock's report.

Embarkation in H.M.S. "Torbay" and H.M.S. "Talisman", 10th November, 1941.

The strength of the party was six officers and 53 other ranks who embarked at Alexandria on the 10th November 1941 in H.M. submarines "Torbay" (Comdr. Miers) and "Talisman" (Lieut. Commdr. N. Wilmott).

The landing was to be made if possible at Chescem-el-Kelb (393-658). Alternative beaches were selected for use if necessary.

Op. Order and Plan.

The party was divided into four detachments which as detailed in Lieut. Col. Keyes' "Scottish Commando Operation Order No. 1" of the 11th November, were as follows:-

(a) No. 1 party Lieut. Col. Keyes with 2 officers and 22 O.Rs. (H.M.S. Torbay").
(b) No. 2 party Lieut. D. Sutherland with 12 O.Rs. (H.M.S. "Talisman").
(c) No. 3 party Lieut. Chevalier with 11 O.Rs. (H.M.S. "Talisman").
(d) H.Q. party Lieut. Col. Laycock with 2 O.Rs. and a Medical Orderly (H.M.S. "Torbay").

There were also two Senussi guides for Nos. 1 and 2 parties; and a "folbot" party of 2 officers and 2 O.Rs.

Tasks.

Their respective objectives and tasks were as follows:-

No. 1   – General Rommel's House and the German H.Q. believed to
            be at Beda Littoria.
No. 2   – The Italian H.Q. at Cyrene.
No. 3   – The Italian Intelligence Centre at Apollonia.
H.Q. Party – To act as a report centre and rear link.

Capt. Haselden's party, described in Col. Laycock's report as No. 4 detachment, had the task of destroying the telephone and telegraph communications on the road from Lamluda (Derna 1/250,000 S.O.8955) to El Faidia (Bengasi 1/250,000 - S.O.8644).

If all went well the detachments were to lie up during the 15th, and during the night 15/16th to move to other concealed localities half way to their objectives. They were again to lie up during daylight on the 16th and move during the night 16/17th to positions whence the objectives could be observed. The primary objectives were to be attacked at 2359 hrs. on the 17th November. The submarines were to be available for re-embarkation from the fourth to the sixth nights after landing, the "Torbay" off the original beach, the "Talisman" three miles to Westward. At the last minute Col. Laycock transferred from the "Torbay" to the "Talisman" as Capt Glennie who was to have commanded the two detachments in the latter ship, went sick. It was necessary that information which for security reasons had not been given to the leaders of Nos. 2 and 3 parties should be imparted to them on the voyage, and Col. Laycock was the only officer available to do it.

Torbay arrives at Chescem-el-Kelb 14th November. Contact with Haselden.

The "Torbay" closed the beaches shortly after 1830 hrs, and Capt. Haselden's signals were received. Lieut. Inglis, was landed, and signalled that the beach was clear and that touch had been gained with Haselden. The latter was dressed as an Arab, and in his report Col. Laycock says of him, "Capt Haselden's activities were invaluable and his calculated daring and physical endurance are worthy of the highest praise." It is a matter of regret that this gallant and gifted officer should have been killed in the raid on Tobruk in September 1942.

The landing from "Torbay".

Lieut. Inglis returned to the submarine and made a full report, but his craft was damaged while it was being got aboard. The raiding party then took station for leaving the submarine according to previously rehearsed drill.

All went well until the "Torbay" trimmed down preparatory to launching the boats, when a sea came aboard and washed four of them and one man overboard. There was considerable difficulty in recovering them in the dark. Further difficulty was experienced owing to boats being swamped and it was midnight before landing from the "Torbay" was completed, having taken five hours instead of one as calculated from rehearsals; but many "broached to" in the surf and most of the landing party were wet from the waist down when they landed. In the meantime those in the "Talisman" including Col. Laycock, were unable to account for the delay in the "Torbay" and an officer sent in a folbot to find out what was wrong failed to located her in the darkness. Moreover the weather was deteriorating, and the swell increased. At 0330 hrs. on the 15th however, just as the Captain and Col. Laycock had decided to postpone landing, a message came to say that the "Torbay" had completed disembarkation.

The landing from "Talisman".

The "Talisman's" rubber dinghies were inflated satisfactorily but before any could be launched a heavy sea washed many of them off the casing; and a few men went overboard after their boats or were washed over the side. Unfortunately most of the men swam back to the submarine instead of to their boats, and only Col. Laycock and seven O.Rs. reached the shore. As both the "Talisman's" "folbots" were by this time out of action it was impossible to get a grass line ashore with which to tow back the boats which had landed, and as it was obviously undesirable for the boats to be washed up in hostile territory Col. Laycock signalled with an electric torch saying that he would hide his boats ashore, and asking the Captain of the "Talisman" to try and collect those which were adrift. From the report sent in by H.M.S. "Talisman" it appears that this was successfully done.

Signalling difficulties.

In regard to signalling Col. Laycock points out that he had no signallers with the raiding party, for those who were formerly in "Layforce" had been transferred with other specialists to other units. Nor were there any sappers with the result that demolitions attempted were for the most part less effective than they might have been. He himself was the only person ashore who knew the naval signals procedure, and his torch had no proper key.

Landing of stores.

Arms, ammunition, field glasses, watches, compasses, explosives and rations had been wrapped in waterproof material and lashed to the boats. In spite of total submersion most of these stores reached the shore undamaged. The party which had reached the shore, numbering about thirty-six of all ranks, remained on the beach for an hour and a half, and the boats were hidden in a cave. As it was then too late for the "Talisman" to land anyone else until the following night, and in any case the weather was too bad, Col. Laycock took his party to the first rendezvous, a wadi about one mile inland, leaving Lieut. Prior and one man (both of the Folbot Section) on the beach. He had the alternatives of waiting for the "Talisman" to land more men in the night 15th/16th and adhering to the original plan; or of sending the party ashore to carry out a modified plan, and using any reinforcements that the "Talisman" might land as a reserve.

He adopted the second alternative for two reasons. In the first place Eighth Army had emphasized the fact that the raid would be of the greatest value if carried out on the night of 17th/18th, in the second the weather was deteriorating and there was a considerable sea running which might well prevent further landings.

Modified Plan.

The modified plan was as follows:-

As originally arranged, Lieut. Col. Keyes with No. 1 detachment was to attack Rommel's house and H.Q; and he took with him Capt. R.F. Campbell and 17 O.Rs. The second detachment under Lieut. R. Cook was given orders to sabotage communications at the cross roads South of Cyrene 632 546. With him were six O.Rs. This was the task of the original No. 2 party under Lieut. Sutherland, and it was unfortunate that none of that party, who had rehearsed the plan and were equipped with special stores, succeeded in landing from the "Talisman". As already arranged Capt. Haselden was prepared to cut communications on the road Lamluda - El Faidia. Col. Laycock himself was to remain at the first rendezvous with a Sergeant and 2 O.Rs. and the reserve ammunition and rations; and was to operate with the remainder of the force if it were landed. On the return journey the detachment was to rally at the rendezvous, not on the beach.

The approach.

The detachments moved off at 1900 hrs. 15th November with Arab guides provided by Haselden (the two Senussi did not reach the shore); but the guides refused to go further than a few miles, and both the detachments lay up for some hours in a suitable wadi. Later the same night they continued their march and lay up again at first light. They were found by a party of Arabs who proved to be friendly and in the evening of the 16th guided them to a spot about 10 miles from Beda Littoria, which was selected as a rallying point (or rendezvous). Surplus clothing and rations were dumped and the party slept there during the remainder of the night 16th/17th. The weather was exceedingly cold and they had been drenched by torrential rain.

Position of Rommel's House.

Capt. Haselden's information had been that General Rommel and his Staff Officers lived in a house at Sidi Rafa (495507) and not in the building at Beda Littoria indicated in our Intelligence Summary; and this was confirmed by the Arabs who had no doubt of it. Lieut. Col. Keyes therefore selected it as his party's objective.

Final approach of No. 1 detachment.

After dark on the 17th they were led by the Arabs to within a few hundred yards of the house and lay up awaiting Zero hour (2359 hrs). Here they were found by a party of Arabs in uniform (presumably Carabinieri) but Capt. Campbell allayed suspicion by explaining in German that the party belonged to a German unit.

No. 2 detachment moves off.

In the meantime No. 2 party under Lieut. Cook had moved off to the cross roads South of Cyrene.

Lieut. Col. Keyes' final orders.

Lieut. Col. Keyes gave orders to No. 1 party as follows:-

(a) He himself with Capt. Campbell and Sergt. Terry, R.A. was to enter and search the house.
(b) Three other ranks were detailed to put the electric light plant out of action.
(c) The remainder of the detachment were dispersed so as to prevent interference by the enemy. Five O.Rs. were to watch the exits from the guard tent and car park; two more were posted outside the hotel near by to prevent any one leaving it; and two were placed on the road on each side of the house. The remaining two were left to guard whichever entrance Col. Keyes used to gain access to the house.

The attack at midnight 17th/18th November.

Everyone was in position just before midnight and Col. Keyes made a reconnaissance of the house. "Unable to find a way in through the back premises or windows Col. Keyes' party walked up to the front door and beat upon it, Capt. Campbell demanding access in German. The door was eventually opened by a sentry who was set upon, but could not be overpowered silently, and was therefore shot by Capt. Campbell which aroused the Headquarters and vicinity. Two men tried to come down stairs from the first floor but thought better of it on being met by a burst of fire from Sergt. Terry's Tommy Gun. No one attempted to leave the rooms on the ground floor, but the lights in them were turned out. No enemy emerged from the guard tent of the hotel, but two Germans carrying lights appeared running towards the house, where they were shot by our sentries.

Lieut. Col. Keyes mortally wounded.

Keyes and Campbell started to make a search of the ground floor, but the occupants of the second room they entered were waiting for them, and Lieut. Col. Keyes, who had opened the door, was met by a burst of fire and fell back into the passage mortally wounded. Sergt. Terry emptied two magazines of his Tommy Gun into the darkened room, and Capt. Campbell silenced the party by throwing in a grenade and slamming the door. Together they carried Lieut. Col. Keyes outside where he died almost immediately." While attending to him Capt. Campbell was hit by a stray bullet which broke the lower part of his leg.

It appeared that the enemy were completely surprised and there was little resistance. Two German Staff Officers were known to have been killed and others wounded[1], while several soldiers were killed and wounded.

It was particularly unfortunate that General Rommel was absent attending a birthday party in Rome. Shooting was heard at some distance from the house where there were none of our troops, and it may be that the enemy were shooting at each other!

The withdrawal.

Capt. Campbell ordered Sergt. Terry to concentrate the party and tell them to throw all the remaining grenades through any available windows before returning to their rallying point, in preparation for withdrawal to the beach. Realizing that he himself could not be carried eighteen miles over precipitous country including a descent of some 2,000 ft. he told his men to abandon him.

The attack on electric light plant.

The party that had attacked the electric light plant had been partially successful. Though rain had rendered the strikers of their charges useless and they were unable to blow up the dynamo, they succeeded in putting it out of action by exploding a grenade on the armature.

Enemy documents captured later indicated that an explosion took place at the cross roads South of Cyrene, that a petrol distribution post was

---

1 Later information received from Arabs stated that three German Lieut. Colonels were killed.

attacked and that raiders made good their escape.[1] It is probable that they belonged to Lieut. Cook's party.

No. 1 detachment's return to the beach 18th November (1700 hrs.)

Sergt. Terry led his party back to the beach in the early hours of the 18th. He had been unable to find the last hiding place in the darkness, and therefore decided to abandon the reserve clothing and rations which had been left there. After a short sleep they marched throughout the day and reported to Col. Laycock at the original rendezvous at 1700 hrs. that evening. Up to that time our casualties had been Lieut. Col. Keyes killed, Capt. Campbell wounded, and Lieut. Cook with 6 O.Rs. missing.

During the remaining hours of daylight Col. Laycock returned to the beach to make a reconnaissance. The weather since the original landing had been bad, and he had abandoned all hope of getting more men ashore. Moreover the night of the 18th/19th had been fixed as the first on which evacuation might be possible and the "Talisman" was expected to arrive off the "alternative beach". On reaching the beach he was told by the folbot officer Lieut. Prior, that friendly Arabs had been there and said that the cave in which the boats were hidden was unsuitable. They had taken them to a new hiding place but had then gone off without indicating where it was!

The weather however appeared to be improving and there was less swell, and Col. Laycock writes "I considered that we had a fairish chance of evacuation provided the submarine could launch a folbot and get a line ashore. One difficulty was that we were now without boats and it would therefore be necessary to ask for a number of life jackets to be sent ashore."[2]

Party discovered by an unfriendly Arab.

While Col. Laycock was away on the beach an Arab came upon the rest of the party in the Wadi. He made off at a great pace keeping under cover as much as he could, and undoubtedly belonged to one of the unfriendly tribes who were to be found in that part of Cyrenaica. Sergt. Terry did not fire as he did not wish to draw attention to the party, and in Col. Laycock's opinion he acted wisely. But there is little doubt that the Arab gave away the presence of the raiders. When Col. Laycock heard of the incident he ordered the detachment down to the caves near the beach so as to save time in re-embarkation which he hoped would be possible, and to elude any party the enemy might send to search the Wadi. He left a Sergeant and two

---

1 See Appendix to Section VII.
2 See Appendix to this Section for a reference to this request in the Naval account of the Operation.

men to move the reserve rations and water down the wadi towards the beach and to keep a look out for Lieut. Cook's party.

The "Torbay" arrives 18th November.

Soon after dark he saw the "Torbay" through his glasses, fully surfaced and about half a mile out to sea. He signalled immediately for a folbot with a grass line and life jackets. A long wait ensued and Col. Laycock repeated his signals, but the unsuitability of his torch may have made them difficult to read.

Signals between beach and ship.

It had been previously decided that for communication between the beach and the ships no signals or acknowledgements would be sent by the latter; but as a considerable time had elapsed without the appearance of any of the enemy Col. Laycock decided to ask for an acknowledgement, and signalled, "If you cannot launch folbot please make three dashes". This signal was not answered, and he therefore left a look-out on the beach and went back to the troops, who were very much exhausted, and told them that evacuation that night was unlikely. He had not been long in the cave before the look-out came there and said that the "Torbay" was now sending Morse signals. He ran back to the beach and took a message saying "No more tonight. Too rough. Try again tomorrow. No more from me tonight" or words to that effect. This signal he acknowledged by sending "Thank you. Goodnight." As he was leaving the beach he was surprised to see the "Torbay" begin to signal again. She made "How many are you, what have you done with your Mae Wests?" He replied that there were twenty two of all ranks and that the boats and Mae Wests had been found. He also reported the success of the operations and gave an account of the casualties. The "Torbay" replied "If there is danger tomorrow and you would like to swim I am prepared to close point to West of beach, otherwise try again tomorrow night." The offer was tempting, but as the troops were almost certainly too exhausted to swim off from a rocky foreland against surf, wind and sea, Col. Laycock decided not to risk accepting it; and he replied "Will try again tomorrow night." The "Torbay" then made "Am sending in boat with food and water." and though in the end it was not towed the boat drifted in to the beach within twenty yards of him. He acknowledged the arrival of the boat and then returned to the cave; and after visiting his sentries went to sleep.[1]

Defensive position taken up 19th November.

An hour before first light Col. Laycock ordered positions to be taken up

1   See Appendix to this Section.

for all round defence, with two small detachments on the East and West flanks who had sentries posted where there was an extensive field of view. Three O.Rs. were left in the Wadi inland from the beach. All was quiet until midday when a few shots were heard from the Wadi, and from the most westerly sentry group. The only enemy so far observed were Arab Carabinieri which did not worry Col. Laycock unduly as he was confident of being able to keep them off until darkness allowed our forces to return to the beach for evacuation. The weather was improving and re-embarkation seemed to be feasible.

Enemy attack.

Shortly afterwards however Germans were seen approaching down the Western side of the Wadi, more Carabinieri appeared from the West and what appeared to be a considerable body of Italians showed themselves on the skyline about a mile away but took no part in the ensuing fight. The enemy opened fire but cover was good and no casualties were suffered, though it was feared that the three men left in the Wadi had been over-run.

Lieut. Prior wounded.

The enemy made good use of cover as they advanced and it was unlikely that they had many men hit. Lieut. Prior, with two other men, had been sent to make an outflanking movement to the West and was shot in the thigh while he gallantly tried to deceive the enemy by continuing to move on after the men with him had been pinned to the ground and their Tommy Gun had jammed. Eventually however he managed to crawl back to the main position near the caves.

The enemy had no automatic weapons but the volume of rifle fire was considerable and it became evident that the beach could not be held till dark against such a superior force, and that the only remaining line of retreat to the East would soon be cut. The Western detachment could not be seen and as a runner sent to find them was unsuccessful it was presumed that they had been killed, captured or driven Westward.

The detachment divides and retires East 1400 hrs. 19th November.

At about 1400 hrs. when the enemy was within 200 yards of the main position Col. Laycock decided that the only course open to his party was to hide in the Jebel-el-Akhdar hills, until they could rejoin our advancing main forces. He therefore split up his men into parties of not more than three and ordered them to make a dash to the East, picking up the Eastern detachment on the way.

Alternative courses.

They were then to gain cover in the Jebel and adopt whichever of the following three courses appeared most advantageous:-

(a) To return under cover of darkness to the "alternative beach" off which the "Talisman" would be lying until just before first light on the 21st November.
(b) To make their way to the Slonta Area where the Arabs were friendly, and there was a chance of being picked up by the L.R.D.G.
(c) To hide in the wadis North of Cyrene until news of our main forces was obtained.

Escape of Lieut. Col. Laycock and Sergt. Terry.

Lieut. Prior had to be left behind with a Medical Orderly as there was a risk of his bleeding to death, and they were told to surrender. Col. Laycock then made good his escape and when passing through the position held by his Eastern detachment was joined by Sergt. Terry. The country at first was open, but the enemy's marksmanship was not good.

After the party divided Col. Laycock and Sergt. Terry remained together. On the first and second nights (20th/21st and 21st/22nd) they tried to gain the alternative beach, but were frustrated by the enemy; and therefore continued their journey Eastwards. They had little difficulty in avoiding search parties in the excellent cover given by the Jebel, but their greatest fear was of being stalked by Arab Carabinieri who tracked cleverly, and got close to them on several occasions during the first few days. They were helped by Senussi tribesmen and "adopted the enjoyable policy of moving each night into the very wadis which the enemy were known to have searched during the day!" Their greatest problem was lack of food and though this never became desperate they were at times reduced to living for two days or more at a time on berries, which weakened them appreciably. At other times they were fed on goat and Arab bread; and as it rained almost continuously water was never a serious difficulty.

They rejoin the British Forces 25th December, 1941.

Nothing more was heard of the rest of the party, but Col. Laycock and Sergt. Terry eventually succeeded in rejoining the British Forces at Cyrene forty one days after landing, that is to say on Christmas Day 1941. In his report Col. Laycock pays a tribute to the co-operation of the Royal Navy; and added "their admirable seamanship on the night of our landing undoubtedly prevented the loss of many lives."

Capt. Haselden's return to Slonta.

It will be remembered that Capt. Haselden left for Slonta on the 15th. He rejoined his own party on the 17th, and learnt that the Trieste Division had moved out of the area to the South East. His only remaining objective was the telephone which was cut on the main road close to Sidi Mohammed-el-Homri (Bengasi 1/250,000 5536). On the 1st December he and his party

286

were picked up by 2/Lieut. Croucher with three H.Q. trucks of the L.R.D.G. and taken back to Siwa.

In his report he states that he was informed by Arabs that Lieut. Col. Keyes' party had succeeded in entering the German H.Q. at Beda Littoria and shot three German officers who, as the Arabs put it, "were all better than Majors". They said that four German O.Rs. had been killed and that we had lost one O.R. and one officer had been wounded but got away. Their information was that early next morning two men were captured and later five others: that one of the two had a map on which Chescem-el-Kelb was marked, which enabled the enemy to send a force to the beach. No one they said had been taken off by the Navy, and Capt. Haselden had to presume that the rest were killed or captured.

Appendix to Section IV

Summary of Naval Report on Attack on Rommel's H.Q.

Col Keyes' party, with certain officers and O.Rs. of the Folbot Section, embarked in H.M. Submarines "Torbay" (Lieut. Commander A.C.C. Miers, V.C., D.S.O.) and "Talisman"[1] at 1500 hrs. on the 10th November, and sailed an hour later. On the 11th and 12th the submarines were at sea, submerged during daylight. The intention was that the party should land at Chescem el Kelb, S.(0)2555, which is on the coast about 40 miles E.N.E. of Barce. On the 13th November the submarines arrived in the neighbourhood of El Aamer (S.(0)4771) and then submerged for a periscope reconnaissance of the beaches. Commander Miers states in his report that the weather was "ideal for carrying out the intended operations, but owing to overriding military considerations the opportunity was not accepted". On the morning of the 14th, when the "Torbay" was about 13 miles North-West of Ras Aasmer and closing the land, a Ghibli aircraft was seen flying down the coast. The submarine "went deep", which resulted in an "immediate" signal to her being partially missed. Nor did it reach the "Talisman". It was not repeated, which caused some anxiety as it might have been an order to abandon the operation. "It was ultimately received at 2145 hrs. and proved to be confirmation of the landing date – too late to be of value". (Commander Miers' report). Nevertheless, although the weather conditions appeared far from satisfactory, it was determined "in view of the importance of the operation, the eagerness of the military to be landed and the improbability of the weather improving in the next few days, to effect the disembarkation in the prevailing conditions". At 1904 hrs. the "Torbay" made her final approach to the beach and, at 1915 hrs., signals were observed on shore and identified as those agreed upon with Capt. Haselden, who had gone to Chescem el Kelb overland. The direction of the beach was pointed out and final instructions were given to Lieut. Inglis, A and S Highlanders, who was in charge of the "reconnaissance folbot". The folbot was launched successfully at 1956 hrs. and the ship manoeuvred to regain position near the beach. A larger sea than hitherto then swept over the casing and washed overboard the four after-most rubber boats with a soldier in one of them; and they were carried Eastwards by the swell and the prevailing "set"; but by 2115 hrs. all were picked up and the soldier, although a non-swimmer, was rescued. The submarine had to go West for two miles to get back to her previous position, and launching did not begin again until 2155 hrs. Meanwhile, Lieut. Inglis came back with the reconnaissance "folbot" to find out the

1   Lieut. Commdr. Wilmott, R.N.

cause of the delay. Finally the first seven "folbots" were got away "with only a few spills". Further delay then occurred owing to the Eastward drift, and launching was resumed at 2240 hrs. Commander Miers writes that the swell seemed by this time to have increased, and "perhaps the less well trained soldiers were being launched – at any rate boats capsized again and again, and in several cases the gear (boots, blanket, shirt and rations wrapped up in an anti-gas cape) was lost overboard". The reconnaissance "folbot", which had again returned, was also lost through "breaking her back" while being lifted out of the water. The submarine obtained "a slight lee" by closing the spit at the end of the bay and, by midnight, all the rubber boats but one had been successfully launched. The last boat capsized three times and was not got away until 0030 hrs. on the 15th. In describing the determined efforts of his own men, Commander Miers writes, "no less splendid was the spirit of the soldiers under strange and even frightening conditions. They were quite undaunted by the set backs experienced and remained quietly determined to get on with the job. The grit of the final pair deserves special mention. They had had several spills during the earlier stages of the operation and were obviously clumsy and unfitted for such difficult conditions, yet they never lost heart and when I sent a personal message finally, asking them to do their best not to delay and therefore jeopardise the operation, I received a reply that they would do their utmost. A few minutes later they were pulling for the shore in splendid style, drenched, but in good spirits."

At 0035 hrs. "operation completed" was signalled to the "Talisman", which had been in visual signal touch throughout, and she was ordered to report the results of her own landing operation. The "Torbay" then put to sea to send a message from Capt. Haselden to Eighth Army and to report the landing (to Rosyth W/T Station). The "Talisman" began to close the beach at 0137 hrs. on the 15th in fairly good conditions; but at 0145 hrs. when she touched bottom, the ground swell increased without warning and the first wave went over the casing aft of the fore hatch, taking away seven boats out of the eight placed there and eleven men. In order to reduce the amount of water sweeping over the casing, the "Talisman's" Commander was obliged to go astern into deeper water and to send a "folbot" to assist the men in the sea; unluckily the "folbot" was wrecked while being launched. He then told Lieut. D. Sutherland (S.A.S.) to "throw in the remaining boats clear of the submarine and get his men to jump in after them. The men very pluckily carried out this order, but only one boat got away the right way up with the men on board ... the moon was well up (about 0400 hrs.) when the last of these men and boats were retrieved from the water." The submarine was then obliged to go out to sea in order to charge. She remained in the vicinity of Chescem el Kelb, but the weather prevented any further attempt at landing that night. At 0935 hrs. next day (Sunday, 16th November) she received orders from Commander Miers to return to Alexandria.

The "Torbay" returned to Chescem el Kelb during the morning of the 15th, and at midday was in signal communication with the Talisman. It was hoped that the latter would be able to continue disembarkation but the weather deteriorated, and at about 1800 hrs. Commander Miers signalled the "Captain (S)" and advised cancellation of further landings. This was agreed to next morning and the "Talisman" was ordered back to Alexandria. The "Torbay" surfaced at 1821 hrs. and "remained hove to in a North-Easterly gale". On the 17th November, a weather report was received "which unfortunately did not even approximate to the prevailing weather conditions, which were most unfavourable"; and the submarine remained where she was, either on the surface or below it.

On the 18th the weather was still bad, with a heavy swell running from the North; but the forecast received in the afternoon promised better conditions on the following day. An aircraft was sighted in the morning and the "Torbay" had to dive. Between 1900 hrs and 2230 hrs. signals, which were identified, were received from the beach asking for a boat to be sent with grass and "Mae Wests". This disturbed Commander Miers as the men had landed with two each, which were to have been hidden at the dump with the rubber boats. Moreover, there was no indication of the number of men on the beach for whom lifebelts were required. He therefore sent in Lieut. Inglis and Corporal Severn in a rubber boat to clear up the situation on shore, and take lifebelts, food and water. They were also to inform those on shore that the weather was unsuitable for boat work but was improving, and that in order not to delay re-embarkation, if a large proportion of the force was present, the "Torbay" would close at dawn to within 100 yards of the spit of sand at the Western end of the beach, so that they could swim out to her. Another signal was then received saying that there were none of the enemy anywhere near the shore. The rubber boat was launched at 2250 hrs. but there was so much swell that the crew could not leave the submarine, and when the boat broke adrift Commander Miers decided to let her go ashore without a crew, as the swell was bound to land her on the beach, and everything in her was well secured. She was loaded with 23 Mae Wests, 12 water bottles and a quantity of food. A signal was made by lamp explaining what had been done and asking how many men there were, what had happened, and where the Mae Wests and boats originally landed were. The answer was[1] "Goodness only knows. Some killed in camp and missing from H.Q."

Concluding that the enemy could not be very far away, Commander Miers again signalled that he would close the beach and enable them to swim out either that night or the next. To this the answer came "Try tomorrow night". The "Torbay" again stood out to sea and resumed charging, but remained in sight of the beach. On the next day, 19th November, a reconnaissance of the beaches was made without sighting anything. The weather was good enough to make boat work possible, and the remaining five rubber boats were put into repair. At 1820 hrs. the submarine surfaced and closed the beach; but no signals were seen, though a light was observed in the fort on the shore. Lieut. Langton (Irish Guards) was then sent ashore in a "folbot" to establish contact. After an anxious hour and a half he returned and the "folbot" was safely hauled on board; just in time to prevent her sinking, as she had capsized in the surf near the shore and been holed. Lieut. Langton, who had been ashore, had seen a blue light (the agreed colour) inland, and had flashed "T's" with his torch, but had not been able to make contact with anyone. The night was spent patrolling up and down the beach but no signals were seen. Next morning it was seen that all the beaches were in the enemy's hands and they were evidently carrying out a search, in which they were being helped by aircraft. Their activities ceased during the afternoon and there was just hope that it might have been a routine patrol.

The weather became calm and, in Commander Miers' words, "the situation, while seeming hopeless, was also unpleasant as the weather … was ideal for E-boat operations. Nothing, however, was sighted. On the 21st November, guns were seen apparently being dragged into position on the hillocks commanding Chescem el Kelb. They would have been an excellent target but there were hostile aircraft about.

1 The message was corrupt and was read as [stated here.]

At midday the "Torbay" moved East to investigate a position East of El Aamer, and at 1630 hrs, she surfaced and destroyed a Ghibli aircraft on what appeared to be a landing ground.

She then continued Eastward and arrived at Alexandria on the 24th November.

MEF   Section IV

LITANI RIVER AREA (Syria) 1 : 200,000
(GSGS 4195—Beyrouth NI-36-XII)

Scale 1 : 200,000

Contours at 50 m. interval

The graticule on this sheet is in terms of Grades. Degree values are marked on the outside of the margin.

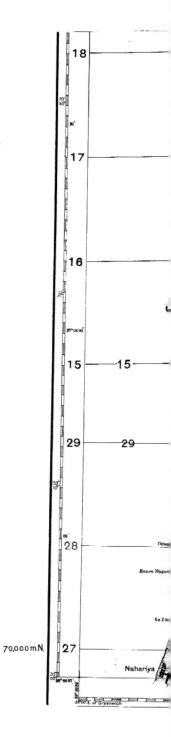

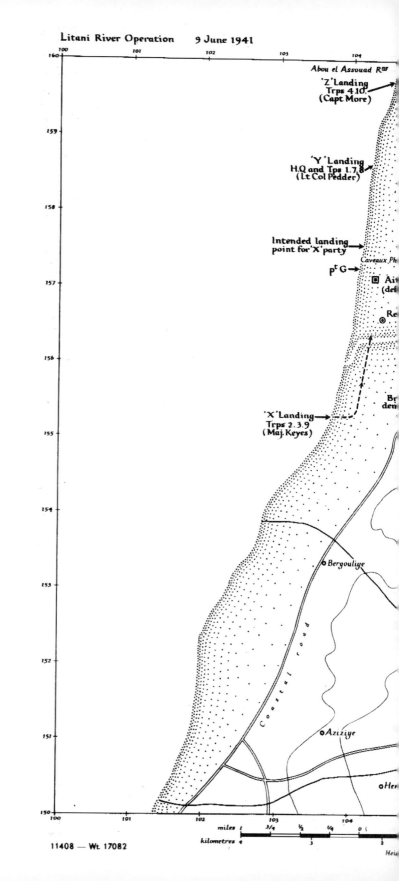

Litani River Operation   9 June 1941

Abou el Assouad R^{as}

'Z' Landing
Trps 4.10.
(Capt More)

'Y' Landing
H.Q and Trps 1.7.8.
(Lt Col Pedder)

Intended landing
point for 'X' party

Caveaux Ph

P^t G→

Aï
(def

Re

Br
deu

'X' Landing→
Trps 2.3.9.
(Maj. Keyes)

Bergoulije

Coastal road

Aziziye

Her

11408 — Wt. 17082

miles 1   3/4   1/2   1/4   0

kilometres

Hei

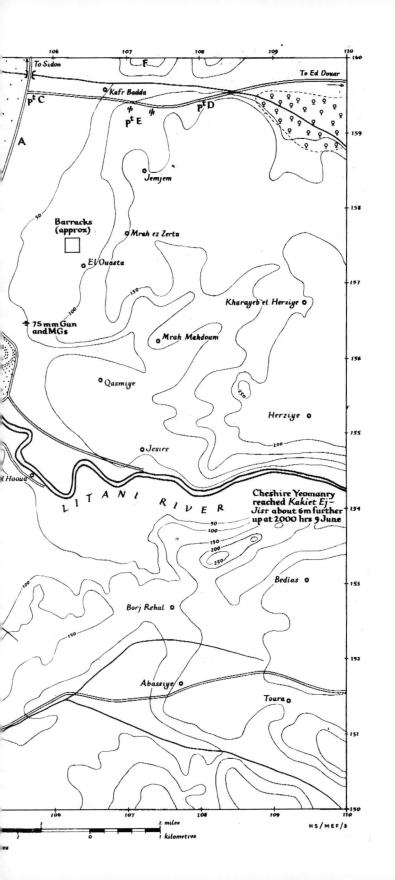

To Sidon

F

To Ed Douar

Kafr Badda

Pt C

Pt D

Pt E

A

Jemjem

Barracks
(approx)

Mrah ez Zerta

El Ouasta

Kharayeb el Herziye

75 mm Gun
and MGs

Mrah Mahdoum

Qasmiye

Herziye

Jesire

Hooua

LITANI RIVER

Cheshire Yeomanry
reached Kakiet Ej-
Jisr about 6 m further
up at 2000 hrs 9 June

Bedias

Borj Rehal

Abassiye

Toura

HS/MEF/3

2 miles

1 kilometres

Section V

52 Middle East Commando
(Afterwoards part of "D" Battalion "Layforce").

Formation.

This Commando was formed in 1940 from troops in the Middle East. It consisted of a H.Q. and three Troops, each of four sections, with an establishment of 19 officers (including the M.O.) and 361 O.R., and it was commanded by Lieut. Col. G.A.D. Young, R.E. At the end of December 1940 it was in Camp at Tuklein near Gallabat on the Sudan-Abyssinia border, about 100 miles North-West of Lake Tana, and was attached to the 9th Indian Infantry Brigade (Brigadier Mayne).

During the first weeks of January 1941 it was employed in patrolling round the enemy's Northern flank, but was only once in contact with the enemy. On the 8th an attempt was made to carry out a long distance raid on the enemy's L. of C. between Khor Kumar and Khor Abd-er Razzag, but the raid was a failure largely owing to transport difficulties.

Raid on Italian L. of C. 17th January 1941.

On the 17th January the Italians retired from their forward zone about Kassala on Agordat and Barentu, and the British forces followed them into Eritrea on the 19th. At the same time, and in co-operation with the 9th Indian Inf. Bde., the Commando was again ordered to raid the enemy's L. of C. about Khor Kumar, on the Gondar Road. It started after dark on the 17th, and the attack on the road was to be made on the 19th; but on the 18th the Abyssinian guide lost his way and the attack was postponed to the 20th January. At 1800 hrs. on that day the River Atbara was crossed and, after some opposition, the Gondar-Metemmeh road was reached at 2100 hrs. No hostile transport was found and the withdrawal began at 2200 hrs. The Atbara was re-crossed and the Commando got back to its original rendezvous at Wad Ghumsa at 0900 hrs. on the 21st January. Casualties were 2 killed, 1 wounded and missing and 3 wounded.

The Commando got back to Tuklein on the 22nd. In a report written after the raid, Lieut. Col. Young pointed out the difficulty of making a long distance raid through the bush with a long column, and suggested that a detachment of at most one company would do the work better. He also pointed out that the carriage of wounded men caused difficulty and delay, especially to small patrols. It appears too that at this time a good many men in the unit were not suitable for Commando work and had to be returned to their units.

The enemy withdraws 31st January 1941.

During the remainder of the month the Commando was employed in patrolling and an abortive raid was made by one company on the 26th January, which resulted in several men being wounded. It had been expected that the enemy would withdraw in Abyssinia as they had done in Eritrea and, on the 31st January, a patrol from the Commando discovered that they had evacuated two neighbouring hills (Djebel Dufeir and Djebel Negus). Orders were issued by Bde. H.Q. for following them up on the 1st February.

The Commando took part in the operations of that day but was not opposed. In the evening it was withdrawn to Camp on the R. Atbara, where it remained until the 7th. It then left for Gedaref (where the 51st Commando was encamped) arriving after a three day march on the 10th February. At 1600 hrs. on the afternoon of the 24th February, the Commando left Gedaref by train and arrived at Kassala at 0100 hrs. on the 25th February. There they remained until the 4th March, and a certain amount of training in Mountain Warfare was given.

On the 3rd March a telegram arrived ordering the Commando to Egypt. It moved on the 4th and, travelling by rail and river, arrived at Abbassia on the 9th and went into Camp at Taheg. On the 23rd March it was moved to Geneifa on the Suez Canal. No. 50 M.E. Commando was already there and, on the 28th March, the two M.E. Commandos were amalgamated to form "D" Battalion "Layforce". "Layforce", with four battalions, was more or less the equivalent of a brigade. It was commanded by Col. R.E. Laycock, R.H.G. and formed part of the 6th Div. under Major General J.F. Evetts, C.B. Lieut. Col. G.A.D. Young, formerly commanding No. 52 Commando, was given Command of the new battalion, with Capt. W.N. Seymour, Scots Guards, as Adjutant. Major S.M. Rose, Royal Fusiliers was 2nd in Command. As the original Commando organization of Ten Troops (of roughly 50 men each) was considered to be unsatisfactory from the point of view of Command in the field and of administration, the Battalion was re-organized as a Headquarters and five companies. The Company Commanders were as follows:-

"A" Coy Capt. K.C. Hermon, Durham L.I.
"B" Coy Capt. C. Parish, Royal Sussex Regt.

"C" Coy Capt. W.J. Burton, York and Lancs. Regt.
"D" Coy Capt. R. Boyle, The Black Watch.
"E" Coy Capt. L.N.R. Wilson, Royal Sussex Regt.

During April the Battalion moved to Sidi Bishr in the outskirts of Alexandria and continued its training. On the 23rd May, at 0240 hrs., orders were received that it was to be ready to move at four hours' notice as from 0400 hrs. It would move "as it stood", that is to say with ammunition up to G 1098 scale, but without blankets or kitbags. At 1200 hrs. orders were received to entrain at 1400 hrs. but the start was postponed. Eventually the move was made by M.T. on the 24th, and the Battalion embarked at Alexandria for Crete, together with Brigade H.Q. and 150 men of "A" Battalion "Layforce", in four destroyers, H.M.S. "Isis", "Decoy", "Hero" and "Nizam". Delay was caused by the shortage of M.T. and, although the destroyers should have weighed anchor at 0900 hrs., the first party of the Battalion did not arrive at the quay until 0915 hrs. Eventually the last destroyer left the quayside at 1055 hrs. 24th May, the 2nd in Command and R.S.M. joining it from a naval pinnace when it was already on the move.

The weather was very bad indeed, some ammunition was lost overboard, some of the boats were washed away and men had narrow escapes. All were very seasick. Early on the 25th it was realized that it was too late to land under cover of darkness, and there was not enough fuel to go out to sea again and make a "run in" that evening. The destroyers therefore went about and returned to Alexandria, which they reached at 1915 hrs. Troops in the "Isis" and "Decoy" were re-embarked in the H.M. Mine-laying Destroyer "Abdiel".

Orders were now received for the Battalion to disembark at Suda. This would entail a march over difficult country after landing and the Adjutant (Capt. Seymour), who had an injured leg, and 10 other ranks who were not fit enough for a long march, had to be left at Alexandria. The convoy put to sea again at 0530 hrs. 26th May, and for the few days the Battalion was in Crete no diary is available. Such information as there is was recorded by Capt. Seymour and obtained by him from the survivors of the Battalion. The first ship arrived at Suda at 2300 hrs. on the 26th, and the rest followed shortly after. Information, obtained on arrival, was that Crete was to be evacuated and all heavy equipment, such as Bren gun boxes and cooks' gear, was left on board. Orders were that D. Battalion was to act as rear guard during the evacuation.

On the 26th May the troops in Crete were holding a North and South line West of Canea, which extended from the coast about 2 miles West of the town to an area just West of Perivolia, and about 23 miles S.S.W. of Canea. The total extent of the front was some 4200 yards, or about

$2^1/2$ miles. During the night of the 26th/27th this position was evacuated and a line was taken up to cover Suda, about 4 to 5 miles further East.

At 0200 hrs. on the 27th "D" Battalion moved in a South-Easterly direction towards Stilos, which is about 28 miles South-East of Canea on the main road to Rethimnon (Retimo). It halted at 0515 hrs. and took up a defensive position covering the road. The Battalion was bombed and machine gunned from 0800 hrs. to 2030 hrs., but cover was good and there were no casualties.

At 2100 hrs. the Battalion again moved South-East for about 10 miles and halted at 0230 hrs. on the 28th May. It then took up a defensive position, in relief of "A" Battalion, "Layforce" which withdrew through it.

At 1335 hrs. the enemy attacked under cover of mortar fire and at one time Battalion H.Q. was nearly surrounded, but the enemy was eventually repelled with considerable losses.

At 2115 the Battalion withdrew Southwards, leaving road blocks behind it, and after a long march reached Askipho at 1500 hrs. on the 29th May. This place is 12 miles North of Sphakia, on the South coast of the island.

During the night 27th/28th and during the 28th, the main body of the New Zealand division withdrew South and passed through "A" and "D" Bns. of "Layforce", rested at Askipho during the morning and afternoon of the 29th and then resumed its march towards the sea.

"D" Battalion rested at Askipho until 1630 hrs. on the 29th, and was subjected to M.G. fire from the air. At nightfall it took up another defensive position in and near a "ravine leading to the beaches" (presumably 3 or 4 miles North of Sphakia). The Battalion remained in position throughout 30th May without being attacked, except, to a limited extent, from the air.

On the 31st May the Battalion withdrew to the hills surrounding Sphakia and occupied a final rearguard position to cover the embarkation. Late in the evening the Brigade Major sent a runner to the Battalion Commander ordering the Battalion to withdraw for embarkation. It seems that the message was delivered, and the last boats waited until 0245 hrs. on the 1st June. It is probable that the Battalion as a whole was unable to force its way through the crowd of refugees which thronged the entrances to the beach, for, with the exception of a few men already wounded or evacuated, only 2 officers and 25 men got back to Egypt.

KASSALA AREA 1 : 2M
(GSGS 2871—Sudan)

20 10 0   20   40   60   80   100
Miles

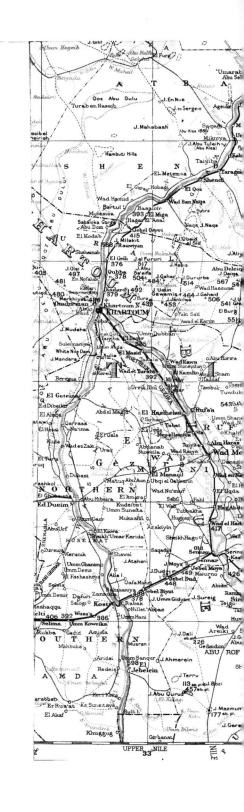

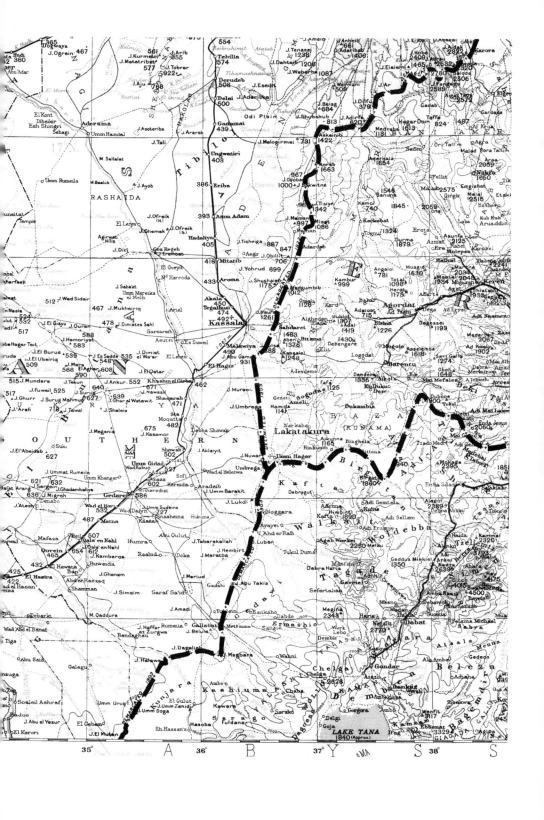

Section VI

Reorganization of Commandos 1941.

Reorganization.

When Col. Laycock returned to Egypt on the 1st June 1941, after the evacuation of Crete, he was told that it had been decided to disband the S.S. Bde., i.e. "Layforce", on the ground that it could not be kept up to establishment. The strength of "Layforce" had in fact been so greatly reduced by the casualties suffered in Crete and elsewhere, which could not be immediately replaced except from regular units in the Middle East Command, that there was good reason for the decision.

Col. Laycock went to England and urged the inadvisability of this step. In July 1940, he was sent back to Egypt with the rank of Lieut. Col. to reform the Commandos on a smaller basis. In October 1941 G.H.Q. Middle East suggested that the Special Service troops in the M.E. should be formed into a unit consisting of a British Squadron, two mixed Palestinian Squadrons of Arabs and Jews and a Parachute Battalion. It was to include "L" Detachment S.A.S., and the Special Boat Section" which are referred to below, and were already in existence. This scheme was not in the end adopted but Col. Laycock, who did not agree with it, could take no further part in the matter as he was recalled to England to take command of the Special Service Brigade at home.

"L" Detachment S.A.S.

When it was decided that the remains of "Layforce" must be reconstituted, Capt. D. Stirling, Scots Guards, who had been an officer in No. 8 Commando, was given permission, in July 1941, to raise and train a "parachute detachment" which would be able to raid the enemy's L. of C. and was to be known as "L" Detachment S.A.S. (Special Air Service). In this enterprise he was greatly assisted by Lieut. J. Lewis, Welsh Guards, who was killed some months later; and the men were largely recruited from Scots Guardsmen formerly in No. 8 Commando ("B" Battalion, "Layforce").

The parachute detachment (originally known as "L" Detachment S.A.S.

and eventually expanded into the 1st S.A.S. Regt.) was formed on the 28th August 1941. The other officers were Lieut. E.C. McGonigal, Royal Ulster Rifles (later killed in action), Lieut. C.J.L. Bonnington, Gen. List (later a P.O.W.), 2nd Lieut. W. Fraser, M.C., Gordon Highlanders, C.S.M. Yates (killed in action), Sergt. (afterwards Lieut.) P. Riley, D.C.M., Lieut. E.C. Parton (Adjt. and Q.M.) and Lieut. (later Lieut. Col.) R.B. Mayne (Royal Ulster Rifles).

A good deal of preliminary training was carried out and casualties occurred, two of which were fatal, but equipment is described as primitive and no qualified instructors were available. Only one parachute operation, which is described later, was carried out (on the night 16th/17th August 1942). For various reasons it was not a success and, of a total of 53 Officers and men who took part in it, 32 were killed or taken prisoner, including Lieuts. McGonigal and Bonnington (See Section VII).

"L" Detachment's training included also the following subjects - navigation, demolitions, languages, specialist and foreign weapons, special boat practice, motor transport and wireless operating. Exercises and schemes took place in the desert, some of which included marches of 100 miles with a full load over difficult country, where the only water available was carried by the men themselves.

In addition to operations in North Africa, which continued until the Eighth Army joined the First Army in Tunisia, raids were carried out on islands in the Mediterranean, held by the enemy, in conjunction with major operations.[1] The enemy's aircraft were the usual target but shipping, stores of petrol, arms and bombs, vehicle parks and water points were also successfully attacked. Skilful planning ensured surprise and a great deal of hostile equipment was destroyed, but casualties were relatively light. In the earlier stages of its existence the operations of "L" Detachment were usually carried out on foot, transport and navigation to the vicinity of the target being provided by the Long Range Desert Group. In the summer of 1942, the detachment was supplied with heavily armed and specially modified Jeeps, which enabled long distance raids to be carried out; and wireless communication was also provided, which made it possible to relay valuable information. The enemy was obliged to use fighters and bombers to counteract the detachment's activities, but though parties were often located and attacked, the number of casualties was not great. Raiding parties remained in the desert for periods as long as two months. It was calculated that during the period of the North African Campaign, in which "L" Detachment and the 1st S.A.S. Regiment played a part, the destruction of 350 hostile aircraft was confirmed. Nor was the damage inflicted confined to the enemy's aircraft, for many dumps and vehicles were blown up, and

1 These are described in the S.B.S. Narrative. (See Note I).

the enemy's rail transport was successfully attacked on several occasions. Originally officers and men were drawn from the British Army, but they were soon reinforced by Free French personnel and, towards the end of the campaign, by Greeks, who formed the "Sacred Squadron".

The "Special Boat Section"[1] was organised by Major R.J. Courtney, M.C., K.R.R.C., in July 1940, with the support of Admiral Sir Roger Keyes. Major Courtney demonstrated the possibilities of a folding boat ("folbot") or collapsible canoe for landing agents on the enemy's coasts, and came to the conclusion that the submarine was the most suitable craft from which to launch them. In February 1941 he and the men he had trained were sent to the Middle East, where they became part of the "Commando" organisation, but were attached to the Special Submarine Flotilla.

Between March and December 1941 the S.B.S. was variously employed, acting independently or in co-operation with the Commandos, as for instance with "A" Battalion at Bardia in April. In September 1942 it became part of the 1st S.A.S. Regiment.[2]

A reconnaissance of Rhodes 1941.

The first operation, carried out by Major Courtney and Lieut. Commander N. Wilmott, R.N., was a three day reconnaissance of Rhodes, which included the beach in front of the hotel just outside the gates of the town of Rhodes, at the North end of the island. Sketches were made, wire was tested and it was established that the garrison kept a very indifferent look out. Indeed, the only "opposition" met was from a dog, which walked up and down one side of the wire in front of the hotel while Major Courtney was walking along the other. As it confined itself to growling and did not bark, the alarm was not given!

Raid on Benghazi harbour May 1941.

In May 1941, Sergt. Allen and Marine Miles entered the harbour at Benghazi in a "folbot" and sank a ship by means of "limpets". Unfortunately their boat sank after striking a rock on the way out and they were taken prisoner. Later in the Summer Lance Cpl. Bremmer (London Scottish) of the S.B.S. landed in Crete from a submarine, got in touch with agents on shore and enabled 200 Australians, who had been left on the island, to escape in three submarines which they boarded by means of a "grass line". During the same period, Capt. Wilson, D.S.O., R.A. and Lieut. Scolfield

---

1   The abbreviation "S.B.S." originally meant "Special Boat Section". It was subsequently used to mean "Special Boat Squadron", though the "Special Boat Sections" continued to exist. The "Special Boat Squadron" in the Middle East was formed in January 1943 by Capt. Lord Jellicoe, for operations in the Eastern Mediterranean.

2   See Section VIII; and for its seaborne operations, Note I.

wrecked five trains and blew up three bridges on the mainland of Italy; and many reconnaissances and trips to land intelligence agents were also made.

At the end of 1941 Major Courtney had to return to England leaving 15 officers and 45 "Folbotiers", as they were called, at Malta.

Note on Commandos for P.M. September 1941.

On the 11th September 1941 the D.D.O. M.E. Forces, wrote for the C-in-C., a note on Commandos which was to be sent to the Prime Minister by the hand of Col. Laycock. The opinions expressed in it were briefly as follows:-

1. In the Spring of 1941, there were in the Middle East three Special Service Battalions (i.e. "A", "B" and "C" Bns. "Layforce", formerly Nos. 7, 8 and 11 Commandos), each of about 600 men, and three Middle East Commandos (50, 51 and 52), each of about 150 men.
2. Many seaborne raids had had to be cancelled or postponed for naval reasons, and only three had been carried out.[1]
3. Crete caused many casualties. As a result there remained in the M.E. the equivalent of about one S.S. Battalion, and the remnants of one M.E. Commando (No. 51).
4. There had been at first too many Commandos and not enough work for them. The men had found themselves inactive, had become disheartened and had applied to return to their units.
5. There were two sorts of sea-borne operations:-
    (a) Operations on a large scale carried out by Armoured and Infantry Units or formations, in which special Service troops could be usefully employed as air-borne troops, or could be landed from the sea to attack the enemy's flanks.
    (b) Small sea-borne raids along the coast of Africa and in the Aegean (eventually perhaps from Turkey).
6. Owing to the lack of suitable shipping and the nature of the coast, which made landing operations very difficult, raids would have to be limited to parties of forty or fifty men. A Commando of 250 men would therefore be strong enough.
7. British regular units, the only source of reinforcements, were very short of men and luxuries could not be afforded.

Conferences on future organization, October 1941.

Colonel Laycock was, however, still in Egypt when the future of Special Service Troops in the Middle East Forces was discussed at a conference held by the D.D.S.D. at G.H.Q. on the 11th October 1941. It was

---

1 Described in Sections II, III, IV and V.

suggested that, subject to the C-in-C's approval, "L" Detachment S.A.S., the remnants of "Layforce", No. 51 Commando and the Special Boat Section should be formed into one Middle East Commando under one Headquarters. This unit was to be entirely separate from the Depot G (R) and the "Desert Troops" (L.R.D.G.).

The Commando was to have six troops of which No. 1 would be the Depot Troop, No. 2 was to be formed from "L" Detachment S.A.S., No. 3 was to be British, Nos. 4 and 5 Palestinian and No. 6 the Special Boat Section. As No. 51 M.E. Commando was still in the Sudan and its men would require leave on their return to Egypt, the scheme could at the moment not be put into full effect. Another meeting was held on the 25th October, during which it transpired that G (Ops) and G (R) held diametrically opposite views as to the organization to which the Special Boat Section should belong. The decision was postponed till the return of the D.D.O., who was away, and the scheme was in the end abandoned.

On the 30th October, the C.G.S. (Lieut. General A. Smith) answered a letter the C.-in-C. had received from Col. Laycock, which condemned the recommendations of the recent conferences and made other suggestions, and wrote, "the real difficulty about S.S. Troops is that we simply have not got the men, and we are now thousands of men short of requirements in ordinary infantry battalions in the Middle East! I have told the C.-in-C. that I really cannot recommend calling for volunteers for a S.S. Unit in view of this shortage. But that does NOT mean that when we get reinforcements we shall not be able to expand the S.S. organization" He went on to tell Col. Laycock that the C.-in-C. would like to discuss the matter with him.

It was not until the 29th December that the decisions described below were made with the authority of the C.-in-C. (Sir A. Wavell).

1. The following were to be combined in one unit under command of Lieut. Col. J.M. Graham (Scots Greys):-
   (a) G (R) Depot at Geneifa
   (b) The remains of "Layforce" and No. 51 M.E. Commando, less "L" Detachment S.A.S.
   (c) The Folbot Section (S.B.S.)
2. The unit was to be controlled by the Ministry of Economic Warfare Mission to the Middle East, to whom G.H.Q. would give every assistance.
3. The Mission was to be responsible for its training, in which Army Training Establishments were to assist.
4. The Mission was also to be responsible for the unit's operations except when they took place
   in an Army area.

By January 1942, the unit was in process of formation at Geneifa and was called the "Middle East Commando".

It was to operate under the orders of G (R) and was to consist of four British Squadrons, and the Special Boat Section, but might be increased by one or more Indian, Dominion or Allied Squadrons. A signal section was to be attached to it and its basic weapons were to be the rifle, the Thompson gun and the grenade. It was also hoped to train a proportion of its men as parachutists. In May 1942 it was proposed that its name should be changed to "1st S.S. Regiment" (not to be confused with 1st S.A.S. Regiment, which was the final development of "L" Detachment S.A.S.) and this change appears to have taken effect. In the end there were only three British Squadrons "A", "B" and "C". "D" Squadron included Spaniards, Palestinian Egyptian and Syrian Arabs, and seven different sorts of Jews. Part of the unit was quartered in Syria and its few active operations in North Africa were in co-operation with the L.R.D.G.

"L" Detachment, which had already been formed from men who had been in the S.S. Brigade, was not to form part of Lieut. Col. Graham's "Middle East Commando" as originally suggested. It developed on separate lines, under the direct control of G.H.Q., Middle East, and its history is dealt with in the next Section.

A detachment of the Middle East Commando or 1st S.S. Regiment as it had then become, was with Lieut. Col. Haselden's Force which made the landward attack on Tobruk during the night of the 13th/14th September 1942. The detachment was Commanded by Major R.L. Campbell (Gordon Highlanders), and other officers who took part were Lieuts. M.M. Roberts (Northumberland Fusiliers) T.C.D. Russell (Scots Guards) H.D. Sillito (A and S.H.) G.J.P. Taylor (Wiltshire Regiment) and W.N. Macdonald (Gen. List). The operation is described in Section VII.

The Regiment was disbanded in October 1942 and a good many of its officers and men were transferred to "L Detachment" S.A.S. which was being expanded to form the 1st S.A.S. Regiment (See Section VIII).

Section VII

"L" Detachment 1941–1942.

Parachute operations at Gazala and Tmimi, November 1941.

The Eighth Army's offensive under Lieut. General Sir Alan Cunningham was timed to start on the 18th November 1941. In anticipation of this attack "L" Detachment S.A.S. was ordered to raid the enemy's aerodromes at Gazala and Tmimi, of which there were two at each place. The attacks were to take place during the night of the 17th/18th November at an hour to be fixed by Maj. Stirling, with due regard to the fact that the aerodromes in question were to be raided by the R.A.F. at dusk on the 17th and again after the moon rose during the night of the 17th/18th. The raiders were to be airborne and dropped by parachute.

L.R.D.G. co-operation.

After completing their task they were to be picked up in lorries by the Long Range Desert Group; and two rallying points were fixed by Major Stirling on consultation with Capt. R. Easonsmith (N.Z.E.F.) commanding R.1 patrol of the L.R.D.G. No. 1 was at Garet Meriem (S.U. 6148), a low hill near the road junction on the Trigh Capuzzo known as the Rotondo Segnali, and was the same distance, 34 miles, from both Gazala and Tmimi. It was intended that the returning raiders should arrive there between 0600 hrs. and 0700 hrs. (G.M.T.) on the 20th November; the L.R.D.G. lorries, for security reasons, could not wait longer. The second rallying point was to be at (S)U. 3418 at the Northern end of Wadi el Mra, and about thirty miles South-West of the first; and Lieut. Fraser of "L" Detachment was sent there with some trucks to pick up stragglers.

About 55 officers and men took part in the raid and were carried in five planes.

S.S.M. Tait's account.

On the morning of the 16th November the party moved to the forward aerodrome of Bagush, rested for the remainder of the day, and took off at

1930 hrs. The information from which some of the details in this narrative have been compiled is taken from accounts of their experiences written by No. 2888693 Squadron Sergt. Maj. R. Tait, who travelled in the same plane as Major Stirling, C.S.M. Yates, Sergt. Cheyne and six other ranks, and by R.S.M. Riley, who was in another plane with Lieut. J. Lewis and eleven O.Rs. The target of both these parties was Gazala but it is reasonable to suppose that the experiences of men in the other planes, whose destination was Tmimi, were not materially different. S.S.M. Tait states that the plane was due to arrive over the dropping area, Bir Temrad about 20 miles South-West of Gazala, at 2230 hrs. but it was much delayed by wind and by A.A. fire, which was heavy. After flying in from the sea over Gazala, which was lit up by flares from our covering aircraft, the raiders were finally dropped at 2130 hrs. and, owing to the high wind, all made very bad landings which resulted in various minor injuries. They had considerable difficulty in assembling, and Sergt. Cheyne was not seen again. Finally they set off at about 0100 hrs. on the 17th to get in contact with the rest of the party at the rendezvous, which was on a hill overlooking Gazala. Major Stirling's intention was to wait there throughout the day and attack the landing grounds at 0300 hrs. on the 18th. Owing, however, to the delay in dropping and assembling, and also to the fact that the landing had been made slightly out of position, the party was not able to reach the rendezvous before daylight and had to lie up for the rest of the day in open country. Very little enemy activity was seen. A good many of the men were the worse for their descent from the air and could march only with difficulty. The containers dropped with supplies had not all been recovered, and Major Stirling decided to try and carry out the task himself with the help of S.S.M. Tait, and to send the rest of the party back to the first rallying point under C.S.M. Yates. Maj. Stirling and his companion reached the high ground behind the escarpment at 2000 hrs., when a violent thunderstorm broke accompanied by rain and hail. They were unable to see more than a few yards and within fifteen minutes the whole area was under water. They tried to get down to the coastal strip where the landing grounds were but the torrents prevented them, and at 0100 hrs. Maj. Stirling decided to abandon the enterprise and make his way to the rallying point near the Rotondo Segnali. He and Tait reached it in the early hours of the 20th November but found that C.S.M. Yates and his party had not arrived; later it became known that they had been captured.

R.S.M. Riley's account.

The experiences of Lieut. Lewis's party, whose destination was also Gazala, were described in a report made by R.S.M. Riley. They too were met by A.A. fire when flying over Gazala, and when they were dropped the high wind dragged them along after they had reached the ground.

There were some minor injuries but the party assembled quickly. The procedure was as follows:- Before leaving the plane every man was told the bearing on which it would be flying when he was dropped. Lieut. Lewis was dropped first and each successive man, after reaching the ground, buried his parachute and remained where he was. Lieut. Lewis, having buried his own parachute, moved along the bearing given and picked up his men in turn. The "Flight Sergeant", who was dropped last, deflated the supply parachutes and got the small arms ready for action.

Having buried their supplies the party moved on and marched all night without seeing any of the enemy or men dropped from other planes. At 0930 hrs. on the 17th the party lay up and R.S.M. Riley was sent forward to reconnoitre, as it appeared that the party had been dropped some distance South of the intended landing area. At about 1400 hrs. they moved North for eight miles and reached a track which they believed was about ten miles from Gazala. They too were then stopped by the thunderstorm and most of their explosives and detonators were rendered useless. They therefore made their way back to the first rallying point, and reached it a little before Major Stirling and S.S.M. Tait.

At daylight R.1 patrol of the L.R.D.G., which was to take them back to Jarabub, withdrew to cover leaving a smoking fire on the hill, on which two hurricane lamps had been hung during darkness. The smoke guided Lieut. Mayne and eight men, who came in during the morning, but no other men returned.[1]

In the late afternoon of the 20th November, after waiting eight hours longer than had been intended, R.1 patrol took the S.A.S. parties to the second rallying point. During the 21st November, trucks were sent over an eight mile front to look for stragglers, but none were seen. The return march to Siwa was delayed by the presence of hostile aircraft and Major Stirling's party did not reach its destination, Jarabub, until midday on the 25th November.

No further parachute operations were attempted but "L" Detachment continued to operate on the flank of the main Army and behind the enemy's communications. It was, however, at this stage dependent on the Long Range Desert Group for transport to its objectives and for navigation.

Raid on Jedabya L.G. 21st December 1941.

No. 1 Section of "L" Detachment S.A.S., commanded by Lieut. W. Fraser, Gordon Highlanders, left Jalo on the 19th December 1941, with the object of raiding the landing ground at Jedabya. It was navigated by S.1 patrol of the L.R.D.G. as far as Ain Naga in the Wadi el Faregh, about forty miles

---

1 See Appendix to this Section for an Italian report on these operations.

South of Jedabya, and arrived there on the 20th. The Section then joined S.2 patrol of the L.R.D.G. (Lieut. Olivey, N.Z.E.F.). The journey was continued on the same day and at 0100 hrs. on the 21st the party reached a point about sixteen miles[1] from Jedabya, on the road to El Haseiat. Lieut. Fraser and his Section then went on alone on a compass bearing, their intention being to reach a point of observation about three miles from the aerodrome. This was found to be impossible owing to the amount of hostile traffic and the lack of cover; and after covering two miles the Section lay up for the night. Daylight revealed about 150 Germans digging defences half a mile to the North, and there were others at greater distances to the East and West. Movement was therefore not possible but, although it was eight miles away, the landing ground could be observed in the intervals between rainstorms and its position was fixed. The day passed without incident, though vehicles passed close by and an Arab goatherd was within 200 yds of the Section all day. At 1830 hrs. the advance continued, and the enemy's positions were avoided fairly easily as the men in them could be heard talking.

The attack 21st December 1941.

The aerodrome was reached at 2115 hrs. and, in Lieut. Fraser's words, "Two tripwires were tripped over without results!" His report goes on to say "some difficulty was experienced in finding the planes, detours being necessary to avoid A.A. guns and strolling sentries. The first plane was located at 0005 hrs. (on the 22nd December). At first the aircraft were fairly well dispersed, but nearer the hangars they were closer together, one batch of C.R.42s standing wing to wing ... Charges were laid in thirty seven aircraft and in one dump of Breda ammunition. The first charge exploded at 0042 hrs. and the aerodrome was evacuated at 0055 hrs., by which time four aircraft were blazing". The Section then withdrew and apparently the fires spread to a small bomb and petrol dump, "as the bangs continued for one and a half hours"; and fires were still burning when the Section lost sight of the landing ground at 0430 hrs. The raid was followed by an attack by our own aircraft, whose target appeared to be the Ageila-Benghazi road in the neighbourhood of Jedabya, but it was noticed that one stick of bombs fell on the landing ground. Slight trouble was experienced in getting through the enemy on the return journey to the rendezvous; but the Sections were duly picked up by S.2 patrol at about 0425 hrs. and returned to the Wadi el Faregh, now occupied by Brigadier Reid's "E" Force. Later in the morning the party was bombed by two low flying

---

1 In the L.R.D.G. account of the operation this distance is given as five miles. It was possibly something between the two estimates.

Blenheim aircraft with British markings, and two men of the L.R.D.G. were killed.

Return to Jalo 23rd December 1941.

On the 23rd December the Section arrived at Jalo. It was believed that more than thirty aircraft had been destroyed.

S.S.M. Tait's account.

S.S.M. Tait, Gordon Highlanders, one of Lieut. Fraser's Section, wrote a separate report on the Jedabya raid, and the following points made by him are interesting. It appears that rather by luck than good management the Section came onto the landing ground from the North and so in the rear of a number of M.G. posts sited to defend it against attack from the East. No individual sentries on aeroplanes were found, but under the heavy bombers there were men asleep, presumably members of the crew, and S.S.M. Tait adds "We did not wake them!" The planes were mostly Italian but there were a few German F.E. 109's. Where the planes were close together, as was in the case in front of the hangars, bombs were placed on alternate planes. Each man had eight Lewis bombs (half delay), but ten could have been comfortably carried. On a warm night the bombs ignite after eighteen minutes, so that the half-hour the party allowed themselves did not enable them to cover all the ground.

General situation Xmas 1941.

The general situation during the last week of December 1941, was as follows. Rommel's main forces were concentrated in the Marada-Jedabya-El Agheila area. He abandoned Benghazi on the 24th December and Jedabya on the 6th January 1942, but his garrisons were still holding out at Bardia, Halfaya and Sollum, and the last two named places were not taken until the 12th January 1942. On Christmas Day 1941 our advanced troops were at Benghazi, Saunnu, Antelat and Soluk, with Brigadier Reid's force in the neighborhood of the Wadi el Faregh, further South. They were lacking in infantry and supply was becoming difficult.

Raids on Tripoli coast, December 1941 - January 1942.

On Christmas Day two sections of "L" Detachment under Lieut. Fraser and Lieut. J. Lewis respectively, left Jalo with T.2 patrol of the L.R.D.G. (2nd Lieut. Morris, M.C., N.Z.E.F.) to raid the landing grounds at Arae Philaenorum, better known as the "Marble Arch" (S.V.5492), and at Nofilia sixty miles further along the coast to the West. The Marble Arch landing ground was to be attacked by Lieut. Fraser and Nofilia by Lieut. Lewis.

Raid near Marble Arch 27th December.

Lieut. Fraser was dropped with four men about six to ten miles South of the Marble Arch on the 27th December and moved on to a position on high ground South of the coast road, from which the landing ground could be observed. Large formations of aircraft came and went, which gave the impression that it was used by day to land reinforcements or as a refuelling point, but it appeared to be empty at night. After three days Lieut. Fraser decided that as he could not enter the landing ground, he would wait for the return of the L.R.D.G., and then attack some other objective. He remained for three more days at the prearranged rendezvous but owing to the fact that the L.R.D.G. patrol and Lieut. Lewis' Section had met with disaster, of which he was of course unaware, no transport arrived. Though there was food, water had run out and on the 2nd January 1942 he started to march back on foot. Some water was obtained from a German lorry, but by 7th January, when the party had reached the Wadi-el-Faregh, both food and water had been exhausted. There were a good many Italian troops about and a stationary lorry was attacked at 1930 hrs. on the 7th January in the hope that it contained supplies. "The occupants" says Lieut. Fraser, "were sleeping inside, and became hysterical when captured. They were for some time under the impression that we were German soldiers. Some food was obtained and the radiator was drained for water. The Italians were very anxious to be captured and were told that if they did not raise the alarm they would be captured the following day! They went back to bed, and the Section marched due North to the main road." The next day (8th January) was spent in the salt marsh South of the Mersa Brega-El Agheila road, known as the Sebkha es Segira. On the night of the 8th/9th the party stopped a German lorry about eight miles South-West of Mersa Brega and forced the driver to take them to the 11 Km. stone North-East of it. They then left the road, and the truck was driven South for seven miles until it stuck in a salt marsh and had to be abandoned about 50 miles South of Jedabya. Two miles further on they were challenged by a sentry, whom they avoided, and about an hour later came upon a strong enemy position running from North to South. They started to walk through it but, owing to bright moonlight, they were seen and fired on by sentries which gave the alarm. Capt. Fraser's report continues "after crawling for about a quarter of a mile we found the net to be closing in, the nearest enemy not being more than twenty yards away, so we rose to our feet ... intending to shoot our way out. Nobody interfered and the Section was able to walk out of the lines and across the minefields in front." They covered another twelve miles before dawn "which came just in time to prevent the Section entering another position." On the night of the 10th/11th January they were given dates and water by friendly Senussi and on the 11th they met a patrol of the K.D.Gs. South of Jedabya.

Lieut. Fraser's Section arrives at Msus 12th January 1942.

The Section went on to Msus by M.T. and thence were flown to Eighth Army H.Q., where Lieut. Fraser reported to General Ritchie.

He speaks highly of the conduct of the four men of his Section, S.S.M. (then Lance Sergt.) R. Tait, M.M., Lance Sergt. J. Du Vivier and Pte. J. Byrne of the Gordon Highlanders, and Pte. A. Phillips of the Royal Warwickshire Regiment, who were also with him in the raid on Jedabya before Christmas.

S.S.M. Tait's account.

As in the case of the raid on Jedabya, S.S.M. Tait wrote an account of the expedition to the Marble Arch, which gives details of considerable interest. He relates that on the third day after the Section had withdrawn to its rendezvous from the hills overlooking the landing ground (30th December 1941) they "saw a continual patrol of Stukas pass overhead and bomb some objective out of sight beyond a ridge about fifteen miles away, where three columns of black smoke rose". They had had no news of the Eighth Army for a fortnight and hoped that the leading troops of it had reached the position which the enemy were bombing. Actually, however, as described later, the attack was being made on T.2 patrol of the L.R.D.G. and Lieut. Lewis' Section of "L" Detachment, which were on their way from Nofilia to pick up Lieut. Fraser's Section. But, as S.S.M. Tait points out, they were expected to arrive from the West or South and not from the East. He also describes the Section's efforts to distill water in the salt marsh South of Jedabya, and the method of doing so, as follows: "I happened to have an Italian water bottle which had a very small opening, over which we placed one end of the narrow rubber tube we all carried (a very useful piece of equipment); the other end we placed in an issue water bottle. With a fire of camel thorn under the Italian water bottle and with the issue water bottle in constantly wetted sand, we managed, after four hours, to obtain one bottle of drinkable water; a very slow process. By night we had only two bottles filled."

Lieut. Fraser had by this time become ill with stomach trouble and, as he was unable to march, it was decided that S.S.M. Tait should take two men down to the road and try to get some water. To continue the story in Tait's own words, "We arrived at the road and found a fair amount of traffic, and ... I was determined to hold up a truck. Fortunately just then a heavy truck stopped, and drew off the road about fifty yards from us and three men got out ... we merely walked up quietly and held them up at revolver point. They were Germans and, after they had recovered from their initial fright, were very friendly. We told them a cock and bull story of being escaped prisoners of war from Tripoli, and they were very sympathetic. We took two "Jerricans" of water and made them carry them for us for about two kilometres on a wrong bearing. We then left them assuring us that they would not report us." This remarkable exploit shows that even the "herrenvolk" have their masters!

S.S.M. Tait also gave details, which are worthy of record, of the capture on the night 8th/9th January of the German car, referred to above. He writes, "we found ourselves near a convoy parking place. We tried to enter this but, as there were too many men walking about, we withdrew to the entrance. Pte. Phillips wrapped a blanket round himself (obtained from Italians) and he then looked like a native. The rest of the party divided, two on each side of the road; then as a car slowed up to leave the park Phillips stepped out and stopped it. We all then rushed it and drove it rapidly away … It was a small car of the Folkswagen type with a driver and a W/T operator … we discovered that, though they had no food and water, they had benzine for 100 kilos. So therefore we drove off down the road, the German driving … through Mersa Brega, luckily without meeting any road blocks. The town was full of troops, who paid no attention to us … The two Germans were very friendly and gave us much information which we found out later was correct."

S.S.M. Tait, in concluding his report, emphasises the value of the specialised training they had received in the unit; water discipline, long desert marches, intensive night work ("we always had the advantage over the enemy, who were obviously not accustomed to night movement"), and navigation, which enabled them at all times to know where they were.

Lieut. Lewis's Section at Nofilia 28th December 1941.

No information of Lieut. Lewis's Section is available other than that contained in the report made by 2nd Lieut. Morris commanding T.2 patrol of the L.R.D.G. The Section was dropped close to Nofilia at 1500 hrs. on the 28th December, and were picked up again at about 1800 hrs. on the 30th. On the 31st the party moved back to the neighborhood of the "Marble Arch" in order to pick up Lieut. Fraser's party. At about 1000 hrs. they were attacked by a Messerschmidt aircraft from a low level. The trucks scattered and the plane went back to the landing ground which was not far away. A second low level attack was then made by two Stukas and a reconnaissance plane with bombs, "cannon", and M.Gs. firing incendiary ammunition.

Lieut. Lewis killed 31st December 1941.

In spite of camouflage, and such cover as was available, the fire was effective. Two trucks were destroyed and Lieut. Lewis was killed. Later in the morning there were further attacks and, though no more casualties occurred, all the trucks but one were destroyed. 2nd Lieut. Morris got away with one truck and some of his party, and reached Jalo on the 1st January. Nine men of the L.R.D.G. and Corporal White of "L" Detachment started off on foot. In spite of being short of food and water, of the cold and of their footwear falling to pieces, all but Corporal White reached Jalo after a march of 200 miles in eight days. Corporal White, whose feet were almost raw, had to fall out by the Marada-El Agheila road and was left behind.

Raid at Bouerat-el-Hsun 23rd January 1942.

"L" Detachment's next operation took place at Bouerat-el-Hsun, and a party left Jalo on the 17th January 1942, four days before Rommel began the counter offensive which carried him back to the frontier of Egypt. It was accompanied by Capt. A.D.N. Hunter and 13 O.R. of G.1 Patrol of the L.R.D.G., and included Major Stirling, Capt. G. Duncan (S.B.S.), R.S.M. Riley, Sergt. Kershaw, an officer of the R.A.F. and twelve O.R. (including one of the R.A.F.). They crossed the Kufra-Marada road at Bir Zelten, sixty miles South of Marada, and then went North-West through Abu Naim, (X)F.7523, and El Hofra (X)F.0546, to the Wadi Tamet which reaches the coast about thirty miles East of Bouerat. While crossing the Wadi they were attacked from the air and the vehicles had to be dispersed. When the party was about to move on again it was found that the W/T operator and three men of the L.R.D.G. were missing and, as there was little time to spare, they had to be left behind. On the 23rd January, the column reached the sand dunes near Gheddahia and just East of the Hon-Misurata road. Here the L.R.D.G. Patrol halted, and the S.A.S. and S.B.S. party went on in a 30 cwt truck to their objective, their intention being to destroy aircraft, transport and, if possible, shipping.

The truck was harboured about two miles from Bouerat and the party split into four groups commanded by Major Stirling, Capt. Duncan, R.S.M. Riley and Sergt. Kershaw respectively. They then entered Bouerat and "mined" the wireless station, some oil and petrol transporters, cable and other communications, dumps and vehicles. The Italian guards did not challenge or make any effort to find out who their visitors were, and this was perhaps due to the fact that the intruders walked boldly about without any attempt at concealment. On one occasion R.S.M. Riley and Sergt. Badger passed within a few yards of two Italians, who did not even speak to them! On returning to the rallying point, Capt. Duncan and his party were missing. While waiting for them to return Major Stirling with the rest of his men attacked a camp "about 300 yds. down the road." A wireless installation was damaged and the men manning it were killed with "Tommy guns". They then returned to the L.R.D.G. rendezvous, but found that Capt. Duncan and his men were still missing. After lying up for the night and next day, Major Stirling and Capt. Hunter went back to the rallying point after dark on the 25th and to another place which had been pre-arranged as a second rallying point, in order to find Capt. Duncan and also to attack the coastal road. The missing men were found on the way. No M.T. were on the move, but a parked tanker with a trailer was "mined" and the explosion caused it to catch fire, and exposed the raiders to view. They drove off in their own truck towards the desert but, when they had gone about 500 yds., they ran into an ambush and were fired at with mortars and heavy M.Gs. All their Tommy guns jammed, as a result of a dust storm earlier, but a Vickers "K" gun got into action, "which had a demoralising effect on the enemy owing to the rate of fire and the incendiaries used." They got away without casualties, however, and rejoined the L.R.D.G. patrol.

L.R.D.G. base withdrawn from Jalo to Siwa 26th January – 1st February 1942.

The party started its return journey during the night 26th/27th January and reached Jalo without incident on the 31st. They were a week later than was expected and found that, owing to the progress of the German counter-offensive, Jalo had been abandoned. But G.2 patrol of the L.R.D.G. (Capt. Timpson), which had been left behind to destroy stores, was still there when they arrived and both parties left Jalo for Siwa next day.

Raids on Benghazi Area, March 1942.

On the 15th March 1942, a raiding party of "L" detachment left Siwa to destroy aircraft and shipping in the Benghazi area. It was escorted by S.2 patrol of the L.R.D.G. under 2nd Lieut. Olivey (S. Rhodesian Forces), and consisted of two officers (Major Stirling and Capt. R. Mayne) and six O.Rs. of the S.A.S., and three officers and three O.Rs. of the S.B.S. (Folbot Section). The party was accompanied by Capt. Melot of the General Staff (a Belgian by nationality and a business man in Cairo who subsequently joined the S.A.S.), and two O.Rs. of the Senussi Regiment. Included in the transport were two staff cars, one British and one German. On the 17th March the German Staff Car struck a thermos bomb and had to be abandoned; and Lieut. D. Sutherland and Sergt. Moss of the S.B.S., who were injured, had to be sent back to Siwa.

On the 18th March the party reached Gasr el Gehesc (S) S.2161, six miles South-East of Benghazi. The two Senussi were then sent forward on foot to reconnoitre the landing ground at Benina, and the main and satellite landing grounds at Berca on the outskirts of Benghazi; while Major Stirling, Capt. Melot and 2nd Lieut. Olivey reconnoitred the escarpment East of Benghazi in a 15 cwt truck. Next day a further reconnaissance of Benghazi was made on foot.

Attack on Berca landing ground 20th March 1942.

On the 20th the two Senussi returned with information; and Lance Naik Ahmed Din of the 4/16 Punjab Regiment, who had been hiding for two months, reported at the L.R.D.G. "harbour". That night Capt. Mayne with two officers and sixteen O.R. of the S.A.S. and L.R.D.G., guided by Corporal Merrick a L.R.D.G. navigator, raided the Berca landing ground. Major Stirling and two O.R. went in a 15 cwt truck - which had to be "helped down" the escarpment, to attack the landing ground at Benina. At midnight, 20th/21st March, the R.A.F. made a covering attack on Benghazi.

Attack at Benghazi 25th-26th March 1942.

Major Stirling found no aircraft at Benina and returned to the harbour at 0510 hrs. on the 21st. The raiding party then returned to Gasr el Gehesc, less Capt. Mayne and his men who reappeared on the 24th. They had not reached Berca main landing ground but had destroyed fifteen aircraft on the satellite aerodrome. That night (24th/25th), Major Stirling went out again in a 15 cwt truck with the "Folbot" party and encamped at Siret Aalia, (S)S.2481. On the following night he drove into Benghazi with two officers and three O.R. Meanwhile 2nd Lieut. Olivey took the remainder of the party to a point on the El Abiar-Benghazi road, six miles East of Regima on the escarpment. Major Stirling's raid on shipping was not carried out as the folbot was found to be unseaworthy. On his way back he dropped an officer and two O.R. to reconnoitre the aerodrome at Benina on the following day. They reported that thirty aircraft were there; but when a raid was made on the following night they were found to be dummies. A swift search of the hangars, however, revealed the presence of five aircraft of various types, including two M.E. 109Fs, all of which were destroyed. The party rejoined 2nd Lieut. Olivey at 0900 hrs. on the 27th and returned by Cheda-bu-Maun to Siwa, less Major Stirling and three O.R. who left the convoy at Hatiet el Retem (long 23°15'E. lat. 30°52' N) and went direct to El Adem. One man of the S.A.S. was missing after the operation and was subsequently captured by the enemy.

Raids at Slonta and Barce March 1942.

During the same period a raiding party of six men of "L" Detachment under Lieut. Dodds was escorted by T.1 patrol L.R.D.G. under Cap. Morris (N.Z.E.F.) to the Slonta area, but appears not to have had any success. Yet another party under Lieut. Fraser was taken to the Barce area by S.1 patrol of the L.R.D.G. (Capt. Holliman) leaving Siwa on the 16th March. The S.A.S. men were dropped on the 20th and picked up at Sidi Zamut (S)S.8475 about the 28th. They had destroyed an aeroplane and four workshop lorries.

Raid at Benghazi 21st-22nd May 1942.

A second raid on shipping in the harbour at Benghazi was attempted on the night 21st/22nd May 1942 and the S.A.S. party, consisting of Major Stirling with three officers and four O.R., was escorted by G.2 patrol of the L.R.D.G. under Lieut. Hon. R. Gurdon. They left Siwa on the 15th May with five 30 cwt trucks of the L.R.D.G., and a Ford Utility staff car belonging to "L" Detachment. Owing to the presence of hostile Arabs in the Jebel el Akhdar, of which they were warned by T.2 patrol of the L.R.D.G. whom they met near the Wadi el Mra on the 17th May, the route had to be altered; and they moved West from the Wadi. On the 21st they lay up all day near Haua (S)S.7575, about forty five miles East of Benghazi; and at 1730 hrs. Major Stirling moved off in the staff car, with two L.R.D.G. trucks carrying Corporal Wilson and other guardsmen of G.2 patrol. On arrival at the El Abiar-Benghazi road, he left the L.R.D.G. trucks and Corporal Wilson's party, who had instructions to mine the railway near El Abiar, and drove on to Regima with his three officers (Lieut. G.W. Alston, R.A., (1st S.S. Regt.) and Capts. R. Churchill, 4th Hussars and F. Maclean, Cameron Highlanders) and three O.R. of "L" Detachment. His report states "on entering the town (Benghazi) an Italian road block was passed by sheer bluff. After numerous attempts to launch rubber boats we were forced to retire to an empty house where the car was parked. The following night we tried again but were foiled by sentries and had to retire via the road block to the Jebel." Major Stirling goes on to say that bluff was sufficient to pass the guards, "no force of arms being necessary to overcome suspicion", and he also says that the German and Italian languages were used with great success. Lieut. Col. Prendergast of the L.R.D.G. in his report of the operation describes the situation in which the raiders found themselves as "Gilbertian", which indeed seems to have been the case!

On their way back they blew up some machinery on the Benina aerodrome and rejoined G.2 patrol at 0600 hrs. on the 23rd May. That afternoon they started the return journey to Siwa and arrived there on the 26th.

Raids in Benghazi area June 1942.

On the 8th June 1942, a party of "L" Detachment S.A.S. left Siwa to make raids on aircraft and shipping in the Benghazi-Benina-Berca Area. The S.A.S. Troops, three officers and 10 O.R., were under the command of Major Stirling, and were conveyed by G.2 patrol of the L.R.D.G. under Lieut. Hon. R. Gurdon, Coldstream Guards. There were in all seven 30 cwt Chevrolet trucks and Major Stirling's Ford utility car. For the purposes of the operation the S.A.S. detachment was divided into three parties, one under Major Stirling, another under Capt. Mayne and a third (Free

French) under Lieut. Zirneld. Major Stirling's Staff Car was destroyed by a "thermos bomb" on the 10th June, and two L.R.D.G. trucks were also damaged and had to be temporarily abandoned. The party nevertheless reached Gasr el Gehesh, (S) S.2361, by 1930 hrs. on the 11th June. There the S.A.S. parties were dropped and the L.R.D.G. patrol moved back to harbour in a Wadi four miles North of Zauiet umm es Schechaneb, (S) S.3255, which was to be used as a rallying point by the returning raiders.

Benina and Berca 13th–14th June 1942.

During the night of the 13th/14th June attacks were made on the landing grounds at Benina, and at Berca (Main and Satellite). At Benina hangars were attacked and five German planes were destroyed, and also twenty to thirty new aero engines, a workshop hangar and tools. The guards were all killed with hand grenades and the hangars were left burning.

At Berca (main) according to Major Stirling's report, the French party destroyed or damaged fourteen aircraft and twelve Italians were killed or wounded. At Berca (satellite) one aircraft and some small bomb dumps were destroyed and a few of the enemy killed. The parties concentrated at the L.R.D.G. rendezvous on the evening of the 14th June, with the exception of Corporal Warburton, missing from the raid on the satellite L.G. at Berca.

On the 15th June, G.2 patrol and the S.A.S. parties moved to Haua ben Chesciar, (S) S.7575, and arrived there at 0800 hrs. on the 16th. That night two officers and five O.R. of "L" Detachment "tried to sabotage dumps in the Benghazi area". The enemy, however, were on the watch and the plan had to be changed.

Lete 16th–17th June

A road house was attacked at Lete (S) S.0375, about four miles East of Benghazi; five trucks there were riddled with M.G. fire and "many of the enemy" were killed. The party retired by the Wadi el Gattara (S) S.1560, and were pursued for some distance. On reaching the top of the escarpment the L.R.D.G. truck in which they were travelling blew up; but no one was hurt and the party made their way to a cave near Zauiet Umm es Schecaneb where they were fed by Arabs until they were picked up on the 18th June by Lieut. Gurdon. He, in the meanwhile, had successfully mined the Barce-Benghazi railway at point (S) S.3279, about nine miles South-West of El Abiar. They then began their return journey and arrived at Siwa on the 21st June.

French account of attack at Berca,13th–14th June 1942.

Major Stirling's brief report on this raid has been amplified in an account written by a French member[1] of the S.A.S. (described by him as "Infanterie de l'Air") which has special reference to the part played by Lieut. Zirneld's detachment.

It was composed and armed as follows:-

Commander. 2nd Lieut. Zirneld	–	Revolver and Tommy Gun
Grenadier Cpl Hurria	–	Revolver and 15 Grenades
Machine } Sergt Bouard } Gunners } Cpl Le Gall }	–	Revolver and Tommy Gun each
Bombcarrier Cpl Fauquet	–	15 delay action bombs.

The detachment left Kabrit on the 5th June and travelled to Siwa by air. The writer, giving details of the method of attack on the aerodrome at Berca on the night 13th/14th June, states that the "grenadier" cleared the way for the "Bomb-carrier", who placed the bombs in the planes, and that flank protection was provided by the two machine gunners who were extended one on each flank. It is claimed that in this raid eleven machines were destroyed and seventeen of the enemy killed, our own casualties being two men slightly wounded and brought away safely. On the way back to the rallying point the detachment were warned by friendly Senussi tribesmen that they had been located by the enemy, and they lay up in the Senussi tents for a day before rejoining the L.R.D.G.

French party at Barce June 1942.

A similar operation at Barce was undertaken at the same time by a party of five French members of "L" detachment commanded by Lieut. Jacquier. They left Siwa on the 8th June escorted by S.1 patrol of the L.R.D.G. under Capt. Holliman, M.C. (R.T.R.). The Barce landing ground was too well guarded to make the destruction of aircraft possible and the French account states that the neighbourhood was patrolled by A.F.Vs. But the detachment was able to blow up a bomb dump which was reported to have damaged a number of vehicles, and they withdrew without loss.

French party at Martuba and El Daba June 1942.

A third raid in this series was carried out against the landing grounds of Martuba and Daba. The party which was escorted by R.1 patrol of the L.R.D.G. (Capt. A.I. Guild, N.Z.E.F.) also left Siwa on the 8th June. It consisted of a French detachment of the S.A.S., 14 men under Lieut. Jordan, and a party of the S.I.G. ("Special Interrogation Group") consisting of 14 Palestinian Jews of German origin under Capt. Buck, who were dressed in German uniforms, and were as a rule used for sabotage. The French detachment and S.I.G. men were dropped ten miles North of Baltet

1 Corporal Fauquet.

es Zelagh, S.T. 6555, on the 11th June, and it was arranged that the L.R.D.G. would wait for their return until the 18th. The attack was only a partial success, for it was betrayed by one of the Palestinians with the result that the whole of Lieut. Jordan's detachment was captured, though not until after they had destroyed some twenty planes. Lieut. Jordan, who spoke fluent German, managed to bluff his captors and escaped but all his men were lost.

This series of attacks on the enemy's landing grounds were not haphazard operations, but part of an extensive plan to assist the arrival of a convoy at Malta by reducing the scale of the enemy's air attacks; and similar attacks were made in Crete at the same time.

The results of the operations in June were as follows:-

Aircraft destroyed		27 at least (others damaged)
Aero engines	"	20 to 30
Trucks	"	5
Fuel dumps	"	numerous

A good many casualties were inflicted on the enemy.

Our losses were:-

Officers	Missing	2
O.R.	Wounded	2
	Missing	13.

Increase of S.A.S. transport June–July 1942.

In June 1942 Capt. Mayne suggested to Major Stirling that jeeps should be provided to carry men of "L" Detachment during the last stages of the approach to an objective, in order to save walking. This suggestion was adopted and extended, and during the raids of July and August 1942 fifteen jeeps, each armed with two Vickers "K" guns, and a number of 3 ton lorries were available.

Future objectives.

The original plan was that "L" Detachment, supported by patrols of the L.R.D.G., should attack:-

(a) The enemy's landing grounds from El Daba to Sidi Barrani.
(b) The road from El Daba to the Halfaya Pass.

Before the operations started, Major Stirling saw the Commander, Eighth Army and the B.G.S., and it was the intention that at a later stage of the projected operations Major Stirling's objective should be transport on the roads leading West. The raiding force was therefore given sufficient supplies to enable it to shift its main base from the area of Qatara Springs (1/250,000, Sheet 5, 7223) to the frontier area, which would enable it also to raid the Martuba, Derna, Tobruk group of landing grounds as opportunity offered. Raids were throughout to be "opportunist"; directives would be given as to suitable targets, but the responsibility for the choice of the target and for timing was to rest with Major Stirling.

Fall of Tobruk 21st June, 1942.

The fall of Tobruk, however, on 21st June, was followed by a further German advance and by the 30th June the Eighth Army had fallen back to the El Alamein line. One result of this advance was that the L.R.D.G. had to abandon Siwa at the beginning of the last week of June and its patrols were based partly on Kufra and partly on the Fayoum, in the Nile Valley South of Cairo.

Concentration at Qaret Tartura 6th July 1942.

In spite of the altered situation, a counter attack was still envisaged and on the 6th July, Major Stirling's force consisting of "L" Detachment and G.1 and Y.2 patrols of the L.R.D.G. concentrated at Qaret Tartura (1/250,000, Sheet 7 - 7423) on the North-Western edge of the Qattara Depression. G.2 patrol of the L.R.D.G. was also at Qaret Tartura and took part in the subsequent operations.

The whole force then marched North for sixty miles through the enemy's "back areas" to attack the coast road between Galal (Sheet El Daba 1/250,000 810316) and Fuka, which are respectively fifty and fifty-seven miles West of El Alamein. In addition to their C.O., the British officers who took part in the operations about to be described, were Capt. Lord Jellicoe (Coldstream), second in command, Capt. R. Mayne (Ulster Rifles), Capt. Schott (K.A.R.),[1] Capt. P.E. Warr (E. Surrey Regt.),[1] Capt. Scratchley (4 County of London Yeomanry), Lieut. W. Fraser (Gordon Highlanders), Lieut. D.C. Mather (Welsh Guards),[1] Lieut. S.L.E. Hastings (Scots Guards), Lieut. H.T. Caden (Green Howards), Ft. Lieut. Rawnsley, R.A.F., and Capt. Pleydell, R.A.M.C. The French officers were Lieuts. Jordan, Zirneld, Harent, Klein and Martin.

Lord Jellicoe's account of attacks in July, 1942.

Lord Jellicoe, who wrote an account of the operations, emphasised the fact that "L" Detachment S.A.S. had not hitherto been motorized and only four days were available for preparations. "Fifteen jeeps had to be prepared with special equipment and twenty 3 ton lorries loaded. This meant that drivers and maintenance crews had to work sometimes as long as seventy-two hours almost without a break". A great strain was therefore imposed on the men.

---

1 Of the 1st S.S. Regiment (Middle East Commando.)

The Plan.

Major Stirling's plan was as follows. G.2 patrol L.R.D.G. (Lieut. Hon. R. Gurdon) was to lead a detachment of the S.A.S. North-West to a position from which the latter could attack the two landing grounds at Sidi Barrani on receiving orders to do so.

The main body with G.1 patrol (Capt. Timpson) was to move under Major Stirling's orders so as to be able to attack, on the night 7th/8th July, the three landing grounds at Fuka, one landing ground at Bagush, and also to form the western end of a road block on the coast road between Bagush and Galal.

A third party commanded by Lord Jellicoe and escorted by Y.2 patrol of the L.R.D.G. (Capt. Hunter), was to move North-East and attack the four aerodromes at El Daba. Just before it started, however, information came from H.Q. Eighth Army to the effect that our counter attack had begun and that the El Daba aerodromes were on no account to be attacked. Lord Jellicoe's party was therefore directed against the coast road between Fuka and Galal to form the Eastern end of the projected road block. The conclusion drawn was that the attack must be going well.

Enemy's attack on the Ruweisat Ridge, 2nd July 1942.

Major Stirling had expected that the roads would be full of the enemy's transport driving Westward and, it was hoped, in some confusion. This anticipation was, however, unduly optimistic. The general course of events during the previous week had been as follows. On the 2nd July the enemy made an attack on the Ruweisat Ridge running from East to West about 20 miles South of El Alamein, which was held by an improvised force under Brigadier R.P. Waller, C.R.A., 10th Division, known as "Robcol". The attack was repelled. Next day "Robcol" followed the enemy Westwards and at 0900 hrs. gained contact with them on the ridges further West. Another engagement took place and the enemy's tanks were still further discouraged. "Robcol" was then reinforced and renamed "Wall Group"; and the Ruweisat ridge area became strong enough to resist an armoured attack. During the next few days Rommel struck in the North against the South Africans, and then to the South against the New Zealand Division near the Qatara depression, but without success. The "Alamein line" was further reinforced and by the 5th July was cohesive and secure.

General Auchinleck realized that though the enemy no longer had the strength to make simultaneous attacks against the whole front, he might well make successive attacks on one sector or another. He therefore prepared to reply to such attacks by counter attacking elsewhere. On the 5th July the newly arrived 9th Australian Division made a successful raid in the central sector; and shortly afterwards a New Zealand column, going round the enemy's position, attacked one of the Fuka airfields and destroyed 40 planes. On the 9th July the Australian Division and 1st South African Division attacked and took their objectives, Tel el Eisa (8399) and Tel el Makh Khad (8795) and held them against counter attacks. The operation was completed by the 11th, but an attempt to exploit it with armour did not succeed.

Raids on Fuka and Bagush 7th–8th July 1942.

"L" Detachment's operations were intended to co-operate with these attacks. As described above, the objectives of the main body of the raiders under Major Stirling were the landing grounds at Fuka and Bagush. They moved at first light on the 7th July, and reached a point about 15 miles South of Fuka by 1700 hrs. that afternoon. This was early enough to enable three parties to go forward to the escarpment to reconnoitre the approaches to their targets; but as a large column was seen moving Westward, and was believed to be hostile, the move forward was delayed. This prevented effective reconnaissance of the route down the Fuka escarpment which was negotiated only with great difficulty. Night had fallen, and the targets too had not been sufficiently reconnoitred. As a result the raid on the three Fuka landing grounds (Nos. 17, 18 and 19) miscarried. Only Nos. 17 and 18 were attacked and on them only ten aircraft were destroyed.

L.R.D.G's successful attack on transport 7th–8th July 1942.

Lieut. Gordon, who had led the party down the escarpment, took his patrol (G.2) across the railway line and reached the main road, where he discovered a "staging point" for the enemy's transport. Having destroyed thirty or forty vehicles and damaged others, he then picked up the S.A.S. parties and took them back to the rendezvous, about fifteen miles to the South.

Bagush 7th–8th July 1942.

The raid on Bagush was carried out by Major Stirling and Capt. Mayne, who were equally handicapped by the delay in starting reconnaissance. Major Stirling was in a "cut down" utility truck on which were mounted eight M.Gs., Capt. Mayne was in a jeep. In describing what happened Lord Jellicoe writes "When actually short of the main coast road, Major Stirling turned West, thinking he had reached it, and entered the Bagush "box" before realizing his error; the "box" consisted of anti-tank defences, mines and barbed wire. However, as it was not defended he was able to reverse and make his way out. The party then made for the landing ground which lay East of the "box", and located it by the positions of sentries standing on the road alongside it. They then parked their trucks South of the road, and Capt. Mayne went on with a small party to make his attack. Normal equipment was carried, each man having one Tommy gun or Colt automatic, two hand grenades, and ten special bombs. The bombs were placed on the wings of the aircraft and Capt. Mayne came back to report to Major Stirling. He then did the same thing again. Major Stirling had meanwhile been examining the road to see if there was any chance of establishing a road block, but had not made one as he did not think it worth while to disclose his position for the sake of an odd truck. When Capt. Mayne had returned the second time, Major Stirling and he drove on to the aerodrome and destroyed, by machine gun fire from their vehicles, a further ten or fourteen aircraft. Subsequently a reconnaissance showed that in all thirty-seven aircraft had been destroyed, mostly C.R. 42s and M.E. 109s. Major Stirling was by this time encountering considerable opposition from M.Gs. and 20 mm. guns distributed round the landing ground. He therefore withdrew but was unable to resist the temptation to return, to Capt. Mayne's disgust, in order to dispatch a few more aircraft! Having accomplished this the party withdrew along the road Eastward and then turned South, crossing L.G.16". There it appears they destroyed another aeroplane which turned out to be an abandoned Hurricane. They then rejoined the Fuka parties and withdrew to a prearranged "harbour" at Qaret Hiremas (730269). On their way back they were attacked from the air by C.R.42s. and, though they lost no men, several vehicles were destroyed in spite of vigorous A.A. defence and Major Stirling, whose truck was among those lost, had a narrow escape. Lord Jellicoe remarks: "The Italians were obviously, for once, in an angry and determined mood!"

Raid on Fuka-Galal road and capture of prisoners.

Lord Jellicoe's own party, whose original objective was the establishment of a road block between Fuka and Galal, was also delayed by the column marching Westwards, which was in fact one of our "Jock" columns. They identified 25 pdr guns but, as the enemy were known to be using captured guns, they decided that it would be imprudent to approach. They moved forward as it was getting dark on the 7th July, and struck the railway at a point some miles West of Galal. They crossed the line and dispersed for some ten miles up and down the road but no vehicles were seen though they picked up "a few stray prisoners"; and after waiting an hour and a half the party withdrew.

While avoiding some German tanks during the return journey to Qaret Hiremas, Lieut. Caden with one jeep became detached and failed to return to the rendezvous. He was able to get back to the El Alamein position later, but had to abandon his vehicle.

Raid on Sidi Barrani 7th-10th July.

The third party, which was to attack the two Sidi Barrani aerodromes, was composed of two S.S. detachments under Capts. Warr and Schott respectively, and was escorted by G.1 patrol of the L.R.D.G. (Capt. Timpson, Scots Guards). It seems to have been expected that these landing grounds would be full of aircraft at night; and if the enemy had been forced to retire from the El Alamein line this might well have been the case. Capt. Warr discovered, however, that it was used only by day, for landing supplies from transport planes, and no raid was possible. But the party was able to destroy the pipeline between the frontier and Sidi Barrani, and three abandoned but intact British vehicles. Moreover the information obtained as to the movements of the enemy's transport planes enabled the R.A.F. to destroy a large number of them in transit.

Major Stirling's report to G.H.Q.

The prisoners who had been taken by Lord Jellicoe's party gave information showing that the main fighter base of the Axis Air Force was at El Daba; and Major Stirling, in forwarding this intelligence to Army H.Q., emphasised that a good opportunity for crippling the enemy's air power had been lost owing to the order prohibiting an attack on these landing grounds. He also pointed out that he had not been warned of the presence of the "Jock" column which had delayed reconnaissance of the objectives for the night of the 7th/8th July; and the lack of detailed information about suitable objectives. He "never knew how many German aircraft there were, or on what aerodromes they were concentrated, and no information as to store dumps or Headquarters was forthcoming."

Corporal Fauquet, in an account of the part played by the French in the S.A.S. operations of July, relates that among the prisoners brought in (by Lord Jellicoe after his raid on the coast road) was a certain Baron von Luterotti of the German Headquarters Staff. He was well known to Lord Jellicoe, helped with the wounded and was given a share of the beer and other supplies dropped by the R.A.F. On the morning of the 3rd August, however, it was discovered that he and another prisoner had escaped during the night, and though a search was made during the rest of that day and the morning of the 4th they could not be found. Corporal Fauquet also states that during the morning of the 4th two Italian lorries were seen with twelve British prisoners, who had been recaptured in an exhausted condition after escaping from Tobruk. They were rescued, their guards were killed and the two vehicles were destroyed.

Base shifted to Bir el Quseir 9th July 1942.

Owing to a reconnaissance of Qaret Hiremas by Italian aircraft on the 8th

July, the base had to be shifted twenty-five miles Westward to Bir el Quseir (689283); and Major Stirling's next operation started from the new base on the morning of the 11th July, with the Fuka landing ground as its objective.

Raid on Fuka L.Gs. 11th July.

There were three parties which were to raid L.G. 16 on the Fuka escarpment, and L.Gs. 17 and 18 in Fuka itself. L.G.16 was attacked by a French detachment under Lieut. Jordan, who drove off the sentries with hand grenades and destroyed eight aircraft. Lieut. Fraser's party, which were to attack L.G.17, were detected by the sentries who fired a red Verey light. Lieut. Fraser therefore decided to drive on to the landing ground and attack with machine guns, as had been recently done by Major Stirling and Capt. Mayne at Bagush. But in attempting to cross the aerodrome defences one of the two jeeps fell into a rifle pit and was extricated with great difficulty under fire. In returning this fire, the machine gun mountings in the other jeep became dislodged and the attack had to be abandoned.

Landing Ground 18 was attacked by Capt. Mayne, who had Ft. Lieut. L.D. Rawnsley, R.A.F. with him, and it was estimated that between fifteen and twenty aircraft were destroyed. Two methods of attack were used. The landing ground was reached "by stealth" and delay action bombs were put on the wings of aircraft; then an attack was made with grenades on the sentries. Y.2 patrol of the L.R.D.G. took part in these operations, and destroyed three aircraft on L.G.68.

Unsuccessful attempt to raid El Daba, 12th-13th July 1942.

On returning to the "harbour" Major Stirling received a message stating that the El Daba aerodromes were no longer excluded from attack, and on the 12th July two parties set out to raid them. The first party under Lord Jellicoe was attacked by an Italian fighter patrol, two of the jeeps being destroyed and the third badly damaged. The party was forced to return over a distance of 90 miles with nine men in one jeep, which had two punctures and two incendiary bullets through the radiator.

Lieut. Gurdon mortally wounded 12th July 1942.

The second detachment, which was French and commanded by Lieut. Martin, was escorted by G.2 patrol L.R.D.G., under Lieut. Hon. R. Gurdon and left Bir el Quseir on the 11th July. On 12th, while in the neighbourhood of Minqar Sida (787267) the party was attacked by three Macchi aircraft. Lieut. Gurdon was mortally wounded and died next day; one truck was destroyed and the raid had to be abandoned.

Recent experience showed that the guards on the enemy's aerodromes were usually on the alert, and that El Daba, owing to its position, was a very difficult target to reach. A considerable number of our vehicles had been destroyed or were out of action, and on the 13th July, Major Stirling went to M.E. Headquarters in Cairo. Capt. Mayne also went there with wounded and unfit men. His party was attacked from the air on the way back and lost a few vehicles but no men.

On the 16th July 1942, the following instructions were issued by H.Q. Eighth Army to Major Stirling personally.

Eighth Army Operation Instruction No. 99.

1. Formation of a base at Qara Oasis.
    You will discuss this with Lieut. Col. Prendergast who will forward proposals to Eighth Army Tactical H.Q.
2. Priorities for Raiding.
    The order of priorities is Tank Workshops, tanks, aircraft, water, petrol. You will use your own judgment in assessing the value and reliability of information, importance of target assessed in terms of numbers of tanks, aircraft, etc. and possibilities of successful attack.
3. Raids by other parties.
    Eighth Army H.Q. will, whenever possible, keep you informed of other raiding parties operating in your area, but as these operations may have to be put on at short notice, no guarantee can be given that you will be warned in every case.
4. Blocking Operations.
    In addition to the normal raiding tasks in para. 2 above, you will be prepared for the following operations:-
    (a) Operations at Sollum and Halfaya.
        (i) One detachment to initiate a traffic block at Sollum. This block will be maintained until a party of Royal Marines has been landed to exploit the situation and maintain the block for 48 hours. As soon as the R.M. party is in position you will hand over to them, and withdraw. You will provide a second detachment to block Halfaya and arrange to keep this block going for 48 hours if possible. The action of this detachment will be co-ordinated with the Sollum detachment.
        (ii) A party under Capt. Buck may collaborate with you if it is placed at your disposal by G.H.Q., M.E.
    (b) Blocking at Bagush and Gerawla.
    You will prepare to initiate traffic blocks at Bagush and Gerawla.
    If these operations are approved instructions will be sent to you.
5. Intercomn.
    You will arrange with Lieut. Col. Prendergast that all W/T messages sent by L.R.D.G. links reach you as soon as possible.

New tactics.

Major Stirling returned to Bir el Quseir with reinforcements and fresh vehicles on the 23rd. He had been considering the tactical problem of dealing with the enemy's latest methods of aerodrome defence, which were making it more difficult and dangerous to effect a successful raid; and had decided on making "mass attacks" with jeeps in full moonlight, which he thought would have the following advantages:-

1. Attacks on landing grounds had never before taken place when the moon was full; and the first attack at least would have the advantage of surprise.
2. The enemy's tendency during periods of moonlight was to scatter aircraft over a number of landing grounds in order to minimize the effects of R.A.F. bombing. They were too numerous to be adequately defended, and successful attacks would result either in a concentration of aircraft on a few well defended landing grounds, which would render them more vulnerable to bombing, or of tying up much needed troops by strengthening the defence of a large number of them.
3. A "mass attack" would nullify the value of sentries on individual aircraft, (the enemy's normal custom) and would necessitate perimeter defence, which past experience had shown to be comparatively easy to penetrate by "stealth". Thus the alternative employment of two methods of attack - either by a small party on foot reaching its objective without being observed, or by a "mass" attack in vehicles - should leave the enemy hesitating between the two methods of defence. A combination of perimeter defence with sentries on individual aircraft would be most uneconomical in men.
4. The psychological effect of successful attacks should increase the enemy's nervousness about the defence of his extended lines of communication; and it was later proved that the enemy had been forced to employ two German reconnaissance groups to deal with the problem.

More jeeps were therefore brought up and on the 24th and 25th July practices, which included the firing of a considerable amount of ammunition, took place about 100 miles behind the enemy's front, in order to arrive at the best method of attack. It was decided that two formations were desirable. The first formation was to take the form of two columns of jeeps with a distance of ten yards between vehicles and an interval of ten yards between columns, the Commander directing from a position between the heads of the two columns. This formation was to be used during a night approach, and for the actual attack. The second formation was in line, with all jeeps abreast except for two in echelon at each end. Its object was to facilitate the crossing of perimeter defences and to develop the maximum fire power of the vehicles. It was considered that the effect of sixteen vehicles each firing two machine guns would be enough to overcome the average defence; but the practices showed that control, whether by word of mouth or by Verey lights, was not possible if vehicles were more than ten yards apart.

Raid on Sidi Haneish, 26th-27th July 1942.

It was decided on the 26th July that the next attack should be made on the dispersal area South of Sidi Haneish (7532) about 30 miles E.S.E. of Mersa Matruh. The column, consisting of 4 jeeps and T.1 patrol of the L.R.D.G. under Capt. Wilder, moved off at 1930 hrs. The plan was that the whole force should move by the main Qatara-Garawla track as far as Bir Khalda (724293). From that point T.1 patrol with one Bren carrier was to move forward to a position North-West of the landing ground; with the general role of creating a diversion on that flank, while the main body was approaching from the East.

The approach march of 70 miles was covered in four hours across open desert in bright moonlight. Six punctures occurred, each of which involved halting the whole column, and one of the L.R.D.G. trucks was lost through hitting a mine. When about a mile from the objective the column formed line and halted for last minute instructions. The force then moved on cautiously at four to five miles an hour, and a few jeeps fell into dispersed rifle pits. It is to be remembered that owing to the enemy's searchlights a concealed approach was not possible and as soon as he opened fire it was returned by each jeep firing its two guns forward. No difficulty was encountered in crossing the aerodrome defences and the force then reformed column. The firing of Verey lights and of tracer and incendiary ammunition having disclosed the approximate positions of the aircraft, the column was directed to the centre of the dispersal area and shot the planes up one by one, the pace, while shooting was going on, being reduced to one or two miles an hour. In this way about thirty were destroyed, though only eighteen actually burst into flames. Fire was also directed at the guards as they ran for cover. After the line of dispersed aircraft had been passed the jeeps came under fire from a 20 mm. gun and from machine guns round it. Some jeeps, including Major Stirling's, were hit and casualties were incurred, but fortunately the fire was not very accurate. The column returned the fire and then wheeled towards another group of aircraft.

Owing to previous practice the manoeuvre was successfully controlled, and Major Stirling reformed the column by sounding a horn. The remaining group of aircraft was then attacked in the same way, but as it was by this time within an hour and a half of daylight, the situation could not be fully exploited. The column recrossed the perimeter, broke up into small groups and withdrew as quickly as possible to the South and South-West. Fortunately fog, which lasted for an hour, obscured the rising sun, and gave the vehicles an opportunity to take cover. Later in the morning there was "furious and continuous" activity over the whole area, and an hourly patrol of six Ju 87s flew down the main track. One detachment of Free French was discovered and its commander, 2nd Lieut. Zirneld, was killed; and a German-Italian column of some thirty vehicles, with two or more 47 mm. guns, attacked T.1 patrol near Qaret Hireimas but was driven off, with loss of one 47 mm. gun and some vehicles, by the patrol's 20 mm. gun. The remaining detachments made their way back to base and arrived within the next two days.

Lieut. D. Russell's exploit, July 1942.

On the 29th July, eight jeeps in four parties went out, with the intention of attacking dispersed tanks and M.T. "leaguers" in the enemy's back areas near the El Alamein line. The front, however, had by this time stabilized. The tanks and M.T. were carefully guarded and no results were achieved, except by Lieut. T.C.D. Russell, Scots Guards, who destroyed eight vehicles in one night by a subterfuge of his own, which was facilitated by the fact that he spoke German extremely well. His method was to halt his truck some little distance from the main track, stop a German lorry and borrow a pump. While the pump was being produced he would contrive to insert a bomb into the vehicle!

Supply problems.

At this time difficulties arose in regard to supplies, which were getting short, and water in particular. Luckily, when only twenty gallons were left, 4000 gallons were found on the "Siwa track".[1]

Major Stirling appears to have had, at this time, a difference of opinion with G.H.Q. Middle East as to replenishment and other matters. G.H.Q. had future operations in view in which "L" Detachment was to take part and wished them to start from Cairo, which would simplify supply. Major Stirling thought that to return to Cairo would be waste of time and petrol and that the operations could be equally well carried out from where he then was. His position, however, was becoming insecure owing to the recent occupation of Siwa by the Italians, and the consequent threat to the Qara oasis. Moreover the gap between their right flank and the Qattara Depression had been closed by the Axis Forces and could no longer be traversed with impunity. Major Stirling's objections were therefore

---

1 Presumably the track from Siwa which runs direct to Mersa Matruh; but possibly another further East, which runs along the edge of the Qattara Depression, to Qaret Hireimas, and thence North to the coast just East of Matruh.

over-ruled, and his force was brought back to Cairo, partly by air, and partly in lorries under Capt. Mayne; and the lorry column marched through the Qara oasis the day before the enemy occupied it.[1]

"L" Detachment assembled in the Cairo area during the first fortnight of August.

The results of raids by "L" Detachment S.A.S. and the Long Range Desert Group during July were as follows:-

Enemy losses	Aircraft 86 (at least)
	M.T. 36 to 45

In addition one 47 mm. gun was destroyed and five prisoners were taken, two of whom subsequently escaped.

Our losses were:-

Killed	–	Officers	2
		O.R.	1
Wounded	–	Officers	1
		O.R.	3
Missing	–	O.R.	2
M.T. lost	–	Jeeps	10
		Staff car	1
		30 cwt lorries	2.

The Prime Minister's visit August 1942 and change of command.

At the beginning of August 1942, the Prime Minister visited Egypt. Shortly afterwards General the Hon. H. Alexander succeeded General Auchinleck at H.Q. Middle East, and General Montgomery became G.O.C., Eighth Army. The Army was reinforced by both infantry and armour. Rommel also received reinforcements of German infantry and artillery, and once more took the offensive on the night 31st August/1st September. By the 3rd September it was obvious that his attack had failed and he withdrew to the line Deir el Angar-Deir el Munasib-Himeimat. Except for small offensive operations on our part, the situation on the main front then remained unchanged until the Eighth Army attacked from the El Alamein position on the 23rd October.

On the 23rd August the D.M.O. (Brigadier G.M.O. Davy) held a conference at which both "L" Detachment and the L.R.D.G. were represented.[2] The control of raiding forces was considered and it was recommended that the L.R.D.G. should be primarily responsible for conveying "L" Detachment, and other organisations that operated behind the

---

1 Qara was still in our hands on the 6th August, for the L.R.D.G. records show that Capt. Kennedy-Shaw visited the Sheikh there on that day.

2 By Major Freeland and Lieut. Col. Prendergast respectively.

enemy's lines, to the vicinity of their objectives; for long range reconnaissance; and for action against "long range targets".

"L" Detachment should be used for the destruction and sabotage of targets closer in; by "stealth" if possible and by force if necessary. Reconnaissance was not its duty. It was also agreed that until "L" Detachment had its own signal organisation it must rely for signal purposes on the L.R.D.G. The Folbot parties S.B.S. were to be put under command of "L" Detachment. These recommendations were adopted.

The next operations in which the S.A.S. took part were preparatory to General Alexander's final offensive; and they were aimed at Rommel's supplies, the bulk of which were landed at Tobruk and Benghazi though Mersa Matruh was also used. The plans were made during August, and Rommel's abortive attack did not in any way affect them.

The operations were to take the form of attacks on the harbours of Benghazi and Tobruk, with a diversion against Jalo. They were known respectively by the Code names "Bigamy", "Agreement" and "Nicety".

Plans for preparatory raids by S.A.S. and L.R.D.G. August 1942.

Their main object was to destroy shipping in the harbours of Tobruk and Benghazi respectively. If the operations were successful the defeat of Rommel's army would be facilitated.

Destroyers and M.T.B's to carry landing parties were available at Malta and Haifa, and troops could be drawn from Egypt, Palestine and Malta. Besides regular troops and the L.R.D.G. it was calculated that there would be the following "irregulars" available.

"L" Detachment S.A.S.	100 men
"Buck" party[1]	30 men
M.E. Commando	60 men

There was some doubt as to whether there were enough men to make simultaneous attacks from the sea and overland on Tobruk and, by land only, at Benghazi. The G.O.C.-in-C., Middle East, considered that to attack Tobruk first and Benghazi later would probably entail the failure of the second attack; and it was finally decided that both places should be attacked at the same time.

The approach of land forces in both cases would depend on a route being open "somewhere between El Alamein and Siwa". The enemy was not at the time occupying Qara, but there was no reason why he should not do so in the immediate future, as in fact he did, and if so it would be

---

1 A small force of German speaking men, mainly Palestinian Jews, operating under the Command of Capt. Buck, who was himself under the Intelligence Branch, M.E.F. They were also known as S.I.G. i.e. Special Interrogation Group.

necessary to fight a way through which would prejudice surprise. The alternative was to go round by Kufra, which was a long way, and the latter course was adopted.

Forces to operate.

On the 17th August the G.O.C. troops in the Sudan, who would be responsible for supplies to Kufra, was told that the strengths of the forces operating from the landward side at Tobruk and at Benghazi would be as follows:-

At Tobruk "Force B" under Lieut. Col. Haselden - 15 Officers, 77 O.R. and 8 vehicles.
At Benghazi "Force X" under Lieut. Col. D. Stirling - 14 Officers, 200 O.R. and 95 vehicles.

In order to provide "Force X" with a base for further activities after the attack on Benghazi, it was decided that a third operation should be carried out on the 16th September, to be known as Nicety". This was to be the capture of Jalo by a battalion of the Sudan Defence Force with attached troops, stationed at Kufra ("Force Z"). It was also arranged that simultaneously with the three main attacks, the L.R.D.G. should carry out a raid in the Martuba-Barce area, which was given the Code name "Caravan".

On the 16th August, 15 drivers I.C. were attached to "L" Detachment S.A.S. for the period of the operations.

G.H.Q. OP Inst 19th August 1942.

On the 19th August G.H.Q., M.E.F. Operation Instruction No. 140 for the attack on Benghazi (Operation "Bigamy") was issued personally to Lieut. Col. Stirling, and a copy of it was sent to the Commander L.R.D.G.

The principal points in it are as follows:-
1. The objects:-
   (a) To block the main harbour.
   (b) To sink all shipping and lighters in the harbour.
   (c) To destroy all oil storage facilities and pumping plants.
2. The Force under Lieut. Col. Stirling's Command, known as "Force X", would comprise:-
   "L" Detachment, S.A.S.
   One L.R.D.G. patrol [1]
   Detachment Royal Navy
   Two Stuart tanks
   Detachment Special Boat Section
   One R.A.F. reconnaissance officer.

1 Eventually two, S.1 and S.2.

3. The operation was to be carried out during the night 13th/14th September and the following details were given:-

(a) The force was to close the harbour area.

(b) The Special Boat Section was to sink all shipping in the harbour except one selected ship which the R.N. Detachment was to sink in the mouth of the harbour.

(c) After the operation "Force X" was to withdraw on Jalo, which by that time should be in the hands of "Force Z" from Kufra. If not, Lieut. Col. Stirling's Force was to help in its capture and to use it as a base for further operations against the enemy's L. of C. "Force X" was to be under direct Command of G.H.Q. except from 1200 hrs. on 4th September to 1200 hrs. on 15th September, when Command would be exercised by "Commanders-in-Chief" from H.Q. C.-in-C. Mediterranean at Alexandria. After the capture of Jalo, and at a time to be notified by G.H.Q., "Force X" would come under Command of H.Q., Eighth Army.

In the first instance "Force X" would be based for supply on Kufra. Arrangements were to be made, however, for emergency supplies by air.

Operation "Bigamy". "X Force's" march from Kufra.

For the march from Kufra to the assembly point "X Force" (less S.2 patrol L.R.D.G. which joined later) was divided into three parties. The Advance party commanded by Major Mayne, Royal Ulster Rifles, left Kufra on the 4th September, and consisted of 5 Officers and 118 O.Rs. (including S.1 patrol of the L.R.D.G.) carried in 3-tonners and "Bantams". It arrived at the first rendezvous at (S)S.6147 on the 9th September.

The second party under Capt. W.J. Cumper, R.E., 5 other Officers and 73 O.Rs., with five 3-tonners and twelve "Bantams", left Kufra on the 5th September, and reached the rendezvous on the 11th. The main party under Lieut. Col. D. Stirling, D.S.O., Scots Guards left Kufra on the 6th September, and reached the rendezvous in the afternoon of the 10th. It included 20 Officers and 35 O.Rs. with eleven 3-tonners and twenty "Bantams". On the morning of the 12th the Force was joined by S.2 patrol of the L.R.D.G. which had marched from Siwa.

During the march from Kufra Lieut. Ardley, R.N.R. whose "Bantam" struck a group of three thermos bombs in the area East of Msus, was killed, the driver, Cpl. Webster, was seriously injured and the car was destroyed; but as far as could be ascertained, all three parties had completed the journey without being observed.

Preliminary recces. 9th September 1942.

On arrival at the first rendezvous Major Mayne sent forward Capt. Melot

(G(R)), 2nd Lieut. Maclean and a private of the Libyan Arab Force to establish contact with a representative of the Inter-Services Liaison Department (I.S.L.D.) who was known to be in the neighbourhood, and get the latest information of the enemy's movements and of the position in Benghazi. The I.S.L.D. man, however, could not be found and the L.A.F. private was therefore sent into Benghazi in plain clothes to visit his relations, and find out what he could. He left in the evening of 10th September and returned in the morning of the 12th, having been four hours in Benghazi and seen his relatives. He reported that the enemy appeared to be expecting an attack, that there were 5,000 Italian troops at El Abiar (thirty miles East of Benghazi and on the railway to Barce), and that the German battalion encamped North-East of Benghazi had been reinforced by seventy truck loads of Italians on the 11th. He said also that most of the shipping had recently left the harbour, and he gave details of the defences. This information was communicated to Lieut. Col. Stirling, and transmitted by him to G.H.Q., M.E.F. but the reply gave the impression that no great importance was attached to it.

Attack on Fort on the escarpment.

The first stage of the operation was an attack on the Fort at the top of the escarpment, with the object of destroying the W/T station from which warning of the main attack might be given. The fort was taken by a party of 3 Officers and 10 men under Capt. Melot, and the wireless installation was destroyed. Five of the garrison were killed and one was taken prisoner; but one man was not accounted for, and Capt. Melot and Capt. Bailey were wounded. The remainder of "X Force" (in M.T.) then continued on its way to Benghazi. As Capt. Melot was out of action the only guide available was the Libyan Arab referred to above, who was not very familiar with the approaches to Benghazi from the escarpment, and took the force over a route which was not only very difficult going, but led to a "dead end". The approaches to Benghazi were not reached until 0430 hrs. 14th September, and the attack was already four hours behind time. The original plan for entering the town had to be abandoned, and Lieut. Col. Stirling decided to force a passage to the nearest of the tracks entering the perimeter from the East. As the party advanced they encountered a cantilever gate weighted down and secured by a barrel of earth. The gate was opened by Capt. Cumper, and as the six leading Bantams went through heavy fire was opened on them by M.Gs., Breda guns, mortars and rifles. The fire was returned, which had a deterrent effect, but the enemy's fire positions could not be exactly located and the two leading Bantams were put out of action, though not before one of them, under Sgt. Almonds, had penetrated well into the enemy's position.

"Force X" withdraws.

In view of the strength of the opposition, of the probability of even stronger opposition further on, and of the approach of daylight, Lieut. Col. Stirling decided that the only course was to withdraw to the pre-arranged rallying point in the hills to the East. It was daylight before the last of the party had started, and three hostile aircraft were already in the air. By the time the escarpment was reached, the vehicles were under heavy fire from seven fighters, and they split up so as to get what cover they could in the numerous wadis; but five 3-tonners and seven "Bantams" were lost in the process. From the escarpment the party moved singly or in small groups to the original rendezvous twenty-five miles further on; and were much delayed on the way by reconnoitring planes. In the course of the next afternoon (15th September) they were located and heavily attacked from the air for five hours, during which time there were never less than fifteen aircraft over them. One aircraft was shot down by a Free French Vickers K.-gun detachment, and our own losses were three killed and four wounded. At nightfall the remains of the force (less the L.R.D.G. patrols which moved independently) were split into three groups, one under Major Mayne, another under Capt. Scratchley, and a third under Lieut. Col. Stirling to act as a rear party and collect stragglers. The first two parties marched to Jalo, after lying up for a night or two in the hills, but six more vehicles were lost on the way there.

Arrival at Jalo.

On arrival at Jalo they joined the rearguard of the Sudan Defence Force troops, which had received orders to evacuate the area, and returned with it to Zighen whence they made their way to Kufra. They were later joined by Lieut. Col. Stirling, who had collected the remnants of the force with the exception of Capt. Duveen and sixteen O.Rs. who were missing. It had also been necessary to leave at the rendezvous Capt. Bailey and three O.Rs. who were too badly wounded to be moved; and a medical orderly was sent into Benghazi in a "Bantam" with a flag of truce to ask the enemy to bring the wounded in. It was later discovered that this request had been complied with. Before leaving the Benghazi hills Lieut. Col. Stirling found the local I.S.L.D. representative, who told him that all the information at his disposal had gone to show that the attack was anticipated on the 13th September, and that the enemy had taken every possible step to meet the threat. In particular all the civilian population of Benghazi had been evacuated, and 200 German machine gunners had been brought in.

Lessons.

The following points, made later in a G.H.Q. note on the lessons of the operations at Tobruk, Benghazi and Jalo, apply to the failure at Benghazi.

1. "Such operations must necessarily be planned a long time ahead, and the strictest control must be exercised on those who are brought into the planning." Too many people knew of the Benghazi operation, and a very much higher sense of security was necessary.

2. "A special unit 'cover plan' is necessary to explain the formation of the force, the many preparations which must go on and the early moves of the troops."

3. The failure at Benghazi was due to the fact that the enemy was pre-pared for the attack, and that the opposition was stronger than had been calculated from the information available. "Any hope of surprise was lost through a detachment of the force attacking an enemy post on the top of the escarpment", (i.e. the Fort attacked by Capt. Melot's party).

4. Arab guides cannot be relied on as they do not know what going is suitable for vehicles and what is not.

5. Air attack caused the majority of casualties to men and vehicles. As attacks by enemy aircraft are so great a danger when a large number of vehicles are employed in a raid, they must be neutralized, either by ensuring that the enemy air forces are committed elsewhere, or by a reduction in the size of the (raiding) force which can justifiably oper-ate in any one area.[1]

6. The numerous mechanical failures in lorries of "L" Detachment S.A.S. Regiment were due to overloading. Long distances and maintenance in difficult conditions make it necessary for vehicles to be if anything under loaded.

7. There was no co-ordinated plan for the collection of relevant informa-tion. In such cases G.S. (Intelligence) must be brought into the picture so that arrangements can be made in time to obtain information that is lacking.

Orders for attack on Tobruk dated 21st August 1942.

The orders for the attack on Tobruk (Operation "Agreement") were issued on the 21st August 1942 in "Commanders-in-Chief Combined Operation Instruction No. 1", to the Naval Commander (Captain Micklethwaite, R.N.), and to Lieut. Cols. Unwin and Haselden, commanding "A" and "B" Forces respectively.

---

1 Lieut. Col. Stirling's force had 95 vehicles in all.

The objects were the destruction of petrol and oil installations, the sinking of shipping and of lighters (less those required for our own use), the destruction of port facilities and of tank repair workshops.

The Forces taking part were as follows:-

"Force A"   (based on Haifa)
　　Commander,　Lieut. Col. Unwin, R.M.
　　　　　　　　　11 Battalion R.M.
　　　　　　　　　Det. A.A. and C.D. gunners.
　　　　　　　　　Sub-section 295 Field Company R.E.
　　　　　　　　　Detachments Royal Signals and R.A.M.C.

They were to be carried by H.M. Destroyers Sikh and Zulu under the Capt. D.22 (Capt. Micklethwaite, R.N.).

"Force B"   (based on Kufra) which was to attack Tobruk from the landward side.
　　Commander,　Lieut. Col. Haselden, M.C.[1]
　　　　　　　　　One squadron 1st S.S. Regiment (Major Campbell)
　　　　　　　　　One patrol L.R.D.G. (Y.1 Capt. D. Lloyd Owen)
　　　　　　　　　Detachment A.A. and C.D. gunners (Lieut. Barlow, R.A.)
　　　　　　　　　Sub-section 295 Field Company R.E. (Lieut. Pointon, R.E.)
　　　　　　　　　Special Detachment G(R) (Capt. Buck)
　　　　　　　　　Detachment Royal Signals (Capt. Trollope)
　　　　　　　　　R.A.M.C. Medical Officer (Capt. Gibson, R.A.M.C.)

"Force C"
　　Commander,　Capt. Macfie, A & S Highlanders
　　　　　　　　　"D" Company, 1 A & S.H.
　　　　　　　　　1 platoon Royal Northumberland Fusiliers (M.G.)
　　　　　　　　　Two sub-sections 295 Field Company R.E.
　　　　　　　　　A.A. Detachment R.A.
　　　　　　　　　Detachment R.A.M.C.

This Force, based on Alexandria, was to be carried in fifteen to twenty M.T.Bs.

Forces "D" and "E" were purely naval forces and included H.M.S. "Coventry" and destroyers of No. 5 Destroyer flotilla, and one submarine to land a special "Folbot" (folding boat, party.

1　Originally known as the M.E. Commando (see page 367).

The general plan as far as land and air forces were concerned was:-

(a) That the R.A.F. should bomb the Northern shore of Tobruk harbour from 2130 hrs. on 13th September till 0340 hrs. on 14th September.

(b) As soon as bombing started "Force "B", from the landward side, was to attack C.D. and A.A. batteries at Mersa-umm-es-Sciausc at the South-Eastern end of Tobruk harbour, and hold the area for a bridgehead for "Force C".

(c) M.T.Bs. with "Force C" were to arrive at Tobruk at 0200 hrs. 14th September, attack shipping outside the harbour and land "Force C" at Mersa-umm-es-Sciausc. As soon as bombing ended the M.T.Bs. were to enter the harbour and attack shipping.

(d) Destroyers carrying "Force A" were to arrive off Mersa Mreira (one and a half miles North of Tobruk) at 0300 hrs. on 14th September and disembark the force, which was then to attack the C.D. and A.A. batteries on the North side of the harbour, and unite with "Force B" as soon as possible after first light.

It was considered that the failure of one seaborne force need not involve the failure of the whole operation. On the other hand the failure of "Force B" would mean that "Force C" could not go ashore and that destroyers would not be able to enter the harbour. Therefore, unless the success of "Force B" was known to Forces "A" and "C" by 0200 hrs. on the 14th September, both forces were to withdraw.

The air plan, in addition to provision for fighter cover, included attacks on the enemy's air forces in Africa and Crete on the 12th, 13th and 14th September, and also "low flying off shore to Eastward of Tobruk, to confuse the R.D.F. and distract seaward lookouts."

Operation "Agreement". Landward attack.
"Force B" Operation Order.

Lieut.Col. J. Haselden issued his Operation Order for "Force B" on the 1st September, at which time the force was concentrated at Kufra.

The "Intention" as defined in the Order was that Forces "B" and "C" would "capture and hold the South shore of the harbours from (incl) Umm es Sciausc to (incl) the Bulk Oil Tank (F.786) which was to be destroyed".

Plan for "Force B".

The "Method" paragraph gave orders to "B Force" as follows:-

"7.(a). "Force B" will leave Kufra on the 6th September in eight 3 ton lorries and proceed to an assembly area in the vicinity of Sidi Rezegh, arriving there at approximately 1200 hrs. on D-1.

(b) At last light on the 12th September "Force B" less the L.R.D.G.

patrol will enter the Tobruk perimeter defences at the East Gate, disguised as British prisoners of war under guard of the Special Detachment G(R).[1]

(c) The Force will proceed to the Wadis South of Umm es Sciausc via the main road, thence by the track running to the North-East of El Gubi main landing ground.

(d) On arrival at this area the force will debus."

"8. "Force C" … are being taken in M.T.Bs. to Mersa Umm es Sciausc where they will land at approximately 0230 hrs. on 14th September. On landing Commander "Force C" will report to H.Q. "Force B". A guide, Lieut. T.B. Langton (Irish Guards and 1st S.S. Regiment) will be available on the beach."

"9. The L.R.D.G. patrol (Y.1 under Capt. D. Lloyd Owen) will accompany "Force B" as far as the assembly area. Two hours after "Force B" has entered the perimeter it will also enter. Its objective will be the long range R.D.F. Station … at 414426 (Ref. Map 1/250,000 Egypt and Cyrenaica, Salum-Tobruk sheet) … the attack should take place before midnight 13th/14th September … after destruction of the R.D.F. Station it will lie up during the (rest of) that night. At dawn on 14th September it will … attack both Gubi landing grounds. It will then withdraw and take up a position astride the Bardia road in order to prevent any reinforcements entering Tobruk by that road."

"10. Phase I.

Air bombing attack is to begin in Tobruk at 2130 hrs. As soon as this has been started Det. 1 S.S. Regt. with under command

Det A.A. and C.D. gunners
Sub-section 295 Field Coy R.E.

will attack and capture the A.A. and C.D. guns at the Eastern and Western entrances at Mersa Umm es Sciausc … the coast guns will be manned and fire at any enemy ships attempting to leave the harbour. The A.A. guns will be destroyed."

The S.S. Detachment (less three Sections, those of Lieuts. Taylor, MacDonald and Sillito) were to deal with the East end of the bay. The remainder of the force (less L.R.D.G.) was responsible for the West end.

Further orders were then given as to what was to be done in Phase II and Phase III, and for the withdrawal. During Phase I Headquarters "Force B" was to be established in the building at Pt.21.51.

Password.

For the password the question "Who goes there?" and the answer "George

---

1 Capt. Buck's German speaking Palestinians, also known as "S.I.G."

Robey". The German and Italian passwords were also known.

One condition of success was deemed by G.H.Q., M.E.F. to be essential, namely that the guns at Mersa umm es Sciausc should be captured. If this part of the operation failed that whole operation was to be called off.

Approach march.

"B Force's" approach march of 700 miles from Kufra was undetected. Aided by aerial bombardment it reached the perimeter on the 13th September and drove through without incident. Some slight delay was then caused by the difficulty of finding the track in the darkness, but the house which was to be Lieut. Col. Haselden's Headquarters was reached, and the parties formed up for the first stage of the operation. Capt. Buck and Lieut. T.C.D. Russell (Scots Guards) with four Palestinians, went into the house and found one Italian who was questioned in German about the position of troops and telephones, and afterwards by Col. Haselden in Italian. Part of the force remained with Col. Haselden, the rest under Major Campbell went East to carry out their tasks.

Pte. J. Mackay (No.2881750) who joined the 11th Scottish Commando from the London Scottish in October 1940 and was with Lieut. G. Taylor's party of the S.S. Regt. during the attack on Tobruk, gives the following account of the operations of "B Force". "On the afternoon of the 13th we moved in to about ten miles outside of the town and at seven we went in along the Derna-Tobruk road. There were three trucks each marked with German divisional signs and we were packed in, sitting on our guns, explosives etc., to look like P.O.Ws. with our own German guards, dressed and equipped with German kit, armed with passes signed by bogus German officers; and in this fashion we went in without a hitch. Once inside we split up into two groups, one under Major Campbell and the other under Lieut. Taylor. The Italian N.C.O. in command of the C.D. battery was taken completely by surprise and was induced with a little persuasion to take us to the crews quarters; these were most effectively dealt with, but in a one sided fight Lieut. Taylor was wounded. At 2200 (?) hrs. we put up the success signal, our job was done, we had only to wait for the landing force and the success signal from Major Campbell's party; this went up at 2400 hrs., but he had suffered a few casualties, two killed, two wounded." The success signal, indicating the capture of the guns, was in fact made a little before midnight, the hour at which the operation would otherwise have been abandoned.

Failure of M.T.Bs. with "Force C".

Unfortunately the eighteen motor torpedo boats which were to land "Force C" at Umm es Sciausc, lost touch with each other in the dark. They tried to find the inlet independently or in small groups, but were confused by the number of lights, and by the firing which was then general on both sides of the harbour, and included a great deal of tracer ammunition. Two M.T.Bs., one of which ran ashore, managed to enter the bay and landed the M.G. section of the Northumberland Fusiliers and their machine guns, who duly reached Lieut. Col. Haselden's H.Q. The remainder withdrew from the coast shortly before daylight.

"Force A" fails to land.

The Marines of "Force A" who were to be landed from the destroyers "Sikh" and "Zulu" on the coast to the North, were defeated partly by the heavy swell, which capsized the folding boats, and partly by the fact that the bulk of the "first flight" were landed at a point three and a half miles too far West, and three miles outside the wall of the town. All who landed were killed or captured after a hard fight; and both Destroyers were lost.

Lieut. T.B. Langton (Irish Guards), one of the officers of the S.S. Squadron under Major Campbell, was responsible, together with F/O Scott, R.A.F. for "signalling in" the M.T.Bs. at Mersa Umm es Sciausc, and for meeting the parties as they came ashore. Signalling was not due to begin until 0130 hrs. on the 14th, and as Major Campbell was suffering from dysentery, Lieut. Langton went with him during the first part of the operation. Directly after leaving its trucks Major Campbell's party was delayed by a minefield which had to be negotiated with the help of a detector and in single file, and this caused considerable delay. A small party of the enemy with a Spandau gun were then put out of action, and later at point 41874036 or thereabouts, a small W/T station and some men were also accounted for. The positions at the East end of the bay were reported to be empty and unused, and at about 0130 hrs. the "success signal" which had already been fired by Lieut. Col. Haselden, was fired by Major Campbell. Lieut. Langton then returned to the beach, and in doing so had to skirt a small camp in the wadi near point 91854310, which he had not noticed on the way East. When he arrived at the Eastern signalling point he saw that F/O Scott was already signalling from the Western side.

Arrival of two M.T.Bs.

Two M.T.Bs. came in and Lieut. Langton had then to decide whether to go on sending signals, or meet the landing troops and conduct them to Col. Haselden's H.Q. as he had been ordered. He compromised by wedging his torch in a rock and leaving it alight. On reaching the landing point he found the two M.T.Bs. unloading. As Lieut. Macdonald (S.S.) was already organising the landing, Lieut. Langton took one man with him and continued to send signals. By this time searchlights were sweeping the entrance of the harbour and the beach; and from the opposite side of the harbour there was heavy fire out to sea. He could occasionally see the other M.T.Bs., but they were well to the East, and there did not seem much likelihood of their getting in. At first light on the 14th he gave up signalling and, on returning to the landing point, saw that one M.T.B. had run ashore. He then went back to Lieut. Col. Haselden's H.Q. and as he did so heard rifle fire from the direction of the wadi where the trucks had been left. The H.Q. house was deserted but the heads of about a platoon of the enemy, lying down and covering it, were visible about 300 yards away. He therefore returned to the landing point and was there joined by Lieuts. Russell and Sillito with Ptes. Hillman and Watler.

About an hour before dawn "B Force" H.Q. were fired on by what were believed to be two platoons of infantry, and the fire was returned. A quarter of an hour later, while the firing was still going on, Col. Haselden, who had waited for the return of Major Campbell's S.S. party, had the wounded (Lieut. G. Taylor and three O.Rs.) loaded on a truck with the M.O. He himself and a few men who were not actually shooting, got into a W/T lorry and the two vehicles went off " down the hill through the enemy". Lieut. Russell with Lieut. Sillito and two O.Rs. gave covering fire.

Lieut. Col. Haselden killed.

Col. Haselden's object was to get the wounded away, and then to carry out the second part of his task which included the capture of the guns along the Southern shore of the harbour, with the oil storage tanks as his final objective; but he was killed shortly afterwards, and most of his party were either killed or captured.

In his account of the last phase of the operation Pte. Mackay writes: "As the morning approached it became apparent that something had gone wrong. On the horizon a destroyer was on fire and fighter planes were straffing the M.T.Bs., but for us it was too late to make an escape, already we could see Italian soldiers taking up positions. The C.O. who had been all this time in his H.Q., took a party and tried to make a break for it, by charging a machine gun post, but he was killed in the attempt. For about two hours we held on, and not until the Italians had fetched German soldiers did they finally get us out, our ranks badly depleted." Pte. Mackay was taken prisoner, but a year later (September 1943), he and Pte. Allardice, who was with him at Tobruk, made their escape and "reached our lines on the 14th June 1944."

The withdrawal.

Lieut. Russell and his party left the house that had been Col. Haselden's H.Q. and made for the beach, where they found Lieut. Langton who was trying to start the stranded M.T.B. While he was doing so Lieut. Russell fired the twin Lewis gun mounted on the forward deck in the supposed direction of the enemy, who were also firing spasmodically. They failed to start the M.T.B., and paddled a landing craft down the coast under fire, to a small bay on the East side of Mersa Umm es Sciausc, where they landed. They then met about fifteen other officers and men and split into two parties. One party under Lieuts. Macdonald and Sillito walked Eastwards along the cliffs intending to look for our M.T.Bs. with, as Lieut. Russell states in his report, not the "slightest chance of succeeding". Lieut. Russell, with Lieut. Langton, Lieut. Barlow R.A. and eight men went South-East and lay up in a Wadi for the rest of the day.

The party splits.

That night they divided the remainder of the rations and water. The party was again split, each officer taking two or three of the men and going generally South-East, but in slightly different directions.

Lieut. Russell's journey.

Lieut. Russell had two men with him, and by walking at night and lying up by day they reached Bardia just before dawn on the 19th September. They had started their walk with a bottle and a half of water, and enough food for one small meal a day for two days, but near Gambut aerodrome they had found a quarter of a tin of jam and some water. On the 19th they were fed by an Arab, and that night set out to look for a bay to which they had been told an M.T.B. would come on the 20th September to look for stragglers.[1] During their search they were fired on by Italian coastguards, and in his efforts to get one man along, Lieut. Russell lost the other, Pte. Watler, a man of great pluck, but suffering from a bad cough and also very deaf.[2] Lieut. Russell made several unsuccessful efforts to find him, and also tried during the next few days to find and seize an Italian truck on the Bardia-Tobruk road. One day they met an Arab who gave them bread and showed them a pool of water and also told them that there was no water on the way to El Alamein. Lieut. Russell therefore decided to go into the hills to the South (Djebel el Akhdar) and try to get into contact with a British agent. Being unable to get the one man who remained with him (a Palestinian) any further, he went on to the West alone, and was fortunate enough to meet Senussi tribesmen who looked after him. Later he went through Gazala where two battalions of Italians "who were doing some form of battle drill" took no notice of him, and just West of Mekili he found an Arab who was in British employ. On the 18th November, he sent Arabs to find some armoured cars he had seen in the distance the day

---

1 Naval Operation Orders included the following paragraph:-
"withdrawal of stragglers will be by small craft from Mersa Shegga, nine miles North of Bardia on night 18th/19th September. This beach is recognisable by the wreck of a schooner lying at its northern end."
2 He was picked up later by Lieut. Langton.

before, and was picked up by a South African Armoured Car Company who took him to Benghazi.

Lieut. Langton's journey.

When Lieuts. Langton, Barlow and Russell decided to separate, Lieut. Langton took three men with him, and on the night of the 14th/15th September, made for the perimeter. Later in the night his party and Lieut. Barlow's met; but soon afterwards they had to scatter in a wadi to avoid a sentry post, and when the parties reassembled Lieut. Barlow was missing. Eventually, after dodging several posts, they got through the perimeter wire and lay up for the day in a cave. Lieut. Langton's party now consisted of Sergt. Evans (Welsh Guards), Cpl. Wilson, Fusiliers Leslie A, Leslie G., and Macdonald (Northumberland Fusiliers), and Pte Hillman of the S.I.G. (Capt. Buck's party). The last named had only one boot and a lacerated heel as well, and as he "had also the added burden of knowing that he would be shot if caught", his name was temporarily changed to Kennedy! After walking for another four nights and lying up by day in caves in the wadis, they had run out of food and water; but on the 19th September they were fortunate enough to find an Arab village, where they were taken in and given water and food. Pte. Hillman acted as interpreter and through him it was discovered that the Arabs knew all about the Tobruk raid, and also said that they could not understand how the English had managed to come all the way from Kufra! Going from village to village they reached the Wadi el Mreisa which runs into the sea some ten miles North of Bardia and is nearly 70 miles as the crow flies from Tobruk; and found that there was a large Carabinieri post at the shore end of the wadi. Here the Arabs told them that boats, thought to be British, had been seen off-shore. One of them had landed a party and someone had shouted "Any British here?" The Arabs guided them to the Wadi Kattara about five miles North of Bardia, where they found a soldier of the 3/18th Garhwal Rifles who had escaped three times from Tobruk and had lived in the wadi for three months, and also Pte. Watler, who, as related earlier, had been lost by Lieut. Russell. They remained in the Wadi Kattara for four weeks, and the Arabs fed them as best they could. They tried to attract the attention of aircraft by lighting fires at night, the only result of which was that a stick of bombs fell very close to them. They got some information about German and Italian soldiers, to whom the Arabs sold eggs on the road, and were given the impression that the enemy's morale was low, and that they were short of food.

There was much rain, and the cold and damp gave Sergt. Evans and one of the two Leslies (who were twins) dysentery. They had to be taken to the road and left for the enemy to pick up, and as the other Leslie went with his brother, the party was reduced to five, for Fusilier Macdonald had been lost on the way. On the 26th October, Lieut. Langton continued his journey with Cpl. Wilson, Pte. Watler and Pte. Hillman. The Garwhali stayed behind. They had one map (1/5,000,000) some tins of bully beef, some goats meat and ten bottles of water. Apart from being fired at on the second night, the rest of the journey was uneventful, and after negotiating the frontier wire they saw no one until they were picked up at Himeimat (about 30 miles South of El Alamein) on Friday, 13th November, except a convoy which looked very like a S.A.S. patrol.

Causes of failure.

The lack of success at Tobruk was to a great extent due to the difficulty, for various reasons, of making effective light signals from the beach to the approaching landing craft. Moreover, in the case of "Force A" the heavy swell capsized the folding boats, which carried the beach marking parties after they had left H.M.S. "Taku", and it was only with great difficulty that the men were rescued. For the same reason it was difficult to get boats away from H.M. destroyers "Sikh" and "Zulu" in which the Force was carried.

It appears too that hostile E-boats attempted to enter the harbour of Umm es Sciausc before the arrival of the M.T.Bs carrying "Force C", and then opened fire on them. This gave the impression that "Force B" had lost control of the harbour, and only two M.T.Bs., neither of which was opposed, arrived at the landing point.

Nevertheless, the raids on Benghazi and Tobruk, though they failed to achieve their immediate objects, were not entirely barren of results; and it became known later that the indirect effects had been considerable. The enemy sent back troops from the El Alamein position to the coast, and expended much air effort and fuel, of which they were short, in precautionary measures.

Operation "Nicety".

The attack on Jalo was made on the 16th September by a motor borne battalion of the Sudan Defence Force, together with a light A.A. Battery and a troop of 3.7" hows from the Sudan Artillery Regiment, under Lieut. Col. A.B. Brown, K.O.Y.L.I. The enemy were on the look out and the force failed to capture Jalo, although it inflicted a good many casualties. It remained in the neighbourhood for some days, and a second attack was planned; but orders to withdraw were then received. Though the attack failed the presence of the Force contained the enemy and prevented any interference with Lieut. Col. Stirling's "X Force", which had to pass close to Jalo during its withdrawal to Kufra after the abortive attack at Benghazi.

Appendix to Section VII

Extracts from a Captured Document

The Italian Inspector General P.A.1.[1] sent to the "General Staff North Africa", and to the Commissioners of Police at Tripoli, Benghazi, Misurata and Derna, a report dated 18th November 1941 on a raid carried out the previous night, which refers also to others made about the same time. He wrote "Last night at 0045 hrs. the Intendance Department at German H.Q. at Beda Littoria was surprised by an enemy raiding party who entered the premises and threw two hand-bombs which killed two German Officers and two soldiers, and wounded several others. In the fight which followed the Captain in charge of the party was wounded and a soldier killed. At 0315 hrs. the same night one of the enemy exploded a bomb under the telephone wire between this office and the Cyrene cross-roads. Immediately afterwards one of our light cars with a Captain on board was fired on and compelled to stop, though no one was hurt. The British patrol then made good its escape, favoured by the darkness and bad weather."

The Inspector General then proceeded to point out that by personal investigation he had discovered that both the officer and the driver who were attacked near the Cyrene cross-roads were unarmed, as also were the attendants at the "petrol distribution post" at the cross-roads. He went on to state that the wounded Captain, and the soldier who was killed, wore plain clothes under their uniform of which he gave a description; and he also gave a list of the documents, money, etc. that they were carrying, which included a letter from the "notorious outlaw Idris Senussi", recommending the people of Cyrenaica to render every aid.

He went on to say that his opinion, supported by that of Officers of the German H.Q., was that the party had been dropped by parachute from a plane which had flown for about two hours between Beda and Cyrene five days before.[2] A Sergeant Major of Carabinieri reported that in the morning of the 17th one of his patrols had met some "strangely dressed soldiers" in the Arab market, but as they replied in German that they belonged to the German Army they were not arrested.

The Inspector General recalled that a "few days ago" four British soldiers had landed between Cyrene and Derna; that "about two weeks ago" a raid had been

---

1 Italian Police in Africa.
2 This was not the case. The attack referred to was Lieut. Col. Keyes' attack on Rommel's H.Q. (See Section IV).

NORTH EAST AFRICA   Area covered by L.R.D.G. Patrols   Map A.

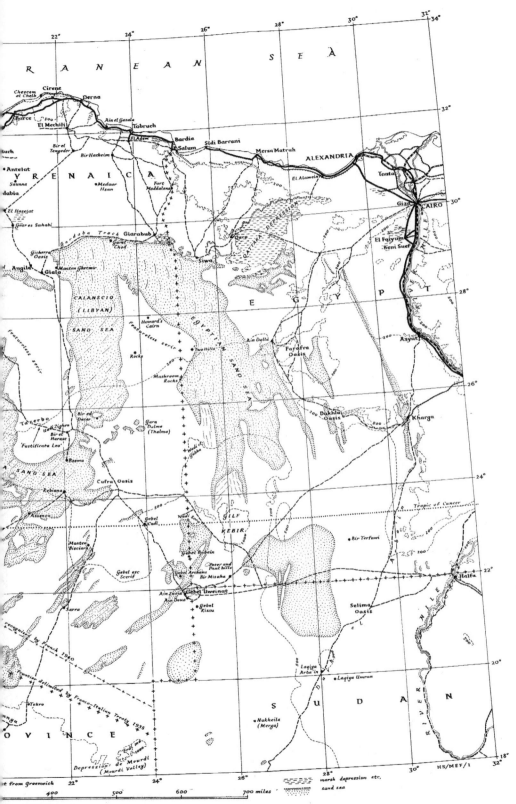

MEDITERRANEAN SEA

Chescem el Chelb · Cirene
Derna
Barce · Soo
El Mechili
Ain el Gazala
Tobruch
Bir el Tengeder
Bir Hacheim · Bir el Adem · Bardia · Sidi Barrani
Salum
Mersa Matruh
ALEXANDRIA
El Alamein
Antelat
Saunnu
CYRENAICA
dabia
Meduar Hsan
Fort Maddalena
El Hag*iat
Gasr es Suhabi
Bardaba Track · Giarabub
Gichorra Oasis
Garet Chod
Augila · Giala
Manten Ghetmir
Siwa
Qara
QATTARA DEPRESSION
Tanta
Giza · CAIRO
NILE
El Faiyum
Beni Suef
EGYPT
CALANSCIO
(LIBYAN)
SAND SEA
Howard's Cairn
Featureless serir
Two Hills
Rocks
Ain Dalla
EGYPTIAN SAND SEA
Farafra Oasis
Mushroom Rocks
Asyut
Bir ed Dacar
Gara Dalme (Thalma)
Wadi el Gubba
Dakhla Oasis · Soo
Kharga
Tazerbo
Uad Zighen
Bir el Harase
'Fustificata Leo'
Bzema
SAND SEA
Cufra Oasis
Rebiana
GILF
Tropic of Cancer
Assenci
Gebel el Cudi
KEBIR
Bir Terfawi
Wadi Sora
Manten Bisciara
Gebel Babein
Gebel esc Scerif
Gebel Archenu
Peter and Paul hills
Bir Misaha
HALFA
Gebel Uweinat
Ain Zuia
Ain Deua
Gebel Kissu
Selima Oasis
Sarra
NILE
RIVER
recognized by French 1940
Tekro
Frontier delimited by Franco-Italian Treaty 1935
Laqiya Arba'in
Laqiya Umran
anga
PROVINCE
S U D A N
Nukheila (Merga)
Erdi and Depression de Mourdi (Mourdi Valley)

at from Greenwich

marsh depression etc.
sand sea

400   500   600   700 miles

ow sea level

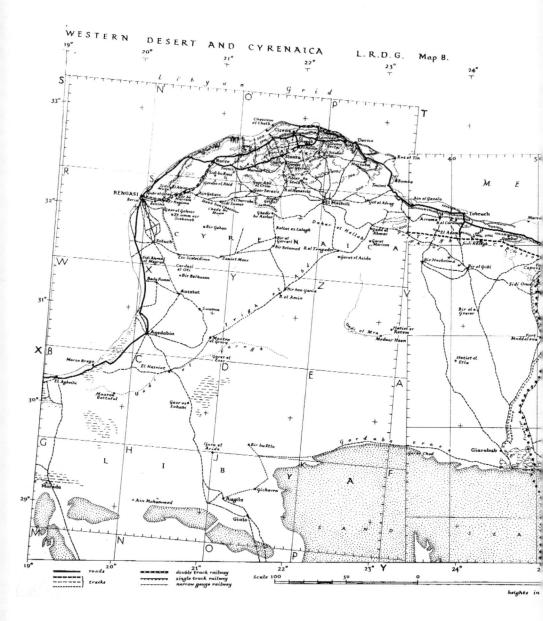

Libyan Grid

S   N   O   P   T

33°

R   M   E

32°

BENGASI   El Mechili   Tobruch

C   Y   R   E   N   A   I   C   A

W

X

31°   V

Agedabia

X B

C   D   E   A

30°

El Agheila

G

L   I   J   B   K   Y   A   F   Giarabub

29°

Marada

M   S   A   N   D   S   E   A

N   O   P

roads
tracks
double track railway
single track railway
narrow gauge railway

Scale 100   50   0

heights in

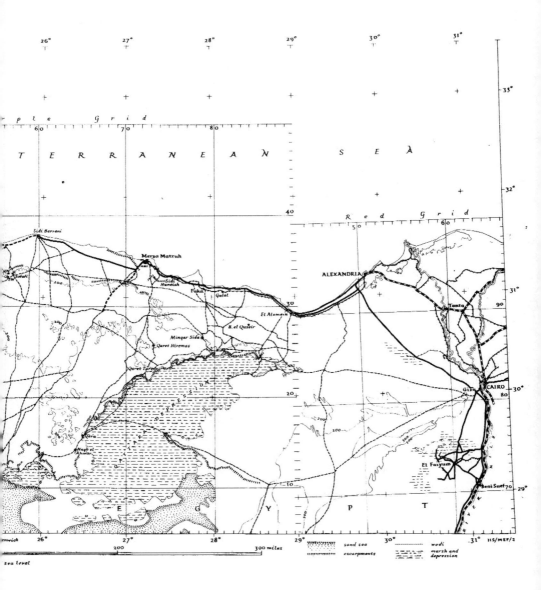

made by five armoured cars and some lorries South of Buerat-el-Hsun;[1] and said that news had just been brought to him of the capture of sixteen parachutists[2] and one Italian, forced to land near Tobruk as the result of being machine gunned by "one of our planes" He then drew the following conclusions:

(a) That the British were attempting by acts of sabotage to draw troops from the front and spread panic among the people.
(b) This sabotage was brought about "by means of coast landings, parachutists, and long-range raids by motor vehicles along Southern roads, carried out by the famous Commandos instructed and directed by the Intelligence Service."
(c) That natives helped the British with shelter and information.
(d) That British were going about populated centres in civilian clothes or a "vague sort of uniform such as shorts and shirts with badges hardly visible" which would foil the police force, who mistook them for Germans.
(e) That there were still too many Italian soldiers who did not seem to realize that it was always necessary to be armed, even in back areas.

The Inspector General then proceeded to recommend frequent visits to sentries at night and other measures against surprise.

1 S.1 patrol of the L.R.D.G
2. They belonged no doubt to Major Stirling's party of parachutists, who were dropped in the Gazala-Tmimi area on the night 17th/18th November.

Section VIII

1st S.A.S. Regiment.

1st S.A.S. Regt. formed September 1942.

On the 28th September 1942 an order was issued by G.H.Q., Middle East Forces for the expansion of "L" Detechment, 1st S.A.S. Brigade into the 1st S.S.S. Regiment. The new unit was to absorb the Special Boat Section and was to be trained "to attack objectives such as the following:-

(a) Landing grounds and aircraft thereon.
(b) Locomotives and rolling stock.
(c) Railway and road communications including bridges.
(d) Supply dumps and other administrative installations.
(e) Enemy tanks and other troops in leaguer.
(f) M.T. in leaguer or on the move in back areas.
(g) H.Qs. and important officers.
(h) Land line communications.
(i) Base ports and shipping."

The unit as a whole or in part might be required to operate anywhere in the Middle East Command, and in various types of country; and the order goes on to say, "This necessitates a difference in organisation between squadrons and troops destined to operate in certain areas of the Middle East."

Organization and control.

The regiment was also to be organised so as to be capable of approaching an objective either by land, by sea or from the air. It was to be a G.H.Q. unit, though a portion of it might come under another command for a particular period or operation.

At G.H.Q., control would be exercised by the D.M.O. under the special branch of the operations staff known as "G" (Raiding Forces). "It is this branch to whom all matters connected with organisation, development, operations and intelligence will be referred. No other contact is permitted with the General Staff at G.H.Q. or with C.-in-C. Mediterranean (including his staff) or H.Q., R.A.F. (M.E.), unless arranged by G (Raiding Forces). Contacts with "A" and "Q" Staff at G.H.Q. will be as for any other unit under command of G.H.Q. direct, and will be confined to normal unit administration unless otherwise arranged by G (R.F.)".

Orders were also given at the same time for the disbandment of the 1st S.S. Regiment.

H.Q. at Kabrit.

The H.Q. of the 1st S.A.S. Regiment were to be established at Kabrit (on the Canal about 15 miles North of Suez) and no form of H.Q. or office was to be maintained in Cairo. For the sake of security all correspondence with G.H.Q. was to be addressed on the inner envelope to "G.H.Q., M.E.F. (Personal for G.S.O.1 (R.F.))".

The provisional establishment of the regiment is given in the Appendix to this Section. As related in Section VI a number of Officers and O.Rs. were absorbed from the 1st S.S. Regiment.

September 1942.

A meeting was held on the 28th September 1942 at which Lieut. Col. D. Stirling S.A.S. and Lieut. Cols. Hackett and Richardson of the General Staff, M.E.F., were present, and notes were made on the employment of the 1st S.A.S. Regiment in conjunction with the forthcoming attack of the Eighth Army from El Alamein, which began on the night 23/24 October.

Plan.

They are summarized as follows:-

(a) In Phase I five land parties (A, B, C, D, E, F) and one "Folbot" party, were to be employed from the 9th October onwards. They were to attack railways, M.T., landing grounds and R.D.F. Stations, operating from L.G.125 (approximately at long 23°E, lat 30° 30' N) and from Fort Maddalena (24° 58' E, 30° 50' N), at which points they were to make supply dumps. "F" party would have the special task of attacking the enemy's L. of C. as far East as possible in the area Sidi Abd ur Rahman (Sheet El Daba 1/25,000. 867309) and then South along the Qattara track. The exact date was to be notified later.

The "Folbot" party would be landed to attack line communications and other targets in the area between El Daba and Sidi Abd ur Rahman.

(b) In Phase II, i.e. after that attack had begun, detachments were to attack M.T. and administrative units.

(c) In Phase III, when the enemy began to withdraw the S.A.S. regiment were to create as much alarm as possible in rear of the enemy, and so cause traffic congestion as a target for the R.A.F. They were also to lie up and wait for enemy aircraft withdrawing to landing grounds further back.

Orders for putting these plans into effect were issued to Lieut. Col. Stirling personally by G.H.Q., M.E. Forces on the 8th October 1942.

Orders to Command 1 S.A.S. Regt. October 1942. Phase I.

The outline plan during Phase I was as follows:-

1. Party "A" was to operate against the railway in the Tobruk area from the evening of the 10th October and subsequently against M.T.
2. Party "B" was to arrive at L.G.125 on the 10th October and operate in the same manner as Party "A", returning to L.G.125 by the 17th October.
3. Parties "C", "D" and "E" were to leave Kabrit in time to arrive at Kufra by the evening of the 14th October, travelling by L.G.125. The parties were then to operate as follows:-

Party "C" against the railway, Administrative installations and M.T. in the Mersa Matruh area, returning by the dump near Fort Maddalena and thence by L.G.125 to Kufra.

Party "D" against similar objectives in the area Bagush-Fuka (between El Daba and Mersa Matruh) from the evening of the 20th October, returning to Kufra by the same route as Party "C".

Party "E" was to protect the dump near Fort Maddalena and carry out reconnaissance.

4. Party "F" was to attack land line communications in an area to be indicated later.
5. A Folbot party supplied by the Royal Navy was to operate in the same way as Party "F" under arrangements to be made by Lieut. Col. Stirling with the Naval Staff.
6. One Squadron S.A.S. regiment less the parties detailed above, was to be ready to move from Kabrit by the 16th October against objectives ordered by the Eighth Army or arranged with them.
7. Parties engaged in operations or being held in readiness at Kabrit, were to come under command of Eighth Army at 0001 hrs. on the 16th October, and a liaison officer from the S.A.S. was to be at Army H.Q. from the afternoon of the 15th onwards.

Phase II.

In Phase II the parties were to be reorganised and to be prepared to operate against the enemy's L. of C. as ordered by the Eighth Army.

Phase III.

In Phase III objectives were to be attacked as arranged at the meeting on the 28th September, and would be selected by H.Q., Eighth Army, or if selected by the Commander S.A.S. to be communicated to them.

In case L.G.125 became unsuitable as a rendezvous, Qaret Khod (YA 1919) was to be used as the first alternative; and others were to be selected as necessary.

In addition the normal methods of intercommunication, pigeons were to be used by parties "C", "D", "E" and "F".

Eighth Army were to be responsible for administration after 1st S.A.S. Regiment came under its command.

Damage inflicted on the enemy October 1942.

A report on the damage inflicted on the enemy by patrols of the 1st S.A.S. Regiment during the last fortnight of October 1942, that is to say just before and during the early stages of the Eighth Army's attack from the El Alamein position, gives the following details:-

(a) On the night 14th/15th October, charges were laid on the railway in the Tobruk area.

(b) An attempt was made to blow up the railway near Sidi Barrani, but the patrol was chased by armoured cars and failed to achieve its object. The patrol Commander was killed when his jeep overturned in the Sand Sea. One O.R. was lost, but was recovered later, having walked 150 miles to the rendezvous at Bu Etla. (50 m. NNE of Jalo).

No date is given for this incident.

(c) About the 24th October the railway was blown up at Fuka, mined East of Piccadilly (611338) and blown up further to the West. A convoy was attacked on the Siwa track, and Italian prisoners were taken.

(d) A similar operation, not located, took place about the 26th October.

(e) On the night 29th/30th October, the railway line was blown up in nine places North (actually North-West) of Sidi Aziz (502388) over a stretch a quarter of a mile long.

(f) The main and looplines at Niswel el Suf[1] Station (615340) were blown up on the 31st October; and fifteen Italians and five Germans were captured. The same patrol also destroyed four machine guns, one W/T installation and three trucks.

---

1 The report gives this place the name "El Sup" but Niswel el Suf is probably meant.

This information, which was recorded early in November, was obtained by W/T and is described as not necessarily complete or correct in every detail. It implied, however, that the enemy's railway communications were interrupted at least once every three days between the 15th and 31st October.

S.A.S. Programme November 1942.

Early in November 1942, Lieut. Col. Stirling sent a proposed programme, for further co-operation with advance of the Eighth Army from El Alamein, to G(Ops) G.H.Q., Middle East. The substance of it was as follows:-

"A" Squadron ($1\frac{1}{2}$ Troops only) was operating from a base between Jarabub and Jalo, and would be available until the advance of the Eighth Army reached the line Derna – Mekili, or alternatively till the end of November. At the time the letter was written two patrols were about to attack (on 10th November) the landing grounds at Gambut and Jalo. Four patrols were on their way back to refit at the rendezvous. Three of them were to remain there until the return of the two patrols mentioned above. The fourth was to go as soon as possible to the escarpment overlooking the main road and landing grounds at Gazala, where it was to watch and record enemy traffic from the 13th to the 21st November; and it was equipped to attack a landing ground, or M.T. on the road. On the 13th the remaining five patrols were to go out for nine days to attack L.Gs. at Tmimi, Martuba and Derna if the number of aircraft on them warranted it.

One troop of "B" Squadron would attack targets from Sirte Westwards to (inclusive) Tripoli, after establishing a forward base.

17th November 1942.

On the 17th November the C.G.S. issued to Lieut. Col. Stirling an Operation Instruction (M.E.F. No. 150) which is summarized below:-

(a) The objective was to be the enemy's "transportation facilities" in the Tripoli area.

(b) Boundaries were on the East, (inclusive) Wadi Haraua[1] (lying between Easting grids 920 and 930), on the West a line North and South through Zuwara (447778).

(c) Maximum strength (estimated as two squadrons of about 80 men each) was to be used.

(d) The attack was to begin on the 30th November or as soon after as possible, and to continue till the 12th December, or longer if the available resources made it possible.

(e) Priority of targets was to be aircraft, M.T. Fuel, M.T., Administrative Installations (other than fuel).

1 This Wadi runs from South to North and its mouth is 42 miles East of Sirte.

If the Misurata-Tripoli railway was working it was to take precedence of all the above targets; but loaded ships would have the highest priority of all, and equipment for attacking shipping was therefore to be carried.

(f) The operation was to be based on Kufra with an advanced base at Marada.

(g) The code word for this operation was to be "Palmyra".

Postponement of Ops. 26th November 1942.

It appears from a note by M.O.3 dated 5th December that with the agreement of G.H.Q., the opening of this operation was postponed; and as a result of a conference on 26th November between Lieut. Col. Stirling, Lieut. Col. Hackett and G.S.O.1(O) at Eighth Army H.Q. the first attack was to be made not earlier than the 4th December and not later than the 6th.

1st December 1942.

On the 1st December, Lieut. Col. Stirling signalled that he had decided to delay his attack until the night of the 10th/11th December, but gave no reasons. A repetition of the message was asked for, but on the 5th December no reply had been received. This postponement raised administrative difficulties, though it had been calculated that enough supplies were available to allow the S.A.S. operation "to begin on the agreed date" (4th-6th December).

4th December 1942.

On the 14th[1] December Lieut. Col. Stirling sent a signal to G.H.Q. to the effect that owing to casualties to vehicles he could not operate West of Tripoli until later. The C.G.S. referred this message to Eighth Army and asked whether Libyan Arabs should be sent to carry out sabotage West of Tripoli and as far as Zuwara[2], or whether it should be left to Lieut. Col. Stirling.

S.A.S. Patrols Gheddahia-Misurata area, December 1942.

During the latter half of December 1942, three patrols of the 1st S.A.S. Regiment operated in the area Gheddahia (RX.49) – Misurata (RN.20). They were commanded respectively by Capt. Hon. A.P. Hore-Ruthven,[3(a)] Major Street,[3(b)] and Major Oldfield.[3(c)] A report on the operations of Capt. Hore-Ruthven's patrol (of "B" Squadron) was written about the

---

1. *Publisher's note:* This discrepancy in dates exists in the original text.
2   On the coast and about 60 miles West of Tripoli.
3   (a) Rifle Brigade (b) Devons (c) R.A.C.

6th January 1943 by Sergt. A.R. Seekings, who was at one time Lieut. Col. Stirling's driver.[1]

The patrol left Lieut. Col. Stirling in the Wadi Zazemet about 14 miles South-West of Bir el Faschia (RW.9857) on the 12th December, and moved up the Wadi to its junction (at El Faschia) with the Wadi Zem Zem. It turned along the Wadi Zem Zem for seven miles and then moved on an approximate bearing of 350°. On the 13th the patrol reached the Wadi Sofeggin about 18 miles North of Sedada (R.R.91), and got badly bogged. In the evening Major Street arrived and decided that both patrols should go back to Sedada on the 14th December. On the 15th the patrols arrived at Bir Gebira (R.R.73) in the Wadi El Merdum. A combined operation was planned, and at Bir Dufan (R.R.76) about 20 miles South-West of Misurata, opposition was met with. The patrols changed course due East and on reaching the road running North-East to Misurata they found twenty large trucks. These were engaged with fire at short range and then with bombs. Fourteen were left in flames and the other six were described as "probables". The road was mined and the telephone wire was cut. On the 16th December Capt. Hore-Ruthven's patrol lay up in the Wadi Durghis (R.R.86) during the day and moved out to a rendezvous in the evening. On the 17th it moved up the Wadi Merdum to the Beni Ulid track (R.R.24) and was unlucky in missing one of the enemy's tankers.

On the 18th a large encampment was located in the neighbourhood of Tauorga (R.S.36), East of the Buerat-Misurata road and about 25 miles South of Misurata, but it was too well guarded to make an attack possible.

Capt. Hore-Ruthven wounded 20th December 1942.

On the 19th the patrol moved to Wadi Henscir-el-Gabu (R.S.07), about eight miles West of Gioda on the Buerat-Misurata road. On the 20th one Jeep went out to the road about three miles South of Gioda, and the road and a neighbouring track were mined near the 35 Km stone. Six vehicles, including two tanks, were attacked and heavy fire was encountered. Capt. Hore-Ruthven was wounded in the right arm. Sergt. Seekings reports that he was carried to cover, but that it was found impossible to move him further. Two of the enemy's trucks were destroyed, but the party became separated and Seekings returned alone to the Jeep. He picked up two men on his way back to the "rendezvous" and a third came in at midday on the 21st December. That night the party moved to the Wadi Sasu (R.S.0986) about seven miles North of Henscir El-Gabu, and lay up during the 22nd. There were parties of the enemy in the neighbourhood and after an

---

1 These raids roused the enemy to activity which had an adverse effect on the road watch that was being maintained in the same area by the L.R.D.G., whose diary refers to it.

unsuccessful attempt on the 23rd to attack the road between Gioda and Crispi, a few miles further North, Sergt. Seekings decided on the 24th to move South to Bir Gebira. On arrival there on the 25th they found that the place had been visited by the enemy, and it was then decided to move on to Bir el Faschia in order to find Lieut. Col. Stirling and warn him of the proximity of the enemy. On the way they destroyed a German lorry, capturing two prisoners, whom they later released, and obtaining food and petrol. As they sighted a hostile patrol about four miles from Bir-el-Faschia and saw a plane land there, they went on to the South towards the Wadi Zazemet, and on the 27th, having for a time lost their bearings, arrived in the Wadi Zem-Zem. On the 28th they moved along the Wadi and when about a mile from Bir el Faschia saw a fire which they thought might have been lit by Lieut. Col. Stirling, but in fact had been lit by the enemy who were still there. On the 30th in the Wadi Zazemet they found "two Jeeps stripped, and several spare wheels," but there were no signs of Lieut. Col. Stirling, and by the 1st January 1943 they were running short of food. They remained in the Wadi during the 2nd and 3rd, when they finished their food, and on the 4th were woken by a German truck which proceeded to take away the two Jeeps, without however noticing Sergt. Seekings and his party who were less than 100 yards away.

Patrol rejoins Eighth Army 5th January 1943.

They managed to get away to the East and on the 5th January met the K.D.Gs. after picking up two Indian soldiers who had escaped from Tripoli on the 19th December.

A.G.S. memorandum dated 7th January 1943 states that Capt. Hore-Ruthven's patrol had arrived without its Commander (who was later reported to have been killed), but that the two other patrols (Street's and Oldfield's) were missing. Neither of these patrols had wireless and it was not known where they were.

Instructions for 1st S.A.S. Regt. January 1943.

In accordance with Eighth Army Operation Instruction No. 6 dated 3rd January 1943, the following Operations to be carried out by the 1st S.A.S. Regiment were summarized in a forecast made by G(Ops)5.M.E.F.

1. From 12th January three patrols were to operate from Mareth to (incl) Zouara. (long. 12° 5' E., lat. 32° 55' N.)
2. From 13th January three (French) patrols under Capt. Jordan were to operate Eastwards from (excl.) Zouara.
3. From 13th January two patrols were to be attached to the leading elements of the Eighth Army and were to enter Tripoli ahead of our forward troops to prevent the enemy from carrying out demolitions.

4.   From 13th January eight patrols under Lieut. Col. Stirling were to operate under command of First Army in the Area Gabes-Sousse.

Capture of Sirte and Tripoli.

The Eighth Army had occupied Sirte on Christmas Day 1942 and reached the Buerat Area on the 26th December. Tripoli was taken on the 23rd January.

The eventual operations did not correspond exactly with the forecast, and those referred to in sub-paras. 2 and 4 above will be dealt with first.

At the end of December 1942, a French Detachment under Lieut. Martin was already with the 1st S.A.S. Regiment and had been operating under Lieut. Col. Stirling's orders. Capitaine Jordan's detachment was in Egypt, and left for the front on the 30th December 1942. It consisted of nine French lorries, one ration lorry and one half-armoured truck, and was divided into four "groupes" commanded respectively by Capt. Jordan, and Lieuts. Harent, Legrand and Klein. Marching by the coast road through Derna, Jedabya and El Agheila it reached the Marble Arch on the 6th January 1943. The detachment was then met by a British Officer of the 1st S.A.S. Regiment who was to guide it to the Regiment's base in the Oasis of El Djofra, about 160 miles South-West of the Marble Arch.

On the 12th January they joined Lieut. Col. Stirling's Command at Bir-el-Gheddafia about 130 miles South by West of Misurata. (W.B.8784).

Attack on Gabes Sfax area, January 1943.

Lieut. Col. Stirling's plan for attacking the enemy's Communications was as follows. One force of 12 Jeeps, including three carrying Lieut. Martin's French patrol, was to operate under his own Command. Another force under Capitaine Jordan was to operate separately at first, but later to join Lieut. Col. Stirling near Ksar Rhilane (Y.D.9732).

Each vehicle of Stirling's force, which included four ration lorries, carried about 90 gallons of petrol, 60 lbs of explosive and 60 days rations. Every Jeep carried three M.Gs. as its normal armament, and one in four lorries carried wireless.

Both forces moved off on the 14th January. Lieut. Col. Stirling's crossed the Tunisian frontier North of Ghadames (long. 9° 30' E, lat. 30° 30' N). Movement was for the most part at night as the tracks were being used by Italians retiring under the pressure of General Leclerc's force operating from the South. On the 17th January French territory was reached at the frontier post of Bir Mechiguig (Y.P.8305) about 70 miles North-East of Ghadames. Continuing by the frontier track as far as Bir Zaar (Y.P.61.67) and making a detour South of Djenein, which was held by Italians, the force turned North over small sand dunes which reduced its speed to a few miles a day; and it arrived at Ksar Rhilane on the 20th. During the march the sky had been continuously patrolled by American "Lightnings". Jordan's force arrived on the 22nd January, and Lieut. Martin's detachment joined it on the 23rd. Both forces then moved North, Lieut. Col. Stirling's leading, towards the area lying between Gabes and Sekhira (T.U.2778, 30 miles North of Gabes) in which the attack was to be made.

In the evening of the 23rd Jordan's force, after crossing difficult country which was full of sand dunes, reached Bordj Saidane (P.Y.6012), 45 miles West by South of Gabes. At 2100 hours they moved on by the track leading E.N.E. to El Hama, about 30 miles away. In the main body there were Eight French trucks and one British one which carried a W.T. set. Two more trucks under Lieut. Martin acted as rearguard.

Jordan's Force encounters the enemy, 23rd January.

At midnight the head of the column was caught in the beam of a headlight, and it was realized that this came from the head of a hostile column moving towards Kebili. The six leading vehicles got past. The seventh was caught by the fire of armoured vehicles. Lieut. Martin's two rearguard trucks left the track, moved due South for five or six miles and then took cover in the Djebel Tebaga just South of Bordj Saidane. One vehicle was lost and as it was hit at a point near the explosives it was carrying, it was unlikely that its occupants (Sergts. Castagner and Vacclui, and Corpl. Vaillant) survived. Martin lay up during daylight on the 24th, and in the evening decided to slip across the track about three miles West of El Hamma. The going was very difficult but thanks to good navigation the detachment reached its area of operations between the Djebel Tebaga and Fatnassa (T.Z.0853).

Martin's attack on Gabes-Sfax road. 24th/25th Janaury.

During the 24th the following plan was made by Lieut. Martin:-

1. The detachment was to be divided into two parties.
    (a) Lieut. Martin with one O.R. (Louis) was to attack the Gabes-Sfax road with M.G. fire.
    (b) Sergt. Fauquet with two O.R. (Golder and Lecorre) was to go on foot to mine the road and blow up the railway line near it.
2. The two parties were to meet again at Fatnassa at 0300 hrs. on the 25th and then go to another rendezvous a little further away.

The two parties moved off at 2100 hrs. At 2300 hrs. the Demolition party under Sergt. Fauquet reached the railway on which they placed about fifteen charges. They then put about ten mines and several "booby traps" on the road. At midnight they withdrew. Four explosions were seen on the road, and all the demolition charges on the railway exploded. They were stopped on the road by a sentry who was killed; and they were forced to make a detour on the way back to Fatnassa as parties of the enemy gave chase and opened heavy fire. They reached the rendezvous at 0200 hrs., however, without loss. At 0300 hrs. Lieut. Martin returned, having destroyed a dozen lorries and killed a number of the enemy with machine gun fire. As there was no traffic on the road he had attacked isolated Italian camps. In spite of considerable opposition he achieved his object, and returned without dmage to himself, Pte. Louis or the truck. At 0500 hrs. on the 25th the detachment moved off on a bearing of 290° towards Djebel-ben-Kreir (TY.6774) where there was better shelter, and rested for the remainder of that day and during the 26th. A good many Tunisians came and asked for tea!

Martin's detachment surprised by the enemy 26th January.

It was intended to make another attack after dark on the 26th, but just before it was due to start the party was discovered by A.F.Vs. of the enemy which had been guided by local Arabs. There was just time to get away on foot into the nearest rocks, but no one was able to take anything with him except his revolver, his compass and a few bars of chocolate. They walked throughout the night in the direction of the First Army's lines, and during the 27th lay up in the Djebel Tala. In the evening they resumed their march and after some exhausting climbs came within sight of Sened (T.Y.4990) which was held by the Italians. By this time they were very hungry and cold, and were lucky in finding water in a ravine.

Martin reaches First Army at Zanouch, 28th January.

By infiltrating through the enemy's posts they succeeded in reaching the railway station at Zanouch (T.Y.3088) at 0400 hrs. on the 28th, and were then seized and disarmed by American sentries. This was understandable in view of the fact that German parachutists disguised as British soldiers had recently tried to capture the station. They spent the night in custody, but next morning were sent to Gafsa where they were recognized, fed and enabled to wash and shave. They were then interrogated at length by the Intelligence officers of three nations!

Lieut. Col. Stirling and Capt. Jordan reported missing, 29th January.

In the afternoon of the 29th January what was left of Jordan's party arrived. Jordan himself, Lieut. Klein and one O.R. were missing, and Lieut. Legrand was in Command. Information was also received that Lieut. Col. Stirling's party which had been operating further North and had taken cover in the Djebel Tebaga – Fatnassa area, had been killed or captured by German parachute Troops who were in fact searching for Martin's party. Only two British soldiers and the French Sergt. Taxis, who was acting as Arabic interpreter, had managed to escape.

2nd. Lieut. Michael Sadler S.A.S. who also escaped and arrived at Advanced H.Q., First Army on the 30th January 1943, made the following report on the capture of Lieut. Col. Stirling's party, which was telegraphed to Eighth Army:-

"Stirling's and McDermot's parties attacked by Germans reference Z.0755 24th Janaury. All Jeeps captured (and) all personnel except Sadler (himself), Cooper and Taxis ... Two men left at Ksar Rhilane 22nd January waiting to be picked up. Co-ordinates N.E. Africa purple grid."

It appears that Sergt. Cooper had been with Lieut. Col. Stirling since he left Eighth Army at the Marble Arch. 2nd Lieut. Sadler (who had at one time been a navigator in the L.R.D.G.) and the French Sergt. Taxis joined him later.

On the 22nd September 1942, G.H.Q., Middle East had issued an instruction (No. 144,) which defined the respective roles of the newly con-stituted 1st S.A.S. Regiment and of the Long Range Desert Group. The decision made was that the L.R.D.G. would normally carry out long range reconnaissance under orders from G.H.Q., M.E.F., and that the S.A.S. Regiment would attack the enemy's communications and aerodromes at shorter range; a task for which their training and equipment made them specially suitable. It was left open to the L.R.D.G. to make similar attacks at greater distances from the base, and the boundary between their activi-ties in this respect and those of the S.A.S. Regiment, was to be the 20th meridian of longitude East, that is to say a North and South line running approximately through Jedabya. But until the second week in December the L.R.D.G. was almost entirely employed in maintaining a watch on the enemy's movements along the Coast road, and taking a census of traffic. In the early part of December the advance of the Eighth Army led to activities by the 1st S.A.S. Regiment much further West, and to reactions on the part of the enemy which upset the L.R.D.G's. arrangements for road watching; and towards the end of December the watch was cancelled.

During most of the last quarter of 1942 the 1st S.A.S. Regiment was still relying on signallers of the L.R.D.G. for intercommunication; but they had become independent in regard to transport and navigation.

Captain Galloway's patrol on the Zouara-Ben Gardane road.

On the 11th January 1943 a patrol of "B" Squadron, 1st S.A.S. Regiment under Capt. R.E. Galloway,[1] which consisted of four officers and two O.Rs., was ordered to attack and delay enemy traffic on the coast road in the neighbourhood of Pisida (Libya 1:500,000 Q.P.19) between Zouara and Ben Gardane. It started from about WB.9883, in the Wadi Bei el Kebir about 90 miles South-West of Buerat el Hsun, at 1700 hrs. on the same day

1   Royal Scots.

with four Jeeps, one of which carried ammunitions and supplies and another spare petrol. The first objective was to be attacked on the 15th January and the operation was to coincide with the attack by the Eighth Army which culminated in the capture of Tripoli. On the 12th January, while crossing the Mizda-Tripoli road, the patrol was fired on by five tanks but a deviation was made to the South and no loss was incurred. At 1230 hrs. on the 13th the patrol halted at QZ.4929 and the Jeeps were refuelled. On the 14th it crossed the Sand Sea East of the road from Sinauen to Nalut (Long 10° E., lat. 31° N.).

On the 16th January the patrol encamped in the Wadi bei-umm-ez-Zuggar at YK.8933 and on the 17th near Djebel Sidi Toui (ZA.51. French N. Africa 1/500,000 N.1.32.S.E.) where the sound of M.T. on the move was heard.

Capt. Galloway decided to attack on the night 18th/19th January, with the object of mining the road and destroying the enemy's vehicles on the move or in "leaguer". The attack was to be made on the Coast road and neighbouring country between (incl) Zelten and (excl) Ben Gardane (11° 8' E., 33° 10' N). The area was divided into two sections divided by a North and South line running through Ras Ajdir, a point on the coast about half way between Zelten and Ben Gardane. Capt. Galloway was to attack with two Jeeps in the right Sector, Capt. J.C. O'Sullivan[1] with one Jeep on the left Sector.

After the operation both parties were to withdraw to Wadi umm-ez-Zuggar, using the roads as far as possible so as to avoid making tracks.

Capt. Galloway's party left the starting point at 1930 hrs. and moved on a bearing of 90° with the object of striking the road running North to El Assa (QP.0470) and thence East to Zouara at QP.0355 (Libya 1/500,000, Sheet 1, Pisida). The intention was to follow this road to about QP.2873 and then to go North across country to Zelten.

Going was bad which made navigation difficult and by midnight the party had not struck the road[2]. Capt. Galloway then altered course to the North-East and reached it at 0300 hrs. Traffic was almost continuous, which made mine laying impracticable. As the moon was about to set and it would be daylight some three hours later, Capt. Galloway decided to attack the enemy's M.T. by fire, and engaged a convoy of three tonners moving from West to East. Capt. Chevallier, who was acting as Gunner in Capt. Galloway's Jeep, opened fire at about 50 yards range on the leading vehicle. The Jeep was then turned to the left and two more trucks were engaged. All three were hit, and halted. Capt. Galloway then moved East

1 K.R.R.C.
2 It appears that the road in question was the Coast road from Zelten to Bir Gardane, though the report does not specifically say so.

along a track running parallel to the South of the road, followed by the other Jeep. Unfortunately both got bogged and had to be abandoned. The party got away on foot with their "escape kit", and marched South until dawn on the 19th January. They lay up for the day about QP.1878, and next night marched to a point about four miles South-East of El Assa. For the next few days they marched at night in a South-Easterly direction hoping to get in contact with the Eighth Army on its way to Tripoli. They had six water bottles and five emergency rations, and obtained some dates, cheese and milk from friendly Arabs. Capt. Chevallier was ill with fever and desert sores, which reduced the rate of progress to ten miles a night. On the 24th they were told by Arabs that Tripoli had been taken, and were entertained in their tents until the night 27th/28th, when they were guided to H.Q. 4th Light Armoured Brigade. They had covered some 500 miles during the raid, 80 miles on foot.

Capt. O'Sullivan's attack.

The attack in the left Sector was made by Capt. J.C. O'Sullivan, who had Pte. R. Higham with him, and they left the rendezvous at 1900 hrs. on the 18th January. They reached the road leading to Ben Gardane from the East about point QJ.8205 at 2340 hrs., having driven through a German "leaguer" about a quarter of a mile short of it. They found a stream of west-bound traffic on the road, which made mining impossible, and Capt. O'Sullivan decided to attack the leaguer. He halted just North of it and saw four heavy lorries, a staff car and three or four smaller vehicles. There were also number of bivouack tents. Capt. O'Sullivan put a "Lewis" bomb into one of two Scammell trucks, against which there was a large tent. As he and Pte. Higham, who were in their Jeep, approached the next lorry a German soldier appeared from behind it. O'Sullivan threw a bomb under the lorry, and as he drove away the German gave chase and was shot. It was not possible to plant the remaining bombs so the machine guns were used at such vehicles and tents as were visible in the moonlight. One vehicle, which appeared to be armoured, started to give chase but was fired at, started to glow and was brought to a halt. Continuing to fire their M.Gs. O'Sullivan and Higham drove away, and as they did so heard one of their bombs explode. They then returned to the Wadi-bei-umm-ez-Zuggar, arriving the next afternoon. There they remained until 22nd January, when Arabs came and told them Italians were approaching from the South, and were going to search the Wadi. They therefore moved on to the edge of the "Sand Sea" about QP.8895 and lay up for two days, but in the morning of the 24th they were chased away by Italian armoured cars. They crossed the road leading South from Nalut, about ten miles from that place, and were pursued for about four miles. They then moved Eastwards for about 120 miles, into the hills at Gaf Mazousa, not far South of Mizda (long. 13°E.

lat. 31° 25' N.). They were reduced to two gallons of petrol and, having no wireless, decided to lie up and find out from the local Arabs where the Eighth Army was. No Arabs appeared and on the 31st January they decided to make for Mizda (about 20 miles to the North) and try to steal some petrol. After going some five miles they ran out of fuel and started to walk. They then met some Arabs who told that Mizda had been occupied by the French. Shortly afterwards they met a L.R.D.G. patrol which gave them some petrol, and they arrived at a Bde H.Q. of the Eighth Army on the 1st February.

Attack on Capt. Murphy's patrol, 17th January 1943.

Another patrol of eleven O.Rs. of "B" Squadron of the 1st S.A.S. Regiment, Commanded by Capt. Murphy,[1] was attacked by the enemy on the 17th January near Nalut.

It entered the area West of that place on the night of 16th/17th January and found "a network of military roads" (? tracks) in square ZF.22. An attempt was made to locate the road to Dehibat, which lay some 20 miles to the North-West, but without success; and at 0300 hrs. on the 17th the patrol halted for some three hours. It then moved South, and at 0930 hrs. halted in a Wadi at ZF.2514 or thereabouts. Some of the men slept while others carried out repairs, a guard having been mounted on the sides of the Wadi. At midday the guard was withdrawn and preparations were made to move off. At 1220 hrs. heavy fire was opened on the patrol from the West side of the Wadi, the enemy using rifles, M.Gs. and mortars. In the words of Sergt. A.E. Badger, R.A., who reported the incident, "Captain Murphy ran from Jeeep to Jeep endeavouring to get the crews organized and the Jeeps started". Sergt. Badger himself was able to start his engine, and while it was warming up opened fire with a Vickers "K" M.G. at the enemy, who were by this time firing from both sides of the Wadi. One other Jeep was firing, but another was burning. After he had fired three magazines Sergt. Badger's machine gun jammed and he decided to try and get his Jeep out of the Wadi to the North, shouting to Pte. A. Hearne (D.C.L.I.) who had been slightly wounded, and Pte. R. Guard (Liverpool Scottish) to come with him. In spite of getting ditched soon after they started they contrived to get away, noticing that all fire had ceased in the Wadi, and reached a point about six miles away to the South-East at about 1530 hrs. There they waited until 0830 hrs. next day (18) but no one else turned up. Sergt. Badger adds that at the moment of leaving the Wadi they saw Capt. Murphy unhurt and trying to start a Jeep, Pte. Hearn D.C.L.I)[2], Pte. M. Nixon (Royal Scots) wounded, Pte. E.

---

1   Royal Northumberland Fusiliers.
2   It is not clear whether Pte. Hearne escaped or not.

Robinson, R.A.S.C. under cover, and Pte. L. Buxton, R.A. running for cover. Owing to the conformation of the ground no other men were visible.

Sergt. Badger's report, written on return to his Squadron, is dated the 14th February 1943.

Appendix to Section VIII

Provisional Establishment – 1st S.A.S. Regiment

**Appendix "A" to G.H.Q., M.E.F. CRME/1679/G(O)
dated 28th Sept 1942.**

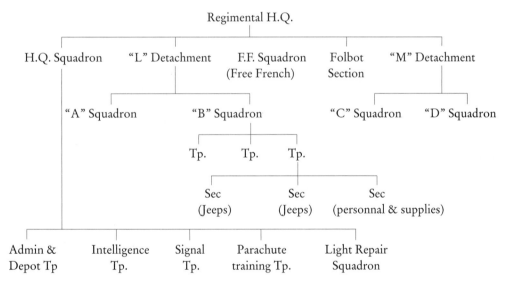

At the end of 1942 a Greek Squadron was added to the regiment.

LIST OF BRITISH OFFICERS OF 1ST S.A.S. REGIMENT IN DECEMBER 1942.

Lieut. Col.	A.D. Stirling	Scots Gds.
Major	P.C. Oldfield	R.A.C.
	R.W. Lea	R.A. (from 1st S.S.)
	R.B. Mayne	R.U.R.
	H.R. Pouch	Essex Regt.
	V.W. Street	Devons
Capt.	A.E. Bonham-Carter	R.N.F.
	W. Fraser	Gordons
	E.L.W. Francis	Gen. List.
	P.M. Gunn	R.A.M.C.
	Hon. A.H.P. Hore-Ruthven	R.B.
	S.L.E. Hastings	Scots Guards
	A.D. Hamilton	Scots Guards
	P.S. Morris-Keating	R.B.
	J.C. O'Sullivan	K.R.R.C.
	M.J. Pleydell	R.A.M.C.
Lieut.	G.W. Alston	R.A. (from 1st S.S.)
	W.G. Austin	R.A.C.
	D.G. Barnby	E. Yorks
	B.E. Dillon	R. Norfolk
	A.E. Galloway	R. Scots
	A.D.V. Hough	R.B.
	D.S. Kennedy [1]	R.A.
	H.F.E. Leljevahl	R.A.S.C.
	D.C.D. McD. Mather	Welsh Gds.
	P.J. Moloney	R. Warwicks
	E. MacDonald	W. Yorks
	W.H.C. McDermott	R.A.
	J.A. Marsh	D.C.L.I.
	J. McKinlay	Camerons
	H.W. Poat	K.O.S.B.
(QM)	W.C.J. Rees	Gen. List
	S.B. Skyrme	R. Sussex
	B.P. Schott	Gen. List (from 1st S.S.)
	A.J. Scratchley	R.A.C.
	J.H. Vaughan	R.W.R.
	P.M. Wand-Tetley	Wiltshires (from 1st S.S.)
2/Lieut.	D.W.S.A. Berneville-Claye	W. Yorks
	J.M.K. Bell	K.O.S.B.
	K. Lepine	S. Staffs
	F.H.R. Maclean	Camerons
	A.M. Wilson	Gordons
	J.W. Wiseman	D.C.L.I.

1   Lieut. Kennedy was killed in November 1942.

Officers attached from other Corps.

Major	V.W. Barlow	K.S.L.I.	21.9.42.
	A.W. Knowles	R.E.	9.11.42. (from 1st S.S.)
	Thesiger	Gen. List	21.9.42.
	P.J.H. Weir	Kings Own	20.12.42.
Capt.	H.G. Chevalier	Gen. List	21.11.42. (from 1st S.S.)
	P. Warr	E. Surreys	2.11.42. (from 1st S.S.)
Lieut.	T.C.D. Russell	Scots Gds.	9.12.42. (from 1st S.S.)
	J.E. Tonkin	R.N.F.	13.12.42.
	R.N. Gutteridge, M.C.	R.A.	20.12.42.
	Brooke-Johnson	Kings Own	20.12.42.
	R. Rowe	Scots Gds.	21.12.42.
	P. Davis	Queens	21.12.42.
Capt.	W. Brinkworth	Gen. List	20.12.42.

GABES AREA (Southern Tunisia) 1 : 1M

(GSGS 2465 NI-32 and pt of NJ-32)

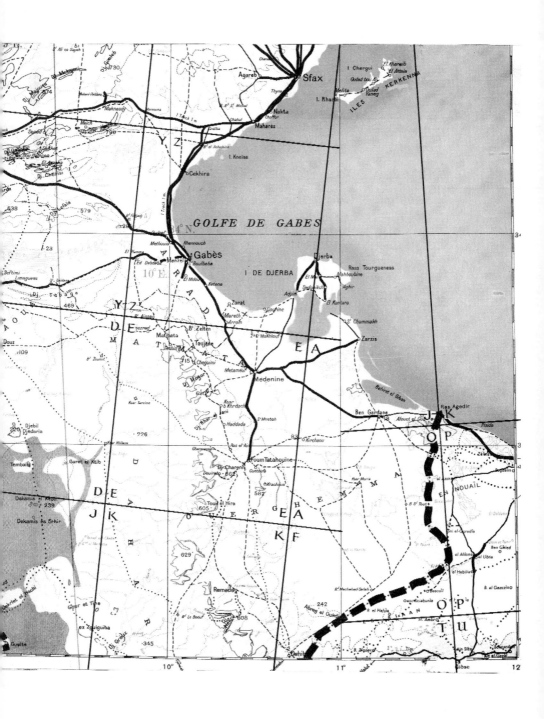

Section IX

No.1 Commando in Algeria and Tunisia (Map reference to "French N. Africa 1/500,000, Sheets Tunis, Constantine, Algiers, unless otherwise stated).

No. 1 Commando consisting of six British and four American troops under Lieut. Col. T.H. Trevor (Welch Regiment), left England at the end of October 1942. H.Q. and the right half of the Commando sailed in the S.S. Otranto, the left half under Major K.R.S. Trevor (Cheshire Regiment), in the U.S.S. Leedstown.

Right half Commando's landing in Algeria, 8th November 1942.

H.Q. and the right half Commando landed at Villa des Dunes in the early morning of the 8th November, without encoountering opposition; and Lieut. Col. Trevor received the formal surrender of Fort Sidi Ferruch from the French Commander, General Mast, who gave our troops a friendly reception. H.Q. and three troops then moved to Blida airport, leaving the other two troops at the fort. In the neighbourhood of Blida, however, the attitude of the French was threatening, and the Commando "stood to" in the evening of the 8th November. During the night 8th/9th, one company of the Lancashire Fusiliers and two Bren carriers arrived as reinforcements. The German Armistice Commission, six German officers and nineteen O.Rs., and the German Minister with his family, were held in custody at the Sidi Ferruch Fort. The Commando continued to "stand to" during the 9th and 10th, in the area of the Airport hospital; and at 2200 hrs. on the 9th an American field battery arrived and took up a position covering the airport.

Surrender of Blida, 9th November 1942.

On the 10th November it seemed likely that the aerodrome would have to be attacked, and Commando H.Q. joined H.Q. Lancashire Fusiliers about three quarters of a mile away. At 1500 hrs. however the Mayor and Council of Blida formally capitulated to Lieut. Col. Trevor, and later in the afternoon the Commando left Blida and moved by M.T. to the airfield at Maison Blanche, having been relieved by the 135th Brigade U.S.

Army.[1] In the evening of the 10th the airfield at Maison Blanche was bombed by the enemy.

Left half Commando lands at Ain Taya, 8th November.

The left half of the Commando landed successfully on the 8th November, in heavy surf, at Ain Taya (938146 Sheet 21. Algeria), and moved off along the road to La Perouse (8915). After efforts to effect a peaceful entry had failed, the Commando attacked the Batterie de Lazarette, which had opened fire seawards, and also the neighbouring Fort d'Estrées. The attacks were not successful and after a further attempt to parley the troops withdrew. At 1100 hrs. the French garrisons were bombarded from the sea, and again from the sea and air at 1430 hrs. At 1600 hrs. three troops of the Commando again attacked the Batterie de Lazarette, and it surrendered at 1700 hrs. Our casualties were two O.Rs. killed, and one officer and six O.Rs. wounded. A projected attack on Fort d'Estrées was abandoned.

Occupation of Fort de l'Eau, 9th November 1942.

Early on the 9th November, Fort de l'Eau was occupied without opposition, but at 0730 hrs. on the 10th, warning was received that negotiations with the French were likely to end in the reopening of hostilities, and the Commando took up positions accordingly in the neighbourhood of La Perouse. In the afternoon however hostilities ceased; H.Q. with the right half Commando arrived from Blida at 0200 hrs. on the 11th, and on the 13th the whole unit moved to Fort de l'Eau.

Move to Bone, 17th November 1942.

On the 17th the Commando marched to Algiers, and moved thence by train to Bone, where on the 19th, it took up a defensive position and during the next few days was attacked daily from the air. On the 26th the Commando embarked in L.C.As., reached Tabarka on the 27th and on the 30th re-embarked in L.C.As. for operations in the Bizerta area, in conjunction with the 36th (British) Infantry Brigade.

Operation near Bizerta, 1st December 1942.

The Commando's task was to turn the enemy's right flank by landing from the sea in the area D.4805 and to capture the road junctions at J.5094 and 5796 (Ref. Sheet No. 2. 1/200,000) on the highway from Cap Serrat to Bizerta. It was then to deny the road to the enemy, destroy transport and delay enemy forces withdrawing before the 36th Infantry Brigade. It was to rejoin the 36th Infantry Brigade at the road junction at J.5094 about seven miles South of the landing beach.

---

1 See Appendix I, para. 1.

The operation as a whole was not successful as the 36th Brigade, to which No. 6 Commando was also attached, were unable to overcome the enemy's opposition astride the Bone – Bizerta main road near Djebel Azzag ("Green Hill"), about J.3777. This area, in which much fighting took place, is from twelve to fifteen miles South-West of point 5904, the nearer of the two road junctions which were the objectives of No. 1 Commando.

The Commando landed without opposition in the early morning of the 1st December, reached the road junction at J.5904 and held it until the 3rd December, when it was attacked from the West by a German armoured column consisting of three armoured cars, two tanks and three lorry loads of infantry, and had to fall back. The road junction at J.5796 was held throughout the 1st December; and though an attack by A.F.Vs. and infantry forced a withdrawal northward into the hills, it was kept under fire during part of the next day. One troop advanced to the aerodrome of Sidi Ahmed (D.6701) about four miles from Bizerta, and established the fact that the enemy was using as his L. of C. the road which runs South from point D.6502, along the East bank of the Garaet Achkel lake, and thence to Mateur; but not the road along the northern shore of the lake.

The various troops of the Commando which had been operating independently, were withdrawn by road to Cap Serrat on the 3rd December without interference, the last troops arriving on the 5th.

The report on the operation draws attention to the unreliability of the local Arabs, and to the fact that Germans were disguised as Arabs, Italians or Frenchmen and in more than one case in British uniform. A good deal of useful information was obtained, particularly about the aerodrome at Sidi Ahmed.

The landing was "wet", that is to say most men were wading up to their waists or higher; and the report includes also the following remark, which is worthy of record, "It is one of the first and fundamental principles of all Combined Operations that material to be landed on an open beach should be both buoyant and waterproof. On this occasion there were certain objects to which this could not apply – the eight donkeys, and the cinema apparatus brought by a Sergeant of the Army Film Unit. The latter was immediately submerged and rendered useless, but five of the donkeys managed to swim ashore. Only two of these however were in any condition to be made use of; and as it turned out they were useless, for the terrain proved to be unsuitable for pack animals."

Casualties were heavy. The killed and missing included four officers and fifty-six O.Rs. from the British troops, and two officers and seventy-two O.Rs. from the American troops. Four British O.Rs. were wounded and brought back.

From the 6th to the 25th December 1942, the enemy made a series of attacks on Medjez-el-Bab (J.5834) in the Medjerda valley, but in spite of fierce fighting there and on the Jebel Ahmera (J.6144), better known as "Long Stop Hill", he did not make much progress. During this period No. 1 Commando was not seriously engaged.

Reorganization.

After the Bizerta operation the Commando was reorganized into six troops; and the Americans attached to it were given the alternative of volunteering for service, or of remaining at Tabarka to do guards and other duties. Sixty-nine men volunteered, and were distributed to the six new troops. Three troops had American Sections and seven surplus Americans were included in two other troops. Lieuts. Skuse and Garner-Jones were promoted Troop Commanders vice Capts. Morgan and Bradford, who had been killed, but the troops continued to bear the names of the dead officers.

On the 11th December 1942 the Commando left Tabarka, and during the next eight or nine weeks was employed in a defensive role in the areas of Djebel Abiod (J.082650), Beja (J.3346), Sedjenane (J.2276) and El Alouana (J.3274).

Craven's patrol ambushed, 16th January 1943.

On the 16th January a party of Craven's patrol was ambushed at J.194929 near Cap Serrat. Capt. Craven and two men were taken prisoner, and two men were killed. A good deal of information about the enemy's positions East of Cap Serrat was reported by Lieut. Scaramanga, who succeeded Capt. Craven in command of the Troop.

From the 18th to the 21st January the enemy attacked again at Bou Arada and in the Oued Kebir and Ouesseltia valleys South of Medjez-el-Bab, but without much success.

Operation "Crumpet" near Green Hill, 28th January 1943.

On the 24th January 1943, Davidson's Troop left to take part in an operation known as "Crumpet". It was to be undertaken by the 139th Infantry Brigade against the Djebel Azzag ("Green Hill") about J.3777, which was occupied by the enemy and blocked the road to Bizerta. The intention is described in the Operation Order as "to harass enemy positions and patrols by simultaneous infantry and artillery engagements, to the left flank and rear of 'Bald Hill'"; an area which includes Jefna Station and ground to the South of it.

Patrolling was carried out and on the 28th January the Troop, supported by Artillery, had a successful skirmish with Germans in Arab dress on the slope of Djebel el Mazdar (J.387715); but no other incident occurred.

On the 31st the Commando was relieved by the 2/5th Leicesters and concentrated at Sedjenane. Orders were at the same time received that all Americans in it were to return to the U.S. Army.

Operation "Scorch", 9th February 1943.

The first week of February was uneventful, but on the 7th the C.O. had a conference on a projected operation whose code name was "Scorch". In the report on it the intention of this operation was defined as follows:- "No. 1 Commando attached to 139 Infantry Brigade to attack Italian position on the North flank of the brigade forward position from (exclusive) Oued Sedjenane[1] to (inclusive) the Coast, and to clear this area of all hostile Arabs by burning their villages and removing their livestock".

Objects.

The "objects" were described in detail as being:-

1. "To ambush and destroy enemy transport and personnel on the road running N.E. from J.3386" (a cart track running along the bed of the Wadi Sedjenane).
2. "To attack and destroy Italian positions in the area Dir en Nsara J.3399" (close to the coast, and roughly nine miles East by North from Cap Serrat).
3. "To create diversions by burning the following Arab villages:-

Sidi el Moudjed	3596
Sidi ben Habbes	3292
Sidi Rherib	3392."

   The two last named villages are close to the Cap Serrat-Bizerta road, and about 13 miles North by East of Sedjenane; Sidi el Moudjed is three miles nearer to the coast.
4. "To attack Italian posts at Maison Forestière J.3996[2] and mine road East of this point."

Method.

The Commando was divided into two detchments: (a) the Sea force, Bradford's and Morgan's Troops under Major K.R.S. Trevor; (b) the Land Force, H.Q., four Troops (Scaramanga's, Davidson's, Davies' and Pollitt's) and a 3" mortar section, under Lieut. Col. Trevor.

The Sea Force was to march to Cap Serrat and there embark in L.C.As.

---

1 The Oued (i.e. Wadi) Sedjenane crosses the road from Sedjenane to Cap Serrat at about J.2383, four miles North of Sedjenane, and thence runs E.N.E. into the Garaet Achkel lake, 20 miles away. The part of it referred to as the Commandos southern boundary was probably about J.3096, some eight miles North-East of Sedjenane.
2 This "Maison Forestière", one of several forest officers' huts in the neighbourhood, is on the Bizerta road 13 miles East of Cap Serrat.

It was to land about point D.383006 some ten miles further East, and then attack enemy positions in the Dir en Nsara area. The Land Force was to march to the road junction at J.229890, then East along the road.

The "Sea Force" failed to embark owing to the breakdown of one L.C.A. and the stranding of another and it had to retire Southwards. It rejoined the rest of the Commando on the 10th February, in the area about J.285902. The Land Force also failed to achieve much, though a few villages were burnt; and Davidson's troop lost a number of men owing to the explosion of a "booby trap" about point 356927.

From the 13th to 22nd February the Commando occupied defensive positions in the Beja-Sedjenane area.

On the 20th February Davies' Troop was sent out to obtain identifications in the hilly country South of the Mateur-Sedjenane road near Sidi Ahmor (J.360725). Several villages were searched which were not occupied by the enemy, but the Arabs in them were unfriendly.

Rommel's counter attack in Tebessa area, 14th February 1943.

While these minor operations were taking place in the North, Rommel on the 14th February, attacked the Americans in the area of Tebessa in Central Tunisia; but after an initial success failed to achieve his object of widening the corridor connecting his own army with that of General von Arnim. On the 23rd February he withdrew, and the important Kasserine Pass was recovered by the Allies.

Arnim attacks in the North, 26th February 1943.

On the 26th Arnim's Army made a series of attacks. Four of them were in the Northern sectors of the Allied position in which No. 1 Commando was operating, as follows:-

1. Westward along the coast road towards Cap Serrat.
2. Southwards along the track from Kef Silia (in the Wadi Sedjenane) to Sedjenane.
3. Westward along the road from Mateur to Jefna (J.4676) and Sedjenane.
4. South-Westwards along the track from Mateur towards Sidi Nair (J.410595) and Beja.

Action of Morgan's Troop, 23rd February 1943.

On the 23rd February Morgan's Troop had been attacked by a hostile patrol near Ela Aouana Station (J.3275). The enemy lost one officer and six O.Rs. killed, several of them were wounded, and two prisoners with a good deal of equipment remained in our hands.

On the 26th Pte. Ellerman and Fusilier Oliver of the Intelligence Section who had been sent out on the 22nd to locate hostile gun positions in the area J.3981 (North of Djebel Azzag) returned to Headquarters. Their report and sketch showed two gun positions and the location of strong points, weapon pits and trip wire. A certain amount of troop movement was also reported.

Successful German attack, 26th February.

At 1630 hrs. on the same day 139 Bde. H.Q. gave information that the enemy had broken through to Bordj des Monopoles, the local French Headquarters on the road from Sedjenane to Cap Serrat; and two troops (Davidson's and Bradford's) took up positions on the left flank of the Durham Light Infntry, from the track junction at 181786 to the high ground at 196778, about five miles North of Sedjenane Station.

At 0830 hrs. on the 27th Davidson's Troop moved South-East towards the Djebel el Guerba (2280). They attacked at 1230 and reached a position at about 222806, where they were joined by about thirty men of the Durham Light Infantry. By 1500 hrs. the enemy were driven off the East side of the Djebel el Guerba, with a loss to the troop of three killed and three wounded. At 1900 hrs. Davidson's Troop was relieved by Bradford's, and evacuated its wounded. On the 28th the Commando acted as rear guard during the withdrawal from Green Hill and took up a position about Pt. 231 (2577) with H.Q. at 2477, about three miles East of Sedjenane Station.

Morgan's and Davies' Troops in action 2nd March to cover withdrawal.

On the 2nd March four troops of the Commando were engaged by the enemy all day. Morgan's Troop took six prisoners, but Davies' Troop lost a sub-section who were ambushed and were believed to be prisoners. Having covered the withdrawal of all the forward troops, the Commando itself retired on the Mine area (1974), less Davidson's Troop, which was attached to the 6th Battalion Lincolnshire Regiment for the defence of Sedjenane.

On the 3rd the Commando (less Davidson's Troop) took up positions to defend the mine area, but at midday the enemy attacked and eventually it was obliged to withdraw to the area South of the mine. At the same time the 6th Lincolns, with Davidson's Troop, withdrew to Tamera (J.1275) from Sedjenane, which was occupied by the enemy at about 1600 hrs.

Commando withdrawn to Tamera and reorganized, 4th March 1943.

At 1700 hrs. on the 4th March the main body of the Commando withdrew to Tamera, and took up a defensive position there at 1000 hrs. on the 5th. The unit was then temporarily reorganized into three Groups; No. 1 Group consisted of Scaramanga's and Bradford's Troops, No. 2 of

Morgan's and Davidson's Troops and No. 3 of Davies' and Pollit's Troops.[1]

Davidson wounded 14th March 1943.

On the 7th March the Commando moved to the right flank of the Sector about Sidi es Siah (J.1167). They occupied this position without incident until the 14th when Davidson's Troop, which was patrolling in the area about J.1468, engaged the enemy and suffered casualties including their Commander who was seriously wounded.

At 2130 hrs. on the 15th three Troops (Scaramanga's, Davidson's and Pollitt's) under Major Trevor were sent to reinforce "B" Company of the 2/5 Bn. Leicestershire Regiment about point 1177, West of Tamera; and at 1830 hrs. next day they moved North to assist the French about Djebel El Azib (110785).

French attacked 17th March 1943.

Late on the 16th the remainder of the Commando was relieved at Sidi el Siah by the 1/6 Durham Light Infantry, and moved to the "Maison Forestière" at 0992 where they arrived at 1115 hrs. on the 17th March. Soon afterwards the enemy attacked in considerable force and the French forward positions were overrun.

At 1600 hrs. on the 17th, Major Trevor's detachment was also involved in fighting, alongside the 2/5 Leicesters and the French, in the area 100775. The enemy continued to make progress and Major Trevor received orders to rejoin Commando H.Q. at Kef el Jemman (0777). At 1645 hrs. the Germans attacked Kef el Jemman, with the result that Scaramanga's and Morgan's Troops were forced off the hill, and fell back on the Foresters' hut at 049706 half an hour later. By 2115 hrs. the whole Commando, less Capt. Pollitt and one Section of his troop, had concentrated, and at 2215 hrs. they arrived at the French casualty clearing station at 045746, about six miles N.N.W. of Djebel Abiod.

Commando withdrawn to Tabarka and again reorganized, 18th March 1943.

At 0300 hrs. on the 18th, Commando H.Q. and five troops moved East to the road junction at 095727, and took up defensive positions which they held until 1430 hrs. They were then withdrawn to Pt. 044646 where they were embussed, and arrived at Tabarka at 2130 hrs.[2] There they remained until the 24th March and the Groups were again reorganized as follows:-

No. 1 Group   (Capt. Garner-Jones) Scaramanga's and Morgan's Troops.

1 See Appendix I, para. 2.
2 See Appendix I, para. 3.

No. 2 Group   (Capt. Davies) Bradford's and Davies' Troops.
No. 3 Group   (Capt. Pollitt) Davidson's and Pollitt's Troops.

For administrative purposes, however, the Commando retained the former six troop organization.

British position 23rd March 1943.

On the 23rd March our position North of Djebel Abiod had its forward defended localities along the line of the Oued bou Zenna, which runs roughly East and West from J.2563 to J.0869 (about two miles North of Djebel Abiod), and joins the Oued el Glia between the road and railway to Bizerta. Thence they extended to the sea. The enemy in the area of Djebel Abiod held localities from East to West as follows:-

Djebel Tabouna J. 2364, Djebel Bou Rdim (1569), Djebel Choucha (1870), high ground about Sidi bou Della (0668), and thence to the West and North-West.

British attack 28th March 1943.

The 46th Division, to which No. 1 Commando was attched, counter attacked this position in the early hours of the 28th March, the Commando's objective being the Djebel Choucha (J.1870).

The tasks allotted to the three groups of the Commando were as shown below:-

No. 1	to capture and hold Point 515 (188701).
No. 2	to capture and hold high ground in the area 193703.
No. 3	to capture and hold the track in the area 183703, and to provide a reserve for either of the other groups.

During the night 26th/27th March the Commando was brought from Tabarka by M.T. to the road and track junction at J.1458 (about six miles South-East of Djebel Abiod), whence it moved on to the assembly position at the mine of Sidi Ahmed (J.1565), arriving there at 0520 hrs. on the 27th March. At 2230 hrs. that night the Commando, which was under Command of the 36th Infantry Brigade, moved to its starting line about 166671. This had been taped by the 5th Bn. The Buffs, who also provided guides. The 46th Division's attack was in three phases – In the first phase the 36th Infantry Brigade were to capture Djebel bou Rdim (1569), about two miles South-West of the Commando's objective at Djebel Choucha. In the second phase the 36th Brigade's objective was Kef Toungache (1670) just West of Djebel Choucha, the attack being made by the 5th Buffs. Further left the 138th Bde. in the third phase, was to capture Djebel el Hamria immediately North of Djebel Choucha. To the South the enemy about Djebel Tebouna were to be contained by the action of the 5th Hampshires.

Commandos attack, 28th March 1943.

The Commando crossed its starting line at 0030 hrs. on the 28th March and reached its objective without opposition. At 0700 hrs. Nos. 1 and 2 Groups were disposed for defence, No. 3 Group being in reserve with Commando H.Q. at Point 182703.

Later in the day there was some contact with the enemy and six prisoners were taken. In the afternoon Capt. Davies and five O.Rs. were wounded and one O.R. was killed, by gunfire alleged to be British. Early on the 29th Point 436 (J.2070) on the Commando's right was occupied by "Goums" of the French native army, who subsequently fell back from it. Later in the day artillery fire was directed by No. 2 Group on to enemy transport advancing along a track to the North of Djebel Choucha. No further incident occurred until midday on the 30th when an enemy column of about a battalion strength moving South-West from about Point 218685 (half way between Djebel Choucha and Djebel Tabouna) was effectively engaged by our artillery.

Enemy retires 31st March and Commando is relieved.

The enemy continued his attempts to advance on the Commando's right flank where the ground was held by African troops, but with the aid of the artillery the ground was held throughout the 30th March, and at midday on the 31st a patrol of Goums found that the enemy had retired and had abandoned a great deal of equipment, which perhaps indicated that his withdrawal had been hasty.

At 1400 hrs. on the 1st April the Commando was relieved and arrived by M.T. at Tabarka at 2100 hrs. that night.

Commando embarks for England, 24th April 1943.

No. 1 Commando took no further part in active operations in North Africa. On the 4th April they, with No. 6 Commando were visited, at Souk-el-Arba, and congratulated by Lieut. General C.W. Allfrey, Commanding V Corps. Later that day they entrained for Algiers, and for about three weeks were quartered in its neighbourhood. They were then embarked on the 24th April and reached Liverpool on the 2nd May.

In a letter to Lieut. Col. Trevor dated 15th April 1943, General Eisenhower wrote:-

"It is a real pleasure to me to express to you and your gallant men commendation for a job well done. You have exemplified those rugged self-reliant qualities which the entire world associates with the very name 'Commando'."

Appendix I

1. The following is an extract from a letter written on the 30th December 1942 by Major General Charles W. Ryder of the U.S. Army Commanding the "Eastern Assault Force" during the landing in Algeria to the Commander in Chief, Allied Forces:-

> "The tasks assigned to the I Commando (British) ... were performed in such a satisfactory manner as to merit special mention.
>
> Arriving on his scheduled beach at the exact hour prescribed for the landing of his Command, Lieut. Col. Trevor promptly received the surrender of the vital coast defences at Port Sidi Ferruch.
>
> Later acting with promptness and vigour on the recommendation of a high ranking French Military Officer, Lieut. Col. Trevor took over the trucks made available to him by the French at Fort Sidi Ferruch, and rushed a strong detachment of the I Commando to the airfield at Blida. This detachment secured and held the important landing field of Blida, thus greatly facilitating our air operations in the vicinity of Algiers".

2. Extract from 46 Div. daily news summary dated 5th March 1943:-

> "2/5 Foresters, 16 D.L.I. and 6 Lincolns and I Commando yesterday fought wonderfully well. The battalions were constantly being attacked. Attempts to surround them were constantly being made. Nevertheless they continued to counter-attack over and over again throughout the day ... the enemy is thought to have suffered heavy losses."

3. Extract from 46 Div. daily news summary dated 19th March 1943.

> "The withdrawal (in the Tamera area) was successfully covered by 1 Para Bn. and I Commando. No frontal attack developed during the day, although two attacks were made on the flanks of our new positions."

Appendix II

The following immediate awards were made to officers and men of No. 1 Commando during their operations in North Africa.

February	1943	Capt. Scaramanga	M.C.
April	1943	Capt. Davidson	M.C.
		Capt. D.H. Cowan	M.C.
February	1943	L/Cpl. Stewart	M.M.
April	1943	2614133 L/Cpl. A. Baker	D.C.M.
		14251854 Cpl. J. Beattie	M.M.
		6096409 L/Cpl. J. Scantlebury	M.M.
		4032283 Pte. J. Williams	M.M.

Section X

No.6 Commando in Algeria and Tunisia (Map Reference to "French N. Africa 1/500,000, Sheets Tunis, Constantine, Algiers.)

No. 6 Commando under Command of Lieut. Col. I.F. MacAlpine (Black Watch) sailed for North Africa in H.M.T. "Awatea" on the 26th October 1942. It formed part of the Anglo-American force under the Supreme Command of General Eisenhower of the U.S. Army, which was landed in Algeria to operate against Tunis from the West and included the First British Army under Lieut. General K. Anderson. The landing began on the night 7th/8th November and on the 7th all ranks were warned that they were not to fire on French Troops unless the latter were actively hostile.

Four of the Commando's ten Troops (Nos. 7, 8, 9 and 10) were American.

General situation, November 1942.

The general sequence of events in N. Africa from the 8th to 30th November was as follows.

Rommel's army was retreating from Egypt, which was finally cleared of the enemy on the 12th November, as a result of the battle of El-Alamein. German and Italian reinforcements were being sent from Italy to General Von Arnim's Army in Tunisia by carrier planes and small vessels. They were steadily increasing in strength, but by the 13th November had no more than covering troops to hold the Tunis-Bizerta area. On that day the leading troops of the First Army were in touch with the enemy on the road to Tebourba.

First Army Plan for attack on Tunis.

General Anderson's objective was the Tunis-Bizerta area and in the Northern Sector the advance of the First Army was to be made in three columns. The right Column by Beza, Mejez-el-Bab and Tebourba, on Tunis.

The centre Column by the Mejerda Valley on Mateur, whence it would be possible to strike either at Tunis or Bizerta.

The left column along the coastal road through Tabarka and Cap Serrat, on Bizerta.

Further South yet another force was to go by rail to Tebessa, and thence strike at Gabes at the southern end of the East coast of Tunisia.

On the 23rd November the left column on the coastal road and the Gabes force were making satisfactory progress. The left column reached Mateur on the 28th November, and the right column occupied Djedeida only 10 miles from Tunis.

On the 30th however Arnim's Army reoccupied Djedeida, and after heavy fighting at Tebourba and Mateur, the advance of the First Army came to an end. By this time Rommel was holding a North and South line through El Agheila.

As will be seen in the detailed account of its actions, No. 6 Commando operated during this period in the area of the left column.

Disembarkation 7th November 1942.

The Commando began to disembark near Algiers at 2130 hrs. on the 7th November. The landing was scattered and no troop was landed complete, but there was fortunately little opposition. A new plan had to be improvised and of the original objectives only Fortin Duperré, a small fort overlooking the beach and about 2 miles North-West of the centre of the town, was attacked. The attack on Algiers itself had to be abandoned, but the town was occupied later. Fortin Duperré surrendered at 1700 hrs. on the 8th November. At 1715 hrs. the Commando received orders from 168 "Combat Team" of the U.S. Army to rendezvous on the high ground West of Algiers at 0220 hrs. on the 9th November; and it was warned that opposition might be expected from two Senegalese Battalions. The Commando marched to the rendezvous without opposition, but as 168 C.T. did not appear Lieut. Col. McAlpine returned with the Commando to Fortin Duperré.[1]

At 0930 hrs. orders were received from 168 C.T. that No. 6 Commando was to supply small garrisons for Fort Anglais, Fort Independence, Cap Caxine and Ras Acrala, West of Algiers. The remainder of the Commando was to occupy Fortin Duperré. The garrisons were duly despatched and Fortin Duperré was put into a state of defence.

Move to Bone, 10th November 1942.

At midday on the 10th the liaison officer S.S. Brigade (Capt. R. Churchill) bought a warning order that the Commando (less its American troops) was to embark in H.M. destroyers "Lamerton" and "Wheatland" the same evening. The C.O. and Second in Command (Major J.E.H. Macleod, Scottish Rifles), were to report to the Commander 78th Division in H.M.S.

1 The War Diary states that No. 6 Commando left the R.V. at 0100 hrs. The rendezvous was ordered for 0220 hrs., which may be the reason for their not meeting 168 C.T.

"Bulolo" at 1630 hrs. The outlying garrisons were recalled and replaced by the American Troops of the Commando.

The Commando less the American Troops embarked at Ilot de la Marine, Algiers, at 1900 hrs. on the 10th November. Verbal orders were then issued for the occupation of two aerodromes at Bone. For this operation the Commando was divided into two groups and a reserve as follows:-

(a) Codo Force (Capt. C.C. Coade) Nos. 1, 4 and 6 Troops
(b) Mayno Force (Capt. J. Mayne) Nos. 2 and 5 Troops
(c) Commando Reserve, No. 3 Troop.

"Codo" was to occupy Allelik aerodrome (9 miles South of Bone) and "Mayno" the racecourse at Duzerville (about 12 miles South of Bone).

At 2030 hrs. on the 10th orders arrived postponing No. 6 Commando's operation for 24 hours owing to a delay in loading rations and ammunition. The Commando remained on board for the night, but disembarked at 0700 hrs. on the 11th and spent the day on the quayside. During the afternoon the four American Troops which had been left at Fort Duperré rejoined, and were allotted to groups as follows:- Nos. 7 and 8 Troops to Codo Force and Nos. 9 and 10 to Mayno Force. The Commando was further strengthened by the arrival of a detachment of U.S. Light A.A. Artillery under Lieut. Driscoll, and an Anti-Tank gun detachment under Lieut. Tighe (Northants Regt.).

Commando disembarks at Bone, 12th November 1942.

At 1910 hrs. on the 21st November the Commando and attached troops re-embarked and the destroyer cast off at 2000 hrs. After an uneventful voyage they arrived off Bone at 0700 hrs. on the 12th. A signal was made by the Captain of "Lamerton" asking for permission to enter the harbour. This was at first refused but later granted, and the destroyers entered the harbour at 0730 hrs., the men on board singing the Marseillaise! They were politely, though not cordially, received. Disembarkation was completed by 0830 hrs., and Codo and Mayno Forces moved off to their respective objectives. Commando H.Q. remained at the pier and the Commanding Officer went to visit the French Commandant of Bone. At 0940 hrs. British troop-carrying planes came over, and 2 companies of a parachute battalion under the command of Lieut. Col. R.G. Pine-Coffin (Devon Regt.), were dropped on Allelik aerodrome. After landing they came under command of Capt. Coade at Allelik. At 1020 hrs. Mayno Force reported that the aerodrome and the Duzerville racecourse were both occupied, and would be ready for use when obstacles had been removed. Shortly afterwards Commando Headquarters moved to a tobacco factory at Johannonville. At 1120 hrs. five Ju.88s. flew over Bone but no bombs were dropped. At 1158 hrs. Codo Force reported the aerodrome at Allelik occupied and ready for use. At 1240 hrs. stores and ammunition arrived in civilian lorries and were distributed to the troops so that they should be independent if attacked.

Early in the afternoon Col. Chauvin of the French Army visited H.Q. and suggested that Capt. Mayne should get in touch with Commandant Couet, the officer commanding the French Artillery at Duzerville, and that the dried up lake at Fet-Zara some 20 miles South-West of Bone would be a suitable landing ground. He said also that the French troops would remain "strictly neutral", that is to say they were prepared to intern Germans, and would use force to do so if necessary. Shortly after 1600 hrs. the Commanding Officer visited Codo and Mayno Forces and transferred No. 9 Troop from Mayno to Codo. Two more German planes came over in the late afternoon, but the situation was otherwise quiet. In the evening Capt. Mayne reported a satisfactory meeting with Commandant Couet who had two 75 mm. batteries in the Duzerville area. Patrols from Codo reported that the local Arabs were not very friendly, but that the French population were eager to hear news from England on the wireless.

All was quiet until 0745 hrs. on the 13th November when a single hostile bomber attacked Bone without doing any damage. Two hours later three more bombers attacked of which one was shot down, and others were seen over Allelik aerodrome at 1045 hrs. At 1015 hrs. 600 men of the 6th Royal West Kent Regiment under Lieut. Col. B. Howlett arrived by destroyer, and were sent to occupy the Fet Zara area. Attempts were made to establish telephone communications with them by the railway system. This, however, could not be done without permission of the French Commander of the Constantine area some distance away, and eventually wireless communication was established between Commando H.Q. and H.Q. 6th R.W.K. Regiment at 1930 hrs. Except for a visit from three Macchi fighters, which flew low over Codo Force at about 1400 hrs., the situation remained quiet, and at 1520 hrs. five of our transport aeroplanes, escorted by fighters, landed on the Allelik aerodrome, bringing American A.A. machine guns for the defence of the harbour at Bone. Capt. Churchill also arrived by air and asked for a report on the situation to take back to Major General Haydon's H.Q. at Algiers. At 1630 hrs. seven Stukas attacked Bone and a good many bombs were dropped. An hour later twelve Spitfires under Group Captain Appleton, D.S.O., D.F.C. landed at Allelik and remained there.

Dispositions of 6 R.W.K. Regt., 13th November 1942.

At about 1820 hrs. the O.C., 6th R.W. Kent reported his dispositions at Fet-Zara which were as follows:-

(a) One Coy. blocking road junction 7735 (E. bank of lake).

(b) One Coy. at the station 7340 (Ain Dahah).

(c) One Coy. in reserve about the road junction 7939.

(d) O.Ps. at Ain Mokra 0637 (near the N.W. shore of the lake) and at Mont Bellil 7939 (on Djebel Edough, a hill overlooking the N.E. corner of the lake).

(e) M.T. patrols round the lake.

(f) H.Q. at the station 7739 (Oued Zeid near the N.E. corner of the lake).

The lake area was a large one and Lieut. Col. Howlett informed Commando H.Q. that the dispositions he had made were as much as, in the circumstances, he was able to do.

Red and white flares were seen over Bone at about 21 hrs. on the 13th, but the situation continued to be quiet during the night 13th/14th.

At 0550 hrs. on the 14th November H.M. ships "Emma" and "Princess Beatrix" arrived at Bone with more troops and Oerlikon guns for A.A. work. At 0745 hrs. Major B. Kingzett Commanding 457 Light Battery R.A. visited No. 6 Commando H.Q. At 0800 hrs. the American Consul arrived from Tunis with information that there were about 100 German planes on the Tunis Aerodrome, and that there were about 400 Germans in Bizerta and 1200 in Tunis. During the morning and early afternoon there was a good deal of aerial activity and by 1700 hrs. two Messerschmidts, one Ju.88 and two Italian bombers had been destroyed. Two Spitfires were shot down over Allelik. Just after 1700 hrs. a bombing attack was made on Bone harbour. At 1715 hrs. Major Kingzett reported that his guns were in action at 9440 – 9460 just East of Allelik.

At 1800 hrs. a warning order was issued to the effect that there would be a general move eastward by French troops during the night 14th/15th November. Later in the evening H.Q. 36th Inf. Bde. (Brig. E.N. Kent-Lemon) was established at Ain Mokra, and the Brigadier visited Commando H.Q. at 0830 hrs. on the 15th. Except for some bombing of Bone early in the morning the situation continued to be quiet. At 0915 hrs. two French Air Force corporals arrived at Allelik aerodrome with a tanker containing 500 litres of aviation spirit which they had contrived to bring from Tunis.

Future Plans.

Brigadier Kent-Lemon, who left Commando H.Q. at 1000 hrs., gave the following information as to future plans. The French General Barré (who was pro-ally and had fought his way of Tunis) was defending Beja, about 30 miles South-East of Tabarka and 55 miles West of Tunis, and an officer had been sent to get in contact with him. The 6th Bn. R.W.K. Regiment with the 502nd field battery (Major Greenwood) and a detachment of R.E., were to go to Tabarka under command of Brig. Kent-Lemon. They were to be followed by the 8th Bn. Argyll and Sutherland Highlanders (Lieut. Col. J.G. McKellar) who were due to arrive at Bone by rail on the 17th November and by the 5th Bn. The Buffs who were to arrive by sea on the 18th.

British Parachute Troops had landed early on the 15th at Souk el Arba, on the railway which runs South from Bone to Souk Ahras and thence down the valley of the river Medjerda to Tunis; and they were to be joined by a mobile column under Major Hunt. Major General V. Evelegh Commanding 78th Div. was due to arrive at Bone by air in the afternoon of the 15th. Except for hostile air activity the situation was quiet, but at least six hostile aircraft were shot down during the day.

Major General Evelegh arrived at 1745 hrs. and established his H.Q. alongside those of No. 6 Commando.

In the afternoon of the 16th November six Macchi 202 fighters attacked the Allelik aerodrome but caused no casualties; one of them was shot down by Sergt. Harper of No. 6 Troop, who was manning an Oerlikon gun.

At 1900 hrs. three French refugees arrived from Tunis and among other information which was passed on to H.Q. 78th Div., said that in a raid carried out by the R.A.F. on the 12th November some 700 Germans had been killed or wounded, and 19 planes were destroyed on the ground.

Arrival of Rear Party, 28th November 1942.

At 0900 hrs. on the 18th November the rear party and kit left behind at Algiers on the 11th November, arrived at Bone; but some kit bags were missing which had been dropped into the sea during disembarkation. On the 19th November the Commando was placed under command of the 78th Division and the Allelik and Duzerville aerodromes were handed over to No. 1 Commando. On the 20th orders were received to move on the 21st to La Calle on a special mission. Later in the day this move was postponed and the Commando entrained at Bone at 0530 hrs. on the 22nd November. At 1030 hrs. the train was attacked by two Messerschmidt planes with the result that 11 men were killed, and 25 wounded.

Move to Tabarka, 22nd November 1942.

Nos. 1, 3 and 4 Troops arrived at La Calle at 2330 hrs. 22nd November and went on by road transport to join H.Q. 36th Inf. Bde. at Tabarka, with a view to carrying out an "infiltration raid" on the enemy's lines on the night 23rd/24th. The remainder of the Commando arrived at La Calle at 0230 hrs. on the 23rd. At 1630 hrs. the 23rd the men killed when the train was bombed on the day before, were buried, and several of the inhabitants of La Calle placed flowers on their graves. In the evening of the 24th Commando H.Q. with Nos. 2 and 6 Troops moved by road transport to Tabarka and were billeted at the Fort.

On the 25th Capt. Scott (No. 3 Troop) reported that the raid on the night of the 23rd/24th had been successful. At 1930 on the 26th November the remainder of the Commando (less the American Troops which remained at La Calle) moved by road transport to the Fort at Tabarka, and their baggage arrived from Bone by sea next day.

Attack at Djebel Abiod, 26th November 1942.

In the early morning of the 26th November the 36th Infantry Brigade attacked the enemy holding positions North-East of Djebel Abiod, and were subsequently to advance along the road to Mateur. The operation was in two phases. In Phase I the 5th Buffs with 2 Troops 6th Commando, attacked on the right, and the 6th R.W.K. on the left. The 8th A & S.H. were in reserve. In Phase II which was to begin at 0515 hrs. the 5th Buffs were to attack with artillery support.

The special task allotted to the two Commando Troops was to "move wide on the right flank, and make for Tamera to destroy:-

(i)   the Tank garage
(ii) The Supply point
(iii) Transport in the vicinity."

They were to "block the road and prevent any German vehicles getting back, at the same time harassing any German infantry withdrawal".

They were to move in M.T. and start at 2000 hrs. 25th.

The 5th Buffs and 6th R.W.K. had captured their first objectives by 0530 hrs. with little opposition and continued to advance towards Tamera; but at 1445 hrs. H.Q. 36 Inf. Bde. received a report from 6th Commando stating that they had been unable to reach their objectives during the night and were "lying up overlooking the valley". One report went on to say that there was "every indication of complete enemy withdrawal". By 1500 hrs. 36th Inf. Bde. reported "the enemy retreating hard", and "many German tanks wrecked".

Move to Sedjenane, 28th November 1942.

At 0900 hrs. on the 28th orders were received for the Commando to move that evening to Sedjenane about 30 miles E.N.E. and it embussed at 1830 hrs. An hour later this destination was changed and the Commando was ordered to push on to El Alouana about 8 miles beyond Sedjenane. The Column arrived at El Alouana at 0100 hrs. on the 29th, but as the cover there was insufficient it was sent back to Sedjenane, where it arrived at 0715 hrs. and billeted in a rope factory. Capt. Lieven the liaison officer, whose services had been invaluable, had gone on ahead to arrange billets, but he was injured by the explosion of a grenade and had to go into hospital at Beja. The 36th Inf. Bde. had also moved forward and its advanced H.Q. were about 4 miles East of El Alouana on the Tabarka-Mateur road.

Opposition at Djefna, 29th November 1942.

At 10.30 hrs. on the 29th November the 36th Inf. Bde reported that at about 1600 hrs. on the 28th its advance guard was held up by what was described as "a most formidable position across the pass at J. 3976" (Djefna Station). An attack was attempted by the 8th A and S.H. but it was unsuccessful and casualties were numerous.

The attack, 30th November 1942.

At 1800 hrs. on the 29th, 36th Inf. Bde. issued orders for an attack on the enemy's position.

The attack was to be made on both sides of the Tabarka – Mateur road.

The 6th R.W.K. were to attack on the right of the road and No. 6 Commando on the left.

Commando's Task.

The Commando's objectives were the Djebel Azzag (Green Hill) about 3877, and Sidi Ayed. Its starting line was the track about 365765 and the attack was to begin at 0300 hrs., 30th November. Artillery support took the form of a 3 minute concentration at 0100 hrs. An Artillery F.O.O. was detailed to go forward with 6th R.W.K. and another was to be "supplied for Green Hill as soon as it was captured".

A reconnaissance of Green Hill was made at 1400 hrs. by Major Macleod with Capts. Coade, Scott (3 Troop) Powell (4 Troop) and Mayne (5 Troop).

It was decided that a frontal (feint) attack was to be made by Capt. Mayne's Troop at 0400 hrs., and the main attack at 0415 hrs. 30th November.

Mayne's Troop left their billets at 1830 hrs. and the remaining troops (3, 4 and 6) at 2100 hrs.

The 6 R.W.K. captured their objective, but the Commando's attack did not go well as the enemy position was strongly defended by machine guns. Artillery support was asked for from guns under Lieut. Col. T.C. Usher, R.A. A final attack was made at 1600 hrs. after half an hour's bombardment by artillery, but it also was unsuccessful and more casualties were incurred. The Brigadier, who had watched the operation since the early morning, told Lieut. Col. Macalpine to withdraw his Troops as they could not be expected to do more. The 6 R.W.K. were also withdrawn as their position was untenable as long as Djebel Azzag was in the enemy's hands. The Commando's casualties were Capt. Scott and 2 O.R. killed, 16 O.R. wounded, 7 O.R. missing.

Reorganization, 3rd[1] December 1942.

On the 2nd December, Nos. 1 and 2 Troops occupied a defensive position just West of Green Hill. On the 5th[1] December the Commando (less the American Troops) was reorganized in four Troops numbered 1, 2, 5 and 6 and commanded by Capts. Robinson, Davis, Mayne and Coade.

Sergt. Beresford, who had been left on Green Hill during the attack and had remained there four days, brought back valuable information as to the enemy's dispositions. On the 4th December the four American Troops (7, 8, 9 and 10) rejoined the Commando, and Major Macleod took over command in the absence through sickness of Lieut. Col. Macalpine. A few days later Nos. 7 and 9 Troops were despatched to carry out an "anti-sabotage" patrol in the Djebel Abiod area (South-West of Sedjenane), and found a good many German weapons, including M.Gs., and also ammunition, in the possession of the local Arabs.

An attack by German parachute troops was anticipated and measures were therefore taken for the perimeter defence of Sedjenane in which the Commando had a share. On the 10th December a patrol of No. 2 Troop under Lieut. Pyman discovered some fifteen Germans in a group of Arab huts. With the help of a 2" mortar and by means of grenades the Germans were put to flight and ten were killed. On the 11th a fighting patrol under Lieut. Winser was cut off by Germans wearing British and American uniforms. Lieut. Winser was wounded, and Cpl. Goodall, who was with him, mortally wounded.

Reconnaissance of road to Mateur, 14th December 1942.

In accordance with instructions given by the Brigade Commander, four patrols were sent out on the 14th December to reconnoitre the areas North and South of the road to Mateur. Two patrols under Sergts. Blint and Preen were to reconnoitre South of the road, and the other two under Lieut. Spooner and Sergt. McKie North of it. They were to send information in by dawn on the 16th, and in any case were to return by dawn on the 18th. Each patrol sent back two men by the 16th who brought useful information.

On the 18th the remainder returned excepting Sergt. Preen's party which was missing (less the 2 men who had come back on the 16th). Sergt. Blint gave information of hostile patrols dressed as Arabs or in British uniform, and he also gave the location of positions and O.Ps., which were later shelled by our guns.

On the evening of the 18th December the entire Commando was concentrated in the railway tunnel 1 mile East of Alouana, but on the 24th it

---

1 *Publisher's note:* This discrepancy in dates exists in the original text.

was evacuated for sanitary reasons. On the 26th, however, all Troops except No. 1 returned to it. Patrolling continued and the artillery fired on ground reported by patrols to be occupied by the enemy.

Attack on Djebel Azzag, 4th/5th January 1943.

On the 1st January 1943 the Commander 36th Inf. Bde. (Brig. Howlett) gave a verbal warning order to the effect that the Commando was to attack and seize Djebel Azzag and point 277 on the high ground North-West of it, on the night 4th/5th January, in cooperation with the 5th Buffs who were to attack Djebel Azzag and Sidi Ayed on the same night. The Commando was reinforced by two machine guns of the 6th R.W. Kent Regiment under Sergt. Kendall who reported at the Tunnel on the 2nd January.

The Commando left the Tunnel to carry out the attack at 1800 hrs. on the 4th and moved to a preparatory position at Point 3477.

Their task in detail was:-

(i)   to capture Pt. 277377[1] and Sidi Abd el Medub 389803.
(ii) to capture Djebel Azzag 3978 by 0430 hrs. 5th January.

During this phase an Artillery F.O.O. was to be available to go with the Commando.

The available Artillery support was eight 25 prs. of 321 Field Bty, six 3.7 Hows of 456 Lt Bty and some medium artillery.

The objectives of the 5th Buffs, who were to attack on the right of the Commando, were Djebel Azzag and Sidi Ayed.

At 0545 hrs. on the 5th, 6th Commando reported two troops climbing to their first objective and the remainder in position at 386804. There had been no opposition.

At 0815 hrs. 6th Commando reported that the enemy were withdrawing from Pt. 399766 and Pt 394773, and that our medium guns were firing on these areas. At 0930 hrs. 5th Buffs reported the capture of Pt. 396 and Ain Azzag but their attack on Sidi Ayed was checked at about 1050 hrs. and they began to dig in on the North slopes of Djebel Azzag.

At 1400 hrs. Capt. Mayne's Troop of 6 Commando was surrounded at Pt 390785 on Djebel Azzag and was under fire from the enemy's mortars. They were able to hold on through the night but at 0900 hrs. next morning were forced to withdraw.

At 1000 hrs. orders were issued for the withdrawal of the 5th Buffs, the Parachute Company and the 6th Commando. The 6th R.W.K. and No. 1 Commando were to remain in position. The withdrawal took place after dark without incident and as they withdrew through our medium Artillery's positions the men of the Commando cheered the gunners.

---

1   Map references are to Sheets 5 and 11, 1/50,000.

The casualties are recorded as follows:- 2 killed, Lieut. Cooper and 18 O.Rs. missing, 14 wounded.

Defensive role resumed, 13th January 1943.

The Commando resumed its defensive role on the 13th January and was disposed as follows:-

In the Tunnel – Adv H.Q. 6 Troop and one Section 2 Troop (Lieut. Pyman).

> Area of Cap Serrat – 5 Troop, 2 Troop (less a Section), one Section 7 Troop and one Section 10 Troop.
>
> Djebel Abiod – One Section 7 Troop (Lieut. Milling) on anti-sabotage duties.
>
> Sedjenane – Rear H.Q. one Section 10 Troop (for protective duties) and No. 1 Troop resting.

Lieut. Col. Mills-Roberts takes command.

On the 16th January Lieut. Col. D. Mills-Roberts, M.C., Irish Guards, arrived to replace Lieut. Col. Macalpine in Command of the Unit. On the 17th the Troops in the Cap Serrat area were relieved by a company of the French Corps d'Afrique, and returned to Sedjenane. On the 18th the Commando came under command of the 139th Inf. Bde. (Brig. R.C. Chichester-Constable) which had relieved the 36th Bde.

Move to Beja area, 23rd January 1943.

At 1545 hrs. on the 23rd January orders were received for a move at 2000 hrs. to an unknown destination. The Commando actually started at 2330 hrs. and, marching by Sedjenane, arrived at Munchar near Beja at 0615 hrs. on the 24th January. It then came under Command of the 11th Inf. Bde. (Brig. E.E. Cass) and left Munchar for its new area at 1800 hrs. on Thursday the 28th. At 2300 hrs. Commando H.Q. were established in the area 304507 – 331467 (Sheet Tunis 1/500,000). The second of these coordinates marks the junction, about 10 miles North-East of Beja, off the Beja – Mateur road with a minor road running North and South.

American troops rejoin U.S. Army.

On the night 31st Januaary/1st February the four American Troops left to join the 34th U.S. Infantry Division at Gueima.

The area about Sidi Nsir Station some five miles North-East of the area occupied by the Commando was held by a battalion of the East Surrey Regiment, and one Section of No. 6 Troop under Lieut. Colquhoun was attached to this battalion. The East Surreys were relieved by a battalion of the Hampshire Regiment on the night 1st/2nd February.

On the 2nd February the 11th Inf. Bde. was relieved by the 138 Inf. Bde; and on the 4th the Commando was relieved by the 2/5 Bn. Hampshire Regiment. At 2300 hrs. that night it was withdrawn to BEJA where it bivouacked. At 1100 hrs. on the 5th orders were received from H.Q. 78 Div. that the Commando was to move at 1730 hrs. to the area Sidi Mahmoud, less one Troop (No. 6 under Capt. Coade) which was to report to the C.R.A. at Medjez-el-Bab and act as protective troops to the guns. Capt. Coade went on ahead to report to the C.R.A. and his troop followed at 1430 hrs. The main body, moving by bus, arrived in their new area at 2345 hrs. on the 5th January and bivouacked by the road side.

Commando in Medjez-el-Bab area, 6th February 1943.

At 0700 hrs. on the 6th February Commando H.Q. were established at Dam Rha (Point 5725 about 5 m. South of Medjez-el-Bab) and came under command of 18 C.T. U.S. Army (Col. Green). The available troops, less No. 2 in reserve at H.Q., were disposed to protect American guns in the neighbourhood. The country was intersected by gullies with concealed approaches, which were full of booby traps, covered by hostile mortars firing on fixed lines. The reserve Troop (No. 2) was later moved to the area 595253 – 596243 to increase the protection of the American gun positions. A building in front of the position, known as Swiss Farm, was reconnoitred by a patrol and was found to be owned by a Swiss named Rachas who was in residence. He described his attitude as strictly neutral, but his situation must have been far from comfortable! On the 10th February No. 5 Troop was moved forward to Djebel Djaffa and was reinforced by four American M.Gs. The Camouflage Officer undertook to construct two dummy guns, to attract the attention of the enemy's fighting patrols and enable our own troops to ambush them; but they had to be removed soon after they were put in position so that real guns of the 78th Div. could take their place. At 2200 hrs. on the 13th February the 18th C.T. were relieved by the 11th (British) Inf. Bde, and on the 14th a patrol was sent out to get in touch with a battalion of the Northants Regiment at 572222 (2 or 3 miles to the South). The patrol was unsuccessful as the battalion was actually located at 568218.

Move to Goubellat, 17th February 1943.
Dispositions and patrol action, February 1943.

On the night 16th/17th the Commando was relieved by a French unit.

H.Q. and Nos. 1, 2, 5 and 6 Troops now took up positions as follows.

No. 1 at 603247 (overlooking Goubellat Station) H.Q. with 2, 5 and 6 Troops in the area 5825 (two miles further West).

During the following three days patrols were sent out in lorries and on foot to the Goubellat plain and on the immediate front, which obtained useful information of the enemy's defences. On the 22nd a patrol of 15 O.R. under Lieut. A.D. Lewis, which was protecting a R.A. Observing Officer (Capt. Barker-Benfield), had a sharp engagement with a German patrol some 50 strong. The fight was indecisive and one Commando Sergt. was killed.

At 1930 on the 24th February the Commando moved by M.T. to the area about Point 516126, some miles to the South of Goubellat in the neighbourhood of Djebel Rhihane, and during the 24th and 25th February they lay in wait for hostile patrols which might attempt to filter through.

Action at Fedj-el-Attia, 26th February 1943.

At 0615 hrs. on the 26th a patrol of 20 men under Capt. Spooner, which was on its way in M.T. to act as a standing patrol in the neighbouring hills, was attacked. The Commando went to its support and a successful defensive action was fought with 3 companies of the Hermann Goering Regiment near Fedj-el-Attia.

It was a part of the defensive battle fought along the whole front of the First Army which began on the Southern sector at the end of January. The Germans captured the Faid pass 60 m. W.N.W. of Sfax, penetrated towards Sidi Bouzid and Faid then attacked again, occupying Gafsa on the 15th February and Sbeitla, Kasserine, Feriana and Tozeur on the 18th. They attacked once more on the 20th February at the Kasserine Gap, and through a pass between the Djebel Semmana and a ridge to the West of the Ousseltian valley; but this attack was eventually held, and the enemy began to retire on the 24th. On the 26th February General von Arnim attacked once more in the Coastal Sector, and on the 27th our left was forced to retire from Sedjenane to Tamera. Further South an equally heavy attack was made on the 26th February in the area of Sidi Nsir, the objective being Beja, the loss of which would have endangered our supply lines from the Algerian ports to Medjez-el-Bab. This attack was stopped mainly by the magnificent fighting of a battalion of the Hampshire Regiment and the 155 Field Battery R.A. The 6th Commando's fight took place 30 miles South of Sidi Nsir, and the position they occupied covered the right flank of the Medjez-el-Bab salient on the 78 Div front. The enemy appears not to have expected opposition there, but if he had got through the consequences would have been serious.

Casualties were as follows:-

Killed – 1 Officer (Lieut. J. Bonvin) and 10 O.R.
Wounded – 3 Officers (Capt. R.D. Knox, Capt. D.A. Robinson and Lieut. N. Read) and 31 O.Rs.
Missing – 4 Officers (Major J.E.H. Macleod, Capt. J. Mayne, Capt. G. Spooner and Lieut. A.J. Keay) and 51 O.Rs.

Commando withdrawn to rest, 27th February 1943.

On the 27th February the Commando moved to a farm in the Testour area (4523) to rest and re-equip; and on the 1st March Lieut. Col. Mills-Roberts went to the scene of the recent engagement in a 15 cwt lorry. The enemy were no longer there and he brought back a good deal of equipment.

On the 2nd March the C.O. again went back to Fedj-el-Attia with the M.O. and 6 O.Rs. in a 3 ton lorry to salvage as much of our own and German equipment as possible. Many enemy dead were found and nine of our own dead were brought back later in the day and buried near the Farm.

In consequence of its reduced strength the Commando was reorganized into two Troops, "A" and "B", each about 60 strong. Lieut. Colquhoun commanded "A" Troop and Capt. Davis "B" Troop.

Corps Commander's Congratulations.

On the 16th March Lieut. General C.W. Allfrey commanding 5 Corps visited the Commando. He congratulated them on the success of their action on the 26th February, and said that if the Germans had succeeded in advancing the whole position of the 78 Division would have been adversely affected. An order from the 11th Bde received next day, gave the Commando the role of Mobile Reserve to the Brigade. Movement was to be in Churchill tanks. Meanwhile the unit continued to patrol the Goubellat area.

On the 23rd March the 11th Inf Bde was relieved by the 2nd Inf Bde as follows:-

2 Lancs Fusiliers by 1st Loyals
1 East Surrey by 6th Gordon Highlanders
5 Northants by the 2nd North Staffs.

The new battalions were lectured on patrolling by Officers and N.C.Os. of the Commando.

During this period patrols had two brushes with the enemy in one of which (at Goubellat) a Sergt. and 2 O.Rs. were missing.

On the 1st April information was received that Lieut. Col. Mills-Roberts had received the D.S.O., that Capt. A.C.H. Pyman R.A. had received the M.C. and that Sergts. Rae and Khytovich were awarded the M.M.

On 0715 hrs. on the 2nd April the Commando was warned to be ready to move the same night to Teboursouk or further. It moved at 2300 hrs. and arrived at Teboursouk at 0240 hrs. on the 3rd. At 1830 hrs. on the same day it left Teboursouk and arrived at Souk-el-Arba,[1] The train started at

1 Sheet Constantine 1/500,000 H.8612.

NORTH AFRICA 1 : 2M
(OR 5404 and OR 5379)

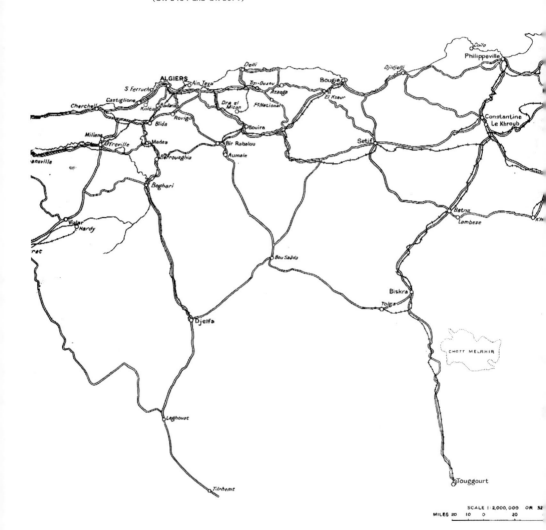

SCALE 1 : 2,000,000   OR 32

MILES 20   10   0   20

Bizerte
Metline
Gulf
of
Tunis
Tabarka
TUNIS
La Goulette
Medjes-el-Bab
Testour
Zaguan
Medjaz-el-Bab
Le Kef
Enfidaville
Gulf of
Hammamet
Sousse
Monastir
Kairouan
Tebessa
Feriana
Sfax
KERKENNA Is.
Gafsa
Gulf of Gabes
CHOTT EL FEDJADT
Gabes
DJERBA
Tozeur
Mamoura
CHOTT DJERID
Medenine
Ben Gardane
Zouara
TRIPOLI
Foum Tatahoume

PANTELLERIA
(Italy)

LINOSA
(Italy)

LAMPEDUSA
(Italy)

80 MILES

L   I   B   Y   A

Geographical Section, General Staff, 1942

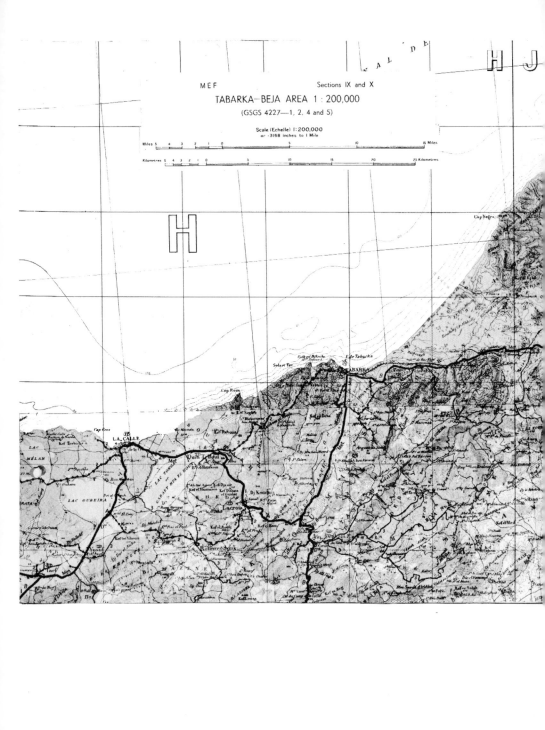

MEF   Sections IX and X

TABARKA—BEJA AREA 1 : 200,000

(GSGS 4227—1, 2, 4 and 5)

Scale (Echelle) 1:200,000
or ·3168 inches to 1 Mile

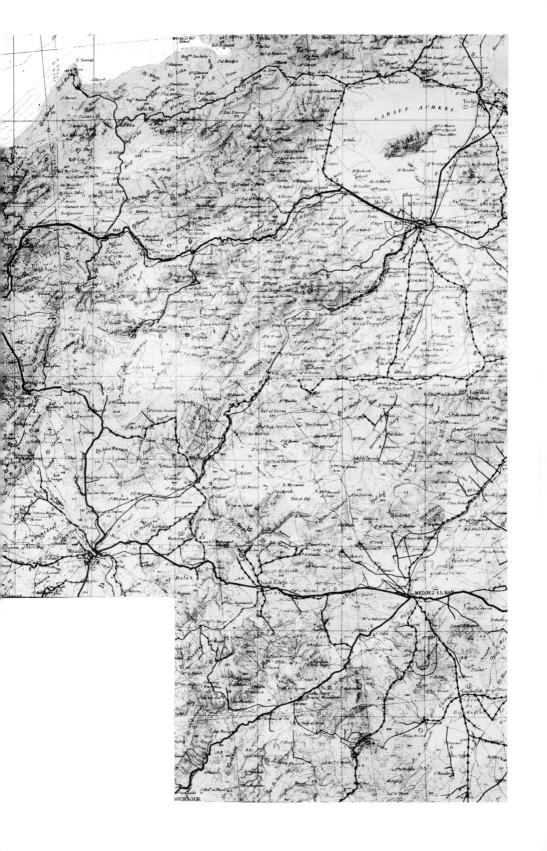

MEF   Sections IX and X

ALGIERS AREA 1 : 200,000
(GSGS 4180—5 and 14)

Echelle (Scale) 1 : 200,000

Miles 5 4 3 2 1 0 5 10 15 Miles

Kilometres 5 4 3 2 1 0 5 10 15 20 25 Kilometres

37° 00′

36° 50′

36° 40′

36° 30′

790,000 m.N.
780,000 m.N.

Degres N.

300

Sidi Ferruch

Zéralda

Bouzouda les Bains

KOLEA

Joinville

Bli

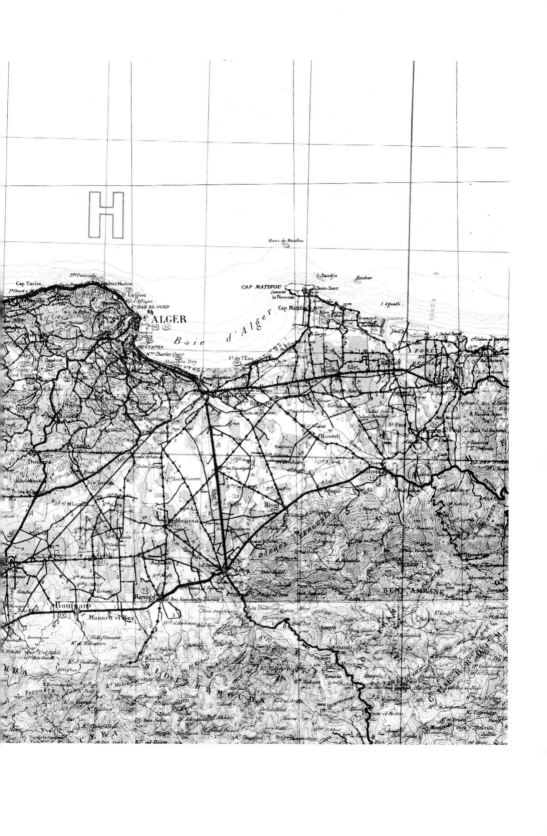

1100 hrs. on the 4th April, and arrived at 0100 hrs. on the 5th at Gueima where the Commando's rear party joined it from Tabarka. At 1200 hrs. on the 7th it arrived at Maison Carrée on the eastern outskirts of Algiers. There it remained until the 23rd April when it embarked for England in the S.S. "Staffordshire". It sailed next day, arrived at Liverpool on the 2nd May and at Hove (Sussex) on the 4th May.

Note I

The Special Boat Section.

The early history of the Special Boat Section has been referred to in Section VI. It was attached to the "Middle East Commando", after the disbandment of Layforce, but eventually became part of the 1st S.A.S. Regiment. Its "folbot" detachments took part in various raids in North Africa carried out by "L" Detachment and later by the 1st S.A.S. Regiment (See Sections VII and VIII). This Note contains accounts of operations in the Aegean which the S.B.S. carried out independently, two in Crete and the other in Rhodes.

In June 1942 a series of attacks on hostile landing grounds was organized, with the object of protecting a convoy on its way to Malta by reducing the scale of air attack. In addition to raids on the African mainland, the aerodromes at Kastelli and Heraklion in Crete were attacked by detachments of the Special Boat Section. The Section is referred to by Lord Jellicoe in his report on the raid on Heraklion, as part of "L" detachment; but it did not in fact become officially part of the S.A.S. until September 1942.

Attack on Kastelli 9th/10th June, 1942.

The raid on Kastelli, which took place on the night of the 9th/10th June 1942, was made by Capt. G.I. Duncan, Black Watch, with C.S.M. C. Barnes of the Grenadier Guards, Corporal Barr of the H.L.I. and three Greeks.

Besides personal weapons they carried two Thompson sub-machine guns, six grenades, 80 lbs of Lewis bombs (plastic and thermite) and sixty igniter sets.

The party left the coast of Crete at 1900 hrs. on the 6th June. Lying up by day, and moving by night, they reached a hiding place on the top of a hill about a mile from the aerodrome, at 0430 hrs. on the 9th June. During the march they were fed by Cretans; and on the last night they were joined by two men who helped to carry the rather heavy loads. The aerodrome was watched through glasses during daylight on the 9th June. At 2030 hrs. they left the hiding place, each man carrying 20 lbs of bombs, and moved to a point about three quarters of a mile from the dispersal areas. After listening for the movements of patrols for an hour, they moved on at 2300 hrs. They could see that a heavy air attack was being made on the aerodrome at Heraklion, and one plane dropped a flare followed by one bomb on the landing ground at Kastelli. After evading a patrol, and crossing sentries' beats on three parallel roads, they reached the dispersal area at 2330 hrs. The report remarks "Sentries were bad; two passed within two feet of the party – who were lying behind a very slender olive tree ... planes were being continually moved presumably to wider dispersal areas. Excitement over the Heraklion air raid seemed considerable." The first bomb was placed at about 2330 hrs. and the last at 0040 hrs. 10th June; and the raiders then withdrew to the hiding place on the hill top. By 0300 hrs. there had been eighteen explosions and fires. A very large fire at 0240 hrs. was thought to be an oil dump. At 0430 hrs. a guide was sent down to find an agent who worked on the aerodrome. He was told that when the explosions began patrols with torches "combed out" the olive groves, and there was some sub-machine gun fire. After the first big fire A.A. guns went into action and fired for half an hour. At first light the enemy started to clear away wreckage, and sent patrols to search the neighbouring villages.

The party lay up throughout 10th June; and at 2000 hrs. received a report from a Greek agent. At 2200 hrs. they started the return march to the beach and reached it at 0530 hrs. on the 13th June. Reports of damage came in from agents on the 10th and 18th June; and it appeared that seven planes were completely burnt; and that 210 sixty gallon petrol drums, three bomb dumps, one fuel oil dump and six transport vehicles were also destroyed. It was also reported that seventy Germans had been killed or wounded, and that the enemy had shot the guards on the area and seventeen Greek night watchmen.

Capt. Duncan and his two men spent five weeks in all on the island, and an appendix to the report on the raid makes recommendations in regard to composite rations and kit for such expeditions.

Attack on Heraklion 12th/13th June 1942.

The attack on the landing ground at Heraklion was made on the night of the 12th/13th June. It was intended to synchronize with the attack on Kastelli, and with another on Timbaki, but this was not possible. The party consisted of Commandant Berge, M.C. with a corporal and two privates of the Free French Forces, Capt. Lord Jellicoe and 2/Lieut. Petrakis Costi, a Cretan.

It embarked in the Greek submarine "Triton" at Alexandria on the 6th June 1942. At 2130 hrs. on the 10th the "Triton" surfaced and began to close the coast; and boats and equipment were assembled on deck. The party left the ship in rubber boats at 2200 hrs. while a R.A.F. raid on Heraklion was going on; they landed at 0115 hrs. on the 11th, and started to march inland at 0200 hrs. No patrols or sentries were met, but going was slow owing to the hilly nature of the country and the loads carried. At 0600 hrs. the party halted on high ground at a point 256323 (1/250,000 Mokhos).[1]

No observation of the landing ground was possible on the 11th, and contact which was unavoidable was made with local peasants but had "no repercussions".

On the night of the 11th/12th a move was made towards the aerodrome. Villagers were asked the way in German and told to produce their identity cards. By first light a lying up position was reached at 192322 (1/100,000 Heraklion). As no observation of the aerodrome was possible Commdt. Berge and Lieut. Costi went forward in plain clothes to obtain a close view; but they were unable to get nearer than three miles and the view was limited. On the next night the party, with the exception of Lieut. Costi who remained at the "lying up" position, started at 2030 hrs. to move up the valley towards Prassas with the intention of approaching the landing ground from the South; but they were delayed by sentries, and it was decided to postpone the attack. On the 13th they moved back to the high ground North of Baboli (1733 – 1/100,000 Heraklion) whence there was good observation

1   References are to maps of Crete 1/50,000 Mokhos and 1/100,000 Heraklion.

of the landing ground. Owing to the presence of villagers it was not possible to use the observation post throughout the day, but it was occupied at first and last light, and during daylight the party lay up in the valley South of Prassas. At 2100 hrs. on the 13th they advanced to a small windmill from which they were able to study the dispositions of the perimeter guard.

The guard was easily evaded and the landing ground was reached at 2130 hrs; but delay was caused by a chance encounter with a roving patrol, and an air attack by the R.A.F. Charges were then placed but the party had to leave the aerodrome before all the planes had been dealt with owing to the explosion of the first charges, and the lateness of the hour (0400 hrs. 14th June). They got away without difficulty "via the main barracks" and rejoined Lieut. Costi at Pt. 192322.

In the evening of the 14th June the party moved to Pt. 125305 (1/100,000) and during the next night to Kharkadiotissa (Square 1217 – 1/100,000) where they stayed to rest during the night of the 16th/17th.

In the morning of the 18th June they reached a point about a mile North East of Vali (Square 6308 – 1/100,000).

During the following night they lost the way and arrived in the neighbourhood of Vasilika Anoghia (Square 9800) at 0200 hrs. on the 19th. Food was obtained from Lieut. Costi's family at Apesokari, (Pt. 975998 – 1/100,000) and "as usual it was impossible to avoid hospitality from the local inhabitants".

At 1600 hrs. on the 19th Lord Jellicoe and Lieut. Costi went forward in plain clothes to Krotos to make contact with other parties which had raided Kastelli and Timbaki. Lieut. Costi remained at Krotos and Lord Jellicoe went back. He arrived at the point where he had left his party, at 2300 hrs., but found no trace of them. It transpired that they had been betrayed by a local "Quisling" who had brought them wine, and subsequently returned with a party of fifty Germans. The party attempted to fight its way out, but eventually Pte. Leostic was killed and the remainder were taken prisoner.

On the 20th Lord Jellicoe rejoined Lieut. Costi at Krotos and they met the Timbaki and Kastelli parties. In the night of the 23rd/24th June they embarked in H.M.S. "Porcupine" and sailed for Mersa Matruh.

Lord Jellicoe's Report.

In a report on the operation at Heraklion Lord Jellicoe drew attention to various points of importance. He stressed the "efficiency and intelligence" of the crew of the Greek submarine "Triton", but added that selected personnel of "L" Detachment should have training in "folbot" work. The Naval arrangements for re-embarkation in H.M.S. "Porcupine" were perfect, but Lord Jellicoe says that a "gross muddle was made on shore" as to those who were to embark, and when they were to do so. "Many of the population of S. Crete decided it was to take place on the night of the 22nd/23rd June and 'rolled up' to fight their way aboard H.M.S. 'Porcupine'. Only thirty could be taken." He went on to deal with alternative means of evacuating raiding parties when service channels failed. For raids in hilly country like Crete training was necessary especially when men had worked in the Libyan Desert only. "Navigation" in the hills was difficult, and a local shepherd would be the best guide. Contact with the local population was hard to avoid and in the end led to betrayal and disaster. But evidence showed that the Germans themselves "were quite unprepared for the presence of British or Allied Troops." Lord Jellicoe wrote, "We were discovered in the night 13th/14th June cutting our way through the fence surrounding the barrack. The patrol who discovered us had

411

a torch and stopped within one foot of my head. A happy snore from one of the Free French satisfied them that we were a party of German drunks!"

He went on to say "The target was a fat and sitting bird. I feel that the results achieved were not commensurate with the opportunity presented." This he thought was partly due to unavoidable lack of time for preparation and planning. He pointed out however:-

(a) That as arranged no air attack was made on the Heraklion landing ground on the night of the 12th/13th June, but that on the next night when the ground attack actually took place the landing ground was "skilfully attacked by Blenheims, but without result. In consequence we lost a good hour's working time and the Germans gained perhaps ten to fifteen Ju.88s." for only three small fires were started. It is difficult for a ground party to be tied down to a definite date in difficult country.

(b) The lack of synchronization with raids on other landing grounds was due to lack of time for consultation with other parties.

(c) He emphasized the "atmosphere of fear and hate that hangs over Crete", but gave his opinion that it should not be allowed to "bubble over and be expended uselessly now."

(d) Finally he paid a tribute to the courage and determination of Commdr. Berge and his men.

Operation "Anglo". 31st August – 20th September 1942.

This operation was a raid on aerodromes in the island of Rhodes. The S.B.S. party which took part in it was Commanded by Capt. R.K.S. Allott (Middx. Regt.) who had with him Lieut. D.G.S. Sutherland (Black Watch), two Greek officers (Capt. Tsoucas and Sub Lieut. Calambakidis) who acted as interpreters, six British other ranks[1] and two Greek guides.

The party left Beyrout in the Greek submarine "Papanikolis" on the 31st August and landed near Mt. Elia on the East coast of the island during the night of the 4th/5th September, in what Lieut. Sutherland's report describes as an "ideal" place; "sheltered from both sides with about four yards of coarse sand leading to large fissures and caves in a rocky cliff directly behind." The party then "lay up" until 2200 hrs. on the 5th September when it started to move inland with the object of crossing the Malona-Massari road just after midnight. The party made very slow progress for the going was difficult and the loads were heavy. The guides were not really familiar with the country and insisted on taking the most mountainous routes. Water too was a difficulty, and on the 7th September there was none to drink. Two valuable nights were wasted after which the guides admitted their ignorance; but as Lieut. Sutherland wrote, "One can hardly blame them as they had volunteered … at great risk to themselves" but he goes on to say "No guide is better than a bad one."

The party divides.

It was decided that on the night 7th/8th the party should be divided in two. Capt. Allott with three other ranks and a guide was to attack Maritza; Lieut. Sutherland with Sub Lieut. Calambakidis, the three Marines and the other guide was to attack

---

1 Sergt. Moss (Devons), Cpl. Mackenzie (H.L.I.), Pte. Blake (Hampshires) and Marines Duggan, Barrow and Harris.

Calato. Capt. Tsoucas was to remain at the starting point, a "grotto" on the hillside.

Maritza is in the North of the island about 12 or 13 miles from the landing beach. Calato is some 7 miles South West of the beach.

Capt. Allott's party moved off at 2030 hrs. and it was arranged that all being well the two parties should meet again at the landing beach on the night 16th/17th.

Unfortunately Capt. Allott's party was not seen again, and the account of what happened refers to Lieut. Sutherland's party only. They moved off at 2100 hrs. on the 7th September and as they had plenty of time covered only short distances each night, observing movement and the defences of the aerodrome by day. Water had to be found every day, and the weather was extremely cold which made sleep difficult.

Attacks on Calato aerodrome 11th September 1942.

The final O.P. in the hills overlooking Calato, was reached just before dawn on the 11th. Lieut. Sutherland decided to observe throughout the day and to make his plan in the evening. At 2300 hrs. the water party, who had left at dusk, returned with two shepherds who were friends of the guide, Savvas. They talked at length with Sub Lieut. Calambakidis and gave valuable information as to the morale of the enemy in the island and the state of his defences. They also brought food.

Lieut. Sutherland's plan was to attack in two parties which were to withdraw independently, and rally at the Chapel of San Giorgio near Malona, where the shepherds were to meet them with food. Throughout daylight on the 12th each member of the party studied the objective through binoculars, so that every one should know the actual positions of the dispersed aircraft, and the nature of the defences to be overcome.

There were some fourteen Italian planes close together along the North East side of the landing ground, and more among the olive trees to the North West. Some seventeen others were inside the aerodrome "towards Calato village, more widely dispersed but better guarded."

The two parties attacked simultaneously at 2315 hrs. from the dry bed of the river Gaddura on the North East edge of the aerodrome. Lieut. Sutherland had Marine Duggan with him; Calambakadis took Marines Mackenzie and Blake.

Lieut. Sutherland and Marine Duggan placed bombs in three planes, but soon afterwards were challenged by a sentry. Not wishing to compromise the other party they withdrew across the wire. There was much movement on the aerodrome and they were unable to do more except to place a bomb in a petrol dump outside the wire, and additional bombs on the three planes which had already been attended to. They then withdrew towards the rallying point hoping to meet the other party. At 0210 hrs, they heard the first of their own bombs explode, and fifteen minutes later the first bomb placed by the other party. Frequent explosions followed and when they reached the rallying point at 0330 hrs. some twelve or fifteen fires were burning and there were continuous explosions.

Calambakidis' party is lost.

Lieut. Sutherland waited an hour for Lieut. Calambakidis' party, but he did not see them again. The enemy realized that it was a land attack and were directing searchlights on to the beach at Malona Bay and on to the low ground over which the withdrawal had to be made. As the beams shook the Greek guide's nerves Sutherland and Duggan left him behind, and moved up into the hills. On the 13th they lay up at a point from which they could see the results of their raid. The remains of burnt out planes however could not be accurately counted as they were close to the ground and close together.

During the night 13th/14th they met Capt. Tsoucas and returned to the cave where they had spent the first night ashore. Tsoucas's observation of the raid confirmed Sutherland's opinion that some thirteen to fifteen planes had been destroyed. In the afternoon of the 15th they narrowly escaped a search party; and found that the enemy who had got to know of the landing place, had carried off the rubber boats in which the party had come ashore. On the 17th Lieut. Sutherland and Marine Duggan were again nearly captured, and were cut off from Capt. Tsoucas. They had to remain concealed until nightfall.

Sutherland and Duggan swim out to the submarine.

The submarine that was to take them off was due on the night of the 17th/18th and they therefore went down to the beach at 2000 hrs. on the 17th so as to signal out to sea. Marine Duggan went to look for Tsoucas but was unsuccessful. At 2130 hrs. the first signals were sent and at 2200 hrs. after a signal had been acknowledged from seaward, Lieut. Sutherland signalled, "Swimming. Come in". He and Duggan swam for about an hour, when they heard the sound of engines which they took to be those of the submarine. In fact they were the engines of an Italian M.T.B. which later made an attack on the submarine. The noise of the engine faded away, which was discouraging. In spite of the calm sea their physical condition was "hardly adequate owing to the recent strain" and the fact that for five days they had had "only one tin of sardines … and little water." In spite of the growing cold however they hung on, and were picked up at 2330 hrs. on the 17th.

Return to Beyrout 20th September 1942.

No other signals had been seen from the submarine and she sailed forthwith, arriving at Beyrout at 0630 hrs. on the 20th September.

March 1942

Other operations carried out by the Special Boat Section were as follows:-

(a) At 2350 hrs on the 29th March 1942 Lieut. T.G.A.W. Walker, Hertfordshire Regiment and No.5989079 Sergt H.V. Penn of the Special Service detachment were landed from H.M.S. Urge (Lieut. E.P. Tomkinson D.S.O, R.N.) on the West Coast of Italy. They laid charges on a railway and returned to the ship at 0032 hrs on the 30th March. At 0050 hrs a South bound train was blown up.

(b) In August 1942 M.T.Bs landed a sabotage party in the El Daba area.

(c) Capt. R. Wilson, D.S.O., R.A. landed off Crotone Harbour with a "new type of self propelled depth keeping limpet" on the night of 3rd/4th September. Capt. Wilson and his companion were not picked up again and were made prisoners. In December 1943 he escaped to a neutral country and he was repatriated in April 1945. For a long time it had been assumed that he had been killed.

In the citation for the D.S.O. which was awarded to him it is recorded that between 10th June and the 17th December[1] 1941 he was "landed by submarine on the enemy coast together with one other man", and "carried out six

1 This is the date given, but Capt. Wilson was captured at the beginning of September.

raids deep into enemy territory involving great personal danger. By his coolness and courage he ensured the success of these operations, and the destruction of vital enemy communications."

November 1942

(d) On the night of the 26th/27th November a special sabotage party was landed in Suda Bay (Crete) from the Greek man-of-war "Papanicolis".

Note II

The Attack on Rommel's H.Q.
(Note by Lieut. Col Laycock)

The following account of the part played by Lieut. Col. G. Keyes, V.C. in the attack on General Rommel's H.Q. was written soon after it took place, by Lieut. Col. R.E. Laycock, D.S.O., then commanding the S.S. Troops in the Middle East.

"Lieut. Col. Geoffrey Keyes commanded a detachment of a force which landed from Submarines 250 miles behind the enemy lines to attack H.Qs and break installations and communications.

The original plan, formulated several weeks in advance at 8 A.H.Q. *included orders* for attacks on various separate objectives. Although the whole operation was considered to be of a somewhat desperate nature it was obvious that certain tasks were more dangerous than others. Col. Keyes, who was present at all the meetings and assisted in the planning, deliberately selected for himself from the outset the command of the detachment which was to attack what was undoubtedly the most hazardous of these objectives – the residence at H.Q. of the General Officer Commanding the German forces in North Africa.

(When the plan was submitted to me as Comdr. of the M.E. Commandos, I gave it as my considered opinion that the chances of being evacuated after the operation were very slender, and that the attack on Gen. Rommel's house in particular appeared to be desperate in the extreme. This attack, even if initially successful, meant almost certain death for those who *took part in it*. I made these comments in the presence of Col. Keyes who begged me not to repeat them lest the operation be cancelled.)

In the execution of the operation Col. Keyes led his detachment ashore. The majority of the boats, including his own, were swamped on the passage in to the beach but whereas his Officers and men were able to take advantage of the shelter of a cave in which they lit a fire, washed themselves and dried their clothing, Col. Keyes remained throughout the night on the beach to meet any men who managed to make the shore from the second submarine.

Shortly before first light the detachment moved to a wadi in which they lay hidden during the hours of daylight.

After dark on the second night Col. Keyes set off with his detachment towards the objective but was deserted by his Arab guide who refused to accompany the party as soon as the weather deteriorated.

Without guides, in dangerous and precipitous country, faced with a climb of over 1800 ft. in pitch darkness and a march of about 18 miles, which they knew must culminate in an attack on the German H.Q., soaked to the skin by continuous torrential rain and shivering with cold from half a gale of wind, the fast ebbing morale of the detachment was maintained solely by Col. Keyes' determination and magnetic powers of leadership.

Hiding throughout the hours of daylight and moving only during darkness, Col. Keyes had led his men to within a few hundred yards of the objective, by 2200 hrs. on the fourth night ashore.

Restricted by the depletion of his party through the fact that some of his men had never reached the shore from the submarines, Col. Keyes now found himself forced to modify his original orders in the light of fresh information elicited from neighbouring Arabs.

Having detached the majority of his men to take up positions so as to prevent enemy interference with his attack on Gen. Rommel's residence, Col. Keyes was left with only one officer and one O.R. with whom to break into the house and deal with the Guards and H.Q. Staff.

At zero hour (2359 hrs.) having despatched his covering party to block the approaches to the house and to guard the exits from neighbouring buildings, he himself with Capt. Campbell and a Sergeant[1] crawled forward past the guards, through the surrounding fence and so up to the house itself.

Col. Keyes hoped to be able to climb in through a window or enter by the back premises but these proved to be inaccessible. He therefore, without hesitation, boldly led his party up to the front door and, taking advantage of Capt. Campbell's excellent German, beat on the door and demanded entranced.

As soon as the sentry opened the door Col. Keyes and Capt. Campbell set upon him, but as he could not be overpowered immediately, Capt. Campbell shot him with his revolver. The noise naturally roused the inmates of the house.

Col. Keyes, appreciating that speed was now of the utmost importance, posted the Sergeant at the foot of the stairs to prevent interference from the floor above – a task which he accomplished satisfactorily by firing a burst from his Tommy gun at anyone who attempted to reach the landing.

Although the lights in the passage were burning, those inside the ground floor room were extinguished by the occupants.

If the raiding party was to achieve any measure of success, these rooms had to be entered. This could be done by stealth which would, however, have taken time and, had the enemy been bold enough to come out into the passage they could have immediately appreciated that they were attacked by 3 individuals only whom they could easily have over-powered.

The only alternative was to attempt to bluff the occupants by dashing into each room in turn with a minimum of delay. This latter course Col. Keyes unflinchingly adopted although he undoubtedly realized that it was almost certain death for the man who first showed himself silhouetted by the passage lights against the darkened doorway.

Col. Keyes who took the lead, emptied his revolver with success into the first room and was followed by Captain Campbell who threw in a grenade; but the inevitable result of such daring occurred on his entering the second room on the ground floor. He must have been perfectly aware that it was occupied, since the Sergeant, who was a few yards further away, reported to me later that he could distinctly hear the occupants breathing and moving about inside.

Col. Keyes was shot almost immediately on flinging open the door, and fell back into the passage mortally wounded. On being carried outside by Capt. Campbell and the Sergeant he died within a few minutes.

1 Sergt. Terry, R.A.

It may be added that on several occasions before the expedition sailed, I suggested to Col. Keyes that he should detail a more junior officer to take his place in leading the actual assault on the German H.Q. and that he himself should remain at the operational R.V. I again made this suggestion to him after he had got ashore just prior to his leaving my H.Q. South of Chescem-el-Chelb.

On each occasion he flatly declined to consider this suggestion, stating that as commander of his detachment it was his privilege to lead his men into any danger that might be encountered; an answer which I considered inspired by the highest tradition of the British Army.

From the first conception of the operation, through the stages in which it was planned, during the weary days spent in waiting for the expedition to sail and up to the last moment when I saw him 250 miles behind the enemy lines heading for almost certain death, I was profoundly impressed by his confidence and determination to face all kinds of danger.

Col. Keyes' outstanding bravery was not that of the unimaginative bravado who may be capable of spectacular action in moments of excitement, but the far more admirable, calculated daring of one who knew only too well the odds against him.

That he was aware of the danger I have no doubt from previously discussing this operation with him, and from his description of his former brilliant action at Litani River; but that he ever allowed fear to influence his action for one single second is unthinkable."

Note III

Note on Lieut. Col. J.E. Haselden.

Lieut. Col. J.E. Haselden, whose name appears frequently in this narrative, was in peace time a Cotton Merchant in Egypt. He was originally in the Libyan Arab Force and worked for G(R), the branch of the General Staff Middle East which dealt with raiding forces, the organization for rescuing prisoners of war known as "Advanced H.Q. "A" Force" and similar services. He then became "Western Desert Liaison Officer" at H.Q. Eighth Army. The W.D.L.O's duty was to control the Arab population of the occupied territory until Civil Affairs could get going; and to obtain intelligence from friendly Arabs. When he was killed, during the raid on Tobruk on the 13th/14th September 1942, he was officially W.D.L.O., but had got away from H.Q. Eighth Army to take part in the raid. Those who knew him agree in describing him as a very remarkable man with a great influence over the Desert Arabs.

Note IV

Officers M.E. Commandos.
(1st S.S. Regt. 1st July 1942)

Lieut. Col.	J.M. Graham	S. Greys
Major	W.A. Knowles	R.E.
	R.L. Campbell	Gordon Highlanders
	C.D. Miller	10 Hussars
	M.R.B. Kealy	Devon Regt.
Capt.	H.C. Buck	3/1 Punjab
	G.I.G. Duncan	Black Watch
	J.N. Lapraik	Cameron Highlanders
	R.M.E. Melot	General List
	M.L. Pilkington	Household Cavalry
	B.P. Schott	General List
Lieut.	G.W. Alston	R.A.
	H.G. Chevalier	General List
	T.B. Langton	Irish Guards
	R.E. Lea	R.A.
	M.M. Roberts	Northumberland Fusiliers
	T.C.D.A. Russell	Scots Guards
	D.G. Sutherland	Black Watch
	R.H. Shorten	General List
	H.D. Sillito	A. & S.H.
	G.J.P. Taylor	Wilts Regt.
2/Lieut.	W.N. Macdonald	General List
	R. Murphy	R.N. Fusiliers

Note V

The Special Boat Squadron (1943-44).

The Special Boat Squadron (known like the Special Boat Section as "S.B.S.") was formed by Major Lord Jellicoe in January 1943 for combined operations in the Eastern Mediterranean and the Aegean Sea. It had three detachments known as "S", "L" and "M", these letters being the initials of the original detachment commanders Major D. Sutherland, Black Watch, (formerly in the S.B. Section), Major T.B. Langton, Irish Guards who was afterwards transferred to the 1st S.A.S. Regiment, and Major (now Brigadier) Fitzroy Maclean M.P. Cameron Highlanders. The last named officer did not retain his command for very long as he was required for other duties, and he was succeeded by Major J.N. Lapraik, Cameron Highlanders.

The Squadron was based on Haifa and was conveyed by the Royal Navy in motor Caiques, "Levant Schooners" and other fast craft to raid various islands and objectives on the mainland of Greece, The Adriatic Coast etc.

July 1943

"S" detachment was sent to Crete to raid landing grounds, the attack being timed to coincide with the landing of the Eighth Army in Sicily, July 9th/10th 1943; and its object was to hamper the enemy's air support. Few aeroplanes were in fact found, but four were destroyed by Lieut. Lassen, a Danish officer of the detachment, and a petrol dump was blown up. The detachment spent about three weeks on the island and lost one officer, Lieut. K.B. Lamonby, Suffolk Regt.

After a pause during which some projected raids were cancelled, the next operation took place in the Dodecanese during the night following the publication of the Armistice with Italy, (9th September 1943). A mixed force from "M" and "S" detachments, about 50 strong, under the command of Major Sutherland, embarked at Haifa in two M.L.Cs, and carried with them certain Intelligence and Political officers and a detachment of A.A. gunners. Their first landing was at Castelrosso (Kastellorizzo) where the Italian garrison made no resistance, and during a stay of three days the island was put into a state of defence. The force then sailed to Cos where also no opposition was met, and similar measures were taken. The next visit was to Samos and the force had orders to find out whether the island could be safely occupied by a Corps Headquarters. On arrival it was met by Major General Arnold of the British Military Mission to Ankara, who had already been on the island for two days! The troops were everywhere warmly welcomed by the Greek islanders, fine people who gave every assistance, especially those in Samos.

September 1943

During this period Lord Jellicoe was sent to Rhodes with a message for the Italian Governor from General Sir Maitland Wilson. He spent two days in the Governor's palace trying to persuade him to hand over the island, but without success. Eventually he was forced to eat Sir M. Wilson's letter in order to prevent it falling into German hands! The Governor himself appeared to be quite friendly, and whenever Germans came to the palace was able to hide Lord Jellicoe (literally) "behind the arras"; but he was incapable of taking action to overcome the Germans who remained in control of the island until the end of the war with Germany in May 1945. He arranged however for Lord Jellicoe's escape in an Italian motor boat to Castelrosso.

By this time (end of September 1943) a H.Q. under Major General D. Turnbull (late R.A.) had been formed at Leros, where the garrison included 100 men of the Long Range Desert Group under Lieut. Colonel Prendergast R.T.R. (see L.R.D.G. Narrative). Lord Jellicoe joined the Military Mission at this H.Q. At the end of September "S" detachment (Major Sutherland) went to the island of Calymnos (Kalino) five miles from Cos; and on the 29th September 1943 a party was sent thence to Chios in M.L. 255 to destroy a reported German O.P. No O.P. however was found, and a raid was made on a post at the West end of the island. The detachment was still at Calymnos when the Germans attacked Cos, and on the 2nd October Major Sutherland sent Capt. Milner-Barry's patrol in L.S.2[1] to carry out sabotage if resistance was still going on, or alternatively to help in evacuating the garrison. On arrival at Cos Captain Milner-Barry found that resistance had ceased and that men of the garrison were doing what they could to escape. Ten days were spent in helping to evacuate men in motor caiques manned by the Navy; and among them were a good many Italians who could not be got rid of. Luckily drinking water was found close to the embarkation point, and food was supplied by Greek shepherds. There were caves near the beach in which it was possible for men to hide; and during three trips about ninety in all were rescued, most of whom belonged to the Durham Light Infantry. Later Major Sutherland with the rest of the detachment evacuated men from Leros and Samos.[2]

September – October 1943

About a week after the armistice with Italy when Major Sutherland's detachment went to Castelrosso, "M" detachment (Major Lapraik) less some men attached to "S" detachment, went in H.M.S. Hedgehog to the island of Simi, close to the coast of Asia Minor and about 12 miles from the N.W. point of Rhodes. They made several reconnaissances in Rhodes, spending as many as ten days at a time on the island. They also defeated on the 7th October an attack on Simi made by a party of Germans in a caique. After Lapraik's detachment had evacuated Simi, it was occupied by hostile Italians, who some time later were raided by Major Lapraik and lost several men including prisoners. After the fall of Leros all the S.B. Squadron's detachments were drawn to camp at Athlit near Haifa.

During the first four months of 1944 a good many raids on islands and attacks on shipping and sea planes were made; in January and February by "L" detachment under Major Patterson, and in March and April by "S" detachment under

1 Levant Schooner.
2 See L.R.D.G. narrative.

Major Sutherland. A good deal of shipping was captured or destroyed and prisoners were brought back. One of these was the German "Chief Navigator" of the Levant who was visiting his mistress on one of the islands! One of the captured caiques carried stores of all sorts for German troops, including large quantities of champagne, hair oil and typewriters.

Note VI

German account of the raid on German H. Q. at Beda Littoria by "C" Battalion "Layforce". 17ty/18th November 1941.

The following account of the raid by 'C' Battalion "Layforce" on the German H.Q. at Beda Littoria during the night 17th/18th November 1941 (see page 287 et seq above) was given in July 1946 by Colonel Schleusener, then a prisoner of war in Germany (P.O.W. Camp No. 2226). In a letter to the Camp Commandant (Lieut.Colonel J. Lyall, R.A.) Schleusener explained that when the raid took place, he was "Oberst Quartier-Meister" of Rommel's Army and that, having read erroneous descriptions of it in British newspapers, he felt compelled to write his own story in the interests of historical accuracy.

According to his statement the house at Beda Littoria, which Colonel Keyes raided, was the administrative headquarters of the army, and General Rommel had in fact never been there. The Operation H.Q. was near Gambut, between Bardia and Tobruk. Rommel was in Rome at the time, and did not return till a day or two after the raid had taken place. General Cruwel was acting as Commander-in-Chief.

Schleusener himself was not actually in the headquarters at the time of the raid, being sick in hospital, a little further East along the coast.

Some days before the raid the local military police had reported some abandoned collapsible boats on the beach West of Beda Littoria, and after this one sentry was posted on the "Q" Headquarters, which had hitherto been unguarded.

In Schleusener's words, "the raid failed totally. The Commander, Lieut.Colonel Keyes, was killed immediately after entering the house. His deputy, a captain, was wounded in the leg and remained down (sic). The whole success (sic) was the death of a lieutenant and of a premier-lieutenant of my staff. The men vanished and were captured during the following days". The Italian headquarters, which were close by, were not raided and Schleusener said he was told that one raiding party could not get from the submarine to the shore, owing to the sea being too rough for rubber boats. This was, in fact, more or less the case. The raiders' third objective was a cable mast with four concrete pillars. One pillar only was damaged.

In conversation with Lieut.Colonel Lyall, Schleusener said that there may have been some mistake in identity, since he and the Senior Medical Officer were of much the same build as Rommel, and wore similar uniform.

Index